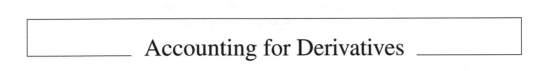

Accounting for Derivatives

For other titles in the Wiley Finance Series
please see www.wiley.com/finance

Accounting for Derivatives

Advanced Hedging under IFRS

Juan Ramirez

John Wiley & Sons, Ltd

Other Wiley Editorial Offices

John Wiley & Sons Inc., 111 River Street, Hoboken, NJ 07030, USA

Jossey-Bass, 989 Market Street, San Francisco, CA 94103-1741, USA

Wiley-VCH Verlag GmbH, Boschstr. 12, D-69469 Weinheim, Germany

John Wiley & Sons Australia Ltd, 42 McDougall Street, Milton, Queensland 4064, Australia

John Wiley & Sons (Asia) Pte Ltd, 2 Clementi Loop #02-01, Jin Xing Distripark, Singapore 129809

John Wiley & Sons Canada Ltd, 6045 Freemont Blvd, Mississauga, ONT, L5R 4J3, Canada

Wiley also publishes its books in a variety of electronic formats. Some content that appears
in print may not be available in electronic books.

Anniversary Logo Design: Richard J. Pacifico

Library of Congress Cataloguing-in-Publication Data

Ramirez, Juan, 1961-
    Accounting for derivatives: advanded hedging under IFRS / Juan Ramirez.
       p.   cm.—(Wiley finance series)
    Includes bibliographical references and index.
    ISBN 978-0-470-51579-6 (cloth)
    1. Financial instruments—Accounting—Standards.   2. Derivative securities—Accounting.
    3. Hedging (Finance)—Accounting.   I. Title.
    HF5681.F54R35 2007
    657'.7—dc22   2007026416

British Library Cataloguing in Publication Data

A catalogue record for this book is available from the British Library

ISBN 978-0-470-51579-2 (HB)

Typeset in 10/12pt Times by Aptara, New Delhi, India
Printed and bound in Great Britain by Antony Rowe Ltd, Chippenham, Wiltshire
This book is printed on acid-free paper responsibly manufactured from sustainable forestry
in which at least two trees are planted for each one used for paper production.

To my wife
Marta and our children Borja, Martuca and David

Contents

Preface

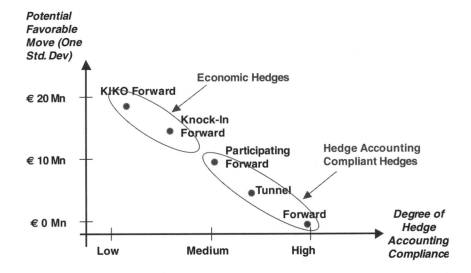

The increasing globalisation of financial markets led companies in many countries to apply from 2005 the IFRS principles. The main goal of IFRS is to safeguard investors by achieving uniformity and transparency in the accounting principles. One of the most challenging aspects of the IFRS rules is the accounting treatment of derivatives, a challenge that has strengthened the relationship between risk management and accounting.

Simultaneously, banks have developed increasingly sophisticated derivatives that have increased the gap between derivatives for which generally accepted accounting interpretations exist and derivatives for which there is no accounting treatment consensus. This gap will continue to widen as the resources devoted to financial innovation hugely exceed those devoted to accounting interpretation.

The objective of this book is not to provide the author's accounting interpretation for as many hedging strategies involving derivatives as possible because the readers will always find many new ones that are not included in our cases. Instead, the objective of this book is to provide a conceptual framework based on an extensive use of cases so that readers can create their own accounting interpretation of the hedging strategy being considered.

This book is aimed at corporate CFOs and treasurers, bank financial engineers and advanced accounting students. This book can also be helpful to well-versed professional accountants because it provides a practical financial markets perspective.

The accounting considerations set out herein are based on our interpretation of the current IFRS standards. Readers should be aware that we address many topics for which IFRS does not provide a clear accounting guidance, and that the current accounting guidance may elicit a broad range of interpretations. Additionally, the current guidance may be subject to change. The accounting treatment of a transaction is ultimately a matter for agreement between the entity and its auditors.

1
The Theoretical Framework

IAS 39 *Financial Instruments: Recognition and Measurement* is a complex standard. It establishes accounting principles for recognising, measuring and disclosing information about financial assets and financial liabilities. In this chapter we provide an overview of the main IAS 39 guidelines, highlighting some of the practical issues surrounding hedge accounting.

The general principles of IAS 39 are:

- The classification and accounting of financial instruments as assets or liabilities are based on management intent.
- Derivative instruments are recognised on the balance sheet and measured at fair value.
- Changes in fair value of derivatives are accounted for depending on whether the derivative is designated as a hedging instrument, and if so, the nature of the item being hedged.
- In order to apply for hedge accounting a derivative must prove it is effective in offsetting the changes in value of the hedged item.

IAS 39 is very wide in scope and interacts with several other standards (see Figure 1.1). When addressing hedging there are primarily two standards that have an impact on the way a hedge is structured: IAS 21 (*The Effects of Changes in Foreign Exchange Rates*) and IAS 32 (*Financial Instruments: Disclosure and Presentation*).

1.0.1 EU's IAS 39 versus IASB's IAS 39

European Union ("EU") entities must apply the version of IAS 39 standard approved by the EU. This version might differ from the IFRS' IAS 39 standard.

1.0.2 US Gaap FAS 133

In this book there are some references to the US Gaap (US generally accepted accounting principles), in particular to its FAS 133 standard. FAS 133 *Accounting for Derivative Instruments and Hedging Activities* is the US Gaap equivalent to IAS 39. Although FAS 133 follows similar principles to IAS 39, there are some differences. We have found it interesting to highlight some of the FAS 133 guidelines that may be useful to justify unclear accounting treatments by IAS 39.

1.1 ACCOUNTING CATEGORIES FOR FINANCIAL ASSETS AND LIABILITIES

Under IAS 39, a financial instrument is any contract that gives rise to both a financial asset in one entity and a financial liability or equity instrument of another entity.

IAS 39 does not cover the accounting treatment of some financial instruments. For example, own equity instruments, insurance contracts, leasing contracts, specific financial guarantees,

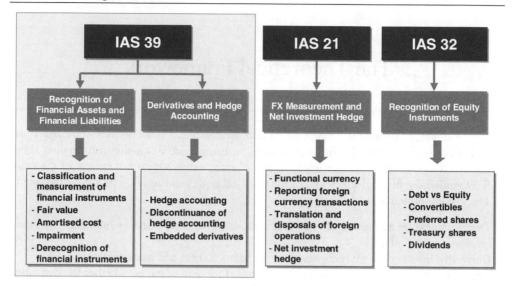

Figure 1.1   Scope of IAS 21, IAS 32 and IAS 39.

weather derivatives, loans not settled in cash (or in another financial instrument), interests in subsidiaries/associates/joint ventures, employee benefit plans, share-based payment transactions, contracts to buy/sell an acquiree in a business combination, contracts for contingent consideration in a business combination, some financial guarantee contracts and some commodity contracts are outside the scope of IAS 39.

1.1.1   Financial Assets Categories

A financial asset is any asset that is cash, a contractual right to receive cash or another financial asset, a contractual right to exchange financial instruments with another entity under conditions that are potentially favourable, or an equity instrument of another entity. Financial assets include derivatives with a fair value favourable to the entity.

IAS 39 considers four categories of financial assets:

1) Financial assets held-to-maturity are non-derivative financial assets with fixed or determinable payments and fixed maturity so that the entity has the positive intention and ability to hold to maturity. The assets classified in this category are subject to severe restrictions, so in reality entities are quite reluctant to include assets in this category.
   - This category includes: non-callable debt, callable debt (provided that if it is called the holder would recover substantially all of debt's carrying amount), mandatorily redeemable preferred shares, etc.
   - This category excludes: originated loans, equity securities (because of their indefinite life), puttable debt (because the entity may not hold it to maturity if option is exercised), perpetual debt (because of their indefinite life), etc. It also excludes financial assets that the issuer has the right to settle at an amount significantly below its amortised cost.
   - The intention and ability to hold the asset to maturity is assessed at initial recognition and at each balance sheet date.

2) Loans and receivables originated by the entity.
   - It includes loan assets, trade receivables and deposits held in banks. It also includes purchased loans and other debt investments that are not quoted in an active market.
3) Financial assets at fair value through P&L (also called financial assets held for trading) are financial assets that: (i) are acquired or originated principally for the purpose of selling them in the short term, or (ii) are part of a portfolio of identified financial instruments that are managed together and for which there is evidence of a recent actual pattern of short-term profit taking; or (iii) a derivative not designated in a hedging relationship, or the ineffective part if designated.
4) Investments available-for-sale. This category includes all debt and equity financial assets not classified in any of the previous categories.

Financial assets held-to-maturity are subject to severe sale restrictions. There is a two full year tainting provision if a held-to-maturity asset is sold or reclassified unless an isolated unanticipated event beyond the entity's control (e.g., a significant deterioration in credit worthiness, a change in tax law relating to interest on asset, a major business combination that requires the sale of the asset, or a certain regulatory change that significantly modifies the capital requirements of holding the asset) takes place, or unless the amount sold or reclassified is insignificant or the maturity/call date is very near. Additionally, the entity must also reclassify all its held-to-maturity assets as available-for-sale assets. In such a case, a transfer back to held-to-maturity is possible after the end of the tainting period.

1.1.2 Financial Assets Recognition

An entity recognises a financial asset when and only when the entity becomes a party to the contractual provisions of a financial instrument. The initial measurement of the financial asset is its fair value, which normally is the consideration given, including directly related transaction costs. The diagram below gives an overview of the accounting treatment of each category of financial assets:

Asset Category	Measurement	Fair Value Changes
Held-to-maturity	Amortised cost less impairment. Any premium or discount is amortised to P&L	Not relevant unless impaired. Impairment can be reversed through P&L.
Available for sale	Fair value (unless fair value cannot be measured reliably)	Changes in fair value recorded in equity (unless impaired or FX gains/losses) until disposal or collection of the asset. Impairment of equity instruments cannot be reversed through P&L. Impairment of debt can be reversed through P&L.
Loans and receivables	Amortised cost less impairment. Any premium or discount is amortised to P&L	Not relevant unless impaired. Impairment can be reversed through P&L.
At fair value through P&L	Fair value	Changes in fair value recorded in P&L.

1.1.3 Financial Liabilities

A financial liability is any liability that is a contractual obligation to deliver cash or another financial asset to another entity or to exchange financial instruments with another entity under conditions that are potentially unfavourable.

Under IAS 39 there are only two categories of financial liabilities: at fair value through profit and loss, and other financial liabilities. The following table summarises the accounting treatment of each category of financial liabilities:

Liability Category	Measurement	Fair Value Changes
At fair value through profit and loss	Fair value	Changes in fair value recorded in P&L
Other financial liabilities	Amortised cost	Not relevant as liabilities not valued at fair value

The category of financial liabilities at fair value through profit and loss has two sub-categories: liabilities held for trading and those designated to the category at their inception. Financial liabilities classified as held for trading include:

- financial liabilities acquired or incurred principally for the purpose of generating a short-term profit;
- a derivative not designated in a hedging relationship, or the ineffective part if designated;
- obligations to deliver securities or other financial assets borrowed by a short seller;
- financial liabilities that are part of a portfolio of identified financial instruments that are managed together and for which there is evidence of a recent actual pattern of short-term profit taking.

1.1.4 The Fair Value Option

Sometimes entities try to record financial assets and liabilities at fair value through P&L to benefit from the natural offsetting of a particular risk affecting the asset and the liability, even if the movements in the value of the asset and the liability are only partially correlated. The fair value option allows an entity to designate a financial asset or a financial liability to be measured at fair value with changes in value recognised in P&L.

Under IAS 39, the usage of the fair value option is severely restricted. In our view, this limitation is aimed to avoid its inappropriate use by financial institutions. An entity can designate an item to be recorded at fair value through P&L if it meets one of two main criteria:

1) It eliminates or significantly reduces a measurement or recognition inconsistency (i.e., an accounting mismatch) that would otherwise arise from measuring assets or liabilities, or recognising the gains and losses on them on different bases. For example:
   - where the cash flows of liabilities are contractually based on the performance of assets that would otherwise be classified as available-for-sale;
   - where liabilities under insurance contracts are related to assets that would otherwise be classified as available-for-sale or measured at amortised cost;
   - where financial assets and/or financial liabilities held by an entity share a risk such as an interest rate risk, but only one of the two would otherwise be measured at fair value (for instance because it is a derivative), or whether the arrangement does not meet

the requirements for hedge accounting because, for instance, effectiveness cannot be demonstrated, or hedge accounting is not possible because none of the instruments are derivatives. An example of this would be where an entity has a portfolio of fixed-rate assets that would otherwise be classified as available-for-sale, plus fixed rate liabilities that would otherwise be recorded at amortised cost.

2) A group of financial assets and/or financial liabilities is managed and its performance is evaluated on a fair value basis, in accordance with a documented risk management or investment strategy, and this is the basis on which information about the assets and/or liabilities is provided internally to the entity's key management personnel. For example:

- where management evaluates and manages a portfolio of assets and liabilities that share similar risks on a fair value basis in accordance with a documented risk management policy. This would include structured products containing multiple embedded derivatives.

If a contract contains one or more embedded derivatives, under some circumstances, it may be simplest to use the fair value option to value the entire contract, eliminating the burden of identifying all of the embedded derivatives, determining which are required to be separated under IAS 39 and valuing those that are required to be separated. This is specially helpful for structured debt issues hedged with other derivatives. An entity may apply the fair value option to the entire combined contract unless:

- that embedded derivative does not significantly modify the cash flows that otherwise would be required by the contract; or
- it is clear with little or no analysis that separation of the embedded derivative is prohibited.

IAS 39 does not allow for the designation at fair value through P&L of:

- financial assets and financial liabilities whose fair value cannot reliably measured; or
- investments in equity instruments that do not have a quoted market price in an active market and whose fair value cannot be reliably measured.

The option to record at fair value is only available on initial recognition of the financial asset or liability. This requirement may create a problem if the entity enters into offsetting contracts on different dates. A first financial instrument may be acquired in the anticipation that it will provide a natural offset to another instrument that has yet to be acquired. If the natural hedge is not in place at the outset, IAS 39 would not allow to record the first financial instrument at fair value through P&L, as it would not eliminate or significantly reduce a measurement or recognition inconsistency. Additionally, to impose discipline, an entity is precluded from reclassifying financial instruments in or out of the fair value category.

1.2 THE AMORTISED COST CALCULATION: THE EFFECTIVE INTEREST RATE

We saw earlier that some assets and liabilities are measured at amortised cost. The amortisation is calculated using the effective interest rate. This rate is applied to the carrying amount at each reporting date to determine the interest expense for the period. The effective interest rate is the rate that exactly discounts the stream of principal and interest cash flows to the initial net proceeds. In this way, the contractual interest expense in each period is adjusted to amortise any premium, discount or transaction costs over the life of the instrument.

The carrying amount of an instrument accounted for at amortised cost is computed as:

- the amount to be repaid at maturity (usually the principal amount); plus
- any unamortised original premium, net of transaction costs; or less
- any unamortised original discount including transaction costs; less
- principal repayments; less
- any reduction for impairment or uncollectibility.

Transaction costs include fees, commissions and taxes paid to other parties. Transaction costs do not include internal administrative costs.

1.2.1 Example of Effective Interest Rate Calculation

Let us assume that an entity issues a bond with the following terms:

Nominal amount: € 1,250
Maturity: 5 years
Issue proceeds: € 1,250

Coupons: 6 % (first year)
8 % (second year)
10 % (third year)
12 % (fourth year)
16.3 % (fifth year)

The effective interest rate (IRR) is computed as the rate that discounts exactly estimated future cash payments through the expected life of the financial instrument:

$$1,250 = \frac{75}{1 + IRR} + \frac{100}{(1 + IRR)^2} + \frac{125}{(1 + IRR)^3} + \frac{150}{(1 + IRR)^4} + \frac{(1,250 + 204)}{(1 + IRR)^5}$$

Solving this equation we get an IRR = 10 %. The amortised cost of the liability at each accounting date is computed as follows:

Year	Amortised Cost beginning Year (a)	Interest (b) = (a) * 10%	Cash Flow (c)	Amortised Cost End of Year (d) = (a) + (b) − (c)
1	1,250	125	75	1,300
2	1,300	130	100	1,330
3	1,330	133	125	1,338
4	1,338	134	150	1,322
5	1,322	132	1.250 + 204	—

1.3 HEDGE ACCOUNTING – RECOGNISING DERIVATIVE INSTRUMENTS

1.3.1 Derivative Definition

Under IAS 39, a derivative is a financial instrument (or other contract within the scope of IAS 39) with all of the following characteristics:

1) Whose value changes in response to changes in an "underlying" price or index: an interest rate, a FX rate, a commodity price, a security price, a credit rating, or an index of any of the above; and
2) That requires no initial investment, or significantly less than the investment required to purchase the underlying instrument; and
3) That is settled at a future date.

Some commodity-based derivatives are not considered a derivative under IAS 39. In Chapter 8 there is a detailed discussion regarding which commodity contracts can be treated as an IAS 39 instrument.

1.3.2 Hedge Accounting

Hedge accounting is a technique that modifies the normal basis for recognising gains and losses (or revenues and expenses) associated with a hedged item or a hedging instrument to enable gains and losses on the hedging instrument to be recognised in P&L in the same period as off-setting losses and gains on the hedged item. Hedge accounting takes two forms under IAS 39:

- Fair value hedge: Recognising gains or losses (or revenues or expenses) in respect of both the hedging instrument and hedged item in earnings in the same accounting period.
- Cash flow or net investment hedge: Deferring recognised gains and losses in respect of the hedging instrument on the balance sheet until the hedged item affects earnings.

The following example highlights the timing of the impacts on P&L when using, or not, hedge accounting. Assume that an entity enters in 20X0 into a derivative to hedge a risk exposure of an item that is already recognised in the balance sheet. The derivative matures in 20X1 and the hedged item settles in 20X2. It can be observed that only the fair value hedge provided a perfect synchronisation between the hedging instrument and hedged item recognitions.

Without hedging

	20X1	20X2	Total
Hedging instrument	1,000		1,000
Hedged item (realised gain)		<1,000>	<1,000>
Net profit/(loss)	1,000	<1,000>	−0−

With fair value hedge

	20X1	20X2	Total
Hedging instrument	1,000		1,000
Hedged item (unrealised gain)	<1,000>		<1,000>
Net profit/(loss)	−0−	−0−	−0−

With cash flow hedge

	20X1	20X2	Total
Hedging instrument (after deferral in equity)		1,000	1,000
Hedged item (realised gain)		<1,000>	<1,000>
Net profit/(loss)	−0−	−0−	−0−

To be able to apply hedge accounting, very strict criteria including the existence of formal documentation and the achievement of effectiveness tests, must be met at inception and throughout the life of the hedging relationship:

- The hedging relationship must be documented in detail.
- The hedge must be expected to be highly effective.
- For cash flow hedges, the forecasted transaction must be highly probable.
- The effectiveness of the hedge must be measured reliably.
- The effectiveness of the hedging relationship must be assessed on an ongoing basis, and the relationship must be deemed to be highly effective throughout the entire hedge relationship term.

1.3.3   Accounting for Derivatives

As we mentioned earlier, all derivatives are recognised at fair value on the balance sheet, no matter whether they qualify for hedge accounting or not. There are two exceptions to this requirement: (i) derivatives whose underlying is an unquoted equity instrument (they are carried at cost until settlement), or (ii) any other derivatives whose fair value cannot be measured reliably (they are carried at cost or amortised cost until settlement).

Accounting for fluctuations on the derivative's fair value can be recognised in four different ways, depending on the type of hedge relationship:

- Undesignated or speculative.
- Fair-value hedge.
- Cash flow hedge.
- Net investment hedge.

1.3.4   Undesignated or Speculative

Some derivatives are termed "undesignated" or "speculative". They include derivatives that do not qualify for hedge accounting. They also include derivatives that the entity may decide to treat as undesignated even though they could qualify for hedge accounting. These derivatives are recognised as assets or liabilities for trading. The gain or loss arising from their fair value fluctuation is recognised directly in P&L.

1.3.5   Fair-value Hedge

The objective of the fair value hedge is to reduce the exposure to changes in the fair value of an asset or liability already recognised in the Balance Sheet, or a previously unrecognised firm commitment (or an identified portion of such an asset, liability or firm commitment), that is attributable to a particular risk and could affect reported P&L. Therefore, the aim of the fair value hedge is to offset in P&L the change in fair value of the hedged item with the change in fair value of the derivative (see Figure 1.2).

The recognition of the hedging instrument is as follows:

- If the hedging instrument is a derivative, losses or gains from remeasuring the derivative at fair value are recognised in P&L.

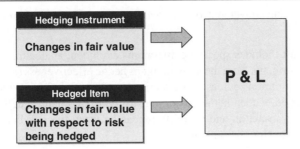

Figure 1.2   Accounting for Fair Value Hedge.

- If the hedging instrument is a non-derivative, the amount recognised in P&L related to the hedged item is the gain or loss from remeasuring, in accordance with IAS 21, the foreign currency component of its carrying amount.

The recognition of the hedged item is as follows:

- If the hedge item is otherwise measured at cost, the carrying amount of the hedged item is adjusted for the loss or gain attributable to the hedged risk with the corresponding gain or loss recognised in P&L. This also applies if the hedged item is an available-for-sale financial asset measured at fair value.
- If the hedged item is measured at amortised cost, the adjustment of the carrying amount affects the effective interest rate calculation for the hedged item. In practice, to ease the administrative burden of amortising the adjustment while the hedged item continues to be adjusted for changes in fair value attributable to the hedged risk, it may be easier to defer amortising the adjustment until the hedged item ceases to be adjusted for the designated hedged risk. An entity must apply the same amortisation policy for all of its debt instruments. However, an entity cannot defer amortising on some items and not on others.
- If the hedged item is an unrecognised firm commitment, the subsequent cumulative change in the fair value of the unrecognised firm commitment attributable to the hedged risk is recognised as an asset or a liability with a corresponding gain or loss recognised in P&L. If the firm commitment is to acquire an asset or assume a liability, the initial carrying amount of the asset or liability that results from the entity meeting the firm commitment is adjusted to include the cumulative change in the fair value of the commitment attributable to the hedged risk that was recognised in the Balance Sheet.

1.3.6   Cash Flow Hedge

A cash flow hedge is a hedge of the exposure to variability in cash flows that:

- is attributable to a particular risk associated with a recognised asset or liability, or a highly probable external forecasted transaction; and
- could affect reported P&L.

The portion of the gain or loss on the hedging instrument (e.g., the derivative) that is determined to be an effective hedge is recognised directly in a separate reserve in equity. Any ineffective portion of the fair value movement on the hedging instrument is recorded immediately in P&L.

- The ineffective part includes specific components excluded, as documented in the entity's risk management strategy, from the assessment of hedge effectiveness (e.g., the time value of an option). Other common sources of ineffectiveness for a cash flow hedge are (i) structured derivative features embedded in the hedging instrument, (ii) changes in timing of the highly probable forecast transaction and (iii) differences between the risk being hedged and the underlying of the hedging instrument.
- When ineffectiveness is present, the amount of gains or losses on the hedging instrument that can be deferred in the accumulated reserve is limited to the lesser of either the cumulative change from the inception of the hedge in the fair value of the actual hedging instrument or the cumulative change from the inception of the hedge in the fair value of the hedged item.

The Under-Hedging Temptation

An entity may be tempted to under-hedge its cash flow exposure to increase the likelihood that the cumulative change in value of the hedged item for the risk being hedged does not exceed the cumulative change in fair value of the hedged item for the risk being hedged, and consequently lessen the possibility of recording ineffectiveness. IAS 39 precludes the voluntary use of under-hedging, however it is quite difficult to detect it when the hedging instrument is a highly structured derivative.

This temptation does not make sense for fair value hedges because both gains and losses on the hedged item and the hedging instrument are recognised in P&L. Therefore, both the effective part and the ineffective part are going to be recorded in P&L.

This gain or loss deferred in equity is reclassified, or "recycled", to P&L in the same period or periods the hedged item affects P&L, therefore offsetting to the extent that the hedge is effective (see Figure 1.3). For example:

- if the hedged item is a variable rate borrowing, the reclassification to P&L is recognised in P&L within "finance costs";
- if the hedged item is an export sale, the reclassification to P&L is recognised in the P&L statement within "sales";
- if the hedged item is a forecast transaction that will result in the recognition of a non-financial asset or non-financial liability (e.g., a raw purchase material, or a purchase of inventory), the

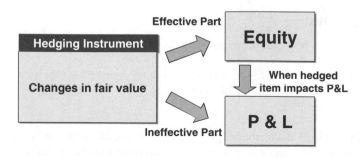

Figure 1.3   Accounting for Cash-Flow Hedge.

entity may choose to adjust the initial carrying amount of the recorded asset or liability (e.g., within "inventories") by the amount deferred in equity, or to keep the amount deferred in equity and gradually transferring it into P&L in the same periods during which the asset or liability affects P&L (i.e., when the depreciation expense or cost of sales is recognised). The choice has to be applied consistently to all such hedges. However, such a basis adjustment is not permitted where a financial asset or liability (e.g., accounts payable) results from the hedged forecast transaction.

A hedge of the FX risk of a firm commitment may be accounted for as a fair value hedge or as a cash flow hedge.

1.3.7 Net Investment Hedge

A net investment hedge is a hedge of the foreign currency exposure arising from the reporting entity's interest in the net assets of a foreign operation. The hedging instrument may be either a derivative or a non-derivative (e.g., a borrowing denominated in the same currency as the net investment). Figure 1.4 highlights the accounting treatment of net investment hedges.

- The effective portion of the gain or loss on the hedging instrument is recognised in equity. As the exchange difference arising on the net investment is also recognised in equity, the objective is to match both exchange rate differences. Gains or losses relating to the ineffective portion of the hedge are recognised immediately in P&L.
- On disposal or liquidation of the foreign operation, the hedge equity balance and the net investment exchange differences are transferred simultaneously to P&L.

1.3.8 Embedded Derivatives

Sometimes, a derivative is "embedded" in a financial instrument in combination with a host contract. The combination of a host contract and an embedded derivative is called *hybrid contract*. The embedded derivative causes the contractual cash flows to be modified based on a specified interest rate, a security price, a commodity price, a foreign exchange rate, index of prices or rates, or other variables. The principle under IAS 39 is that an embedded

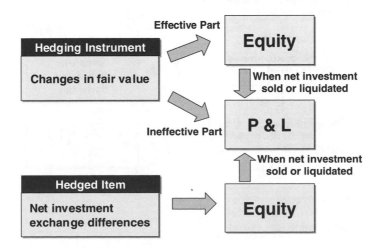

Figure 1.4   Accounting for Net Investment Hedge.

derivative should be split (except in specific situations) from the host contract and accounted for separately.

> For example, an entity might issue a low coupon bond that is exchangeable for shares in another listed company. Under IAS 39, the amount received for the exchangeable bond is split between the receipt for the fair value of the debt security and the fair value of the equity conversion option.

IAS 39 does not require the separation of the embedded derivative (see Figure 1.5):

1) if the host contract is accounted for at fair value, with changes in fair value recorded in profit and loss; or
2) if the derivative does not qualify as a derivative if it were freestanding; or
3) if the economic characteristics and risks of the embedded derivative are closely related to those of the host contract.

The principle of "clearly and closely related" is explained in IAS 39 only by providing examples of contracts that pass and fail the test. As a consequence, it is likely that some subjective interpretation may arise for contracts not covered in the examples. Contracts with embedded derivatives to be separated include:

• options to extend the maturity date of fixed rate debt, except when interest rates are reset to market rates;
• any derivative that "leverages" the payments that would otherwise take place under the host contract;
• Credit-linked notes, convertible bonds, equity or commodity indexed notes, notes with embedded currency options.

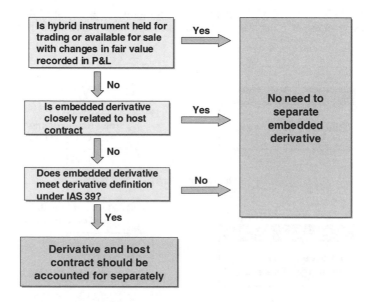

Figure 1.5   Separation of Embedded Derivative – Decision Tree.

Examples of contracts not requiring separation include:

- debt without leveraged interest rates;
- debt without leveraged inflation (although this is questionable);
- debt with vanilla interest rate options;
- debt with cash flows linked to the creditworthiness of a debtor.

A derivative that is attached to a host contract but is contractually transferable independently of the host contract, or has a different counterparty from the host contract, is not an embedded derivative but a separate one.

1.4 HEDGING RELATIONSHIP TERMINATION EVENTS

In certain circumstances, it is necessary for an entity to discontinue prospectively hedge accounting. A hedging relationship may be terminated due to any of the following:

- The hedging instrument expires or is sold, terminated or exercised. It is not a termination or expiration if the hedging instrument is replaced or rolled-over into another hedging instrument, if such replacement or roll-over is part of the entity's documented hedging strategy; or
- The hedge fails the highly effective test or its effectiveness is no longer measurable; or
- The entity voluntarily decides so. The entity may de-designate the hedging relationship by designating a new hedging accounting relationship with the same hedging instrument; or
- The hedged item ceases to exist as a result of either (i) the recognised hedged item matures, is sold or terminated, or (ii) the forecast transaction is no longer expected to occur.

In total there are six different accounting treatments depending upon the kind of hedge and the cause of discontinuance:

1) Hedging instrument of a cash flow hedge expires or is sold. The hedging gains or losses that were previously recognised in equity remain in equity and are transferred to P&L when the hedged item is ultimately recognised in P&L.
2) The fair value hedge fails the highly effective test. Adjustments to the carrying amount of the hedged item previously recorded as of the last assessment (which was highly effective) remain part of the hedged item's carrying value. If the entity can demonstrate exactly when the test failed, it can record the change in fair value of the hedged item up to the last moment the hedge was highly effective. From this moment there is no further fair valuing of the hedged item. The adjustments to the carrying value of the hedged item to date are amortised over the life of the hedged item. When the hedged item is carried at amortised cost, the amortisation is performed by recalculating its effective interest rate.
3) The firm commitment of a fair value hedge is no longer firm or the fair value hedged item no longer exists. Any amounts recorded on the balance sheet related to the change in fair value of the hedged item are reversed out to P&L.
4) The cash flow hedge fails the highly effective test or the hedging instrument expires or is sold. The hedging gains or losses that were previously recorded in equity as of the last test (which was highly effective) remain deferred and are transferred from equity to P&L when the forecast transaction is ultimately recognised in P&L. If the entity can demonstrate exactly when the cash flow hedge failed the highly effective test, it can record the change in fair value on the hedged item in equity up to the last moment it was highly effective.

5) The forecasted transaction of a cash flow hedge is either no longer highly probable or no longer expected to take place. Two different treatments are possible: (i) if the forecasted transaction is no longer highly probable but it is still expected to occur, the cumulative hedge gains or losses that were previously recorded in equity remain deferred in equity until the hedged cash flow is recognised in P&L, or (ii) if the forecasted transaction is no longer expected to take place, the cumulative hedge gains or losses that had been deferred up to that point in equity are reclassified immediately to P&L.

6) Voluntary termination by the entity of the fair value or cash flow hedge. For fair value hedges, the adjustments to the carrying value of the hedged item to date are amortised over the life of the hedged item. When the hedged item is carried at amortised cost, the amortisation is performed by recalculating its effective interest rate. For cash flow hedges, the amounts previously recorded in equity remain in equity until the underlying hedged item impacts P&L. For net investment hedges, the amounts previously recorded in equity remain there until the related "translation adjustments" amount is reversed.

In any type of termination, if any derivatives from the terminated hedges are still outstanding, then they should continue to be fully marked-to-market on the balance sheet, with any subsequent change in fair value recorded in P&L.

If a hedging instrument fails the retrospective test it can subsequently be redesignated in a hedge relationship with the same hedged item as long as the hedge accounting requirements are met, including prospective hedge effectiveness. However, the entity will need a robust basis for concluding that the new hedge will be highly effective.

The following table summarises the accounting treatment of the different hedging termination events:

Termination Event	Fair Value Hedge	Cash flow Hedge
Hedging instrument expires, is sold, terminated or exercised	No further fair valuing of the hedged item. Any previous adjustments to the carrying amount of the hedged item are amortised over the remaining maturity of the hedged item	Deferred equity balance remains deferred in equity until forecast transaction impacts P&L
Hedge fails highly effective test	Same as above	Same as above
Voluntary termination by entity	Same as above	Same as above
Forecast transaction still expected to occur, although not highly expected	Not applicable	Same as above
Forecast transaction no longer expected to occur	Not applicable	Deferred equity balance is reclassified immediately to P&L

1.5   HEDGED ITEM CANDIDATES

In a hedging relationship there are two elements: a hedged item and a hedging instrument. A hedged item is the element that is designated as being hedged. The fundamental principle is that the hedged item creates an exposure to risk that could affect the income statement.

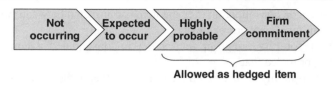

Allowed as hedged item

Figure 1.6   Scale of Probability of a Forecasted Transaction.

The hedged item can be:

- a recognised asset or a liability;
- an unrecognised firm commitment. A firm commitment is a legally binding agreement for the exchange of a specified quantity of resources at a specified price on a specified future date or dates;
- a highly probable forecasted external transaction (see Figure 1.6). A forecast transaction is an anticipated transaction that is not yet legally committed. In assessing "highly probable" the entity must consider among others the frequency of similar past transactions.
- a net investment in a foreign operation (on a consolidated basis only);
- a group of assets, liabilities, firm commitments, highly probable forecasted external transactions, or net investments in foreign operations, as long as they share the risk exposure that is designated as being hedged. This "sharing" condition is very restrictive: "the change in fair value attributable to the hedged risk for each individual item in the group shall be expected to be approximately proportional to the overall change in fair value of the group of items attributable to the hedged risk". It does not qualify for hedge accounting comparing a hedging instrument with an overall net position (e.g., the net of all fixed rate assets and fixed rate liabilities with similar maturities), rather than with a specific hedged item.

> This would preclude for example the use of hedge accounting if a put option on the DAX index is purchased to hedge the fair value of a portfolio of shares members of the DAX index. Even though the hedge is perfect from an economic point of view, the portfolio cannot be designated as a hedged item because the fair value of the individual shares does not move in an approximately proportional manner to the fair value of the portfolio as a whole;

- a non-financial asset (e.g. inventory) or a non-financial liability for the risk of changes in the fair value "in its entirety" for all risks, or for a hedge of FX risk only, because of the difficulty of isolating other risks;
- one or more selected contractual cash flows, or portions of them or a percentage of the fair value, of a financial asset or a financial liability, provided that effectiveness can be measured. For example, it is possible to hedge only part of the life of a loan or only to hedge the Euribor interest rate in a loan paying Euribor plus a margin;
- an amount of assets or an amount of liabilities (rather than as individual assets or liabilities) in a fair value hedge of the interest rate exposure of a *portfolio* of financial assets and/or financial liabilities. Designation of a net amount including assets and liabilities is not permitted;
- an intragroup monetary item (e.g., a payable/receivable between two subsidiaries) in the consolidated financial statements if it results in an exposure to FX gains or losses that are

not fully eliminated on consolidation (i.e., the item is transacted between two group entities that have different functional currencies);

- A highly probable forecast intragroup transaction, in consolidated statements and in a FX cash flow hedge, provided that:
  1) the transaction is highly probable and meets all the other hedge accounting criteria (with the exception of the requirement that it involves a party external to the group), and
  2) the hedged FX transaction is denominated in a currency other than the functional currency of the entity entering into it and the FX risk affects consolidated P&L. The entity can be a parent, subsidiary, associate, joint venture or branch. An example of this sort of transactions is a forecast sale or purchase of inventory between members of the same group if there is an onward sale of inventory to party external to the group. Another example is a forecast intragroup sale of equipment from the group entity that manufactured it to a group entity that will use the equipment in its operation (it affects P&L because the equipment will be depreciated by the purchasing entity, and the amount initially recognised may change if it is denominated in a currency other than the functional currency of the purchasing entity).

IAS 39 imposes the following restrictions or conditions regarding the hedge item:

- Held-to-maturity instruments cannot be hedged items with respect to interest rate risk or prepayment risk because held-to-maturity investments require an intention to hold to maturity without regard to changes in fair value or cash flows due to changes in interest rates. Held-to-maturity instruments can be hedged items with respect to credit risk or FX risk.
- A derivative cannot be designated as a hedging item. The only exception is an embedded purchased option that is hedged with a written option.
- The other counterparty has to be a party external to the entity. The only exceptions are intragroup monetary items that can be hedged items with respect to FX risk in the consolidated financial statements if it results in an exposure to FX gains or losses that are not fully eliminated on consolidation (i.e., monetary items transacted between two group entities that have different functional currencies).
- An entity's transaction in its own equity cannot be a hedged item because it does not expose the entity to a particular risk that could impact P&L. Similarly, a forecast dividend payment by the entity cannot be a hedged item as its distribution to equity holders is debited directly to equity and therefore does not impact P&L.
- An equity method investment cannot be the hedge item in a fair value hedge, as the equity investor does not recognise changes in fair value in P&L, but accounts for its share of the investee's P&L.

1.6   HEDGING INSTRUMENT CANDIDATES

The following can be designated as hedging instruments:

- A derivative that involves an external party, except for most written options. A written option can only be designated as hedging instrument in combination with a purchased option and under certain conditions.
- An external non-derivative financial asset or liability, but only for hedges of FX risk.

- A portion of the entire hedging instrument. The portion must be a percentage of the entire derivative (for example, 40 % of the notional). It is not possible to designate a hedging instrument only for a portion of its life.
- Two or more derivatives, or portions of their nominal, can be viewed in combination as the hedging instrument if none of them is a written option. A combination of a purchased and a written option can be a hedging instrument if the written option meets certain requirements.
- A single hedging instrument my be designated as a hedge for more than one type of risk provided that: (i) the risks being hedged can be identified clearly, (ii) the effectiveness of the hedge can be demonstrated, and (iii) it is possible to ensure that there is specific designation of the hedging instrument and the different risk positions.

1.7 HEDGING RELATIONSHIP DOCUMENTATION

One of the fundamental requirements for a hedging relationship to qualify for hedge accounting is that formal hedge documentation be prepared at inception of the hedging relationship. The formal documentation must identify the following:

- The entity's risk management objective and strategy for undertaking the hedge: an explanation of the rationale for contracting the hedge. It should include evidence that the hedge is consistent with the entity's risk management objectives and strategies.
- The type of hedge: fair value, cash flow, or net investment hedge.
- The specific risk being hedged: foreign exchange risk, interest rate risk, equity price risk, commodity price risk or credit risk.
- The hedging instrument: its terms and how it will be fair valued.
- The hedged item: a sufficiently detailed explanation of the hedged item.
  - For fair value hedges, the document must include the method for recognising in earnings the gains or losses in the fair value of the hedged item.
  - If the hedged item is a forecasted transaction, the documentation should also include references to the timing (i.e., the estimated date), the nature and amount of the forecasted transaction. It also should include the rationale for the forecasted transaction being highly probable to occur and the method for reclassifying into P&L amounts deferred in equity.
- How effectiveness will be assessed, both prospectively and retrospectively. It includes the method to be used and the frequency of the tests. The entity should also disclose if the tests will be performed on a cumulative basis or on a period-by-period basis.

The following is an example of a hedge documentation for a highly expected foreign currency export transaction hedged with a FX forward.

Hedging Relationship Documentation	
Risk management objective and strategy for undertaking the hedge	The objective of the hedge is to protect the EUR value of the USD 100 million highly expected sale of finished goods against unfavourable movements in the USD/EUR FX rate. This hedging objective is consistent with ABC's overall FX risk management strategy of reducing the variability of its Profit and Loss statement.
Type of hedge	Cash flow hedge.
Risk being hedged	FX risk. The variability in EUR value of the highly expected transaction.

(*Continued*)

Hedging Relationship Documentation	
Hedging instrument	The FX forward contract with reference number 012345. The counterparty to the forward is XYZ Bank and the credit risk associated with this counterparty is considered to be very low.
Hedged item	USD 100 million sale of finished goods expected to take place on 31 March 20X5
Assessment of effectiveness testing	Hedge effectiveness will be assessed by comparing changes in the fair value of the hedging instrument to changes in the fair value of the expected cash flow. Hedge effectiveness assessment will be performed on a forward-forward basis. In other words, the forward points of both the hedging instrument and the expected cash flow are included in the assessment. **Prospective test** A prospective test will be performed at each reporting date. Due to the fact that the terms of the hedging instrument and those of the expected cash flow match, the hedge is expected to be highly effective. The credit risk of the counterparty of the hedging instrument will be monitored continuously. **Retrospective test** A retrospective test will be performed at each reporting date using the "ratio analysis method". The ratio will compare the cumulative change since hedge inception in the fair value of the expected cash flow arising from the forecast sale with the cumulative change since hedge inception in the fair value of the hedging instrument. The hedge will be assumed to be highly effective on a retrospective basis if the ratio is between 80 % and 125 %.

1.8   EFFECTIVENESS TESTS

IAS 39 requires hedging strategies to be tested for effectiveness in order to apply hedge accounting. Effectiveness is probably the most challenging aspect of achieving hedge accounting. Effectiveness is simply the extent to which changes in the fair value or cash flows of the hedged item that are attributable to a hedged risk are offset by changes in the fair value or cash flows of the hedging instrument. IAS 39 requires that hedge effectiveness be evaluated at the inception of the hedge and then monitored at each balance-sheet date, including interim financial statements. IAS 39 requires two separate tests to be applied (see Figure 1.7):

- A prospective test, that shows that the hedge is expected to be highly effective looking forward. This test must be performed at inception and at least at each balance-sheet date.
- A retrospective test, that shows that the actual hedge results to have been effective during the accounting period. This test must be performed at least at each balance-sheet date.

1.8.1   Prospective test

The objective of the prospective test is to prove that the hedge is expected to be highly effective during the life of the hedge. The prospective test must be performed at inception and at least at each balance-sheet date. IAS 39 states that to pass the prospective effectiveness test, changes in fair value or cash flows of the hedging instrument must effectively offset changes in the fair

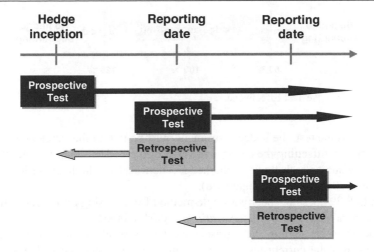

Figure 1.7 Effectiveness Tests.

value or cash flows of the hedged item. IAS 39 does specify an 80 %–125 % range required for the results of a test to be considered highly effective.

Although IAS 39 does not specify a single method for assessing prospective hedge effectiveness, in general it is done in one of three ways:

- Using a qualitative assessment if the terms of the hedging instrument and hedged item match exactly. This method is called the "critical terms" method. If notional amounts, terms, pricing dates, timing and currency of cash flows match then the hedge relationship is expected to be perfectly effective. This expectation is valid while the credit risk associated with the counterparty to the hedging instrument is considered to be very low; or
- Assessing how effective the hedging relationship was, or would have been, in prior periods using historical information. This testing is usually performed using the linear regression method; or
- Applying scenario analysis: modelling how effective the hedging relationship would be under several possible scenarios. This testing is usually performed using the Monte Carlo simulation method.

A thorough review of the prospective test method is usually needed if the retrospective test does not pass. Giving special attention to reviewing the prospective test may also be needed if a significant part of the change in fair value of the derivative or hedged item is due to counterparty credit risk. For this reason, assessment of credit risk forms a crucial part of the prospective tests.

1.8.2 Restrospective Test

Periodically, IAS 39 requires a retrospective test so the entity can prove whether the actual hedging relationship was effective in the last period (i.e., since the last test was performed). As a minimum, the retrospective test should be completed at each reporting date (each time annual or interim financial statements are prepared).

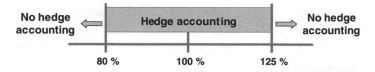

Figure 1.8   Retrospective Test Effectiveness.

In order to pass the test, the hedge instrument must be within the range of 80 %–125 % in terms of effectively offsetting the changes in value of the hedged item. In other words, if the change in fair value or cash flows of the hedged item is 100, the hedging instrument must change between 80 and 125 (see Figure 1.8).

Although IAS 39 does not specify a single method for assessing retrospective hedge effectiveness, in general it is done using the "*ratio analysis*" method.

A key choice in calculating the retrospective test is whether the changes in fair value are calculated over the current test period or cumulatively since the hedge inception. The cumulative basis is recommended since the change in fair value over a longer period should be more stable than over a shorter period and thus less likely to fall outside the of the 80 %–125 % range.

1.8.3   Restrospective Test Failure

If the hedge does not pass the restrospective test, hedge accounting may not be applied as of the end of the previous accounting period (i.e., the last time the hedging relationship was highly effective). The entity must determine whether the hedge will continue to be highly effective:

- The entity may conclude that the test failure was the result of an isolated event that is very unlikely to repeat itself. After reviewing the prospective test, the entity still considers that the hedging relationship is expected to be highly effective in the future. In this case, the hedging relationship continues to be in place and hedge accounting can be applied in the next period if both the next prospective and retrospective test pass.
- The entity may conclude that the test failure was the result of an event likely to be repeated. After reviewing the prospective test, the entity concludes that it does not expect the hedging relationship to be highly effective in the future. In this case, hedge accounting is discontinued.
- The entity cannot identify the event or change in circumstances that caused the hedge relationship to fail. In this case, hedge accounting is discontinued.

The European Airlines Dilemma

When hedging their exposure to jet fuel prices, airlines most of the time use crude oil derivatives instead of jet fuel derivatives as the former is a much more liquid market. Jet fuel and crude oil prices are approximately 90 % correlated in the long-term, but there are periods in which correlation falls below the 80 % minimum. As a consequence, airlines may find that the prospective test is passed while in some periods the retrospective test may fail.

1.9   METHODS FOR TESTING EFFECTIVENESS

IAS 39 does not prescribe a specific method to evaluate hedge effectiveness prospectively or retrospectively. However, IAS 39 requires an entity to specify at hedge inception, in the hedge documentation, the method it will apply to assess the hedge effectiveness and to apply that method consistently during the life of the hedging relationship. The method chosen by the entity has to be applied consistently to all similar hedges unless different methods are justified explicitly.

1.9.1   The Critical Terms Method

The "critical terms" method is the simplest way to assess hedge effectiveness prospectively. Under IAS 39, an entity has a valid expectation that the hedge will be highly effective if the terms of the derivative hedge are such that the changes in the derivative's fair value are expected to completely offset the expected changes in cash flows of the hedged risk on an ongoing basis.

At a minimum, the following critical terms must be the same:

- The notional amount of the derivative is equal to the notional amount of the hedged item.
- The maturity of the derivative equals the maturity of the hedged position.
- The underlying of the derivative matches the underlying hedged risk.
- The fair value of the derivative is zero at inception.

If the critical terms are met, the hedge can be justified as highly effective on a prospective basis. However, even if the critical terms method is used to pass the prospective test, the entity is still required to perform the retrospective effectiveness test. Nevertheless, if the critical terms are the same it is unlikely the retrospective test will fail unless there is a sudden deterioration in the creditworthiness of the derivative counterparty not detected in the assessment of the prospective test.

1.9.2   The Ratio Analysis or Dollar-Offset Method

The most commonly method used in retrospective tests is the "ratio analysis" method, also called the "dollar-offset" method. This method is the simplest and compares changes in fair values of the hedging instrument and hedged item over a given period. The retrospective test is deemed to be highly effective if the ratio is within the range 80 %–125 %.

$$\text{Ratio} = \frac{-\text{Change in fair value of hedging instrument}}{\text{Change in fair value of hedged item}}$$

The main weakness of the ratio analysis method is that the test may fail if fair value changes are relatively small. Consider for example a € 500 million bond hedged with an interest rate swap. A € 100 change in the value of the bond and a € 30 opposite change in the value of the swap will result in a ratio of 30 %. Thus, the hedge will be deemed ineffective even though the net change is insignificant compared to the size of the hedge. The best way to remedy this weakness is to use the cumulative change since the hedge inception in the fair values of both the hedging instrument and the hedged item.

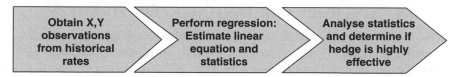

Figure 1.9   Stages of the Regression Analysis Method.

1.9.3   The Regression Analysis Method

The regression analysis method is the most commonly used method in prospective tests, when the critical terms method cannot be used. The idea is to analyse the behaviour of the hedging relationship using historical market rates. Regression analysis is a statistical technique that assesses the level of correlation between one variable (the dependent variable) and one or more other variables (known as independent variables). In the context of hedge effectiveness testing, the primary objective is to determine if changes in fair value of the hedged item and the hedging instrument attributable to a particular risk were highly correlated in the past and, thus, supportive of the assertion that there will be a high degree of offset in changes in fair value of the hedged item and the hedging instrument in the future. The regression analysis is a process that can be divided into three major steps, as shown in Figure 1.9.

The first step in the regression analysis is to obtain the inputs to the analysis: the X and Y observations. Figure 1.10 outlines this process. This step is quite complex and requires a computer program to perform it. The idea is to go back to a specific date (the simulation period start date), assume that the hedge relationship started on that date and observe the behaviour of the hedging relationship using the historical market data of the simulation period. The simulation period ends on a date such that the term of the simulation is equal to the term of the actual hedge. This process is repeated several times.

The second step of the regression analysis is to plot the values of the X and Y variables and to estimate a best "fitting" line. A pictorial representation of the variables in the standard regression equation is illustrated in Figure 1.11.

Regression analysis uses the "least squares" method to fit a line through the set of X and Y observations. This technique determines the slope and intercept of the line that minimises the size of the squared differences between the actual Y observations and the predicted Y values. The linear equation estimated is commonly expressed as:

$$Y = \alpha + \beta * X + \varepsilon, \text{ where}$$

X: Change in fair value (or cash flow) of the hedging instrument attributable to the risk to be hedged
Y: Change in fair value (or cash flow) of the hedged item attributable to the risk to be hedged
α: The intercept (where the line crosses the Y axis)
β: The slope of the line
ε: The random error term

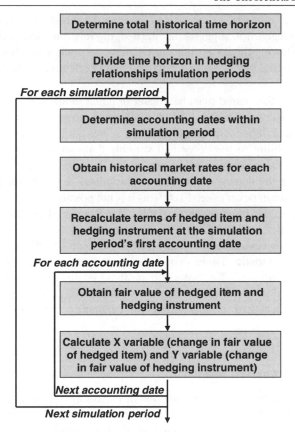

Figure 1.10   Process to Obtain X,Y Observations.

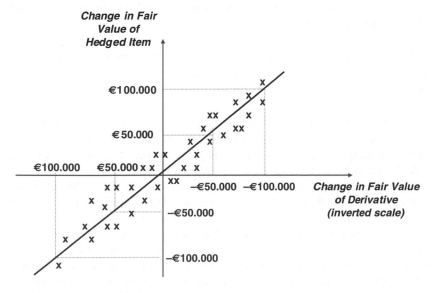

Figure 1.11   Regression Best Fitting Line.

The third step of the regression process is to interpret the statistical results of the regression and determine if the regression suggests that the hedging relationship is expected to be highly effective. All the following three statistics must achieve acceptable levels to provide sufficient evidence for the expectation that the hedge will be highly effective in the future:

• The R-squared. The R-squared must be greater or equal to 80 %. R-squared, or coefficient of determination, measures the degree of explanatory power or correlation between the dependent and the independent variables in the regression. The R-squared indicates the proportion of variability in the dependent variable that can be explained by variation in the independent variable. By way of illustration, an R-squared of 95 % indicates that 95 % of the movement in the dependent variable is "explained" by variation in the independent variable. R-squared can never exceed 100 % as it is not possible to explain more than 100 % of the movement in the independent variable. The R-squared by itself is an insufficient indicator of hedge performance.
• The slope β of the regression line. Usually a slope between -0.80 and -1.25 is accepted.
• The t-statistic or F-statistic. These two statistics measure whether the regression results are statistically significant. The t-statistic or the F-statistic must be compared to "t-tables" or "F-tables" to determine statistical significance. A 95 % or higher confidence level is generally accepted as appropriate for evaluating the statistical validity of the regression.

1.9.4   The Scenario Analysis Method

The scenario analysis method is another method of performing prospective tests. The goal of this method is to reveal the behaviour of changes in fair value of both the hedging item and the hedging instrument under specific scenarios. Each scenario assumes that the risk being hedged will move in a specific way over a certain period of time.

For example, a structured swap hedging the interest rate risk of a floating rate liability may be tested under the following scenarios:

1) A parallel shift of $+200$ basis points (bps) and -200 bps in the interest rate curve.
2) A steepening move of 200 bps in the interest rate curve.
3) An inversion move of 200 bps in the interest rate curve.

When a reduced number of scenarios are used, the main drawback of the scenario analysis method is the subjectivity in selecting the scenarios. The scenarios chosen may not be followed by the underlying hedged risk once the hedge is in place, and therefore the analysis conclusions may not depict a realistic expectation of hedge effectiveness.

One way to draw meaningful conclusions to the analysis is to test the behaviour of the changes in fair value of both the hedging item and the hedging instrument under a very large number of scenarios of the underlying risk. The Monte Carlo simulation is a tool that provides multiple scenarios by repeatedly estimating thousands of different paths of the risk being hedged, based on the probability distribution of the risk. In our view, a well-performed Monte Carlo simulation can be very appropriate to assess prospective effectiveness, as there is a high likelihood that one of the paths will become the actual path of the underlying risk.

1.9.5 The Volatility Risk Reduction Method (VRR)

The volatility risk reduction method (VRR) compares the risk of the combined position (hedged item plus hedging instrument) to the risk of the hedged item taken separately. In other words, the method assesses how small is the combined position risk relative to the hedged item risk. The VR is calculated by comparing the standard deviation of the combined position to the standard deviation of the hedged item only, as follows:

$$VRR = \frac{1 - \text{Standard deviation (hedged item + hedge instrument)}}{\text{Standard deviation (Hedged item)}}$$

$$VRR = \frac{1 - \text{Standard deviation } (X_i + Y_i)}{\text{Standard deviation } (Y_i)}$$

X_i: Change in fair value (or cash flow) of the hedging instrument attributable to the risk to be hedged
Y_i: Change in fair value (or cash flow) of the hedged item attributable to the risk to be hedged

If the VRR statistic is greater that some agreed-upon parameter, say 40 %, then the hedge relationship would pass the effectiveness test. It is considered that a VRR of 40 % is equivalent to a correlation of 80 %. This is the major drawback of the VR method: the threshold to consider high effectiveness may be different to IAS 39's 80 %–125 % benchmark. If, on the other hand, the entity decides to use a minimum VRR of 80 % to conclude that the hedge is expected to be highly effective, it may set a limit too unrealistic to be achieved. This is probably the reason why few entities use the VRR method for testing hedge effectiveness. Telecom Italia was one of the few entities adopting this method (see Figure 1.12).

The VRR method has three main advantages: Firstly, it takes into account the overall volatility. Secondly, it is consistent with the Value at Risk, or VaR approach, a risk measure that is used by a substantial number of entities. Finally, it can be determined with the outcome of only one statistic if the effectiveness test has passed.

"The selected method to test effectiveness, retrospectively and prospectively, of Fair Value Hedge instruments and Cash Flow Hedge instruments is the Volatility Risk Reduction Method (VRR)"

Figure 1.12 Telecom Italia – Annual Report 2005.

The VRR method can be used to determine the notional of the hedging instrument that optimises the effectiveness of the hedging relationship, as follows:

$$\text{NOMINAL}_{\text{INSTRUMENT}} = \text{NOMINAL}_{\text{ITEM}}{}^{*}(-\rho)^{*}\sigma_{\text{ITEM}}/\sigma_{\text{INSTRUMENT}}$$

Where,

ρ: correlation between the changes in fair value (or cash flow) of the hedged item and the hedging instrument

σ_{ITEM}: Standard deviation of the change in fair value (or cash flow) of the hedged item attributable to the risk to be hedged

$\sigma_{\text{INSTRUMENT}}$: Standard deviation of the change in fair value (or cash flow) of the hedging instrument attributable to the risk to be hedged

1.9.6   The Short-Cut Method for Interest Rate Swaps

The US Gaap's FAS 133 allows a method, called the "short-cut" method, for hedges of interest rate risk involving a recognised interest bearing asset or liability and an interest rate swap. The short-cut method can be applied to both fair value and cash flow hedges of debt. In the case of plain vanilla interest swaps (cross-currency swaps are thus not included), perfect effectiveness can be assumed if certain restrictive requirements are met, and therefore no periodic effectiveness testing is required. For time being, IAS 39 does not allow applying the short-cut method, and instead it allows the critical terms method which in a way can be considered a "light" short-cut method.

There are severe requirements in order to be able to use the short-cut method to make sure that the hedged item and the interest rate swap are perfectly matched and there is no chance of any ineffectiveness. These requirements include, for example, that notionals, maturities, interest periods, currency, and underlying interest rates in the swap and the hedged item coincide.

1.9.7   Concluding Remarks

All the methods demonstrate whether or not the hedging relationship is expected to be (or was) highly effective. However, we think that some methods are preferable to others (see Figure 1.13).

When assessing prospective effectiveness, we prefer the critical terms method as it is a qualitative assessment which is very easy to apply. However, the critical terms method can only be used in limited circumstances, so other methods may need to be considered. Our second favoured method is the regression analysis using a robust set of historical data, as the past has probably witnessed most of the extreme movements that will be experienced in the future.

When assessing retrospective effectiveness, we strongly prefer the ratio analysis method. From an accounting perspective, only the ratio analysis method calculates the amount of ineffectiveness, and thus, the amounts necessary for the accounting entries.

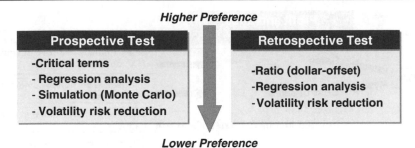

Figure 1.13   Effectiveness Test Methods – Recommendations.

1.10   THE HYPOTHETICAL DERIVATIVE SIMPLIFICATION

The hypothetical derivative approach is a useful simplification when assessing hedge effectiveness. IAS 39 allows for performing effectiveness tests in which the changes in the fair value of the hedged item are modelled as if the hedged item were a hypothetical derivative perfectly matching the terms of the hedged item. The hypothetical derivative is a derivative whose changes in fair value offset perfectly the changes in fair value of the hedged item for variations in the risk being hedged. The changes in the fair value of both the hypothetical derivative and the real derivative (i.e., the hedging instrument) are then used to test the hedge effectiveness. If the hedge is highly effective, then the hedge ineffectiveness is the difference between the two fair value changes.

The use of the hypothetical derivative method can simplify the process of effectiveness testing, particularly of cash flow hedges. For example:

- When hedging a recognised interest bearing debt with an interest rate swap. The change in fair value of the derivative may not sufficiently offset the change in the fair value of the underlying debt, because fair valuing the debt would involve fair valuing the principal repayment. The derivative, of course, has no principal repayment. IAS 39 allows the substitution of the hedged debt by a hypothetical interest rate swap that mirrors all of the terms of the debt, but without the principal repayment cash flow. The use of the hypothetical interest rate swap eliminates the artificial ineffectiveness caused by the principal cash flow.
- When hedging the FX exposure of a highly expected foreign currency cash flow. The hedge effectiveness can be tested assuming a hypothetical forward with the same maturity of the exposure with a forward rate that gives the hypothetical forward an initial zero cost.
- When hedging the FX exposure of a highly expected foreign currency cash flow with options. The hedge effectiveness can be tested assuming a hypothetical option (or combination of options) that replicates exactly the fair value changes of the forecasted cash flow within the range of the risk being hedged.

1.11   EFFECTS OF DERIVATIVES IN THE P&L STATEMENT

Qualifying for hedge accounting does not imply that the hedging strategy will have no volatility impact in earnings. If highly effective, the change in fair value of the hedging instrument is allocated, in accordance with the hedge documentation, into three possible components: the

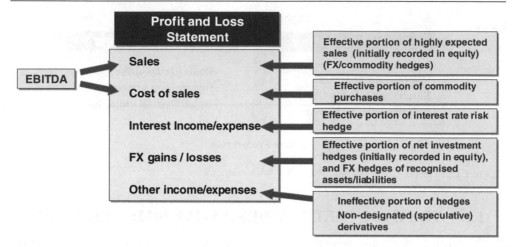

Figure 1.14   Derivatives – Impact in P&L.

"effective" component, the "ineffective" component, and the "excluded" component. IFRS does not prescribe where gains and losses from derivatives should be shown in the P&L statement. The most common practice (see Figure 1.14) is the following:

- The effective portion of the hedge will show up in P&L (after being recycled from equity in case of cash flow and net investment hedges) in the same line item as the hedged item.
- The ineffective portion of the hedge is usually recorded in the "other income and expenses" line of P&L. Sometimes, if the ineffective portion is related to movements in interest rates, entities record the hedge ineffective part in "interest income or expense".
- The excluded portion of the hedge is usually recorded in the "other income and expenses" line of P&L.

2

An Introduction to the
Derivative Instruments

Before addressing the hedge accounting implications of the most common hedging strategies, it is helpful to examine the derivative instruments used in these strategies. Each derivative portrayal shown in this chapter is divided into two parts: a first part describing the instrument and a second part highlighting its accounting implications under IAS 39. Readers who are already familiar with the hedging instrument are suggested to skip the first part.

The accounting implications mentioned herein are a summary. A more detailed explanation can be found in the numerous cases provided in this book. We would like to warn the reader that IFRS accounting is not clear for structured transactions, and that its interpretation can elicit a broad range of responses. The accounting considerations set out herein are based on the author's interpretation of the current rules. The reader should also bear in mind that these rules may be subject to change. In our experience advising multinationals, we have frequently found that interpretations that are adequate to one auditor may not be acceptable to another.

2.1 FX FORWARDS

2.1.1 Product Description

An FX forward is the most common and the simplest hedging instrument in the FX market. It is a contract to exchange a fixed amount of one currency for a fixed amount of another currency. Let us assume that ABC is a European company that expects to purchase a USD 100 million machine from a US supplier. The purchase is expected to be paid in USD on 30 June 20X5. As a result, ABC is exposed to an appreciation of the USD relative to the EUR. To hedge this exposure ABC enters into a FX forward with the following terms:

FX Forward Terms	
Start date	1 January 20X5
Counterparties	Company ABC and XYZ Bank
Maturity	30 June 20X5
ABC buys	USD 100 million
ABC sells	EUR 80 million
Forward Rate	1.2500
Settlement	Physical delivery

The FX forward locks-in the exchange rate at which ABC will buy the USD 100 million: ABC knows that on 30 June 20X5 will buy the USD at an exchange rate of 1.2500, no matter what the USD/EUR exchange rate ends up being on that date (see Figure 2.1). This 1.2500 forward rate is the USD/EUR expected rate for 30 June 20X5, so no premium is paid by any of the two counterparties at the beginning of the transaction.

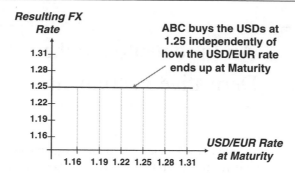

Figure 2.1   FX Forward – Resulting FX Rate.

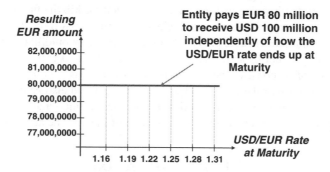

Figure 2.2   FX Forward – Resulting EUR Amount.

Similarly, the hedge can be analysed by calculating the amount of EUR that ABC will need to sell in order to buy the USD 100 million, as a function of the USD/EUR exchange rate at maturity. Figure 2.2 shows that the FX forward locks-in a EUR 80 million amount, no matter what the USD/EUR rate ends up being at maturity.

Forward contracts may be settled by physical delivery or by cash settlement. The FX forward described previously will be settled by physical delivery. As a consequence, both parties will actually exchange both currencies on 30 June 20X5: ABC agrees to buy USD 100 million and, simultaneously, to sell EUR 80 million. If the contract were to be settled by cash settlement, a final exchange rate would be set by observing an official fixing two business days prior to the maturity date, and then one counterparty will pay the other a settlement amount. For example, if two business days prior to maturity the chosen official USD/EUR rate fixes at 1.3000, ABC would pay XYZ Bank EUR 3,076,923.08 (= 100 million * (1/1.2500 − 1/1.3000)) on 30 June 20X5.

2.1.2   IAS 39 Accounting Implications

An FX forward is the friendliest FX hedging instrument from IAS 39's perspective. The only particular point to note is the accounting treatment of the forward points. The forward points are the difference between the forward and spot prices. For example, if on 1 January 20X5 the spot USD/EUR rate was 1.2360 and the USD/EUR forward rate for 30 June 20X5 was 1.2560, then the forward points were 0.0140 (= 1.2500 − 1.2360). The forward points reflect the differential between USD and EUR interest rates from 1 January 20X5 to 30 June 20X5.

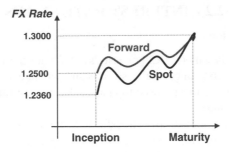

Figure 2.3 FX Forward Spot and Forward Rates Convergence.

At maturity of the transaction the forward points become zero as spot and forward rates converge, as shown in Figure 2.3.

Under IAS 39, an entity may elect to include or exclude the forward points in the assessment of effectiveness when using forwards. The method chosen must be consistently applied for similar types of hedges. As a result, an entity can elect to assess effectiveness in one of four ways:

- Spot-to-spot comparison. The effectiveness assessment is based on changes in spot rates. Thus, it excludes from the assessment the effects of changes in the forward points.
- Forward-to-forward comparison. The effectiveness assessment is based on changes in forward rates. Thus, it includes in the assessment the effects of changes in the forward points.
- Spot-to-forward comparison. The effectiveness assessment is based on changes in spot rates for the hedged item and on changes in the forward rate for the hedging instrument. In practice, it does not make sense to apply this alternative.
- Forward-to-spot comparison. The effectiveness assessment is based on changes in forward rates for the hedged item and on changes in the spot rate for the hedging instrument. In practice, it does not make sense to apply this alternative.

The following example illustrates how the usage of the spot-to-forward or the forward-to-spot comparisons may cause considerable inefficiencies. Let us assume that a EUR based entity hedges the cash flow risk relating to a highly expected purchase of raw material denominated in a foreign currency (FC) using a forward contract. The prevailing spot FX rate at the inception of the hedging relationship is 500 and the one-year forward rate is 520. Suppose that when the forward contract expires, and the hedging relationship ends, the spot price is 570. The following table shows the calculation of the cumulative changes of fair value and the hedge ineffectiveness under the four alternatives:

	Spot-to-spot	Forward-to-forward	Spot-to-forward	Forward-to-spot
Hedging instrument change	70 = 570–500	50 = 570–520	50 = 570–520	70 = 570–500
Hedged Item change	<70> = 500–570	<50> = 520–570	<70> = 500–570	<50> = 520–570
Effective part	70	50	50	50
Ineffective part	0	0	20	20

2.2 INTEREST RATE SWAPS

2.2.1 Product Description

Interest rate swaps (usually called "IRS" or just "swaps") are the most common instrument used to hedge interest rate risk. In general, a swap is an exchange of interest payment flows in the same currency. Swaps are mostly used to change the interest rate risk profile of interest-bearing assets and/or liabilities.

Corporations usually enter into swaps to transform the interest rate basis of a debt obligation from a floating to fixed rate or vice versa. The two counterparties to a swap agree to exchange, at certain future dates, two sets of cash flows denominated in the same currency. The cash flows paid by one counterparty reflect a fixed rate of interest while those of the other counterparty reflect a floating rate of interest. The term "floating rate" means that the interest rate used in an interest period is unknown until the commencement of such period. In the case of Euribor interest rates, the floating rate of a specific interest period is set two business days prior to the beginning of the interest period. All the stream of fixed rate payments is grouped together under the term "fixed leg". Similarly, the "floating leg" groups all the string of floating rate payments. The swap is usually entered at-market rates and as a result there is no exchange of a premium at the inception of the swap.

The following example highlights the mechanics of swaps. On 15 January 20X0, ABC enters into a EUR 100 million notional, three-year interest rate swap. Under the terms of the swap, ABC will pay semiannually a 5 % fixed interest and receive annually a floating interest (the Euribor 12-month rate). The floating interest rate resets two business days prior to the commencement of each interest period. The terms of the swap are summarised below:

Interest Rate Swap Terms	
Start date	15 January 20X0
Counterparties	Company ABC and XYZ Bank
Maturity	3 years (15 January 20X3)
Notional	EUR 100 million
ABC pays	5.00 % semiannually, 30/360 basis
ABC receives	Euribor 12-month, annually, Actual/360 basis
	Euribor is fixed two business days prior to the beginning of the annual interest period

The fixed leg of this swap has six interest periods, and the floating leg three periods. Figure 2.4 shows the cash flow dates of the fixed and floating legs.

All the fixed leg cash flows are known at the beginning of the swap. ABC will be paying EUR 2.5 million (= 100,000,000*5 %/2) every 15th of July and every 15th of January during the life of the swap and starting on 15th July 20X0.

Unlike the fixed leg cash flows, the floating leg cash flows are unknown at the beginning of the swap (except the first one). The first floating cash flow will take place on 15 January 20X1 and its floating rate (2.70 %) is already known at the swap inception as it was fixed on 13 January 20X0 (two business days prior to the beginning of the first interest period). As a result, ABC expects to receive EUR 2,737,500 (= 100,000,000*2.70 %*365/360) on 15 January 20X1. Each of the remaining floating leg cash flows will be determined two business days prior to the beginning of their corresponding interest period. For example, the

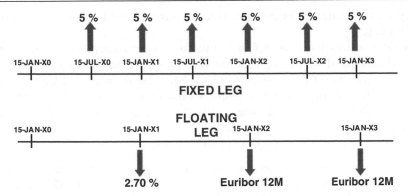

Figure 2.4   Interest Rate Swap Flows.

cash flow to be received by ABC on 15 January 20X2 will be known on 13 January 20X1. There are several examples of swaps and their pricing mechanics in the cases covered in Chapter 5.

2.2.2   IAS 39 Accounting Implications

Interest rate swaps are the friendliest interest rate hedging instruments from IAS 39's perspective. There are two particular points that are covered in detail in Chapter 5 that we would like to highlight: firstly, the need to define hedge relationships involving swaps in such a way that eligibility for hedge accounting is maximised, and secondly, the need to exclude the interest accrual amounts when calculating swap fair value changes.

In a hedge accounting context, a swap is often linked to a specific liability. The market value of a swap and a liability are usually determined using different yield curves. Typically, the market values a liability using a yield curve that incorporates the issuer's credit spread, while swaps are valued excluding the issuer's credit spread from the yield curve. As a result the interest rate sensitivities of a liability and its related swap can be significantly different, endangering the eligibility for hedge accounting of a well-constructed hedge. When the liability and swap interest rate sensitivities are notably different, it is advisable to include in the hedge relationship only the interest rate risk (i.e., excluding other risks, such as the credit risk).

Often valuation dates fall within interest periods. When testing hedge effectiveness, the inclusion or exclusion of accrued interest in the valuation of a swap can make a huge difference. The solution to this problem is a simple one, interest accrual amounts need to be excluded when calculating a swap fair value. The exclusion is especially relevant to make consistent fair value comparisons of liabilities and swaps with unmatched interest periods. The exclusion is also needed to avoid double counting the interest income or expense related to a swap, as the income or expense associated with a cash flow is apportioned into the periods to which it relates. The calculation of accruals is quite straight forward as shown in Chapter 5.

2.3   CROSS-CURRENCY SWAPS

2.3.1   Product Description

A cross-currency swap, also termed "CCS" or just "currency swap", is a contract to exchange interest payment flows in one currency for interest payment flows in another currency. CCSs are mostly used to change the interest rate risk and currency profile of interest-bearing assets and/or liabilities.

Corporations usually enter into CCSs to transform the currency denomination of a debt obligation denominated in a foreign currency. The two counterparties to a CCS agree to exchange, at certain future dates, two set of cash flows denominated in different currencies. The cash flows paid by one counterparty reflect a fixed (or a floating) rate of interest in one currency while those of the other counterparty reflect a fixed (or floating) rate of interest in another currency.

In its simplest (and most common) form a CCS involves the following cash flows:

• An initial exchange of principal amounts. This initial exchange is sometimes not undertaken. The most common reason for not using an initial exchange is that the CCS swap is being undertaken to hedge already existing liabilities.
• A string of interim interest payments. Periodically, one counterparty pays a fixed (or floating) interest on one of the principal amounts, and the other counterparty pays a fixed (or floating) interest on the other principal amount. The payments are usually netted.
• A final re-exchange of principal amounts.

For example, suppose a borrower is about to issue a 5 % fixed-rate 5-year GBP denominated bond. The borrower is only interested in raising EUR funds, so it decides to transform the GBP fixed-rate liability into a EUR floating-rate liability by entering into a CCS. The terms of the bond and the swap are summarised in the following tables:

Bond Terms	
Maturity	5 years
Notional	GBP 70 million
Coupon	5 %, to be paid annually, 30/360 basis

Cross-currency Swap Terms	
Maturity	5 years after start date
GBP nominal	GBP 70 million
EUR nominal	EUR 100 million
Initial exchange	On start date, borrower receives the EUR nominal and pays the GBP nominal
ABC pays	Euribor 12m + 50 bps, annually, on the EUR nominal
ABC receives	GBP 5 %, annually, on the GBP nominal
Final exchange	On maturity date, borrower receives the GBP nominal and pays the EUR nominal

Figure 2.5 shows the initial cash flows of the CCS and their interaction with the bond initial flow. Through the CCS, the borrower delivers the GBP 70 million issue proceeds and receives EUR 100 million. As a result, the borrower is in effect obtaining a EUR 100 million funding.

Figure 2.6 shows the bond and the CCS periodic interest payments. Through the CCS, the borrower receives annually a GBP 5 % interest calculated on the GBP 70 million nominal, and pays annually a EUR floating interest (Euribor 12-month plus 50 bps) calculated on the EUR 100 million nominal. The borrower uses the CCS GBP receipts to meet the bond interest payments.

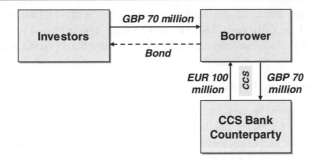

Figure 2.5   Bond with CCS: Initial Cash-flows.

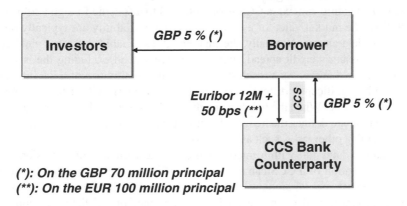

Figure 2.6   Bond with CCS: Intermediate Cash-flows.

Figure 2.7 shows the CCS final cash flows and their interaction with the bond redemption. On maturity date the borrower re-exchanges the principals, paying EUR 100 million and receiving GBP 70 million through the CCS. The borrower then uses GBP 70 million received to repay the GBP bond.

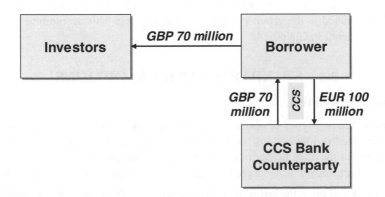

Figure 2.7   Bond with CCS: Cash-flows at Maturity.

Under the structure depicted, the borrower effectively achieves funding at Euribor plus 50 bps. Note that all the GBP cash flows have to be fully synchronised to eliminate the GBP exposure. Chapter 6 includes several examples of CCSs and their pricing mechanics.

2.3.2 IAS 39 Accounting Implications

Cross-currency swaps are the most basic instruments to hedge foreign currency denominated liabilities. In general, CCSs do not imply a major challenge from IAS 39 viewpoint. As mentioned for interest rate swaps, there are two particular points that are worth noting: firstly, the need to define hedge relationships involving CCS in such a way that eligibility for hedge accounting is maximised, and secondly, the need to exclude the interest accrual amounts when calculating CCS fair value changes.

In a hedge accounting context, a CCS is often linked to a specific foreign currency denominated liability. The market value of a CCS and its related liability are typically determined using different yield curves. Normally, the market values a liability using a yield curve that incorporates the issuer's credit spread, while CCSs are valued excluding the issuer's credit spread from the yield curve. As a result the interest rate sensitivities of a liability and its related CCS can be significantly different, endangering the eligibility for hedge accounting of a well-constructed hedge. When the liability and the CCS rate sensitivities are notably different, it is suggested that one defines the hedge relationship as the hedge of interest rate and FX risk only (i.e., excluding other risks, such as credit risk).

Often valuation dates fall within interest periods. The inclusion or exclusion of accrued interest in the valuation of a CCS can make a huge difference. The solution to this problem is to exclude interest accrual amounts when calculating a CCS fair value. The exclusion is especially important to make consistent fair value comparisons of liabilities and CCS with different interest periods. The exclusion is also needed to avoid double counting the interest income or expense related to a CCS, as the income or expense associated with a cash flow is apportioned into the periods to which it relates. Chapter 6 includes detailed computations of the interest accruals of CCSs.

In addition to hedging foreign currency denominated liabilities, CCSs are used to hedge the FX exposure of net investments in foreign operations. For this type of hedge, IAS 39 sets a special type of hedge accounting, called "net investment hedge". When designated as hedging instruments of net investment hedges, some aspects of the accounting treatment of CCSs are still unclear. This is particularly the case of CCSs in which the entity pays a fixed interest rate in the leg denominated in the group's functional currency leg. This accounting uncertainty is covered in more detail in Chapter 4.

2.4 STANDARD (VANILLA) OPTIONS

2.4.1 Product Description

In general there are two types of options: standard options and exotic options. The standard, options, also called "vanilla options" or just "options", are the most basic option instruments. Unlike the terms of most exotic options, the terms of a standard option (e.g., nominal, strike, expiry date, etc) are known at its inception. There are two types of standard options:

- Call options. A call gives the buyer the right, but not the obligation, to buy a specific amount of an underlying at a predetermined price on or before a specific future date.

- Put options. A put gives the buyer the right, but not the obligation, to sell a specific amount of an underlying at a predetermined price on or before a specific future date.

The buyer of the option has to pay a premium to the seller. Usually the premium is paid two or three (depending on the underlying) business days after the option is agreed. The underlying can be any financial asset (e.g., a security, a currency, a commodity) or a financial index (e.g., a stock market index, an interest rate).

2.4.2 Standard Foreign Exchange Options

Most FX instruments involve two currencies: a specific amount of one currency is delivered (or sold) in exchange for receiving (or paying) a specific amount of another currency. An interesting aspect of FX options is that they are simultaneously a call and a put option. If the option is a call on one of the two currencies, it necessarily is a put option on the other currency. Accordingly, when entering into a FX option, the term call (or put) is accompanied by the currency for which the option is a call (or a put). For example, a USD/EUR option in which the option buyer benefits if the USD strengthens is simultaneously a USD call and a EUR put option. Likewise, a USD/EUR option in which the option buyer benefits if the USD weakens is simultaneously a USD put and a EUR call option.

As a first example, suppose that a European entity highly expects to sell a plant to a US customer. The plant is expected to be sold for USD 100 million in one year. The entity is exposed to a declining USD relative to the EUR. Accordingly, the entity decides to hedge the FX risk arising from the highly expected purchase by buying an option with the following characteristics:

EUR Call/USD Put Terms	
Buyer:	European entity
Option type:	EUR Call/USD Put
Expiry:	One year
Notional:	USD 100 million
Strike:	1.16
Settlement:	Cash settlement
Premium:	EUR 1.8 million to be paid two business days after start date

As this option is cash settled, the option will pay a EUR amount at expiry only if the option ends up being in-the-money. The cash settlement amount (i.e., the option payoff) at expiry is calculated using the following formula:

$$\text{EUR settlement amount} = \text{Maximum } \{\text{USD Notional} * [1/1.16 - 1/(\text{FX rate at expiry})], 0\}$$

Figure 2.8 shows the option payoff (i.e., the settlement amount) as a function of the USD/EUR spot rate at expiry, without taking into account the premium that the entity paid for the option.

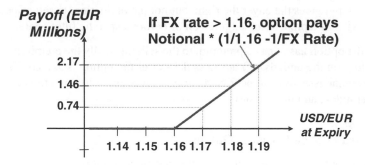

Figure 2.8   1.16 USD Put/EUR Call Payoff at Expiry (Excluding Premium).

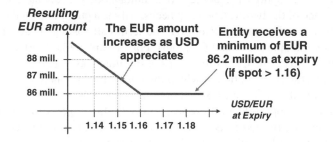

Figure 2.9   1.16 USD Put/EUR Call Resulting EUR Amount (Excluding Premium).

On receipt of the USD 100 million, the entity will exchange the USD for EUR at the spot rate. The entity will also exercise the option if it ends up being in-the-money at expiry. The option payoff, if the option is exercised, will then increase the EUR proceeds of the sale. Figure 2.9 shows the resulting EUR amount obtained through both transactions. It can be seen that by purchasing the EUR call the entity limited the minimum EUR amount to be received from the sale to EUR 86.2 million (excluding the option premium). However, the entity benefited from higher proceeds was the EUR to depreciate below 1.16.

As a second example, suppose that a European entity highly expects to purchase a machine from a US supplier. The machine is expected to cost USD 100 million. The invoice will be paid in USD in one year. The entity is exposed to a rising USD relative to the EUR. Accordingly, the entity decides to hedge the FX risk arising from the highly expected purchase by buying an option, whose characteristics are as follows:

EUR Put/USD Call Terms	
Buyer:	European entity
Option type:	EUR Put/USD Call
Expiry:	One year
Notional:	USD 100 million
Strike:	1.16
Settlement:	Cash settlement
Premium:	EUR 1.6 million to be paid two business days after Start Date

As this option is cash settled, the option will pay a EUR amount at expiry only if the option ends up being in-the-money. The cash settlement amount at expiry is calculated using the following formula:

EUR settlement amount = Maximum {USD Notional * [1/(FX rate at expiry) − 1/1.16], 0}

Figure 2.10 shows the option payoff (i.e., the settlement amount) as a function of the USD/EUR spot rate at expiry, excluding the premium that the entity paid for the option.

At maturity of the transaction and in order to meet the USD 100 million payment, the entity will receive USD 100 million in exchange for a EUR amount at the spot rate prevailing on that date. The entity will also exercise the option if it ends up being in-the-money, then decreasing the total EUR cost of the purchase. The following graph shows the resulting EUR amount from both transactions (excluding the option premium). It can be seen that by purchasing the EUR put, the entity limits the maximum EUR amount to be paid for the machine to EUR 86.2 million, and at the same time, the entity benefits from a lower total payment if the EUR appreciates beyond 1.16 Figure 2.11.

In the two examples just provided, the entity paid a premium for the protection. It is more common though, to buy an option and simultaneously sell the opposite option in order to avoid paying any premium. Applying this strategy to our second example, the entity would have bought the 1.16 EUR put and simultaneously sold a 1.26 EUR call. If we assume that the EUR call premium was also EUR 1.6 million, the entity neither paid nor received a premium for the combination of the two options. This strategy, called "zero-cost tunnel", is the most popular

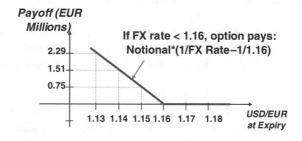

Figure 2.10   1.16 USD Call/EUR Put Payoff at Expiry (Excluding Premium).

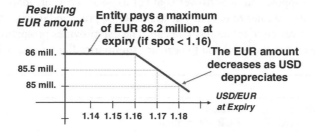

Figure 2.11   1.16 USD Call/EUR Put Resulting EUR Amount (Excluding Premium).

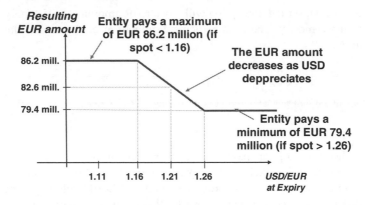

Figure 2.12   1.16–1.26 Tunnel Resulting EUR Amount.

FX option hedging strategy. In our example, the purchased EUR put limits the maximum EUR amount to be paid for the machine to EUR 86.2 million. At the same time, the sold EUR call limits the minimum EUR amount to EUR 79.4 million (= 100 million/1.26), as shown in Figure 2.12.

2.4.3   Interest Rate Options – Caps, Floors and Collars

When referring to interest rate options, the term "cap" is used instead of the term "call option". Similarly, the term "floor" is used instead of the term "put option". The reason behind is that a cap (or a floor) is in reality a string of call (or put) options. For example, a borrower may prefer to pay a floating interest rate in a floating-rate bond, but may require assurance that the interest payments do not exceed a maximum limit. An interest rate cap would achieve this objective by providing the issuer protection against rising interest rates. Bear in mind that the borrower usually is not hedging only one interest payment but each interest payment on the bond. Therefore, the cap is in reality a string of options, each hedging a specific interest payment. Each option in a cap is called a "caplet". Similarly, each option in a floor is called a "floorlet".

Just as a borrower issuing a floating-rate bond is concerned about rising interest rates, an investor buying a floating-rate bond is concerned about declining interest rates. An investor may prefer to receive a floating interest rate in a bond, but may require assurance that each interest receipt is not lower than a minimum limit. An interest rate floor would achieve this objective by providing the issuer with protection against low interest rates.

As an example, suppose that a borrower is about to issue a 5-year floating-rate bond. The borrower expects interest rates to decline but wishes to be protected in case its view is wrong. As a result the borrower buys an interest rate cap. The cap provides protection if interest rates exceed 6 %. The terms of the bond and the cap are summarised in the following tables:

Bond Terms	
Maturity	5 years
Notional	EUR 100 million
Coupon	Euribor 12-month + 50 bps, to be paid annually

Interest Rate Cap Terms	
Buyer:	Borrower
Maturity	5 years
Notional	EUR 100 million
Cap rate:	6 %
Underlying:	Euribor 12-month
Interest periods:	Annual
Premium:	EUR 2 million to be paid upfront

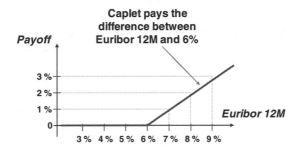

Figure 2.13   Caplet Payoff (Excluding Premium).

In each interest period that the Euribor 12-month fixes above the 6 % cap rate, the borrower will receive from the seller of the cap an interest related to the difference between the Euribor 12-month rate and the 6 % cap rate. In each interest period that the Euribor 12-month is fixed at or below the 6 % cap rate, the borrower will receive nothing. Figure 2.13 shows a caplet payoff as a function of the Euribor 12-month rate, without taking into account the cap premium.

Figure 2.14 illustrates how the interest rate cap will operate in our example in conjunction with the bond. By entering into the cap, the borrower would achieve funding at a maximum rate of 6.50 % (= 6 % + 0.50 %), without taking into account the cap premium.

- On any interest reset date that Euribor 12-month is fixed at a rate above 6 %, the borrower will receive through the cap the difference between Euribor 12-month and 6 %. Because the borrower pays Euribor 12-month plus 50 bps to the bondholders, the borrower will effectively pay a total interest of 6.50 % (= Euribor 12M + 0.50 % − (Euribor 12M − 6 %)).
- On any interest reset date that Euribor 12-month is fixed below the 6 % cap rate, the borrower will receive nothing through the cap. Therefore, the borrower will effectively pay an interest of Euribor 12-month rate plus the 50 bps bond spread. This interest will be lower than 6.50 %.

Because the purchase of a cap requires the payment of an up-front premium, a cap is often transacted in conjunction with a floor to avoid making any up-front payments. The combination of a purchased cap and a sold floor is called a "collar". In the case of a floating rate debt, a collar sets an upper and a lower limit on the interest the borrower would pay. If the premium of the cap is equal to the premium of the floor, the strategy is called a "zero-cost collar", as no premium is exchanged at inception.

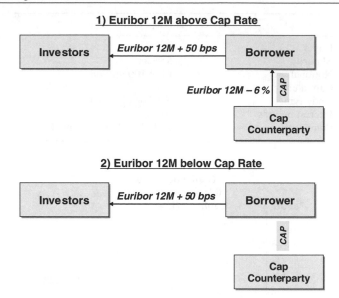

Figure 2.14   Floating Rate Bond with a Cap: Interest Cash-flows.

In our example, let us assume that the borrower, besides buying the 6 % cap, also sells a 4 % floor. Through the floor, in each interest period that Euribor 12-month is fixed below 4 %, the borrower will pay the floor buyer an interest corresponding to the difference between the 4 % and the Euribor 12-month rate. In each interest period that Euribor 12-month is fixed at or above the 4 % floor rate, the borrower will pay nothing.

Figure 2.16 illustrates how the collar will operate in our example in conjunction with the debt. Through the collar, the borrower will achieve funding at a maximum rate of 6.50 % (= 6 % + 0.50 %) and at a minimum rate of 4.50 % (= 4 % + 0.50 %).

- On any interest reset date that Euribor 12-month fixes above 6 %, the cap will be exercised and the borrower will effectively pay 6.50 % (6 % plus the 50 bps bond spread), as shown in Figure 2.14.
- On any interest reset date that Euribor 12-month fixes between 4 % and 6 %, neither the cap nor the floor will be exercised. Thus, the borrower will pay the Euribor 12-month rate plus the 50 bps bond spread.

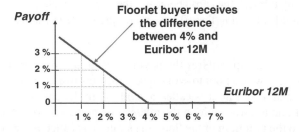

Figure 2.15   Floorlet Payoff (Excluding Premium).

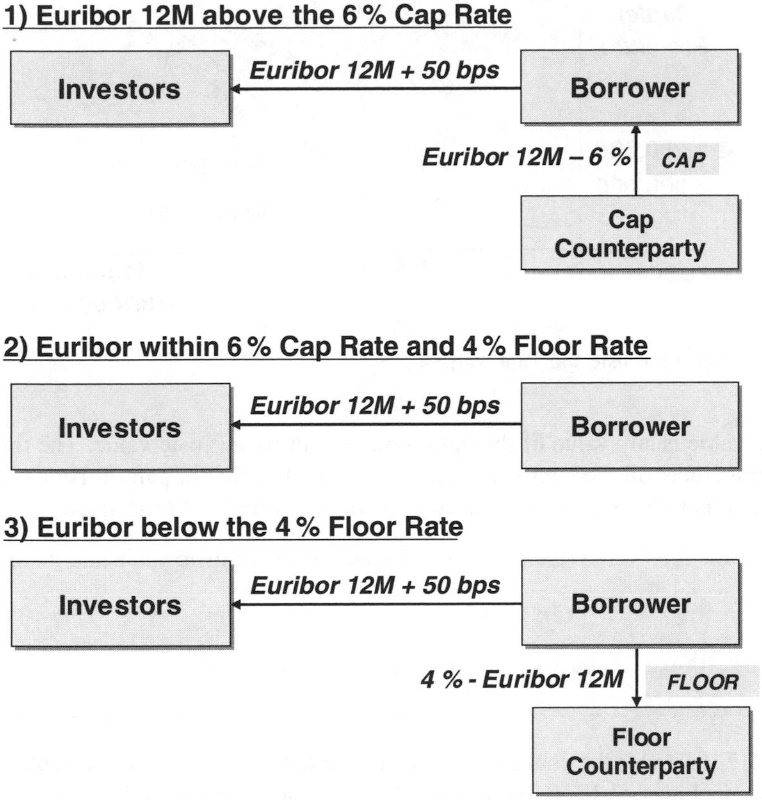

1) Euribor 12M above the 6 % Cap Rate

2) Euribor within 6 % Cap Rate and 4 % Floor Rate

3) Euribor below the 4 % Floor Rate

Figure 2.16   Floating Rate Bond with a Collar: Interest Cash-flows.

- On any interest reset date that Euribor 12-month fixes at a rate below 4 %, the floor will be exercised. The borrower will pay the floor buyer the difference between 4 % and Euribor 12-month. As a consequence, the borrower will effectively pay 4.50 % (= Euribor 12M + 0.50 % + 4 % − Euribor 12M).

2.4.4 IAS 39 Accounting Implications of Options – Intrinsic versus Time Value

When an option is used in a hedging relationship, the intrinsic value and the time value of the option are separated, and only the intrinsic value is included in the hedging relationship. Accordingly, when valuing an option it is convenient to break down the value of the option into its intrinsic value and time value components.

- The intrinsic value is the value that the option would have if it were exercised now. The intrinsic value of an option can be calculated either using the spot rate or the forward rate. In the case of equity and FX options, the intrinsic value is usually calculated using the spot rate. In the case of interest rate options, the intrinsic value is usually calculated using the forward rate.

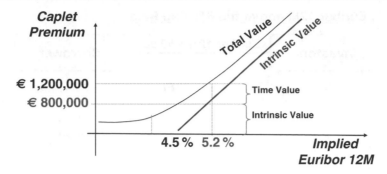

Figure 2.17 Caplet Intrinsic and Time Values.

- The time value is any value of the option other than its intrinsic value. The time value of an option includes all the components of the option that are not part of the instrinsic value. Options that have zero intrinsic value are comprised entirely of time value.

Therefore, the total value of an option is the sum of its intrinsic value and its time value.

Total Value = Intrinsic Value + Time Value

Figure 2.17 illustrates the concept of intrinsic and time value for a 4.5 % caplet.

As shown in Figure 2.17, if the implied forward rate is below 4.5 %, the option has no intrinsic value (the option would be worth nothing if it were exercised now) and therefore the option has only time value. If the implied forward rate is above 4.5 %, the option has both intrinsic and time value. For example, if the implied forward rate were 5.2 %, the total value of the option is EUR 1.2 million, being split between a EUR 0.8 million intrinsic value and a EUR 0.4 million time value.

IAS 39 treats options quite unfavourably as the test of effectiveness may be based solely on changes in the option intrinsic value, therefore excluding the option time value from the effectiveness tests. Consequently, changes in the option time value would be recorded in P&L. The result is not only additional reporting complexity and burden but also unpredictable earnings volatility.

For example, assume that an entity buys an out-of-the-money option as disaster insurance, paying a premium cost of just 0.5 %. As this option moves to be at-the-money, its time value might rise to 5 % and be reported as a big gain in earnings, only to get written off at maturity as the option's time value invariably ends up being zero.

IAS 39 unfavourable treatment of options may tempt entities to change their hedging strategy regarding options. Entities may be inclined to:

1. Shorten the maturities of the options, to lower the option time value
2. Deal with collars/tunnels with strikes that are close to being in-the-money (i.e., avoiding well out-of-the-money options), to lower the strategy time value volatility

The US Gaap FAS 133 allows for cash flow hedges to base the test of effectiveness on total changes in the option's fair value (i.e., option time value may be included in the effectiveness assessment).

FAS 133 – DIG 20: "Cash Flow Hedges: Assessing and Measuring the Effectiveness of a Purchased Option Used in a Cash Flow Hedge"

For cash flow hedges (i.e., not allowed for fair value hedges) in which the hedging instrument is a purchased option or a combination of only options that comprise a net purchased option or a zero-cost collar/tunnel, FAS 133 allows the effectiveness to be calculated by comparing the total change in fair value of the hedging instrument and the change in fair value of a "perfectly effective" hypothetical hedging instrument. The change in fair value of that hypothetical hedging instrument can be regarded as a proxy for the present value in expected future cash flows on the hedged transaction.

As a consequence if the hedging instrument and the hypothetical hedging instrument have the same terms, the entity would simply record all changes in the hedging option's fair value (including changes in the option's time value) in equity.

The hypothetical hedging instrument should have terms that meet the following four conditions:

1. The critical terms of the hedging instrument (such as its notional amount, underlying and maturity date, etc.) completely match the related terms of the hedged forecasted transaction (such as, the notional amount, the variable that determines the variability in cash flows, and the expected date of the hedged transaction, etc.);
2. The strike (or prices) of the hedging option (or combination of options) matches the specified level (or levels) beyond (or within) which the entity's exposure is being hedged;
3. The hedging instrument's inflows (outflows) at its maturity completely offset the change in the hedged transaction's cash flows for the risk being hedged; and
4. The hedging instrument can be exercised only on a single date.

As we have just seen, the option's time value is treated differently under US Gaap. As there is a gradual process of convergence between FAS 133 and IAS 39, we hope that IAS 39 will finally allow the inclusion of option time value in a hedging relationship (which in our opinion makes a great deal of sense).

2.4.5 IAS 39 Accounting Implications of Options – Written Options

IAS 39 permits designating as hedging instruments a purchased option or a combination of purchased options. A written option cannot be a hedging instrument, either on its own or in combination with other derivatives unless it is designated as an offset of a purchased option (e.g., in a tunnel or a collar) and all the following conditions are met:

- No net premium is received either at inception or over the life of the options; and
- Except for the strike prices, the critical terms and conditions of the written option and the purchased option are the same (underlying, currency denomination, maturity date, etc). Also the notional amount of the written option is not greater than the notional amount of the purchased option.

The no net premium requirement may create illogical situations like the following: An entity may buy an option today with the objective of selling another option at a later date once the sold option becomes more valuable. If the premium of the sold option was larger than the premium of the bought option, IAS 39 forbids designating the combination of the purchased and the sold options as a hedging instrument.

2.5   EXOTIC OPTIONS

As was mentioned earlier, there are two types of options: vanilla and exotic options. Vanilla options, also called standard or regular options, have all their terms fixed and predetermined at their start. Exotic options group any other options that are not considered to be vanilla. In general, exotic options have some terms that depend on specific conditions being met during their life. The rationale behind most exotic options is to have a lower premium than their vanilla equivalents.

It is not easy to classify the exotic options into small groups because their characteristics are very wide-ranging. Also, it would be unrealistic to try to list all the different exotic options being developed, as banks come up continuously with new ones. However, if we were to provide some sort of categorisation, we would use the following classification:

- Path-dependent options. The payoff of a path-dependent option depends on how the underlying price (or rate) has traded over the life of the option. The most popular path-dependent options are average-rate options, barrier options, and range accrual options. Average rate options, also called "Asian options", are options with payoffs determined by some averages of the underlying price (or rate) during a pre-specified period of time before the option expiry. Barrier options are the most popular exotic options and we will cover them in detail next. Range accrual options are options with payoffs determined by the number of days that the underlying stays within a specific range during a pre-specified period of time.
- Correlation options. The payoff of a correlation option is affected by more than one underlying. The most popular correlation options are basket options, quanto options and spread options. Basket options are options on a portfolio of underlyings. Quanto options are options with payoffs denominated in one currency whose underlying is denominated in another currency. Spread options are options with payoffs determined by the difference of two prices (or indices or rates).
- Other types of exotic options. This broad category groups all other options not included in the previous two categories. The most common options in this category are digital options. Digital options are options with payoffs that are either a fixed amount of cash (or other asset) or nothing.

2.6   BARRIER OPTIONS

The most popular type of exotic option is the barrier option. Barrier options allow entities to tailor their hedging strategies to very specific market views. The payoff of a barrier option depends on whether the price of the underlying crosses a given threshold, called the "barrier", before maturity.

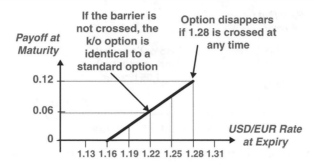

Figure 2.18   EUR Knock-out Call – Barrier *not* Hit. Payoff at Expiry (Excluding Premium).

In general there are two types of barrier options: knock-in options and knock-out options:

- Knock-in options come into existence when the price of the underlying reaches the barrier at any time during the life of the option.
- Knock-out options come out of existence when the price of the underlying reaches the barrier at any time during the life of the option.

The existence of the barrier lowers the probability of exercise, and therefore, barrier options are cheaper than their vanilla counterparts. Entities which are willing to keep some residual risk on their hedging strategy can reduce their hedging costs by using barrier options.

2.6.1   Knock-Out Barrier Options – Product Description

- The knock-out option at inception is a standard option. This option disappears if the barrier is crossed. For example, a EUR-based USD exporter has the view that the EUR will strengthen against the USD over the next 6 months, but expects the EUR not to appreciate beyond 1.28. The entity buys a 6-month EUR knock-out call with strike 1.16 and barrier 1.28. The premium of a knock-out option is lower than the premium of its equivalent standard option because the protection disappears if the barrier is crossed.
- If the USD/EUR never trades at or above 1.28 during the life of the option, the entity effectively has a protection identical to a standard option with strike 1.16 (see Figure 2.18).
- However, if at any time during the life of the option the barrier is crossed, the option ceases to exist and the entity losses its protection (see Figure 2.19).

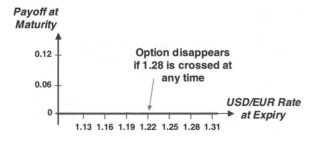

Figure 2.19   EUR Knock-out Call – Barrier *was* Hit. Payoff at Expiry (Excluding Premium).

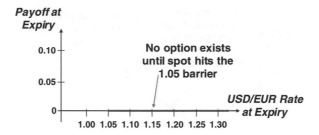

Figure 2.20   EUR Knock-in Put – Barrier *not* Hit. Payoff at Expiry (Excluding Premium).

2.6.2   Knock-in Barrier Options – Product Description

The knock-in option is an inactive option that becomes alive automatically should the USD/EUR trade at or beyond the barrier. For example, a EUR-based USD importer has the view that the EUR will weaken against the USD over the next 6 months, but expects the EUR to have a large movement beyond 1.05. The entity buys a 6-month EUR knock-in put with strike 1.15 and barrier 1.05. The premium of a knock-in option is lower than the premium of its equivalent standard option due to the possibility of no activation of the option.

- If the USD/EUR exchange rate never trades at or below 1.05, the entity has no option. It is equivalent to the entity having no protection (see Figure 2.20).
- If the USD/EUR exchange rate ever trades at or below 1.05, the entity effectively has bought a standard 1.15 option (see Figure 2.21).

The two barrier options we just covered are the most common ones. Our two examples had a single barrier. More complex barrier options can be obtained with double barriers that activate or extinguish an option if, for example, the two barriers are crossed during the life of the option. In our example, the exchange rate was also monitored continuously to check if the barrier was crossed. Some barrier options observe the barrier only on specific dates. In summary many different variations of barrier options can be found in the market.

2.7   RANGE ACCRUALS

A range accrual option is an option that accrues value for each day that a reference rate remains within a specified range (the accrual range) during the accrual observation period. For example, let us assume that an investor buys an accrual option on the Eurostoxx 50 index

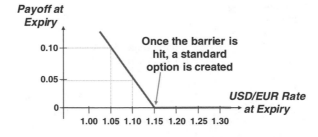

Figure 2.21   EUR Knock-in Put – Barrier *was* Hit. Payoff at Expiry (Excluding Premium).

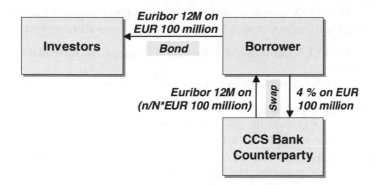

Figure 2.22   Range Accrual – Interest Flows.

(the reference rate). The option has 6 months to expiration and pays EUR 10,000 for each day that the index closes in the range 3,000 to 3,200 (the accrual range). The investor pays a EUR 600,000 premium for the option. There are 130 trading days in the accrual observation period. Therefore, for the investor to break even, the reference rate must trade within the accrual range for 60 days (= 600,000/10,000), or 46 % of the total trading days.

In the interest rate market, interesting alternatives to standard interest rate swaps are range accrual swaps. An example of a popular range accrual structure is the following: let us assume that a corporate wants to hedge its exposure to a 5-year EUR 100 million floating-rate liability by paying a fixed rate of 4 %, well below the 5 % market rate. Unlike a standard swap, the floating rate is conditional on how many days an observation rate (in our example the Euribor 12-month rate) is within a predefined range (3.7 % to 4.7 %) in the interest period. The aim of the range accrual swap is to lower the fixed rate of the swap by assuming the risk that the Euribor 12-month rate fixes outside the accrual range. The interest flows are as follows (see Figure 2.22):

- The entity pays 4 % annually, on the EUR 100 million.
- The entity receives Euribor 12-month on an accruing nominal. The nominal of the interest period is calculated using the following formula:

$$\text{Accrued nominal} = \text{n/N} * \text{EUR 100 million}$$

Where "n" is number of fixings during the interest period that the Euribor 12-month is within the 3.70 % – 4.70 % range, and "N" is the total number of fixings in the interest period.

FX range accrual forwards are an alternative to hedging with FX forwards. For each of the daily fixings up to maturity that the spot rate remains within a predetermined range, the forward nominal accrues a certain amount at a forward rate. The accrual forward rate is a better than market rate. For example, let us assume that a EUR based USD exporter wants to hedge a USD 40 million sale expected to take place in 3 months. The exporter expects the USD/EUR to trade within the 1.23 and 1.26 range during the next 2 months. The USD/EUR

3-month forward is 1.2500. Instead of entering into a standard forward at 1.2500, the exporter enters into a range accrual forward at 1.2400 with the following accruing terms:

- Every day the USD/EUR rate falls within the 1.23–1.26 range, the accrued notional increases by USD 1,000,000.
- Every day the USD/EUR rate falls outside the 1.23–1.26 range, there are no accruals.

The accrual observation period has 65 observation days. The exporter expects that a total of 40 observation days the USD/EUR will close within the accrual range.

Assume further that during 50 days, the USD/EUR remained within the 1.23–1.26 range. As a consequence, the exporter ended up with a contract to sell USD 50 million at a rate of 1.2400. The exporter then used the first USD 40 million of the range accrual forward to hedge the sale, but was left with a USD 10 million excess.

3
Hedging Foreign Exchange Risk

Foreign exchange (FX) risk is the most common financial risk. Entities that have foreign currency transactions and operations are exposed to the risk that exchange rates can vary, causing unwanted fluctuations in earnings and in cash flow. Chapters 3, 4 and 6 deal with the accounting implications of FX hedges through the extensive use of cases. Chapter 3 covers the hedging of anticipated sales and purchases and their resulting receivables and payables. Chapter 4 examines the hedging of net investments in foreign entities. Chapter 6 covers the hedging of foreign currency denominated debt.

Most of the accounting guidance required to understand the treatment of FX exposures and their hedging is based on two IFRS standards: IAS 39 *Financial Instruments: Recognition and Measurement* and IAS 21 *The Effects of Changes in Foreign Exchange Rates*. A summary of IAS 39 was depicted in Chapter 1. Some of the concepts of IAS 21 are outlined in this chapter and Chapter 4.

3.1 TYPES OF FOREIGN EXCHANGE EXPOSURES

The exposure to FX risk is caused mainly by the following transactions:

1) Foreign currency forecasted sales and purchases, and receivables and payables resulting from such transactions.
2) Interest and principal repayment on foreign currency denominated debt and deposits.
3) Revaluation of foreign currency denominated equity investments.
4) Dividends receipt from foreign investments.
5) Translation of profits of foreign operations.
6) Translation of net assets of foreign operations.
7) Competitive risk.

Competitive risk is the risk that the entity's future cash flows and earnings vary as a result of competitor's FX risk exposure. For example, a European car manufacturer is exposed to FX risk if a major Japanese competitor builds its cars in Japan, even if the European entity has all its manufacturing and sales denominated in Euros. In this case, unfavourable shifts in the EUR against the JPY can adversely affect the competitive position of the company.

3.2 INTRODUCTORY DEFINITIONS

3.2.1 Functional Currency

The entity's assets, liabilities and results must be measured in a functional currency. IAS 21 defines the functional currency of an entity as the currency of the primary economic environment in which the entity operates. Within a group, the functional currency of each entity must be determined individually based on its particular circumstances. IAS 21 ensures that the selection of the functional currency is a question of fact rather than management choice. IAS

21 includes some primary indicators that must be given a priority in determining an entity's functional currency, and also some secondary indicators. The primary indicators are:

1) The currency that mainly influences sales prices for goods and services, and of the country whose competitive forces and regulations mainly determine the sale prices of its goods and services.
2) The currency that mainly influences labour, material and other costs of providing goods or services.

If these primary indicators do not provide an obvious answer, then the entity need to turn to the secondary indicators, as follows:

1) The currency in which funds from financing activities (i.e., from issuing debt and equity instruments) are generated; and
2) The currency in which receipts from operating activities are usually retained.

IAS 21 also describes some other factors to consider in determining whether the functional currency of a foreign operation is the same as that of the parent company. For example, this would apply where a foreign subsidiary is used to market goods from the parent company and its cash is all remitted back to the parent.

In reality, most functional currencies used by each subsidiary throughout a group are generally the subsidiary's local currency (i.e., the currency of the country of its location). However, the group sometimes has a functional currency that differs from its local currency. This is often the case of oil companies and high-tech companies. For example, STMicroelectronics the semiconductor French-Italian company used the USD as its functional currency as "the reference currency for the semiconductor industry is the U.S. dollar, and product prices are mainly denominated in U.S. dollars".

3.2.2 Relevant Dates

Three different dates are relevant in a foreign currency transaction:

1) The transaction date: the date on which the transaction is recorded initially on the books.
2) The financial reporting dates: the financial reporting dates between the transaction date and the settlement date.
3) The settlement date: the date on which the payment or receipt is made.

3.3 SUMMARY OF IAS 21 TRANSLATION RATES

All the items in the financial statements denominated in a currency different to the entity's functional currency are translated using specific exchange rates.

3.3.1 Monetary versus Non-Monetary Items

In order to determine the appropriate translation exchange rate to use, IAS 21 groups assets and liabilities, that are not part of the financial statements of the group's foreign operations, into monetary accounts and non-monetary accounts. Monetary items are items that are settled in a fixed or determinable number of units of currency. All other assets and liabilities are non-monetary. Equity and income statement accounts are neither monetary nor non-monetary items. Examples of monetary and non-monetary items are:

Monetary Items

Assets	Liabilities
Accounts Receivable	Accounts payable
Long-term receivables	Long-term debt
Deferred income tax receivables	Deferred income tax payables
Intercompany receivables	Intercompany payables
Investments in bonds	Accrued liabilities

Non-monetary Items

Assets	Liabilities
Inventory	Prepayments for goods
Property, plant and equipment	Provisions settled by delivery of
Investments in equities of	a non-monetary asset
another entity	

3.3.2 Translation Rates

Under IAS 21, the exchange rate to be used to translate the different FX denominated items is determined as follows:

1) Foreign currency transactions are translated at the exchange rate prevailing on the date of the transactions.
2) Monetary assets and liabilities are translated at the exchange rate ruling at the balance sheet date. This FX rate is usually referred to as "the closing rate".
3) Non-monetary assets and liabilities, that are not valued at fair value, are translated at the exchange rate prevailing on the date of the transaction. In other words, there are no further retranslations.
4) Non-monetary items, that are valued at fair value, are translated at the exchange rate prevailing on the date when the latest fair value was determined.
5) Assets and liabilities of all the Group foreign entities are translated at the closing rate.
6) Income statements of all the Group foreign entities are translated at the average exchange rate for the period. It is also possible to use the exchange rate prevailing on each transaction date, but in reality few entities adopt this alternative.

3.4 FOREIGN CURRENCY TRANSACTIONS

The type of foreign currency transaction covered in this chapter is a transaction that requires the payment or receipt of a fixed amount of foreign currency. Usually there is a span of time between when the transaction is initiated and when the foreign currency is to be paid or received, as shown in Figure 1.1.

First, the entity expects, without a high probability, the occurrence of the FX transaction. At a later stage, the entity expects the FX transaction to happen with a high probability. Next, the

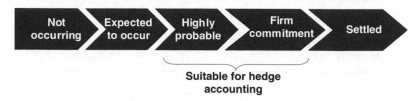

Figure 3.1   Chronology of a FX Transaction.

FX transaction is legally formalised, becoming a firm commitment. Finally, the FX transaction is settled, or in other words, payment/receipt is made.

An entity does not have to wait until the FX transaction is recorded in the balance sheet to apply hedge accounting. IAS 39 allows both highly probable transactions and firm commitments, to be designated as hedged items.

Stage of the FX Transaction	Balance Sheet Recognition	Hedge Accounting Allowed?
Expected to occur	None	✕
Highly expected to occur	None	✓
Firm commitment	Accounts payable/receivable	✓
Settled	Foreign currency cash reduction	Transaction already happened

3.4.1 Summary of Most Popular Hedging Derivatives – Foreign Exchange Risk

The following table summarises the most frequently FX hedging instruments, and the implications of their use from a IFRS perspective.

Hedging Derivative	Hedge Accounting Implications
FX Forward	Most friendly FX instrument to qualify for hedge accounting. Effectiveness assessment can be based either on spot or on forward rates. If based on spot rates, changes in fair value due to forward points are recognised in P&L.
FX option	Treated quite unfavourably by IAS 39. Hedge accounting only includes intrinsic value changes. Time value changes are taken to P&L.
FX tunnel	Written option subject to stringent conditions to qualify for hedge accounting. Better IAS 39 treatment than stand-alone options. Although time value changes are also taken to P&L, in some rate intervals there may be a big offset between both options' time value changes.
Participating forward	Suggested split between a forward and an option. Therefore, strategy implications are already outlined for a FX forward and a FX option.
Knock-in forward	Suggested split between a forward (eligible for hedge accounting) and a residual derivative (undesignated). Hedge accounting treatment is less challenging than KIKO or range accruals.

Hedging Derivative	Hedge Accounting Implications
KIKO forward	If knock-in barrier expected to be reached, suggested split between a forward (eligible for hedge accounting) and a residual derivative (undesignated). If knock-in barrier not expected to be reached, suggested split between an option (eligible for hedge accounting) and a residual derivative (undesignated). Accounting treatment can be specially challenging if knock-out barrier is crossed.
Range accrual forward	Very challenging to meet requirements of hedge accounting. If hedge initially eligible for hedge accounting, there may a notable risk of subsequent hedge relationship termination.

CASE 3.1

Hedging a Highly Expected Foreign Sale with a Forward

This case illustrates the accounting treatment of highly expected FX transactions and their hedges through FX forwards.

Let us assume that on 1 October 20X4 ABC Corporation, a company whose functional currency was the EUR, was expecting to sell finished goods to a US client. The sale was expected to occur on 31 March 20X5, and the sale receivable was expected to be settled on 30 June 20X5. Sale proceeds were expected to be USD 100 million to be received in USD.

The highly expected sale would become a foreign currency receivable upon the sale of the finished goods. The receivable will be an asset exposed to the risk that the EUR could weaken in value in relation to the USD. The following table summarises the effects on the USD receivable caused by fluctuations in the USD/EUR exchange rate.

USD/EUR Exchange Rate	Funcional Currency (EUR)	EUR value of USD Receivable
Goes up	Strengthens	Exchange loss (decreases in value)
Goes down	Weakens	Exchange gain (increases in value)

To hedge this exposure, on 1 October 20X4 ABC entered into a FX forward contract with the following terms:

FX Forward Terms	
Start date	1 October 20X4
Counterparties	Company ABC and XYZ Bank
Maturity	30 June 20X5
ABC sells	USD 100 million
ABC buys	EUR 80 million
Forward Rate	1.2500
Settlement	Physical delivery

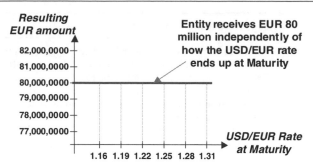

Figure 3.2   EUR Proceeds from USD Sale.

The FX forward locked-in the amount of EUR to be received in exchange for the USD 100 million, as shown in Figure 3.2.

ABC designated the forward contract as the hedging instrument in a foreign currency cash flow hedge, and the highly expected sale as the hedged item. IAS 39 permits the entity to choose whether or not to include the FX forward points in the hedge relationship assessment. ABC decided to base its assessment of hedge effectiveness on total variations in forward FX rates. In other words, the forward points of the FX forward were included in the hedge relationship.

Hedge Relationship Documentation

ABC documented the hedging relationship as follows:

Hedging Relationship Documentation	
Risk management objective and strategy for undertaking the hedge	The objective of the hedge is to protect the EUR value of USD 100 million highly expected sale of finished goods against unfavourable movements in the USD/EUR exchange rate.
	This hedging objective is consistent with ABC's overall FX risk management strategy of reducing the variability of its Profit and Loss statement.
Type of hedge	Cash flow hedge.
Risk being hedged	FX risk. The variability in EUR value of the highly expected transaction
Hedging instrument	The FX forward contract with reference number 012345. The counterparty to the forward is XYZ Bank and the credit risk associated with this counterparty is considered to be very low.
Hedged item	USD 100 million sale of finished goods expected to take place on 31 March 20X5.
Assessment of effectiveness testing	Hedge effectiveness will be assessed by comparing changes in the fair value of the hedging instrument to changes in the fair value of the expected cash flow.

Hedge effectiveness assessment will be performed on a
forward-forward basis. In other words, the forward points of both
the hedging instrument and the expected cash flow are included in
the assessment.

Prospective test

A prospective test will be performed at hedge inception and at each
reporting date. Due to the fact that the terms of the hedging
instrument and those of the expected cash flow match, the hedge is
expected to be highly effective. The credit risk of the counterparty
of the hedging instrument will be monitored continuously.

Retrospective test

A retrospective test will be performed at each reporting date and at
maturity of the hedging relationship using the "ratio analysis
method". The ratio will compare the cumulative change since
hedge inception in fair value of the expected cash flow arising from
the forecast sale with the cumulative change since hedge inception
in fair value of the hedging instrument. The hedge will be assumed
to be highly effective on a retrospective basis if the ratio is between
80 % and 125 %.

Prospective Tests

ABC used the critical terms method to assess prospective effectiveness. Because (i) the terms
of the forecast transaction and the forward coincided exactly, and (ii) the credit risk associated
with the counterparty to the hedging instrument was considered to be very low, ABC expected
that changes in the fair value of the expected cash flow of the forecasted transaction to be
completely offset by changes in fair value of the FX forward.

Retrospective Tests

A retrospective test was performed at each reporting date and at hedge maturity. ABC used
the ratio analysis method. The ratio compared the change (since hedge inception) in the fair
value of the expected cash flow with the change (since hedge inception) in fair value of the FX
forward. The hedge was assumed to be effective retrospectively if the ratio was between 80 %
and 125 %.

The spot and forward exchange rates on the relevant dates were as follows:

Date	Spot rate at indicated date	Forward rate for 30-Jun-X5	Discount factor for 30-Jun-X5
1 October 20X4	1.2350	1.2500	0.9804
31 December 20X4	1.2700	1.2800	0.9839
31 March 20X5	1.2950	1.3000	0.9901
30 June 20X5	1.3200	1.3200	1.0000

The fair value calculation of the hedging instrument was as follows:

Hedging Instrument Fair Value Calculations				
	1-Oct-X4	31-Dec-X4	31-Mar-X5	30-Jun-X5
Initial value in USD	100,000,000	100.000.000	100.000.000	100.000.000
Forward rate for 30 June 20X5	/ 1.2500	/ 1.2800	/ 1.3000	/ 1.3200
FX forward EUR amount	80,000,000	80,000,000	80,000,000	80,000,000
Value in EUR	80,000,000	78,125,000	76,923,000	75,758,000
Difference	0	1,875,000	3,077,000	4,242,000
Discount factor for 30 June 20X5	x 0.9804	x 0.9839	x 0.9901	x 1.0000
Forward fair value	0	1,845,000	3,047,000	4,242,000
Forward fair value change	—	1,845,000	1,202,000	1,195,000

The fair value calculation of the expected cash flow was as follows:

Highly Expected Cash Flow Fair Value Calculations				
	1-Oct-X4	31-Dec-X4	31-Mar-X5	31-May-X5
Expected cash flow in USD	100,000,000	100.000.000	100.000.000	100.000.000
Forward rate for 30 June 20X5	/ 1.2500	/ 1.2800	/ 1.3000	/ 1.3125
Value in EUR	80,000,000	78,125,000	76,923,000	75,758,000
Initially expected EUR amount	80,000,000	80,000,000	80,000,000	80,000,000
Difference in EUR cash flow	0	<1,875,000>	<3,077,000>	<4,242,000>
Discount factor for 30 June 20X5	x 0.9804	x 0.9839	x 0.9901	x 1.0000
Cash flow fair value	0	<1,845,000>	<3,047,000>	<4,242,000>
Cash flow fair value change	—	<1,845,000>	<1,202,000>	<1,195,000>

Changes in the fair value of the hedged item were, in absolute value, equal to those of the derivative. As fluctuations in fair value of both the hedged item and the hedge instrument coincided, there wasn't any hedge ineffectiveness. In other words, the hedge was 100 % effective.

	31-Dec-X4	31-Mar-X5
Forward contract fair value change	1,845,000	3,047,000
Expected sale fair value change	<1,845,000>	<3,047,000>
Ratio	100%	100%

A particular point is worth noting before illustrating the transaction accounting. The hedge relationship ended on 31 March 20X5, before the FX forward matured. Until 31 March 20X5, the changes in fair value of the forward were recorded in equity. On 31 March 20X5, the hedged cash flow was recognised in ABC's P&L and, simultaneously, the amount previously recorded in equity was reclassified to P&L. During the period from 31 March 20X5 until 30 June 20X5, there was no need to establish a new hedging relationship because FX gains and losses on the revaluation of the USD accounts receivable were going to be recorded in P&L and offset by the revaluation gains and losses of the forward also to be recorded in P&L.

Accounting Entries

The required journal entries were as follows:

1) To record the forward contract trade on 1 October, 20X4

   No entries in the financial statements were required as the fair value of the forward contract was zero.

2) To record the closing of the accounting period on 31 December 20X4:

   The change in fair value of the forward since the last valuation was a gain of EUR 1,845,000. As the hedge was all effective, all this change in fair value was recorded in equity and none of it recorded in P&L

Fair Value of Derivative (Asset)	€ 1,845,000	
Cash flow Hedges (Equity)		€ 1,845,000

3) To record the sale agreement and the end of the hedging relationship on 31 March 20X5:

   The sale agreement was recorded at the spot rate ruling on the date the sales are recognised (1.2950). Therefore, the sales euro amount was EUR 77,220,000 (= 100 million/1.2950)

Accounts Receivable (Asset)	€ 77,220,000	
Sales (P&L)		€ 77,220,000

The change in the fair value of the FX forward since the last valuation was a gain of EUR 1,202,000. As the hedge had no ineffectiveness, all this change was also recorded in equity.

Fair Value of Derivative (Asset)	€ 1,202,000	
Cash flow Hedges (Equity)		€ 1,202,000

The recognition of the sales transaction in P&L caused the release to P&L of the deferred hedge results accumulated in equity.

Cash flow Hedges (Equity)	€ 3,047,000	
Sales (P&L)		€ 3,047,000

4) To record the settlement of the sale on 30 June 20X5:

The receivable was revalued at the spot rate prevailing on this date, showing a loss of EUR 1,462,000 (= 100 million/1.3200 − 100 million/1.2950)

FX loss on Accounts Receivable (P&L)	€ 1,462,000	
Accounts Receivable (Asset)		€ 1,462,000

The USD payment from the receivable was exchanged for EUR as soon as it was received. The spot rate on payment date was 1.32, so the USD 100 million were exchanged for EUR 75,758,000 (= 100 million/1.32)

Cash (Asset)	€ 75,758,000	
Accounts Receivable (Asset)		€ 75,758,000

The change in the fair value of the FX forward since the last valuation was a gain of EUR 1,195,000.

Fair Value of Derivative (Asset)	€ 1,195,000	
Gain on derivative (P&L)		€ 1,195,000

The settlement of the FX forward resulted in the receipt of EUR 4,242,000 (= 100 million*(1/1.25–1/1.32)).

Cash (Asset)	€ 4,242,000	
Fair Value of Derivative (Asset)		€ 4,242,000

It can be seen that with the hedge ABC locked-in EUR 80,000,000 proceeds from the USD sale. Without the hedge, the proceeds from the sale would have been EUR 4,242,000 lower. The inclusion of the forward points in the hedge relationship caused the expected deterioration of the exchange rate implied by the forward points to end up within EBITDA, and not in the "other gains and losses" line, as shown in Figure 3.3.

Summary of Accounting Treatment – Forward-to-Forward Method

	Cash (Asset)	Forward Fair Value (Asset)	Accounts Receivable (Asset)	Cash flow (Equity)	Profit and Loss
1 October 20X4					
Start of forward contract	0	0			
31 December 20X4					
Forward contract fair value change		1,845,000		1,845,000	
31 March 20X5					
Forward contract fair value change		1,202,000		1,202,000	
Hedge transfer				<3,047,000>	3,047,000
Sale shipment			77,220,000		77,220,000
30 June 20X5					
Forward contract fair value change		1,195,000			1,195,000
Forward settlement	4,242,000	<4,242,000>			
Receivable revaluation			<1,462,000>		<1,462,000>
Receivable payment	75,758,000		<75,758,000>		
TOTAL	80,000,000	–0–	–0–	–0–	80,000,000

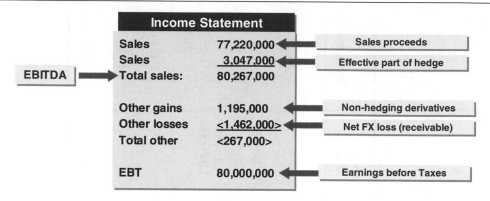

Figure 3.3   Income Statement – Forward-to-Forward Method.

Accounting When Forward Points are Excluded from Hedge Assessment

Let us assume that in the previous hedge ABC decided to exclude the forward points from the hedging relationship. In other words, the effectiveness was assessed based in changes of the spot exchange rate (what is termed "spot-to-spot" assessment).

Derivative's Fair Value Calculation

The changes in fair value of the forward were calculated as follows:

	1-Oct-X4	31-Dec-X4	31-Mar-X5	30-Jun-X5
Initial value in USD	100,000,000	100.000.000	100.000.000	100.000.000
Forward rate for 30-Jun-X5	/ 1.2500	/ 1.2800	/ 1.3000	/ 1.3200
Value in EUR	80,000,000	78,125,000	76,923,000	75,758,000
FX forward EUR amount	80,000,000	80,000,000	80,000,000	80,000,000
Difference	0	1,875,000	3,077,000	4,242,000
Discount factor for 30-Jun-X5	x 0.9804	x 0.9839	x 0.9901	x 1.0000
Forward total fair value	0	1,845,000	3,047,000	4,242,000
Forward total fair value change	—	1,845,000	1,202,000	1,195,000
Expected cash flow in USD	100,000,000	100,000,000	100,000,000	100,000,000
Spot rate at inception	/ 1.2350	/ 1.2350	/ 1.2350	/ 1.2350
Initial value in EUR	80,972,000	80,972,000	80,972,000	80,972,000
xpected cash flow in USD	100,000,000	100,000,000	100,000,000	100,000,000
Spot rate	/ 1.2350	/ 1.2700	/ 1.2950	/ 1.3200
Value in EUR at spot	80,972,000	78,740,000	77,220,000	75,758,000
Difference	0	2,232,000	3,752,000	5,214,000
Discount factor for 30-Jun-X5	x 0.9804	x 0.9839	x 0.9901	x 1.0000
Forward fair value due to spot	0	2,196,000	3,715,000	5,214,000
Forward fair value due to spot change	—	2,196,000	1,519,000	1,499,000
Forward total fair value change	—	1,845,000	1,202,000	1,195,000
Forward fair value change due to spot	—	2,196,000	1,519,000	1,499,000
Difference	—	<351,000>	<317,000>	<304,000>
Forward fair value change due to forward points	—	<351,000>	<317,000>	<304,000>

Expected Purchase Fair Value

The changes in fair value of the expected cash flow were calculated as follows:

	Oct 1, 20X4	Dec 31, 20X4	Mar 31, 20X5	Jun 30, 20X5
Expected cash flow in USD	100,000,000	100,000,000	100,000,000	100,000,000
Spot rate	/ 1.2350	/ 1.2700	/ 1.2950	/ 1.3200
Cash flow value in EUR at spot	80,972,000	78,740,000	77,220,000	75,758,000
Difference	0	<2,232,000>	<3,752,000>	<5,214,000>
Discount factor for 30 June 20X5	x 0.9804	x 0.9839	x 0.9901	x 1.0000
Cash flow fair value due to spot	0	<2,196,000>	<3,715,000>	<5,214,000>
Cash flow fair value due to spot change	—	<2,196,000>	<1,519,000>	<1,499,000>

Retrospective Tests

A retrospective test was performed at each reporting date and at hedge maturity. ABC used the ratio analysis method. The ratio compared (i) the change (since hedge inception) in the fair value due to changes in the spot rate of the expected cash flow with (ii) the change (since hedge inception) in fair value due to changes in the spot rate of the FX forward. The hedge was assumed to be effective retrospectively if the ratio was between 80 % and 125 %.

All the changes in fair value of the FX forward due to changes in the forward points were excluded from the hedge relationship, and consequently were considered ineffective. The hedge relationship terminated on 31 March 20X5, so no further calculations of the hedge effective and ineffective parts were needed after that date.

	31 Dec 20X4	31 Mar 20X5
Cumulative fair value change of expected cash flow due to spot movement	<2,196,000>	<3,715,000>
Cumulative fair value change of hedging instrument due to spot movement	2,196,000	3,715,000
Retrospective test: Ratio	100 %	100 %
Cash flow fair value change during period	<2,196,000>	<1,519,000>
Forward fair value change due to spot rate	2,196,000	1,519,000
Hedge: effective part	2,196,000	1,519,000
Hedge: ineffective part due to spot rate	–0–	–0–
Forward fair value change due to forward points	<351,000>	<317,000>
Hedge: total ineffective part	<351,000>	<317,000>

Accounting Entries

The required journal entries were as follows:

1) To record the forward contract trade on 1 October 20X4:

No entries in the financial statements were required as the fair value of the forward contract was zero.

2) To record the closing of the accounting period on 31 December 20X4:

The change in fair value of the forward since the last valuation was a gain of EUR 1,845,000. Of this amount, a gain of EUR 2,196,000 was considered effective and recorded in equity, and a loss of EUR 351,000 was considered ineffective and recorded in P&L (in the "other income/losses" line). Some accountants recognise the fair value changes on the forward points component of the FX forward in the "interest income/expense" line of P&L as forward points represent an interest rate differential.

Fair Value of Derivative (Asset)	€ 1,845,000	
Other Income and Losses (P&L)	€ 351,000	
Cash flow Hedges (Equity)		€ 2,196,000

3) To record the sale agreement on 31 March 20X5:

The sale agreement was recorded at the spot rate ruling on the date the sales were recognised (1.2950). Therefore, the sales EUR amount was EUR 77,220,000 (= 100 million/1.2950):

Accounts Receivable (Asset)	€ 77,220,000	
Sales (P&L)		€ 77,220,000

The change in the fair value of the FX forward since the last valuation was a gain of EUR 1,202,000. Of this amount, a gain of EUR 1,519,000 was considered effective and recorded in equity, and a loss of EUR 317,000 was considered ineffective and recorded in P&L:

Fair Value of Derivative (Asset)	€ 1,202,000	
Other Income and Losses (P&L)	€ 317,000	
Cash flow Hedges (Equity)		€ 1,519,000

The recognition of the sales transaction in P&L caused the deferred hedge results accumulated in equity to be reclassified to P&L:

Cash flow Hedges (Equity)	€ 3,715,000	
Sales (P&L)		€ 3,715,000

4) To record the settlement of the sale on 30 June 20X5:

The receivable was revalued at the spot rate prevailing on this date, showing a loss of EUR 1,462,000 (= 100 million/1.3200 − 100 million/1.2950):

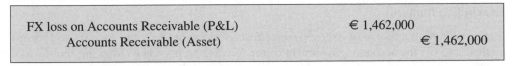

The USD payment from the receivable was exchanged for EUR as soon as it was received. The spot rate on payment date was 1.32, so the USD 100 million were exchanged for EUR 75,758,000 (= 100 million/1.32):

| Cash (Asset) | € 75,758,000 | |
| Accounts Receivable (Asset) | | € 75,758,000 |

The change in the fair value of the FX forward since the last valuation was a gain of EUR 1,195,000:

| Fair Value of Derivative (Asset) | € 1,195,000 | |
| Gain on Derivative (P&L) | | € 1,195,000 |

The settlement of the FX forward resulted in the receipt of EUR 4,242,000 (= 100 million*(1/1.25–1/1.32):

| Cash (Asset) | € 4,242,000 | |
| Fair Value of Derivative (Asset) | | € 4,242,000 |

It can be seen that the hedge locked-in EUR 80,000,000 proceeds from the USD sale. Without the hedge, the proceeds from the sale would have been EUR 4,242,000 lower. The exclusion of the forward points from the hedge relationship caused the expected deterioration of the exchange rate implied by the forward points (EUR 668,000) to end up in the "other gains and losses" line of P&L and not within EBITDA, as shown in Figure 3.4.

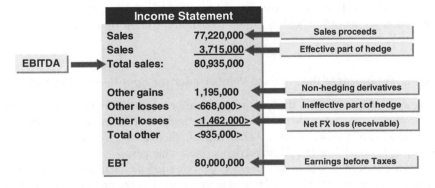

Figure 3.4 Income Statement – Spot-to-Spot Method.

Concluding Remarks

It is worth noting a couple of issues: (i) the effects of the spot-to-spot or forward-to-forward method and (ii) the accounting treatment of the forward points when using the spot-to-spot method.

Spot-to-Spot versus Forward-to-Forward

In a FX forward, the forward points represent the expected depreciation of one currency relative to the other currency during a specific period. The forward points are caused by the interest rate differential between both currencies. Under IAS 39, the measurement of the hedge effectiveness between the forecasted transaction and the FX forward may be based on either the spot rates (i.e., excluding the forward points from the hedge relationship) or the forward rates (i.e., including the forward points in the hedge relationship). No method is best as both approaches have potential benefits and drawbacks. We will analyse the impact of both methods on EBITDA and recognition timing.

In our case, the forward points implied a depreciation of the USD relative to the EUR:

- In the spot-to-spot method, this USD depreciation was recorded outside EBITDA, in the "other income and expense" line of P&L.
- In the forward-to-forward method, the USD depreciation was recorded within EBITDA.

In our case we covered the hedge of a highly expected sale. Choosing the spot-to-spot method instead of the forward-to-forward method kept the USD deterioration outside EBITDA, resulting in a higher EBITDA. If the expected transaction were a purchase, the effect would have been the opposite: a lower EBITDA under the spot-to-spot method.

If the time span between hedge inception and the sale recognition is very long, there could be important timing differences between the recognition of the forward points and the recognition of the sale. The spot-to-spot method recognises in P&L, at each balance sheet date, a part of the expected depreciation (or appreciation) implied by the forward points. As a consequence, under the spot-to-spot method, when the expected sale is finally recognised in P&L, already a sizeable portion of the forward points deterioration (or appreciation) could already have been recognised. This timing differences do not happen under the forward-to-forward method as the recognition in P&L of the forward points deterioration and of the recognition of the sale take place simultaneously. In our case, the period between hedge inception and sale recognition was quite short so the differences in timing recognition caused by the spot-to-spot method were not relevant.

Accounting Treatment of the Forward Points Under the Spot-to-Spot Method

Under the spot-to-spot method, the forward points are excluded from the hedge relationship. As a consequence, the changes in the fair value of the hedging instrument due to changes in the forward points are recognised in P&L. At the moment, there is no agreement in the accounting community as to which line of P&L to recognise these changes.

In our case, under the spot-to-spot method we recorded the changes in fair value of the forward due to changes in the forward points in the "other income and expense" line of P&L. Some accountants argue that as the forward points are caused by the interest rate differential

Summary of Accounting Treatment – Spot-to-Spot Method

	Cash (Asset)	Forward Fair value (Asset)	Accounts Receivable (Asset)	Cash flow Hedges (Equity)	Profit and Loss
October 1, 20X4					
Start of forward contract	0	0			
December 31, 20X4					
Forward contract fair value change		1,845,000		2,196,000	<351,000>
March 31, 20X5					
Forward contract fair value change		1,202,000		1,519,000	<317,000>
Hedge transfer				<3,715,000>	3,715,000
Sale shipment			77,220,000		77,220,000
June 30, 20X5					
Forward contract fair value change		1,195,000			1,195,000
Forward settlement	4,242,000	<4,242,000>			
Receivable revaluation			<1,462,000>		<1,462,000>
Receivable payment	75,758,000		<75,758,000>		
TOTAL	80,000,000	–0–	–0–	–0–	80,000,000

between the two currencies of the FX forward, and consequently, that the changes in fair value of the forward due to changes in the forward points should be recorded in the "interest income and expense" line of P&L. Alternatively, we have seen some entities recognising these changes within EBITDA as "operating income and expense". In our view this quite an aggressive interpretation of accounting guidelines.

CASE 3.2

Hedging a Highly Expected Foreign Sale with a Tunnel

The risk being hedged in this case is the same as the previous one: the hedge of a highly expected sale denominated in a foreign currency. The hedging instrument in this case is a tunnel. This case highlights the unfavourable treatment of options under IAS 39 due to the exclusion of the time value from the hedging relationship.

The starting point of this case is identical to the previous case. Let us assume that on 1 October 20X4 ABC Corporation, a company whose functional currency was the EUR, was expecting to sell finished goods to a US client. The sale was expected to occur on 31 March 20X5, and the sale receivable was expected to be settled on 30 June 20X5. Sale proceeds were expected to be USD 100 million to be received in USD.

ABC had the view that the USD could appreciate against the EUR and wanted to benefit were its view right. At the same time, ABC wanted to have a protection, were its view wrong. As a consequence, on 1 October 20X4 ABC entered into a FX tunnel with the following terms:

USD Put/EUR Call Terms		USD Call/EUR Put Terms	
Trade date	1 October 20X4	Trade date	1 October 20X4
Option buyer	ABC	Option buyer	XYZ Bank
Option seller	XYZ Bank	Option seller	ABC
USD Notional	USD 100 million	USD Notional	USD 100 million
Strike	1.2900	Strike	1.2120
EUR Notional	EUR 77,519,000	EUR Notional	EUR 82,508,000
Expiry date	30 June 20X5	Expiry date	30 June 20X5
Settlement	Physical delivery	Settlement	Physical delivery
Premium	EUR 1,400,000	Premium	EUR 1,400,000
Premium payment date	1 October 20X4	Premium payment date	1 October 20X4

In the FX options market, the term call (or put) is accompanied by the currency to which it is a call (or put), as discussed in Chapter 2. Additionally, a call on one of the two currencies is a put on the other currency. For example, when referring to a USD/EUR option, a call on the USD automatically implies a put on the EUR. In our case, ABC bought a USD put (or EUR call) with strike 1.2900. The USD put gave ABC the right, but not the obligation to sell USD 100 million at a rate of 1.2900 on expiry date. This option protected ABC's sale from a depreciating USD above 1.2900. Consequently, ABC would only exercise the USD put if the USD/EUR exchange rate exceeded 1.2900 on expiry date, receiving then EUR 77,519,000 in exchange for the USD 100 million.

In order not to pay a premium, ABC also sold a USD call (or EUR put) with strike 1.2120. The combination of both options is called a tunnel in the FX market. The same strategy in the interest rate market would be called a collar. Because the premium to be paid for the purchased option equalled the premium to be received for the written (sold) option, this hedging strategy is called a zero-cost tunnel. The USD call gave XYZ Bank the right to sell EUR 82,508,000 (= USD 100 million/1.2120) in exchange for USD 100 million. Thus, at expiry XYZ Bank would only exercise the USD call if the USD/EUR exchange rate were below 1.2120.

The tunnel guaranteed ABC that the EUR proceeds stemming from the highly expected sale would be between EUR 77,519,000 and EUR 82,508,000. If the USD/EUR at maturity was between 1.2120 and 1.2900, nether option would be exercised and ABC would exchange the USD for EUR in the FX market at the prevailing FX rate at that moment.

Figure 3.5 depicts the amount of EUR that ABC would get in exchange for the USD 100 million as a function of the spot USD/EUR at expiry:

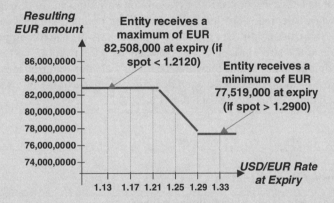

Figure 3.5   FX Tunnel – Resulting EUR Amount.

In terms of the resulting exchange rate at which ABC would exchange the USD 100 million, it had the profile showed in Figure 3.6:

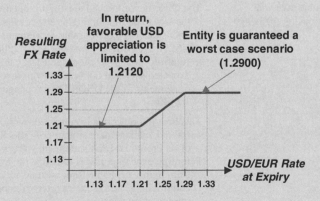

Figure 3.6   FX Tunnel – Resulting USD/EUR Rate.

ABC denominated the tunnel (i.e., the combination of the two options) as the hedging instrument and the highly expected sale as the hedged item in a foreign currency cash flow hedge. The tunnel could be designated as the hedging instrument because:

1) no net premium was received;
2) the underlying of the USD put and the USD call was the same (i.e., the USD/EUR exchange rate);
3) the USD put and the USD call had the same maturity; and
4) the notional amount of the written option (i.e., the USD call) was not greater than the notional amount of the purchased option (i.e., the USD put).

Hedge effectiveness was assessed by comparing the changes in the intrinsic value of the options with the changes in the fair value of a hypothetical derivative for the risk being hedged. In our case, all the terms of the hypothetical derivative coincided with the terms of the tunnel, except that the hypothetical derivative had no credit exposure. ABC also decided to base its hedge effectiveness assessment on variations in spot exchange rates. In other words, when calculating the intrinsic value of the options, the forward points were excluded from this calculation (i.e., the intrinsic value was measured comparing the spot exchange rate and the strike price). As a consequence, effectiveness was required to be assessed only during those periods in which there was a change in intrinsic value. Changes in the time value of the options were excluded from the assessment of effectiveness and were recognised directly in P&L in each period.

Hedge Relationship Documentation

ABC documented the hedging relationship as follows:

Hedging Relationship Documentation	
Risk management objective and strategy for undertaking the hedge	The objective of the hedge is to protect the EUR value of the USD 100 million highly expected sale of finished goods against unfavourable movements in the USD/EUR exchange rate beyond 1.2900.
	In return for this protection, the EUR value of the highly expected sale will not benefit from favourable movements in the USD/EUR exchange rate below 1.2120.
	This hedging objective is consistent with ABC's overall FX risk management strategy of reducing the variability of its Profit and Loss statement. ABC's policy regarding foreign exchange risk is to hedge the exposure arising from highly probable forecast transactions, firm commitments and monetary items denominated in foreign currencies.
Type of hedge	Cash flow hedge.
Risk being hedged	FX risk. The variability in EUR value of the highly expected transaction.

Hedging Relationship Documentation	
Hedging instrument	The FX tunnel contract with reference number 012349. The counterparty to the tunnel is XYZ Bank and the credit risk associated with this counterparty is considered to be very low.
Hedged item	USD 100 million sale of finished goods expected to take place on 31 March 20X5.
Assessment of effectiveness testing	Hedge effectiveness will be assessed by comparing changes in the intrinsic value of the hedging instrument to changes in the intrinsic value of a hypothetical derivative. The intrinsic value of the options will be measured as the difference between the spot exchange rate and the strike price. Effectiveness will be assessed only during those periods in which there is a change in intrinsic value. Changes in the time value of the options will be excluded from the assessment of effectiveness and will be recognised directly in P&L in each period.
	The terms of the hypothetical derivative are such that its fair value changes exactly offset the changes in fair value of the hedged highly expected cash flow for the risk being hedged. In this hedging relationship, all the terms of the hypothetical derivative coincide with the terms of the hedging instrument except that the hypothetical derivative has the same maturity as the hedge and that it has no credit risk.
	Prospective test A prospective test will be performed, at hedge inception and at each reporting date, using the critical terms method. Because the terms of the hedging instrument and those of the hypothetical derivative match and that the credit risk to the counterparty to the hedging instrument is very low, the hedge is expected to be highly effective prospectively. The credit risk of the counterparty of the hedging instrument will be monitored continuously.
	Retrospective test A retrospective test will be performed, at each reporting date and at hedge maturity, using the "ratio analysis method". The ratio will compare the cumulative change since hedge inception in the intrinsic value of the hypothetical derivative with the cumulative change since hedge inception in the intrinsic value of the hedging instrument. The hedge will be assumed to be highly effective on a retrospective basis if the ratio is between 80 % and 125 %.

Prospective Tests

A prospective test was performed at hedge inception and at each reporting date. ABC used the critical terms method to assess prospective effectiveness. Because (i) the terms of the hypothetical derivative and the hedging instrument matched, and (ii) the credit risk associated with the counterparty to the hedging instrument was considered to be very low, ABC expected that changes in expected cash flows from the forecasted transaction beyond 1.2900 and below 1.2120 to be completely offset by changes in the intrinsic value of the tunnel. The credit risk of the counterparty to the hedging instrument was monitored at each testing date, but there was no significant deterioration in its credit.

Retrospective Tests

The spot exchange rates on the relevant dates were as follows:

Date	Spot USD/EUR	Forward rate for 30-Jun-X5	Discount factor for 30-Jun-X5
1 October 20X4	1.2350	1.2500	0.9804
31 December 20X4	1.2700	1.2800	0.9839
31 March 20X5	1.2950	1.3000	0.9901
30 June 20X5	1.3200	1.3200	1.0000

The fair value of the tunnel was calculated using the Black-Scholes model. The intrinsic value was calculated using the spot rates. The time value of the hedging instrument was calculated as follows:

> Option Time Value = Option Total Fair Value − Option Intrinsic Value

The following table details the calculation of the changes in the tunnel intrinsic and time values from the tunnel total value. It is worth noting that although the tunnel had no time value at the beginning and at the end of its life, its time value change showed a remarkable volatility. Remember that during the term of the hedge, changes in time value were recognised in P&L, so the hedge increased the volatility of ABC's P&L during the life of the hedge. Note also, that the hedging relationship ended on 31 March, 20X5. From that date, there was no need to split the option fair value into its intrinsic and time values.

	1-Oct-X4	31-Dec-X4	31-Mar-X5	30-Jun-X5
USD Put fair value	1,400,000	1,580,000	1,584,000	1,761,000
USD Call fair value	<1,400,000>	<490,000>	<89,000>	−0−
Tunnel total fair value change	−0−	1,090,000	1,495,000	1,761,000
Expected cash flow in USD	100,000,000	100,000,000	100,000,000	100,000,000
Spot rate at USD put strike	/ 1.2900	/ 1.2900	/ 1.2900	/ 1.2900
EUR amount at USD put strike	77,519,000	77,519,000	77,519,000	77,519,000
Expected cash flow in USD	100,000,000	100,000,000	100,000,000	100,000,000
Spot rate	/ 1.2350	/ 1.2700	/ 1.2950	/ 1.3200
EUR amount at spot	80,972,000	78,740,000	77,220,000	75,758,000
USD put undisc. intrinsic value	−0−	−0−	299,000	1,761,000
Discount factor	x 0.9804	x 0.9839	x 0.9901	x 1.0000
USD put intrinsic value	−0−	−0−	296,000	1,761,000

	1-Oct-X4	31-Dec-X4	31-Mar-X5	30-Jun-X5
Expected cash flow in USD	100,000,000	100,000,000	100,000,000	100,000,000
Spot rate at USD call strike	/ 1.2120	/ 1.2120	/ 1.2120	/ 1.2120
EUR amount at USD call strike	82,508,000	82,508,000	82,508,000	82,508,000
Expected cash flow in USD	100,000,000	100,000,000	100,000,000	100,000,000
Spot rate	/ 1.2350	/ 1.2700	/ 1.2950	/ 1.3200
EUR amount at spot	80,972,000	78,740,000	77,220,000	75,758,000
USD call undisc. intrinsic value	−0−	−0−	−0−	−0−
Discount factor	x 0.9804	x 0.9839	x 0.9901	x 1.0000
USD call intrinsic value	−0−	−0−	−0−	−0−
Tunnel intrinsic value	−0−	−0−	296,000	1,761,000
Tunnel total fair value change	−0−	1,090,000	1,495,000	1,761,000
Tunnel intrinsic value	−0−	−0−	296,000	1,761,000
Tunnel time value	−0−	1,090,000	1,199,000	−0−
Change in tunnel intrinsic value	—	−0−	296,000	1,465,000
Change in tunnel time value	—	1,090,000	109,000	<1,199,000>

A retrospective test was performed at each reporting date and at hedge maturity. The hedged item was substituted by a hypothetical derivative with the same terms as the tunnel. ABC used the ratio analysis method to assess retrospective effectiveness. The ratio compared (i) the change (since hedge inception) in the hypothetical derivative intrinsic value due to changes in the spot rate with (ii) the change (since hedge inception) in the tunnel intrinsic value due to changes in the spot rate. The hedge was assumed to be effective retrospectively if the ratio was between 80 % and 125 %.

As the changes in the hypothetical derivative intrinsic value coincided with those of the hedging instrument, the hedge was 100 % effective retrospectively, as shown in the following table:

	31-Dec-X4	31-Mar-X5
Change in tunnel intrinsic value	−0−	296,000
Change in hypothetical derivative intrinsic value	−0−	296,000
Retrospective effectiveness	100 %	100 %

For illustration purposes only, the following table shows the calculation of the change in fair value of the hedged item, were the hypothetical derivative approach not chosen.

	1-Oct-X4	31-Dec-X4	31-Mar-X5	30-Jun-X5
Expected cash flow in USD	100,000,000	100,000,000	100,000,000	100,000,000
Upper hedged rate	/ 1.2900	/ 1.2900	/ 1.2900	/ 1.2900
EUR amount at upper hedge rate	77,519,000	77,519,000	77,519,000	77,519,000
Expected cash flow in USD	100,000,000	100,000,000	100,000,000	100,000,000
Lower hedged rate	/ 1.2120	/ 1.2120	/ 1.2120	/ 1.2120
EUR amount at lower hedge rate	82,508,000	82,508,000	82,508,000	82,508,000
Expected cash flow in USD	100,000,000	100,000,000	100,000,000	100,000,000

(*Continued*)

	1-Oct-X4	31-Dec-X4	31-Mar-X5	30-Jun-X5
Spot rate	/ 1.2350	/ 1.2700	/ 1.2950	/ 1.3200
EUR amount at spot	80,972,000	78,740,000	77,220,000	75,758,000
Shortage of EUR amount at spot vs EUR upper hedge amount	−0−	−0−	<299,000>	<1,761,000>
Shortage of EUR lower hedge amount vs EUR amount at spot	−0−	−0−	−0−	−0−
Total shortage	−0−	−0−	<299,000>	<1,761,000>
Discount factor	x 0.9804	x 0.9839	x 0.9901	x 1.0000
PV of shortage (hedged item fair value for risk being hedged)	−0−	−0−	<296,000>	<1,761,000>
Change of hedged item fair value for the risk being hedged	−0−	−0−	<296,000>	<1,465,000>

Using the expected cash flow instead of the hypothetical derivative also shows that the hedge was effective retrospectively, as shown in the following table:

	31 Dec 20X4	31 Mar 20X5
Change in tunnel intrinsic value	−0−	296,000
Change in hedged item fair value	−0−	<296,000>
Retrospective effectiveness	100 %	100 %

Accounting Entries

The required journal entries were as follows:

1) To record the tunnel trade on 1 October 20X4:

No entries in the financial statements were required as the fair value of the tunnel was zero.

2) To record the closing of the accounting period on 31 December 20X4:

The change in fair value of the tunnel since the last valuation was a gain of EUR 1,090,000. This amount was due only to the tunnel change in time value which was considered ineffective and recorded in "other income and expense" in P&L:

Fair Value of Derivative (Asset)	€ 1,090,000	
Other Income and Losses (P&L)		€ 1,090,000

3) To record the sale agreement on 31 March 20X5:

The sale agreement was recorded at the spot rate ruling on that date (1.2950). Therefore, the sale EUR proceeds were EUR 77,220,000 (= 100 million/1.2950):

| Accounts Receivable (Asset) | € 77,220,000 | |
| Sales (P&L) | | € 77,220,000 |

The change in the fair value of the tunnel since the last valuation was a gain of EUR 405,000. Of this amount, a gain of EUR 296,000 was due to the change in the tunnel intrinsic value, thus considered effective and recorded in equity. The remainder, a gain of EUR 109,000, was due to the change in the tunnel time value, therefore considered ineffective and recorded in P&L:

Fair Value of Derivative (Asset)	€ 405,000	
Cash flow Hedges (Equity)		€ 296,000
Other Income and Losses (P&L)		€ 109,000

The recognition of the sales transaction in P&L caused the release to P&L of the deferred hedge results accumulated in equity. The hedging relationship finished on this date.

| Cash flow Hedges (Equity) | € 296,000 | |
| Sales (P&L) | | € 296,000 |

4) To record the settlement of the sale on 30 June 20X5:

The receivable was revalued at the spot rate prevailing on this date, showing a loss of EUR 1,462,000 (= 100 million/1.3200 − 100 million/1.2950):

| FX loss on Accounts Receivable (P&L) | € 1,462,000 | |
| Accounts Receivable (Asset) | | € 1,462,000 |

The change in the tunnel fair value since the last valuation was a gain of EUR 266,000:

| Fair Value of Derivative (Asset) | € 266,000 | |
| Gain on Derivative (P&L) | | € 266,000 |

ABC received USD 100 million from the client. Simultaneously, the tunnel expired and ABC exercised the USD put, exchanging the USD 100 million for EUR 77,519,000.

Cash (Asset)	€ 77,519,000	
Fair Value of Derivative (Asset)		€ 1,761,000
Accounts Receivable (Asset)		€ 75,758,000

CASE 3.3

Hedging a Highly Expected Foreign Sale with a Participating Forward

In this case we will be hedging the same risk as the previous cases, but using instead a participating forward as the hedging instrument. The participating forward is one of the most basic and conservative hedges available. As its name implies, this hedge allows ABC a certain amount of "participation" in favourable movements of the USD/EUR exchange rate. The hedge also provides a guaranteed protection.

The risk being hedged in this case is the same as in the previous cases. Let us assume that on 1 October 20X4 ABC Corporation, a company whose functional currency was the EUR, was expecting to sell finished goods to a US client. The sale was expected to occur on 31 March 20X5, and the sale receivable was expected to be settled on 30 June 20X5. Sale proceeds were expected to be USD 100 million to be received in USD.

ABC had the view that the USD could appreciate against the EUR in the following months and wanted to benefit were its view right. At the same time, ABC wanted to have a protection were its view wrong. As a consequence, on 1 October 20X4, ABC entered into a participating forward with the following terms:

Participating Forward Terms	
Start date	1 October 20X4
Counterparties	Company ABC and XYZ Bank
Maturity	30 June 20X5
ABC sells	USD 100,000,000
ABC buys	EUR 100,000,000/Forward rate
Forward Rate	1.2760, if Final Spot $\geq$ 1.2760
	1.2760 − (1.2760 − Final Spot)/2, otherwise
Final Spot	The USD/EUR spot at maturity
Premium	Zero
Settlement	Physical delivery

At maturity, ABC had the obligation to exchange USD 100 million for EUR at the forward rate. The forward rate was a function of the spot at maturity. The maximum forward rate was 1.2760. The forward rate participated in half of the USD appreciation below 1.2760. Figure 3.7 shows the resulting forward rate as a function of the spot USD/EUR at maturity:

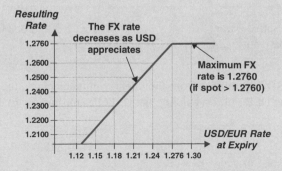

Figure 3.7   Participating Forward Resulting Forward Rate.

Figure 3.8a shows the amount of EUR that ABC would receive in exchange for the USD 100 million, as a function of the spot USD/EUR at maturity:

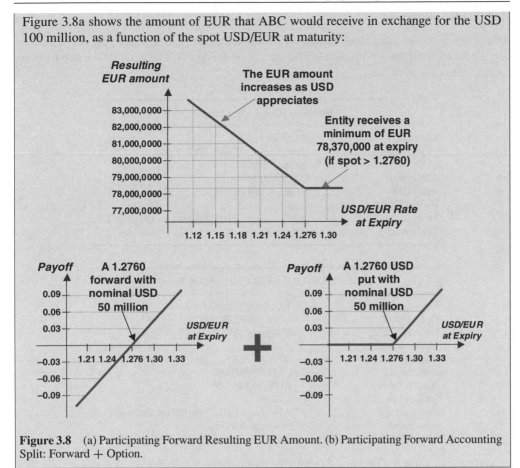

Figure 3.8   (a) Participating Forward Resulting EUR Amount. (b) Participating Forward Accounting Split: Forward + Option.

Hedge Accounting Optimisation of the Participating Forward

One of the fundamental issues that ABC faced regarding the participating forward was how to formalise the instrument to maximise its eligibility for hedge accounting. ABC considered the following choices:

1) To divide the hedging instrument into the following two parts (see Figure 3.8b): (i) a FX forward at 1.2760 and a nominal of USD 50 million, and (ii) a purchase of a USD put with strike 1.2760 and a nominal of USD 50 million. Under this alternative, both the forward and the option were considered eligible for hedge accounting.
2) To divide the hedging instrument into the following two parts: (i) a purchased USD put with strike 1.2760 and nominal 100 million, and (ii) a written USD call with strike 1.2760 and nominal 50 million.

In this case, there was no need to analyse which alternative showed a lower volatility of P&L. The friendlier treatment by IAS 39 of forwards relative to options indicated that the first alternative was better choice than the second alternative.

Hedging Relationships

As a result of the split described earlier, ABC established two different hedging relationships: one for the forward (hedge 1) and other for the option (hedge 2). The terms of the two hedging instruments were as follows:

Hedge 1: FX Forward Terms	
Start date	1 October 20X4
Counterparties	Company ABC and XYZ Bank
Maturity	30 June 20X5
ABC buys	USD 50,000,000
ABC sells	EUR 39,185,000
Forward Rate	1.2760
Premium	ABC receives EUR 799,000 on the Start Date
Settlement	Physical delivery

Hedge 2: USD Put (EUR Call) Option Terms	
Start date	1 October 20X4
Option type	USD put/EUR call
Counterparties	Company ABC and XYZ Bank
Option buyer	ABC
Maturity	30 June 20X5
ABC buys	USD 50,000,000
ABC sells	EUR 39,185,000
Strike Rate	1.2760
Premium	ABC pays EUR 799,000 on the Start Date
Settlement	Physical delivery

ABC documented the first hedging relationship involving the forward as follows:

Hedge 1: Hedging Relationship Documentation	
Risk management objective and strategy for undertaking the hedge	The objective of the hedge is to protect the EUR value of the USD 50 million highly expected sale of finished goods against unfavourable movements in the USD/EUR exchange rate by locking-in its EUR value.
	This hedging objective is consistent with ABC's overall FX risk management strategy of reducing the variability of its Profit and Loss statement.
Type of hedge	Cash flow hedge.
Risk being hedged	FX risk. The variability in EUR value of the highly expected transaction.
Hedging instrument	The FX forward contract with reference number 012779. The counterparty to the forward is XYZ Bank and the credit risk associated with this counterparty is considered to be very low.
Hedged item	USD 50 million sale of finished goods expected to be agreed on 31 March 20X5.
Assessment of effectiveness testing	Hedge effectiveness will be assessed by comparing changes in the fair value of the hedging instrument to changes in the fair value of a hypothetical derivative.

Hedge 1: Hedging Relationship Documentation

The terms of the hypothetical derivative are such that its fair value changes offset exactly the changes in fair value of the hedged highly expected cash flow for the risk being hedged. The hypothetical derivative in this hedging relationship is a forward with maturity the end of the hedging relationship (31 March 20X5), nominal USD 50 million, a 1.2450 forward rate and zero initial fair value.

Hedge effectiveness assessment will be performed on a forward-forward basis. In other words, the forward points of both the hedging instrument and the hypothetical derivative are included in the assessment.

Prospective test
A prospective test will be performed at inception and at each reporting date, using the scenario analysis method. The credit risk of the counterparty of the hedging instrument will be monitored continuously.

Retrospective test
A retrospective test will be performed at each reporting date and at hedge maturity using the "ratio analysis method". The ratio will compare the cumulative change since hedge inception in the fair value of the hypothetical derivative with the cumulative change since hedge inception in the fair value of the hedging instrument. The hedge will be assumed to be highly effective on a retrospective basis if the ratio is between 80 % and 125 %.

ABC documented the second hedging relationship as follows:

Hedge-2: Hedging Relationship Documentation

Risk management objective and strategy for undertaking the hedge	The objective of the hedge is to protect the EUR value of the USD 50 million highly expected sale of finished goods against unfavourable movements in the USD/EUR exchange rate beyond 1.2760. This hedging objective is consistent with ABC's overall FX risk management strategy of reducing the variability of its Profit and Loss statement. ABC's policy regarding foreign exchange risk is to hedge the exposure arising from highly probable forecast transactions, firm commitments and monetary items denominated in foreign currencies.
Type of hedge	Cash flow hedge.
Risk being hedged	FX risk. The variability in EUR value of the highly expected transaction.
Hedging instrument	The FX option contract with reference number 012780. The counterparty to the option is XYZ Bank and the credit risk associated with this counterparty is considered to be very low.
Hedged item	USD 50 million sale of finished goods expected to take place on 31 March 20X5.
Assessment of effectiveness testing	Hedge effectiveness will be assessed by comparing changes in the intrinsic value of the hedging instrument to changes in the intrinsic value of a hypothetical derivative. The intrinsic value of the options will be measured as the difference between the forward exchange rate and the strike price. Effectiveness will be assessed only during those periods in which there are changes in any of the options' intrinsic value. Changes in the time value of the hedging instrument will be excluded from the assessment of effectiveness and recognised directly in P&L.

(Continued)

Hedge-2: Hedging Relationship Documentation

The terms of the hypothetical derivative are such that its fair value changes offset exactly the changes in fair value of the hedged highly expected cash flow for the risk being hedged. In this hedging relationship, the terms of the hypothetical derivative coincide with the terms of the hedging instrument except the expiry date and the credit risk.

Prospective test

A prospective test will be performed at each reporting date, using the scenario analysis method. Two scenarios will be considered: a two standard deviation upward movement in the exchange rate, and a two standard deviation downward movement in the exchange rate. The hedge will be assumed to be highly effective on a prospective basis if the assessment results are between 80 % and 125 %.The credit risk of the counterparty of the hedging instrument will be monitored continuously.

Retrospective test

A retrospective test will be performed at each reporting date using the "ratio analysis method". The ratio will compare the cumulative change since hedge inception in the intrinsic value of the hypothetical derivative with the cumulative change since hedge inception in the intrinsic value of the hedging instrument. The hedge will be assumed to be highly effective on a retrospective basis if the ratio is between 80 % and 125 %.

The terms of the hypothetical derivative of the first hedging relationship were as follows:

Hedge 1: Hypothetical Derivative Terms	
Instrument	FX Forward
Start date	1 October 20X4
Maturity	31 March 20X5
ABC buys	USD 50,000,000
ABC sells	EUR 40,161,000
Forward Rate	1.2450
Initial fair value	Zero

The terms of the hypothetical derivative of the second hedging relationship were as follows:

Hedge 2: Hypothetical Derivative Terms	
Instrument	USD Put/EUR Call
Start date	1 October 20X4
Maturity	31 March 20X5
Nominal	USD 50,000,000
Option buyer	ABC
Strike Rate	1.2760
Initial intrinsic value	Zero

Prospective Tests

ABC performed a prospective test at hedge inception and at each reporting date. For each hedging relationship, ABC used the scenario analysis method to assess prospective effectiveness.

For the prospective test of the first hedging relationship (involving the FX forward), ABC chose two scenarios: (i) a two-standard deviation upward movement in the forward and spot rates in the next six months, and (ii) a two-standard deviation downward movement in the forward and spot rates in the next six months. The test performed at inception for the first hedge relationship involving the FX forward was as follows:

Hedge 1: Prospective Test at Inception	
Spot (on 1-Oct-X4)	1.2350
Market forward rate for 31-Mar-X5 (on 1-Oct-X4)	1.2450
Hedging instrument forward rate	1.2760
Hypothetical derivative forward rate	1.2450
$+2\sigma$ Movement in the forward rate for 30-Jun-X5 (10% volatility + 6 months)	1.4350
$+2\sigma$ Movement in the forward rate for 31-May-X5 (10% volatility + 6 months)	1.4300
Change in Fair value of FX forward = 0.9901*(50 mn/1.276 − 50mn/1.435)	4,299,000
Change fair value hypothetical derivative = 1*(50 mn/1.245 − 50 mn/1.43)	5,196,000
Effectiveness	82.7%
-2σ Movement in the forward rate for 30-Jun-X5 (10% volatility + 6 months)	1.0750
-2σ Movement in the forward rate for 31-May-X5 (10% volatility + 6 months)	1.0700
Change in fair value of FX forward = 0.9901*(50 million/1.276 − 50 million/1.075)	<7,254,000>
Change fair value hypothetical derivative (= 50 million/1.245 − 50 million/1.07)	<6,568,000>
Effectiveness	110.4%

It can be seen that the mismatch created by being the forward off-market had an impact in the hedge effectiveness. Nonetheless, the effectiveness was within the range 80%–125%, so ABC expected the first hedge relationship to be highly effective prospectively.

For the prospective test of the second hedging relationship (involving the option), ABC also used the scenario analysis method. The test was performed in a similar way to the test performed for the first hedging relationship, but computing instead the changes in intrinsic value of the hedging instrument and the hypothetical derivative.

After studying at the test results, ABC concluded that it expected the second hedge to be highly effective on a prospective basis. We would like to highlight that there could be ineffectiveness for small changes in the fair value of the derivatives, as we will see in the retrospective test. The following table shows the prospective test for the second hedging relationship, performed at its inception.

Hedge 2: Prospective Test at Inception	
Spot (on 1-Oct-X4)	1.2350
Forward rate for 31-Mar-X5 (on 1-Oct-X4)	1.2450
Hedging instrument and hypothetical derivative strikes	1.2760
$+2\sigma$ Movement in the forward rate (10% volatility + 6 months)	1.4350
$+2\sigma$ Movement in the spot rate	1.4300
Change in intrinsic value of hedging instrument	4,299,000
$\quad = 0.9901*(50 \text{ mn}/1.276 - 50\text{mn}/1.435)$	
Change in intrinsic value of hypothetical derivative	4,220,000
$\quad = 1*(50 \text{ mn}/1.276 - 50 \text{ mn}/1.43)$	
Effectiveness	101.9%
-2σ Movement in the forward rate (10% volatility + 6 months)	1.0750
-2σ Movement in the spot rate	1.0700
Change in intrinsic value of hedging instrument	−0−
Change in intrinsic value of hypothetical derivative	−0−
Effectiveness	100% (1)

Note (1): Although the ratio is in theory undetermined, in practice the result can be thought of an exact coincidence in the changes in the intrinsic value of both instruments.

Retrospective Tests

Two retrospective tests, one for each hedging relationship, were performed at each reporting date during the hedge life and at hedge maturity. Remember that the hedging relationship finished on 31 March 20X5, so only two retrospective tests were needed. It was assumed no significant deterioration in the credit of the counterparty of the hedging instrument during the hedge life.

The results of the retrospective tests of the first hedging relationship (involving the FX forward) are shown in the next two tables. It can be seen that the changes in the fair value of the hedging instrument were slightly different to those of the hypothetical derivative because their forward rate and maturity were different.

Hedge-1: Fair Values	1-Oct-X4	31-Dec-X4	31-Mar-X5	30-Jun-X5
Spot rate	1.2350	1.2700	1.2950	1.3200
Forward rate to 31-Mar-X5	1.2450	1.2750	1.2950	—
Forward rate to 30-Jun-X5	1.2500	1.2800	1.3000	1.3200
Forward fair value	<799,000> (1)	120,000 (2)	716,000 (3)	1,306,000 (4)
Forward fair value change	—	919,000	596,000	590,000
Hypothetical derivative fair value	−0− (5)	936,000 (6)	1,551,000 (7)	—
Hypothetical derivative fair value change	—	936,000	615,000	—

Notes:

(1) $= (50 \text{ mn}/1.2760 - 50 \text{ mn}/1.25)*0.9804$
(2) $= (50 \text{ mn}/1.2760 - 50 \text{ mn}/1.28)*0.9839$
(3) $= (50 \text{ mn}/1.2760 - 50 \text{ mn}/1.30)*0.9901$
(4) $= (50 \text{ mn}/1.2760 - 50 \text{ mn}/1.32)*1.0000$
(5) $= (50 \text{ mn}/1.2450 - 50 \text{ mn}/1.2450)*0.9842$
(6) $= (50 \text{ mn}/1.2450 - 50 \text{ mn}/1.2750)*0.9902$
(7) $= (50 \text{ mn}/1.2450 - 50 \text{ mn}/1.2950)*1.0000$

Hedge 1: Retrospective Tests	31-Dec-X4	31-Mar-X5
Forward contract fair value change (since hedge inception)	919,000	1,515,000
Hypothetical derivative fair value change (since hedge inception)	936,000	1,551,000
Ratio	98.2%	97.7%
Hedge effective amount	919,000	596,000
Hedge ineffective amount	–0–	–0–

Each retrospective test of the first hedge was within the 80%–125% range, and therefore, the hedge was considered to be highly effective retrospectively. Because the accumulated change in the fair value of the hedged item (the hypothetical derivative) exceeded the accumulated change in the fair value of the hedging instrument, there was no ineffectiveness to be recorded.

The options' total fair value were calculated using the Black-Scholes method. The time and intrinsic values of the hedging instrument and the hedged item were as follows:

Hedge 2: Fair Values	1-Oct-X4	31-Dec-X4	31-Mar-X5	30-Jun-X5
Forward rate to 31-Mar-X5	1.2450	1.2750	1.2950	—
Forward rate to 30-Jun-X5	1.2500	1.2800	1.3000	1.3200
Hedging instrument fair value	799,000	941,000	1,017,000	1,306,000
Hedging instrument intrinsic value	–0– (1)	120,000 (2)	716,000 (3)	1,306,000 (4)
Hedging instrument time value (0)	799,000	821,000	301,000	–0–
Hypothetical derivative intrinsic value	–0– (5)	–0– (6)	575,000 (7)	—

Notes:

(0) = Option time value = option fair value–option intrinsic value
(1) = Max [(50 mn/1.2760–50 mn/1.25)*0.9804; 0]
(2) = Max [(50 mn/1.2760–50 mn/1.28)*0.9839; 0]
(3) = Max [(50 mn/1.2760–50 mn/1.30)*0.9901; 0]
(4) = Max [(50 mn/1.2760–50 mn/1.32)*1.0000; 0]
(5) = Max [(50 mn/1.2760–50 mn/1.2450)*0.9842; 0]
(6) = Max [(50 mn/1.2760–50 mn/1.2750)*0.9902; 0]
(7) = Max [(50 mn/1.2760–50 mn/1.2950)*1.0000; 0]

The results of the retrospective tests of the second hedging relationship (involving the option) are shown in the following table. It can be seen that the hedge was ineffective during the period between 1-Oct-X4 and 31-Dec-X4 because there was no change in the intrinsic value of the hypothetical derivative while there was change in the intrinsic value of the hedging instrument. This problem could have been reduced by calculating the intrinsic value based changes in the spot rates instead of changes in the forward rates, or by entering into a participating forward with maturity coinciding with the end of the hedging relationship. ABC concluded that the problem was very particular and that there was a low probability of repetition. As a consequence, ABC did not terminate the hedge relationship.

Hedge 2: Retrospective Tests	31-Dec-X4	31-Mar-X5
Change in hedging instrument intrinsic value (since hedge inception)	120,000	716,000
Change in hypothetical derivative intrinsic value (since hedge inception)	−0−	575,000
Retrospective effectiveness	Undefined	124.5 %

The calculation of the effective and ineffective parts of the second hedge at each period were the following:

Hedge 2: Effective and Ineffective Parts	31-Dec-X4	31-Mar-X5
Change in hedging instrument time value	22,000	<520,000>
Change in hedging instrument intrinsic value	120,000	596,00
Change in hypothetical derivative intrinsic value	−0−	575,000
Effective Part	−0−	575,000
Ineffective Part	142,000	<499,000>

3.7.5 Accounting Entries

The required journal entries were as follows:

1) To record the forward and the option trades on 1 October, 20X4

The FX forward had a fair value of EUR -799,000 at its inception:

Cash (Asset)	€ 799,000	
Fair Value of Derivative (Liability)		€ 799,000

The option had a fair value of EUR 799,000 at its inception:

Fair Value of Derivative (Asset)	€ 799,000	
Cash (Asset)		€ 799,000

2) To record the closing of the accounting period on 31 December 20X4:

The change in fair value of the forward since the last valuation was a gain of EUR 919,000. All this amount was considered to be effective, and thus, recorded in equity:

Fair Value of Derivative (Asset)	€ 919,000	
Cash flow hedges (Equity)		€ 919,000

The change in fair value of the option since the last valuation was a gain of EUR 142,000. As the retrospective test failed, all this amount was considered to be ineffective and therefore recorded in "other income and expense" in P&L.

Fair Value of Derivative (Asset)	€ 142,000	
Other Income and Losses (P&L)		€ 142,000

3) To record the sale agreement on 31 March 20X5:

The sale agreement was recorded at the spot rate ruling on the date the sales were recognised (1.2950). Therefore, the sales EUR amount was EUR 77,220,000 (= 100 million/1.2950)

Accounts Receivable (Asset)	€ 77,220,000	
Sales (P&L)		€ 77,220,000

The change in fair value of the forward since the last valuation was a gain of EUR 596,000. All the amount was considered to be effective, and thus, recorded in equity.

Fair Value of Derivative (Asset)	€ 596,000	
Cash flow hedges (Equity)		€ 596,000

The change in fair value of the option since the last valuation was a gain of EUR 76,000 (= 1,017,000 − 941,000). Of this amount, EUR 575,000 was considered to be effective and recorded in equity. The remainder, and loss of EUR 499,000 was considered to be ineffective and recorded in P&L.

Fair Value of Derivative (Asset)	€ 76,000	
Other Income and Losses (P&L)	€ 499,000	
Cash flow Hedges (Equity)		€ 575,000

The recognition of the sales transaction in P&L caused the release to P&L of the deferred hedge results accumulated in equity, a total of EUR 2,090,000 (= 919,000 + 596,000 + 575,000). The hedging relationship finished on this date.

Cash flow Hedges (Equity)	€ 2,090,000	
Sales (P&L)		€ 2,090,000

4) To record the settlement of the sale on 30 June 20X5:

The receivable was revalued at the spot rate prevailing on this date, showing a loss of EUR 1,462,000 (= 100 million/1.3200−100 million/1.2950)

FX loss on Accounts Receivable (P&L)	€ 1,462,000	
Accounts Receivable (Asset)		€ 1,462,000

The change in the fair value of the forward since the last valuation was a gain of € 590,000 (=1,306,000 − 716,000).

Fair Value of Derivative (Asset)	€ 590,000	
Gain on Derivative (P&L)		€ 590,000

The change in the fair value of the option since the last valuation was a gain of € 289,000 (= 1,306,000 − 1,017,000).

Fair Value of Derivative (Asset)	€ 289,000	
Gain on Derivative (P&L)		€ 289,000

On 30 June, 20X5 ABC received the USD 100 million from the client and eliminated the related account receivable. The USD 100 million were valued at that date's exchange rate (1.3200):

Cash (Asset)	€ 75,758,000	
Accounts Receivable (Asset)		€ 75,758,000

Simultaneously, the forward and option expired. Through the forward, ABC sold USD 50 million and received EUR 39,185,000. The transaction increased the cash account carrying value by EUR 1,306,000 (= 50 million*(1/1.2760 − 1/1.3200))

Cash (Asset)	€ 1,306,000	
Fair Value of Derivative (Asset)		€ 1,306,000

Simultaneously, ABC exercised the USD put, exchanging the USD 50 million for EUR 39,185,000. The transaction increased the cash account carrying value by EUR 1,306,000 (= 50 million*(1/1.2760 − 1/1.3200))

Cash (Asset)	€ 1,306,000	
Fair Value of Derivative (Asset)		€ 1,306,000

CASE 3.4

Hedging a Highly Expected Foreign Sale with a Knock-in Forward

In Cases 2 and 3, we analysed hedging strategies of highly expected foreign sales built with vanilla options. The hedging instrument used in this case, a knock-in forward, involves an exotic option. At the moment, the IFRS accounting treatment of exotic options is unclear. A potential solution is to split the exotic instrument into two parts: a first part that involves a group of standard derivatives for which the accounting treatment is clear, and a second part that includes the rest. The first part is eligible for hedge accounting and the second part is treated as undesignated. This process of splitting the exotic instrument into the two parts is quite challenging as it generally turns out to be different solutions. Therefore, readers seeking an optimal accounting solution to be etched in stone are bound to be disappointed. Our objective is that the reader develops and exercises his own judgment.

The risk being hedged in this case is the same as in the previous cases. Let us assume that on 1 October 20X4 ABC Corporation, a company whose functional currency was the EUR, was expecting to sell finished goods to a US client. The sale was expected to occur on 31 March 20X5, and the sale receivable was expected to be settled on 30 June 20X5. Sale proceeds were expected to be USD 100 million to be received in USD.

ABC had the view that the USD could appreciate against the EUR in the following months and wanted to benefit were its view right. However, ABC thought that the USD appreciation was going to be quite limited, not reaching 1.1620. At the same time, ABC wanted to have a protection, were its view wrong. As a consequence, on 1 October 20X4 ABC entered into a knock-in forward with the following terms:

FX Knock-in Forward Terms

ABC has the right to sell the USD notional and to buy the EUR notional at 1.2600 on maturity date.
If at any moment from start date until maturity date the USD/EUR spot rate does trade at, or below, the barrier, the right becomes an obligation.

Start date	1 October 20X4
Counterparties	Company ABC and XYZ Bank
Maturity	30 June 20X5
USD notional	USD 100,000,000
EUR notional	EUR 79,365,000 (if barrier is reached)
Strike Rate	1.2600
Barrier	1.1620
Premium	Zero
Settlement	Physical delivery

The knock-in forward guaranteed an exchange rate slightly worse than that of standard forward but, in contrast, it allowed ABC a better exchange rate provided the spot rate did not reach 1.1620. On expiry, ABC had the right to exchange USD for EUR at a rate of 1.2600. In the event that the spot USD/EUR exchange rate ever traded at or below 1.1620 during the instrument's life, ABC's right became an obligation to exchange USD for EUR at a rate of 1.2600. ABC did not have to pay a premium to enter into the knock-in forward.

Figure 3.9 shows the EUR amount that ABC would get in exchange for the USD 100 million as a function of the spot USD/EUR at maturity, were the barrier <u>not hit</u> during the life of the instrument. It can be seen how ABC could benefit if the exchange rate at maturity was below 1.2600, and that this benefit was limited by the 1.1620 barrier.

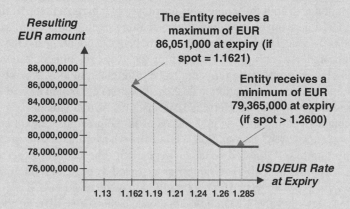

Figure 3.9 Knock-In Forward Resulting EUR Amount – Barrier <u>not</u> Hit.

Figure 3.10 illustrates the EUR amount that ABC would get in exchange for the USD 100 million as a function of the spot USD/EUR at maturity, were the barrier <u>hit</u> during the instrument's life. It shows that the product secured a worst-case rate of 1.2600, or a worst-case amount of EUR 79,365,000.

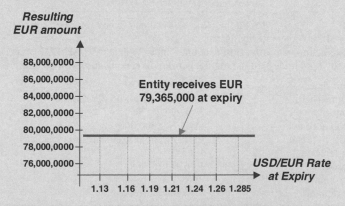

Figure 3.10 Knock-In Forward Resulting EUR Amount – Barrier <u>was</u> Hit.

Figure 3.11 shows the resulting exchange rate at which ABC would exchange the proceeds from the USD sale as a function of the exchange rate at maturity, were the barrier <u>not</u> hit during the life of the knock-in forward. It can be seen that the knock-in forward allowed ABC to participate in a potential appreciation of the USD below 1.2600 provided that the USD/EUR did not reach the 1.1620 level during the life of the instrument.

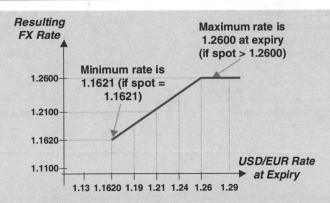

Figure 3.11   Knock-In Forward Resulting FX Rate – Barrier <u>not</u> Hit.

Figure 3.12 shows the resulting exchange rate at which ABC would exchange the proceeds from the USD sale, as a function of the exchange rate at maturity if the barrier <u>was hit</u> during the instrument's life. It can be seen that once the 1.1620 level was reached, the resulting rate was 1.2600.

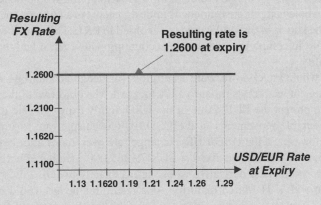

Figure 3.12   Knock-In Forward Resulting FX Rate – Barrier <u>was</u> Hit.

Accounting Optimisation of the Knock-In Forward

One of the main issues that ABC faced regarding the knock-in forward was how to split the instrument into two parts, a first part eligible for hedge accounting and a second part treated as undesignated, so the overall impact in P&L volatility was minimised. ABC considered the following choices:

1) Divide the hedging instrument into two parts (see Figure 3.13): (i) a FX forward at 1.2600, and (ii) a purchased knock-out USD call with a 1.2600 strike and a 1.1620 barrier. The forward would be considered eligible for hedge accounting, and the knock-out option would be undesignated (i.e., considered as speculative). Therefore, all the changes in the fair value of the knock-out option would be recorded in P&L.

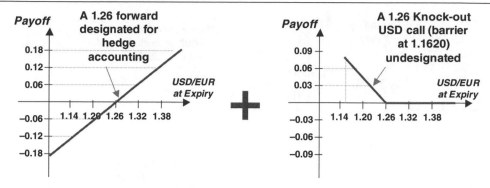

Figure 3.13   Knock-in Forward Alternative 1: Forward + Knock-out Option.

2) Divide the hedging instrument into two parts (see Figure 3.14): (i) a purchased standard USD put with strike 1.2600, and (ii) a written USD knock-in call with a 1.2620 strike and a 1.1620 barrier. Part (i) would be considered eligible for hedge accounting. Part (ii) would be considered undesignated. In this choice, the changes in the time value of the standard option and the changes in the fair value of the knock-in option would be recorded in P&L.
3) Consider the whole hedging instrument as undesignated. As a consequence, all changes in fair value of the knock-in forward would be recorded in P&L. This choice was the simplest, saving the effort in complying with hedge accounting. However, it had the biggest impact in P&L volatility.
4) Consider the whole knock-in forward as eligible for hedge accounting, arguing that this hedging instrument was very similar to a FX forward. The objective of the hedge would be defined as: "to protect the EUR value of the USD highly expected sale of finished goods against unfavourable movements in the USD/EUR exchange rate to minimum of EUR 79,365,000. However, if the USD/EUR exchange rate ever trades at or below 1.1620 until 31 June 20X5, the EUR value is fixed at EUR 79,365,000". Hedge effectiveness would be tested using a hypothetical derivative whose terms exactly matched those of the hedging instrument but with a 31 March maturity. As a result, the hedge would be considered as 100 % effective, and all the changes in fair value of the knock-in forward would be recorded in equity until the hedged item impacted P&L. This accounting treatment, in our view, is very controversial and we think that many auditors will question its validity. Besides, when

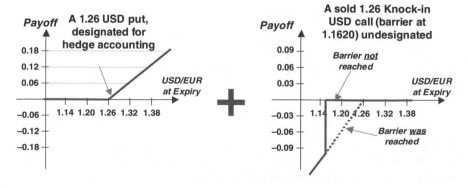

Figure 3.14   Knock-in Forward Alternative 2: Standard Option + Knock-in Option.

the hedging relationship ended on 31 March 20X5, the barrier may still be operative, so there might be still uncertainty about the resulting profile of the hedging instrument on that date, complicating things further.

ABC discarded the third and fourth choices, and decided to analyse which of the first two choices could result in a lower P&L volatility. A simple way to perform this analysis was to compute the changes in the fair value of the ineffective parts in different scenarios. ABC computed the change in fair value of the effective and ineffective parts from hedge inception to 31 December 20X4 under four scenarios of the USD/EUR spot rate:

1) A two standard deviations ($+2\sigma$) upward movement.
2) A one standard deviation ($+1\sigma$) upward movement.
3) A one standard deviation (-1σ) downward movement.
4) A two standard deviations (-2σ) downward movement.

ABC assumed a 10% volatility when computing these movements. This volatility was the market implied volatility of 3-month USD/EUR at-the-money-forward options at the time of the analysis.

To keep the analysis simple, the forward points and the discount factors were considered unchanged in the analysis. The following table summarises the resulting forwards and the fair value of the whole knock-in forward under each scenario:

	$+2\sigma$ Movement	$+1\sigma$ Movement	-1σ Movement	-2σ Movement
Spot on 1 October 20X4	1.2350	1.2350	1.2350	1.2350
Spot on 31 December 20X4	1.3650 *(1)*	1.3000	1.1750	1.1150
Forward for 31-Mar-X5 (on 31-Dec-X4)	1.3700	1.3050	1.1800	1.1200
Forward for 30-Jun-X5 (on 31-Dec-X4)	1.3750	1.3100	1.1850	1.1250
Knock-in forward fair value on 1-Oct-X4	–0–	–0–	–0–	–0–
Knock-in forward fair value on 31-Dec-X4 *(2)*	6,670,000	3,427,000	<4,531,000>	<9,370,000>

Notes: *(1)* Spot*Exp(2*σ *sqrt(number of years)) = 1.2350*Exp(2*10%*sqrt(1/4)) = 1.3650; *(2)*: Using a Black-Scholes modified formula to price barrier options.

The results of the application of the scenario analysis to choice 1 are shown next:

Alternative-1: Split into Forward + Knock-Out Option:

	$+2\sigma$ Movement	$+1\sigma$ Movement	-1σ Movement	-2σ Movement
Forward fair value on 1-Oct-X4	<622,000>	<622,000>	<622,000>	<622,000>
Forward fair value on 31-Dec-X4	6,531,000 (1)	2,980,000	<4,942,000>	<9,370,000>
Change in fair value of forward	7,153,000	3,602,000	<4,320,000>	<8,748,000>
Hedge effective part	7,153,000	3,602,000	<4,320,000>	<8,748,000>
K/O option fair value on 1-Oct-X4	622,000	622,000	622,000	622,000
K/O option fair value on 31-Dec-X4	139,000	447,000	411,000	–0–
Change in fair value of K/O option	<483,000>	<175,000>	<211,000>	<622,000>
Hedge ineffective part	<483,000>	<175,000>	<211,000>	<622,000>

Notes regarding these calculations:

- For example (1): 100 million*$(1/1.26 - 1/1.375)$*0.9839 = 6,531,000
- The forward fair value was calculated using forward rates. See Case 1 for a detail description on how FX forward fair values are computed. All the change in fair value of the FX forward was considered to be effective. This was not 100 % accurate as the FX forward is off-market (i.e., its fair value was not zero at hedge inception), but we thought that it was a reasonable simplification.
- The knock-out USD call was valued using a closed-end formula for barrier options. All the change in its fair value was considered to be ineffective.

The results of the scenario analysis applied to alternative 2 are shown in the following table:

Alternative 2: Split Into Standard Option + Knock-In Option:

	$+2\sigma$ Movement	$+1\sigma$ Movement	-1σ Movement	-2σ Movement
Standard option (USD put) intrinsic value on 1-Oct-X4	–0–	–0–	–0–	–0–
Standard option intrinsic value on 31-Dec-X4	6,531,000 *(1)*	2,980,000	–0–	–0–
Change in standard option intrinsic value	6,531,000	2,980,000	–0–	–0–
Hedge effective part	6,531,000	2,980,000	–0–	–0–
Standard option time value on 1-Oct-X4	2,050,000	2,050,000	2,050,000	2,050,000
Standard option time value on 31-Dec-X4	192,000	725,000	484,000	149,000
Change in standard option time value	<1,858,000>	<1,325,000>	<1,566,000>	<1,901,000>
Knock-in option fair value on 1-Oct-X4	<2,050,000>	<2,050,000>	<2,050,000>	<2,050,000>
Knock-in option fair value on 31-Dec-X4	<53,000>	<278,000>	<5,015,000>	<9,519,000>
Change in knock-in option fair value	1,997,000	1,772,000	<2,965,000>	<7,469,000>
Hedge ineffective part	139,000	447,000	<4,531,000>	<9,370,000>

Notes regarding these calculations:

- The intrinsic value was calculated using forward rates, and assumed to be totally effective. For example (1): 100 million*$(1/1.26-1/1.375)$*0.9839 = 6,531,000.
- Standard option intrinsic value = Option intrinsic value + Option intrinsic value.
- See Case 2 of this chapter for a more detailed description of the intrinsic and fair value calculations of options.
- Ineffective part of hedge = change in standard option time value + change in knock-in option fair value.

The following table summarises the results of the ineffective part for each alternative:

	Alternative-1 (Forward + K/O option)	Alternative-2 (Standard + Knock-in)
Average	<373,000>	<3,329,000>
Maximum value	<175,000>	447,000
Minimum value	<622,000>	<9,370,000>

Clearly, alternative 1 showed a much lower volatility in P&L during the period. In alternative 2, the inclusion of the standard option time value in the ineffective part of the hedge added a significant amount of volatility in the P&L. It is important to note that the result of this analysis is not a general solution to be etched in stone. It depends on the terms of the knock-in forward and the market conditions.

ABC performed the analysis studying only the P&L impact on 31 December 20X5, its year-end date. To keep the case simple we have not studied the P&L impact on all reporting dates, but the process would be similar.

Resulting Instruments Terms

As a consequence of the previous analysis, ABC decided to adopt the first alternative formalising the transaction through two different contracts: a FX forward and a knock-out USD call. The FX forward was designated as the hedging instrument in a hedging relationship of a highly expected cash flow. The terms of the forward were as follows:

FX Forward Terms	
Start date	1 October 20X4
Counterparties	Company ABC and XYZ Bank
Maturity	30 June 20X5
ABC sells	USD 100,000,000
ABC buys	EUR 79,365,000
Forward Rate	1.2600
Premium	ABC receives EUR 622,000 on the start date
Settlement	Physical delivery

The knock-out USD call was considered undesignated (i.e., it was not part of any hedging relationship). Note that because the settlement of the FX forward was by physical delivery, the knock-out option settlement had to be in cash, so ABC did not delivered the USD 100 million twice. The terms of the knock-out USD call were as follows.

Knock-out Option Terms	
Start date	1 October 20X4
Option type	USD knock-out call
Counterparties	Company ABC and XYZ Bank
Option buyer	ABC
Maturity	30 June 20X5
ABC buys	USD 100,000,000
ABC sells	EUR 79,365,000
Strike Rate	1.2600
Premium	ABC pays EUR 622,000 on the start date
Barrier	1.1620
Knock-out provision	The option will cease to exist if the USD/EUR exchange rate reaches, or is below, the barrier level at any time until maturity
Settlement	Cash settlement

Hedge Relationship Documentation

ABC denominated the forward contract as the hedging instrument in a foreign currency cash flow hedge, and the highly expected sale as the hedged item. ABC also decided to base its assessment of hedge effectiveness on variations in forward FX rates. In other words, the forward points of the FX forward were included in the hedge relationship. ABC documented the hedging relationship as follows:

Hedging Relationship Documentation	
Risk management objective and strategy for undertaking the hedge	The objective of the hedge is to protect the EUR value of the USD 100 million highly expected sale of finished goods against unfavourable movements in the USD/EUR exchange rate by locking-in its EUR value.
	This hedging objective is consistent with ABC's overall FX risk management strategy of reducing the variability of its Profit and Loss statement.
Type of hedge	Sash flow hedge.
Risk being hedged	FX risk. The variability in EUR value of the highly expected transaction.
Hedging instrument	The FX forward contract with reference number 012749. The counterparty to the forward is XYZ Bank and the credit risk associated with this counterparty is considered to be very low.
Hedged item	USD 100 million sale of finished goods expected to be agreed on 31 March 20X5.
Assessment of effectiveness testing	Hedge effectiveness will be assessed by comparing changes in the fair value of the hedging instrument to changes in the fair value of the expected cash flow.
	Hedge effectiveness assessment will be performed on a forward-forward basis. In other words, the forward points of both the hedging instrument and the expected cash flow are included in the assessment.
	Prospective test
	A prospective test will be performed at hedge inception and at each reporting date, using the scenario analysis method. Due to the fact that the terms of the hedging instrument and those of the expected cash flow are similar, the hedge is expected to be highly effective. The credit risk of the counterparty of the hedging instrument will be monitored continuously.
	Retrospective test
	A retrospective test will be performed at each reporting date and at hedge maturity using the "ratio analysis method". The ratio will compare the cumulative change (since hedge inception) in the fair value of the hedging instrument with the cumulative change (since hedge inception) in the fair value of the expected cash flow arising from the forecast sale. The hedge will be assumed to be highly effective on a retrospective basis if the ratio is between 80 % and 125 %.

Prospective Tests

ABC performed a prospective test at hedge inception and at each reporting date. ABC used the scenario analysis method to assess prospective effectiveness. ABC chose two scenarios: (i) a two-standard deviation upward movement in the forward rate, and (ii) a two-standard deviation downward movement in the forward rate. The test performed at inception was as follows:

Prospective Test at Hedge Inception	
Spot rate on 1-Oct-X4	1.2350
Forward rate for 31-Mar-X5 (on 1-Oct-X4)	1.2450
FX Forward (hedging instrument) rate	1.2600
$+2\sigma$ Movement in the forward rate (10 % volatility + 6 months)	1.4350
$+2\sigma$ Movement in the spot rate	1.4300
Fair value of FX forward = 0.9901*(100 million/1.26 − 100 million/1.4350)	9,583,000
Fair value of cash flow = 1*(100 million/1.43 − 100 million/1.245)	<10,391,000>
Effectiveness	92.2 %
-2σ Movement in the forward rate (10 % volatility + 6 months)	1.0750
-2σ Movement in the spot rate	1.0700
Fair value of FX forward = 0.9901*(100 million/1.26 − 100 million/1.075)	<13,523,000>
Fair value of cash flow = 1*(100 million/1.07 − 100 million/1.245)	13,137,000
Effectiveness	102.9 %

It can be seen that the mismatch created by being the forward off-market had a small impact in the effectiveness of the hedge. As the effectiveness was within the range 80 %–125 %, ABC expected the hedge relationship to be highly effective prospectively.

Retrospective Tests

A retrospective test was performed at each reporting date and also at the maturity of the hedging relationship. There was no significant deterioration in the credit of the counterparty of the hedging instrument during the life of the hedging relationship.

The spot exchange rates on the relevant dates were as follows:

Date	Spot rate	Forward rate for 31-Mar-X5	Discount factor for 31-Mar-X5	Forward rate for 30-Jun-X5	Discount factor for 30-Jun-X5
1-Oct-X4	1.2350	1.2450	0.9842	1.2500	0.9804
31-Dec-X4	1.2700	1.2750	0.9902	1.2800	0.9839
31-Mar-X5	1.2950	1.2950	1.0000	1.3000	0.9901
30-Jun-X5	1.3200	—	—	1.3200	1.0000

The fair value of the hedging instrument was calculated as follows:

	1-Oct-X4	31-Dec-X4	31-Mar-X5	30-Jun-X5
Initial value in USD	100,000,000	100,000,000	100,000,000	100,000,000
Forward rate for 30-Jun-X5	/ 1.2500	/ 1.2800	/ 1.3000	/ 1.3200
Value in EUR	80,000,000	78,125,000	76,923,000	75,758,000
FX forward EUR amount	79,365,000	79,365,000	79,365,000	79,365,000
Difference	<635,000>	1,240,000	2,442,000	3,607,000
Discount factor for 30-Jun-X5	x 0.9804	x 0.9839	x 0.9901	x 1.0000
Forward fair value	<622,000>	1,220,000	2,418,000	3,607,000
Forward fair value change	—	1,842,000	1,198,000	1,189,000

Bear in mind that the hedging relationship was due on 31-Mar-X5, and that at hedge inception (1-Oct-X4) the expected exchange rate for 31-Mar-X5 was 1.2450, resulting in an expected EUR 80,321,000 cash flow stemming from the USD 100 million sale. The fair value calculation of the expected cash flow was:

	1-Oct-X4	31-Dec-X4	31-Mar-X5	30-Jun-X5
Expected cash flow in USD	100,000,000	100.000.000	100.000.000	100.000.000
Forward rate for 31-Mar-X5 (or spot rate afterwards)	/ 1.2450	/ 1.2750	/ 1.2950	/ 1.3200
Value in EUR	80,321,000	78,431,000	77,220,000	75,758,000
Initially expected EUR amount	80,321,000	80, 321,000	80, 321,000	80, 321,000
Difference in EUR cash flow	−0−	<1,890,000>	<3,101,000>	<4,563,000>
Discount factor for 31-Mar-X5 (or 1.0000 afterwards)	x 0.9842	x 0.9902	x 1.0000	x 1.0000
Cash flow fair value	−0−	<1,871,000>	<3,101,000>	<4,563,000>
Cash flow fair value change	—	<1,871,000>	<1,230,000>	<1,462,000>

ABC performed a retrospective test at each reporting date and at hedge maturity. Remember that the hedging relationship finished on 31 March 20X5, so only two retrospective tests were performed. It can be seen that the changes in the fair value of the hedging instrument were slightly different to those of the hedged item because it was an off-market FX forward.

As the result of each test was within the 80 %–125 % range, each test was considered to be highly effective retrospectively. Because the accumulated change in the fair value of the hedged item exceeded the accumulated change in the fair value of the hedging instrument, there was no ineffectiveness to be recorded.

	31-Dec-X4	31-Mar-X5
Forward contract fair value change	1,842,000	1,198,000
Expected cash flow fair value change	<1,871,000>	<1,230,000>
Ratio	98,5 %	97,3 %
Hedge effective amount	1,842,000	1,198,000
Hedge ineffective amount	−0−	−0−

Change in Fair Value of the Knock-Out Option

The following table summarises the calculation of the change in fair value of the knock-out option. The fair value of the option was computed using a closed-end formula to value barrier options. Remember that all the change in the fair value of the knock-out option was recorded in P&L, as this derivative was undesignated.

	1-Oct-X4	31-Dec-X4	31-Mar-X5	30-Jun-X5
Fair value in EUR	622,000	690,000	360,000	−0−
Change in fair value	—	68,000	<330,000>	<360,000>

Accounting Entries

The required journal entries were as follows:

1) To record the forward contract trade on 1 October, 20X4

The FX forward had a fair value of EUR −622,000 at hedge inception:

Cash (Asset)	€ 622,000
Fair Value of Derivative (Liability)	€ 622,000

The knock-out option had a fair value of EUR 622,000 at hedge inception:

Fair Value of Derivative (Asset)	€ 622,000
Cash (Asset)	€ 622,000

2) To record the closing of the accounting period on 31 December 20X4:

The change in fair value of the forward since the last valuation was a gain of EUR 1,842,000. As the hedge was all effective, all this change in fair value was recorded in equity and none of it recorded in P&L. Now the forward had a positive fair value, so it was recycled from the liability side to the asset side:

Fair Value of Derivative (Asset)	€ 1,842,000
Cash flow Hedges (Equity)	€ 1,842,000

The change in the fair value of the knock-out option since the last valuation was a gain of EUR 68,000. As this derivative was undesignated, all this change in fair value was recorded in P&L:

Fair Value of Derivative (Asset)	€ 68,000
Other Income and Losses (P&L)	€ 68,000

3) To record the sale agreement and the end of the hedging relationship on 31 March 20X5:

The sale agreement was recorded at the spot rate ruling on the date the sales were recognised (1.2950). Therefore, the sales EUR proceeds were EUR 77,220,000 (=100 million/1.2950):

Accounts Receivable (Asset)	€ 77,220,000
Sales (P&L)	€ 77,220,000

The change in the fair value of the forward since the last valuation was a gain of EUR 1,198,000. As the hedge had no ineffectiveness, all this change was also recorded in equity:

Fair Value of Derivative (Asset)	€ 1,198,000	
Cash flow Hedges (Equity)		€ 1,198,000

The recognition of the sales transaction in P&L caused the release to P&L of the deferred hedge results accumulated in equity, or EUR 3,040,000 (= 1,842,000 + 1,198,000).

Cash flow Hedges (Equity)	€ 3,040,000	
Sales (P&L)		€ 3,040,000

The change in fair value of the knock-out option since the last valuation was a loss of EUR 330,000. As this derivative was undesignated, all this change in fair value was recorded in P&L.

Other Income and Losses (P&L)	€ 330,000	
Fair Value of Derivative (Asset)		€ 330,000

4) To record the settlement of the sale on 30 June 20X5:

The receivable was revalued at the spot rate prevailing on this date, showing a loss of EUR 1,462,000 (=100 million/1.3200 − 100 million/1.2950)

FX loss on Accounts Receivable (P&L)	€ 1,462,000	
Accounts Receivable (Asset)		€ 1,462,000

The change in the fair value of the FX forward since the last valuation was a gain of EUR 1,189,000. Because the hedging relationship ended on 31-Mar-X5, since this date the FX forward was undesignated, and thus its changes in fair value recorded in P&L.

Fair Value of Derivative (Asset)	€ 1,189,000	
Gain on derivative (P&L)		€ 1,189,000

The USD payment from the receivable was exchanged for EUR as soon as it was received using the forward. The forward rate was 1.26, so the USD 100 million were exchanged for EUR 79,365,000 (=100 million/1.26)

Cash (Asset)	€ 79,365,000	
Accounts Receivable (Asset)		€ 75,758,000
Fair Value of Derivative (Asset)		€ 3,607,000

The change in fair value of the knock-out option since the last valuation was a loss of EUR 360,000. As this derivative was undesignated, all this change in fair value was recorded in P&L.

Other Income and Losses (P&L)	€ 360,000	
Fair Value of Derivative (Asset)		€ 360,000

The knock-out option expired worthless, so no settlement amount was received at maturity, and no accounting entries were needed.

CASE 3.5

Hedging a Highly Expected Foreign Sale with a KIKO Forward

In Case 4, we analysed a hedging strategy, the knock-in forward, built with a barrier option. In this case, we will analyse another popular hedging strategy, the knock-in knock-out forward ("KIKO forward"), also built with barrier options. This hedging instrument is created in this case by combining the purchase of a knock-out USD put and the sale of a knock-in USD call with the same strikes. In this case we will cover how the KIKO could be split to make part of it eligible for hedge accounting, and how the split affects the accounting treatment of the hedge strategy.

The risk being hedged in this case is the same as in the previous cases. Let us assume that on 1 October 20X4 ABC Corporation, a company whose functional currency was the EUR, was expecting to sell finished goods to a US client. The sale was expected to occur on 31 March 20X5, and the sale receivable was expected to be settled on 30 June 20X5. Sale proceeds were expected to be USD 100 million to be received in USD.

ABC wanted to enter into a FX forward, but wanted to incorporate its view on the USD/EUR exchange rate in the next nine months, to improve the forward rate. ABC thought that a potential USD appreciation was going to be quite limited, not going below 1.1000. At the same time, ABC had the view that it was unlikely that a potential USD depreciation could be beyond 1.3500. As a consequence, on 1 October 20X4, ABC entered into a KIKO forward. The KIKO forward was obtained by combining the purchase of a USD knock-out put and a written USD knock-in call with the following terms:

USD Knock-out Put Terms		USD Knock-in Call Terms	
Option type	USD Knock-out put / EUR call	Option type	USD Knock-in call/EUR put
Start date	1 October 20X4	Start date	1 October 20X4
Counterparties	ABC and XYZ Bank	Counterparties	ABC and XYZ Bank
Option buyer	ABC	Option buyer	XYZ Bank
Expiry	30 June 20X5	Expiry	30 June 20X5
USD Notional	USD 100,000,000	USD Notional	USD 100,000,000
EUR Notional	EUR 81,301,000	EUR Notional	EUR 81,301,000
Strike Rate	1.2300	Strike Rate	1.2300
Barrier	1.3500	Barrier	1.1000
Premium	EUR 850,000	Premium	EUR 850,000
	Option ceases to exist if at any time until Expiry the spot USD/EUR exchange rate trades at, or above, the barrier		Option can only be exercised if at any time until Expiry the spot USD/EUR exchange rate trades at, or below, the barrier
Settlement	Physical delivery	Settlement	Physical delivery

There are four scenarios depending on the behaviour of the USD/EUR spot rate during the life of the KIKO forward.

1.10 Barrier	1.35 Barrier	Equivalent Position	Comments
Not hit	Not hit	Purchased 1.2300 USD put	Best scenario. ABC had a protection and participated in USD appreciation
Hit	Not hit	1.2300 forward	Good scenario, ABC ended up with a forward rate better than market forward (market forward rate would have been 1.25)
Not Hit	Hit	No derivative	Bad scenario, is like ABC had no hedge in place
Hit	Hit	Written 1.2300 USD call	Worst scenario, ABC lost its protection and did not benefit from USD appreciation

Graphically, the KIKO payoff at expiry in each of the four scenarios is shown in Figure 3.15.

Once the hedging instrument and the expected cash flow are combined, the resulting EUR amount to be received by ABC in exchange for the USD 100 million in each of the four scenarios is shown in Figure 3.16.

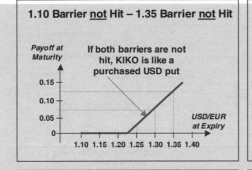

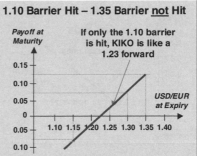

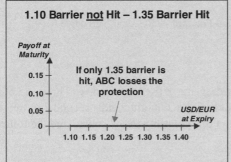

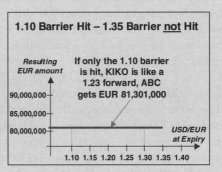

Figure 3.15   KIKO Forward – Scenarios.

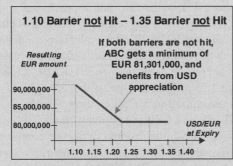

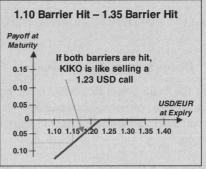

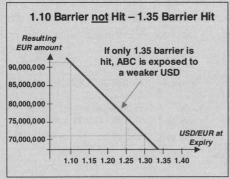

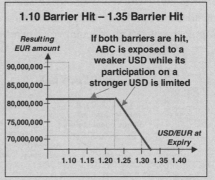

Figure 3.16   KIKO Forward – Resulting EUR Amount.

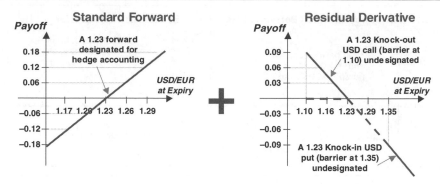

Figure 3.17   KIKO Forward Alternative 1: Standard Forward + Residual Derivative

3.9.1   Hedge accounting optimisation

One of the main issues that ABC faced regarding the KIKO forward was how to split the instrument into two parts, a first part eligible for hedge accounting and a second part treated as undesignated, to minimise the overall impact in P&L volatility. ABC considered the following five choices:

1) Divide the KIKO into two parts (see Figure 3.17): (i) a 1.2300 standard forward and (ii) a "residual" derivative. Under this alternative, the residual derivative combined a written knock-in USD put (with a 1.2300 strike and a 1.3500 barrier) and a purchased knock-out USD call (with a 1.2300 strike and a 1.1000 barrier). The standard forward would be considered eligible for hedge accounting and the residual derivative would be considered as undesignated (i.e., speculative). Therefore, all the changes in the fair value of the residual derivative would be recorded in P&L. This alternative is recommended if ABC expected the 1.1000 barrier to be crossed but not the 1.3500 barrier. One of the strengths of this alternative is that the hedge effective part is recognised in the "sales" line of P&L.
2) Divide the KIKO into two parts (see Figure 3.18): (i) a USD put option with a 1.2300 strike and (ii) a "residual" derivative. Under this alternative, the residual derivative combined a written knock-in USD put (with a 1.2300 strike and a 1.3500 barrier) and a written knock-in USD call (with a 1.2300 strike and a 1.1100 barrier). The USD put option would be considered eligible for hedge accounting and the residual derivative would be considered as undesignated (i.e., speculative). Therefore, all the changes in the fair value of the residual

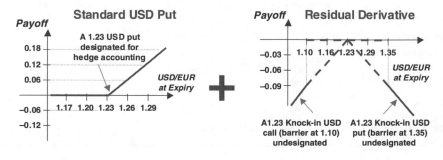

Figure 3.18   KIKO Forward Alternative 2: USD Put Option + Residual Derivative

derivative would be recorded in P&L. This alternative is recommended if ABC expected neither the 1.1000 barrier nor the 1.3500 barrier to be crossed. One of the strengths of this alternative is that the hedge effective part is recognised in the "sales" line of P&L.

3) Consider the whole KIKO as undesignated. As a consequence, all changes in fair value of the KIKO would be recorded in P&L. This alternative was the simplest, saving the effort in complying with hedge accounting. However, it also had the largest impact in P&L volatility.

4) Consider the whole KIKO as eligible for hedge accounting. The objective of the hedge would be defined as: "to protect the EUR value of the USD highly expected sale of finished goods against unfavourable movements in the USD/EUR exchange rate to a minimum of EUR 81,301,000, provided that the USD/EUR exchange rate never trades at or above 1.35. However, if the USD/EUR exchange rate ever trades at or below 1.10, the EUR value of the sale is capped at EUR 81,301,000". Hedge effectiveness would be tested using a hypothetical derivative whose terms exactly matched those of KIKO but with a 31 March maturity. As a result, the hedge would be considered as 100 % effective, and all the changes in fair value of the KIKO would be recorded in equity until the hedged item impacted P&L. This accounting treatment, in our view, will be questioned by most auditors.

5) Try to consider the whole KIKO as eligible for hedge accounting by comparing it to a forward. The objective of the hedge would be defined as: "to lock to EUR 81,301,000 the value of the USD highly expected sale of finished goods against unfavourable movements in the USD/EUR exchange rate". ABC would need to perform a very robust prospective test comparing the changes in fair value of the KIKO to the changes in fair value of a hypothetical derivative. The hypothetical derivative would be a 1.25 standard forward. The problem with this alternative is that movements in the USD/EUR near the 1.35 barrier may cause the retrospective test to fail.

The following table summarises these five choices:

Alternative	Hedging Instrument	Hypothetical Derivative	Comments
Split KIKO into standard forward and residual derivative	Standard forward with 1.2300 rate	Standard forward with 1.2500 rate	Recommended if 1.10 barrier expected to be crossed, but not the 1.35 barrier. Effective part of hedge recognised in "sales" line of P&L
Split KIKO into USD put and residual derivative	USD put with 1.23 strike	USD put with 1.23 strike	Recommended if neither the 1.10 barrier nor 1.35 barrier expected to be crossed. Effective part of hedge recognised in "sales" line of P&L
Treat KIKO as undesignated	—	—	Simplest alternative, but two weaknesses: 1) potential P&L volatility 2) KIKO fair value changes not recognised in "sales" line of P&L
Treat whole KIKO as eligible for hedge accounting	KIKO	KIKO	Very questionable interpretation of IAS 39 Risk of future restaments
Treat whole KIKO as eligible for hedge accounting	KIKO	Standard forward with 1.2500 rate	Subject to passing prospective test Risk of retrospective test failure

Let us assume that ABC expected the USD/EUR to cross the 1.10 barrier but not the 1.35 barrier. As a result, ABC chose the first choice: to divide the hedging instrument into two parts a standard forward at 1.2300 and a "residual" derivative.

The standard forward was designated as the hedging instrument in a cash flow hedge relationship. The terms of the hedging instrument were as follows:

Hedging Instrument Terms	
Instrument	FX Forward
Start date	1 October 20X4
Maturity	30 June 20X5
ABC buys	USD 100,000,000
ABC sells	EUR 81,301,000
Forward Rate	1.2300
Initial fair value	EUR 1,263,000

Hedge effectiveness was assessed by comparing the changes in fair value of the hedging instrument with the changes in fair value of a hypothetical derivative. The terms of the hypothetical derivative were as follows:

Hypothetical Derivative Terms	
Instrument	FX Forward
Start date	1 October 20X4
Maturity	31 March 20X5
ABC buys	USD 100,000,000
ABC sells	EUR 80,321,000
Forward Rate	1.2450
Initial fair value	Zero

ABC documented the hedging relationship as follows:

Hedging Relationship Documentation	
Risk management objective and strategy for undertaking the hedge	The objective of the hedge is to protect the EUR value of the USD 100 million highly expected sale of finished goods against unfavourable movements in the USD/EUR exchange rate by locking-in its EUR value. This hedging objective is consistent with ABC's overall FX risk management strategy of reducing the variability of its Profit and Loss statement.
Type of hedge	Cash flow hedge.
Risk being hedged	FX risk. The variability in EUR value of the highly expected transaction.
Hedging instrument	The FX forward contract with reference number 012569. The counterparty to the forward is XYZ Bank and the credit risk associated with this counterparty is considered to be very low.
Hedged item	USD 100 million sale of finished goods expected to be agreed on 31 March 20X5.

Hedging Relationship Documentation	
Assessment of effectiveness testing	Hedge effectiveness will be assessed by comparing changes in the fair value of the hedging instrument to changes in the fair value of a hypothetical derivative.
	The terms of the hypothetical derivative are such that its fair value changes offset exactly the changes in fair value of the hedged highly expected cash flow for the risk being hedged. The hypothetical derivative in this hedging relationship is a forward with maturity the end of the hedging relationship (31 March 20X5), nominal USD 100 million, a 1.2450 forward rate and zero initial fair value.
	Hedge effectiveness assessment will be performed on a forward-forward basis. In other words, the forward points of both the hedging instrument and the hypothetical derivative are included in the assessment.
	Prospective test
	A prospective test will be performed at inception and at each reporting date, using the regression analysis method. The credit risk of the counterparty of the hedging instrument will be monitored continuously.
	Retrospective test
	A retrospective test will be performed at each reporting date and at hedge maturity using the "ratio analysis method". The ratio will compare the cumulative change since hedge inception in the fair value of the hypothetical derivative with the cumulative change since hedge inception in the fair value of the hedging instrument. The hedge will be assumed to be highly effective on a retrospective basis if the ratio is between 80 % and 125 %.

Prospective Tests

ABC performed a prospective test at hedge inception and at each reporting date using the regression analysis method. Figure 3.19 highlights the regression analysis performed at hedge inception (1 October 20X4), comparing the changes in fair value of the hedging instrument to the changes in the fair value of a hypothetical derivative. The analysis was based on the historical USD/EUR (or the USD/ECU) exchange rates from January 1990 until November 2006 (the "historical time horizon"). The historical time horizon was divided into 65 "simulation periods" of six months each. Each simulation period had an inception date and two subsequent balance sheet dates. In each simulation period, the behaviour of an equivalent hedging relationship using the historical data was simulated. Each observation pair (X,Y) was generated by computing the cumulative change in the fair value of a standard forward (variable X) and the cumulative change in fair value of a hypothetical derivative (observation Y). The terms of these two derivatives were identical to the terms of the real hedging instrument and hypothetical derivative, except that their forward rates were adjusted to conform to the market rates prevailing at the beginning of the simulation period.

The analysis produced:

- an R-squared of 99.8 %;
- an F-statistic that indicates statistical significance at the 95 % confidence level;
- a regression coefficient for the slope of + 1.00.

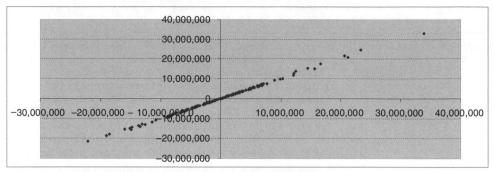

X axis: Cumulative change in fair value of hedging instrument
Y axis: Cumulative change in fair value of theoretical derivative

Figure 3.19   Standard Forward – Regression Analysis.

As a consequence, ABC concluded that it expected the hedge to be highly effective prospectively. A similar test was performed on 31 December 20X5, with very similar outcome.

Retrospective Tests

ABC performed a retrospective test at each reporting date and at hedge maturity using the ratio analysis method. The spot and forward exchange rates at each relevant date were as follows:

Date	Spot rate	Forward to 31-Mar-X5	Forward to 30-Jun-X5	Discount Factor to 31-Mar-X5	Discount Factor to 30-Jun-X5
1-Oct-X4	1.2350	1.2450	1.2500	0.8942	0.9709
15-Nov-X4	1.1000	1.10 Barrier was hit			
31-Dec-X4	1.1500	1.1550	1.1600	0.9901	0.9804
31-Mar-X5	1.3000	1.3000	1.3050	1.0000	0.9901
30-Jun-X5	1.3200	—	1.3200	—	1.0000

Note that on 15 November 20X4 the 1.10 barrier was hit. As a result, the knock/out USD call portion of the residual derivative ceased to exist. In other words, the knock-in USD call of the KIKO became a standard USD call option.

The assumed fair value of the hedging instrument at each date is shown in the following table:

Date	Hedging Instrument Fair Value (EUR)	Hedging Instrument Change in Fair Value	Hedging Instrument Cumulative Change in Fair Value
1-Oct-X4	1,263,000	—	—
31-Dec-X4	<4,810,000>	<6,073,000>	<6,073,000>
31-Mar-X5	4,626,000	9,436,000	3,363,000
30-Jun-X5	5,543,000	917,000	Not relevant

The changes in the fair value of the hypothetical derivative were as follows:

Date	Hypothetical Derivative Fair Value (EUR)	Hypothetical Derivative Change in Fair Value	Hypothetical Derivative Cumulative Change in Fair Value
1-Oct-X4	−0−	—	—
31-Dec-X4	<6,197,000>	<6,197,000>	<6,197,000>
31-Mar-X5	3,398,000	9,595,000	3,398,000

The results of the retrospective tests are shown in the table below. ABC concluded that the hedge was highly effective retrospectively during the two reporting periods because the ratio was inside the 80 %–125 % band.

Date	Hedging Instrument Cumulative Change in Fair Value	Hypothetical Derivative Cumulative Change in Fair Value	Ratio
1-Oct-X4	—	—	—
31-Dec-X4	<6,073,000>	<6,197,000>	98.0%
31-Mar-X5	3,363,000	3,398,000	99.0%

Rest of Fair Value Calculations

The changes in fair value of the residual derivative are shown in the table below. The KIKO was valued using a variation of the Black-Scholes method to price barrier options. Remember that on 15 November 20X4 the 1.10 barrier was hit. As a result, the knock-in USD call of the KIKO became a standard USD call option from that date. The residual derivative fair value was calculated as follows:

Residual derivative fair value = KIKO fair value − Hedging instrument fair value

Date	KIKO Fair Value (EUR)	Hedging Instrument Fair Value	Residual Derivative Fair Value	Change in Residual Derivative Fair Value
1-Oct-X4	−0−	1,263,000	<1,263,000>	—
31-Dec-X4	<4,935,000>	<4,810,000>	<125,000>	1,138,000
31-Mar-X5	1,450,000	4,626,000	<3,176,000>	<3,051,000>
30-Jun-X5	5,543,000	5,543,000	−0−	3,176,000

Accounting Entries

The required journal entries were as follows:

1) To record the forward contract trade on 1 October, 20X4

The hedging instrument (the standard forward) had a fair value of EUR 1,263,000 at hedge inception:

Fair Value of Derivative-Forward (Asset)	€ 1,263,000	
Cash (Asset)		€ 1,263,000

The residual derivative had a fair value of EUR −1,263,000 at hedge inception:

Cash (Asset)	€ 1,263,000	
Fair Value of Derivative-Residual (Liability)		€ 1,263,000

2) To record the closing of the accounting period on 31 December 20X4:

The change in fair value of the standard forward since the last valuation was a loss of EUR 6,073,000. As the hedge was completely effective, all this change in fair value was recorded in equity. Now the standard forward had a negative fair value, so it was recycled from the asset side to the liability side:

Cash flow Hedges (Equity)	€ 6,073,000	
Fair Value of Derivative-Forward (Liability)		€ 6,073,000

The change in the fair value of the residual derivative since the last valuation was a gain of EUR 1,138,000. As this derivative was undesignated, all this change in fair value was recorded in P&L:

Fair Value of Derivative-Residual (Liability)	€ 1,138,000	
Other Income and Losses (P&L)		€ 1,138,000

3) To record the sale agreement and the end of the hedging relationship on 31 March 20X5:

The sale agreement was recorded at the spot rate ruling on the date the sales were recognised (1.3000). Therefore, the sales EUR proceeds were EUR 76,923,000 (=100 million/1.3000):

Accounts Receivable (Asset)	€ 76,923,000	
Sales (P&L)		€ 76,923,000

The change in fair value of the hedging instrument (the standard forward) since the last valuation was a gain of EUR 9,436,000. As the hedge had no ineffectiveness, all this change was also recorded in equity. Now the standard forward had a positive fair value, so it was recycled from the liability side to the asset side:

| Fair Value of Derivative-Forward (Asset) | € 9,436,000 | |
| Cash flow Hedges (Equity) | | € 9,436,000 |

The recognition of the sales transaction in P&L caused the release to P&L of the deferred hedge results accumulated in equity, or EUR 3,363,000 (=−6,073,000+ 9,436,000).

| Cash flow Hedges (Equity) | € 3,363,000 | |
| Sales (P&L) | | € 3,363,000 |

The change in fair value of the residual derivative since the last valuation was a loss of EUR 3,051,000. As this derivative was undesignated, all this change in fair value was recorded in P&L.

| Other Income and Losses (P&L) | € 3,051,000 | |
| Fair Value of Derivative-Residual (Liability) | | € 3,051,000 |

4) To record the settlement of the sale on 30 June 20X5:

The receivable was revalued at the spot rate prevailing on this date, showing a loss of EUR 1,166,000 (= 100 million/1.3200 − 100 million/1.3000)

| FX loss on Accounts Receivable (P&L) | € 1,166,000 | |
| Accounts Receivable (Asset) | | € 1,166,000 |

Due to the fact that the hedging relationship ended on 31 March 20X5, there was no further need to split the KIKO. The change in fair value of the KIKO since the last valuation was a gain of EUR 4,093,000. Because the hedging relationship ended on 31-Mar-X5, since this date the whole KIKO was undesignated, and thus its changes in fair value recorded in P&L.

| Fair Value of Derivative (Asset) | € 4,093,000 | |
| Other Income and Losses (P&L) | | € 4,093,000 |

The USD payment from the receivable was exchanged for EUR as soon as it was received using the KIKO. The KIKO rate was 1.23, so the USD 100 million were exchanged for EUR 81,301,000 (= 100 million/1.23)

Cash (Asset)	€ 81,301,000	
Accounts Receivable (Asset)		€ 75,758,000
Fair Value of Derivative (Asset)		€ 5,543,000

3.9.6 Final Remarks

Figure 3.20 summarises the effects of the strategy on ABC's P&L. The strategy worked very well. The total proceeds from the strategy were EUR 81,300,000, equivalent to a USD/EUR of 1.2300. Sales were translated at a 1.2455 rate, totaling EUR 80,286,000.

The strategy was successful in hedging the FX exposure because the 1.35 barrier was not crossed. The story would have been dramatically different were the 1.35 barrier reached. Let us assume that during February 20X5 the 1.35 barrier was crossed. The retrospective test performed on 31 March 20X5 would have failed and, as a result, all the change in fair value of the KIKO would have been recorded to P&L. Assuming that the KIKO was worth EUR − 200,000 on 31 March 20X5, ABC's P&L would have looked very differently, as shown in Figure 3.21. The results would have been quite disappointing: firstly, ABC lost the protection and as a result the total proceeds from the whole strategy EUR 75,757,000 were exchanged at a 1.3200 rate, and secondly the sales figure (EUR 70,850,000 = 76,923,000 − 6,073,000) was exposed not only to the 31 March 20X5 exchange rate but also to the 31 December 20X4 rate (the "sales" line showed a translation rate of 1.4114 !!!).

Figure 3.20   KIKO - Income Statement Profile 1.35 Barrier <u>not</u> Crossed.

Figure 3.21   KIKO - Income Statement Profile 1.35 Barrier <u>was</u> Crossed.

CASE 3.6

Hedging a Highly Expected Foreign Sale with a Range Accrual Forward

In this case, we will analyse another popular FX hedging strategy, the range accrual forward. The case will show that the eligibility of this instrument for hedge accounting can be very challenging.

The risk being hedged in this case is the same as in the previous cases. Let us assume that on 1 October 20X4 ABC Corporation, a company whose functional currency was the EUR, was expecting to sell finished goods to a US client. The sale was expected to occur on 31 March 20X5, and the sale receivable was expected to be settled on 30 June 20X5. Sale proceeds were expected to be USD 100 million to be received in USD.

ABC had the view that the USD would remain in a 1.22 to 1.25 range in the next several months and wanted to benefit were its view right. As a consequence, on 1 October 20X4, ABC entered into a range accrual forward with the following terms:

FX Range Accrual Forward Terms	
ABC enters into a FX forward with a nominal amount that is a function of the number of days that the USD/EUR stays within a pre-specified range (the accrual range)	
Start date	1 October 20X4
Counterparties	Company ABC and XYZ Bank
Accrual range	1.22–1.25
ABC sells (USD)	USD nominal
ABC buys (EUR)	EUR nominal = USD nominal/1.23
Reference rate	USD/EUR FX rate
Maturity	30 June 20X5
USD Nominal	USD 1,100,000 for each day that the reference rate fixes within the accrual range during the accruing period
Accruing period	From, and including, 1 October 20X4 until, and including, 31 March 20X5 (a total of 130 fixings)
Forward rate	1.23
Premium	Zero
Settlement	Physical delivery

On 30 June 20X5, ABC would exchange for EUR an amount of unknown USD, at 1.23. This rate was notably better than the 1.25 market forward rate. To obtain such an advantageous rate, ABC ran the risk of an uncertain total USD nominal. On 31 March 20X4, the USD notional was to be determined by observing the number of business days in the accruing period that the USD/EUR rate fixed within the 1.22–1.25 range (see Figure 3.22).

- ABC expected the number of days with fixings within the range to be 91, and thus, the USD nominal to be USD 100,100,000 (= 91 days * 1.1 million). In other words, ABC expected the USD/EUR to stay 70 % (= 91 days/130 days) of the total period within the range.

- A proportion higher than 70 % (more than 91 days) would imply that ABC was over-hedged. Probably ABC would need to unwind the excess, becoming exposed to a declining USD/EUR exchange rate.
- A proportion lower than 70 % (less than 91 days) would imply that ABC was underhedged. Probably ABC would need to enter into an additional hedge, becoming exposed to a rising USD/EUR exchange rate.

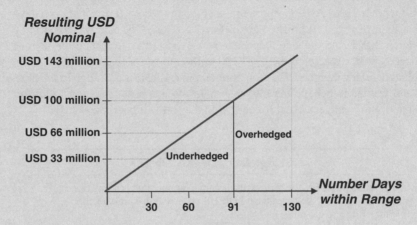

Figure 3.22 Range Accrual Forward Resulting USD Nominal.

In order to analyse the accounting implications of the range accrual instrument, we have taken two different approaches to designate it eligible for hedge accounting. The first approach is to designate the whole range accrual as the hedging instrument. The second approach is to split the range accrual into a standard forward (designated as the hedging instrument) and a remaining derivative (undesignated).

APPROACH 1: DESIGNATE THE WHOLE RANGE ACCRUAL AS HEDGING INSTRUMENT

In order to highlight the challenge of trying to apply hedge accounting when taking the first approach (to designate the whole range accrual as the hedging instrument), we have performed a prospective test and the retrospective tests assuming certain behaviour of the USD/EUR rate during the life of the strategy. The hedge relationship ended on 31 March 20X5.

Prospective Tests

Let us assume that ABC performed a regression analysis (see Figure 3.23), comparing the changes in fair value of the hedging instrument to the changes in the fair value of a hypothetical derivative. The market data used to perform this analysis was the same as in Case 5.

The terms of the hypothetical derivative were such that fair value changes exactly offset the changes in the fair value of the hedged highly expected cash flow for the risk being hedged. The hypothetical derivative in this case was a standard forward with the following terms:

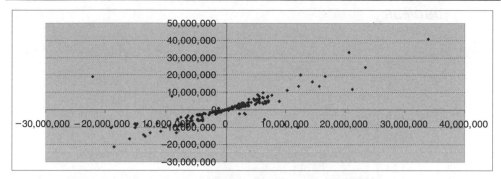

X axis: Cumulative change in fair value of hedging instrument
Y axis: Cumulative change in fair value of theoretical derivative

Figure 3.23   Range Accrual – Regression Analysis.

Hypothetical Derivative Terms	
Instrument	FX Forward
Start date	1 October 20X4
Maturity	31 March 20X5
ABC buys	USD 100,000,000
ABC sells	EUR 80,321,000
Forward Rate	1.2450
Initial fair value	Zero

The R-squared of the regression analysis was 82 %. Although inside the 80 %–125 %, in our opinion the "weak" R-squared already indicated the potential problems that we were to witness in the retrospective test.

Retrospective Tests

A retrospective test was performed at each reporting date and also at the maturity of the hedging relationship. There was no significant deterioration in the credit of the counterparty of the hedging instrument during the life of the hedging relationship. The behaviour of the USD/EUR during the life of the instrument is shown in Figure 3.24.

At each relevant date, the spot exchange rates, the accumulated number of days within the accrual range and the USD nominal were as follows:

Date	Spot rate	Accumulated Number of Days within Range	USD Nominal
1-Oct-X4	1.2350	—	–0–
31-Dec-X4	1.2300	66	72,600,000
31-Mar-X5	1.2600	100	110,000,000
30-Jun-X5	1.2850	—	100,000,000 *(1)*

(1) Assuming that USD 10 million nominal was sold on 31-Mar-X5

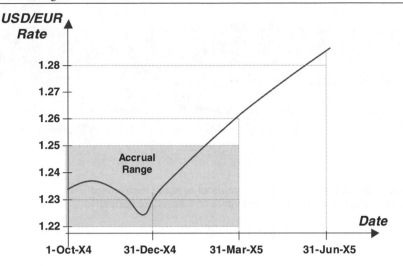

Figure 3.24   Behaviour of the USD/EUR Rate.

The fair value of the hedging instrument was calculated using the Monte Carlo method, resulting in the following fair values:

Date	Range Accrual Forward Fair Value (EUR)	Range Accrual Change in Fair Value	Range Accrual Cumulative Change in Fair Value
1-Oct-X4	–0–	—	—
31-Dec-X4	786,000	786,000	786,000
31-Mar-X5	2,474,000	1,688,000	2,474,000
30-Jun-X5	3,480,000 *(1)*	1,231,000 *(1)*	Not relevant

(1) Assuming that the USD 10 million excess nominal was sold on 31-Mar-X5, with EUR 225,000 proceeds.

The changes in the fair value of the hypothetical derivative were as follows:

Date	Hypothetical Derivative Fair Value (EUR)	Hypothetical Derivative Change in Fair Value	Hypothetical Derivative Cumulative Change in Fair Value
1-Oct-X4	–0–	—	—
31-Dec-X4	<644,000>	<644,000>	<644,000>
31-Mar-X5	956,000	1,600,000	956,000

The results of the retrospective tests are shown in the table below. The retrospective tests showed that the strategy was not eligible for hedge accounting in any of the two reporting periods as the ratio was outside the 80 %–125 % band.

Date	Range Accrual Cumulative Change in Fair Value	Hypothetical Derivative Cumulative Change in Fair Value	Ratio
1-Oct-X4	—	—	—
31-Dec-X4	786,000	<644,000>	<122.0%>
31-Mar-X5	2,474,000	956,000	258.8%

The failure of the retrospective tests implied that all the changes in fair value of the range accrual were to be recorded in P&L. Thus, the result was the same as if the range accrual was considered undesignated from the start. We would like to note that the range accrual was notably leveraged (i.e., the accrual range was notably narrow), and probably a less leveraged range accrual could have shown more positive results.

Accounting Entries

The required journal entries were as follows:

1) To record the range accrual forward contract on 1 October, 20X4

   There were no accounting entries as the range accrual forward had zero fair value at hedge inception.

2) To record the closing of the accounting period on 31 December 20X4:

   The change in fair value of the range accrual forward since the last valuation was a gain of EUR 786,000. As the hedge was completely ineffective, all this change in fair value was recorded in P&L.

Fair Value of Derivative (Asset)	€ 786,000	
Other Income and Losses (P&L)		€ 786,000

3) To record the closing of the accounting period on 31 March 20X5:

   The sale agreement was recorded at the spot rate ruling on the date the sales were recognised (1.2600). Therefore, the sales EUR proceeds were EUR 79,365,000 (=100 million/1.2600):

Accounts Receivable (Asset)	€ 79,365,000	
Sales (P&L)		€ 79,365,000

The fair value change of the range accrual forward since the last valuation was a gain of EUR 1,688,000. As the hedge was completely ineffective, all this change was recorded in P&L:

Fair Value of Derivative (Asset)	€ 1,688,000	
Other Income and Losses (P&L)		€ 1,688,000

The nominal of the range accrual forward was USD 110 million. Because the derivative was hedging the USD 100 million sale, ABC unwinded USD 10 million of the derivative, getting EUR 225,000 (= 10 million *(1/1.2300 − 1/1.2650)), as the forward rate for 30 June 20X5 was 1.2650 (assuming a discount rate of one):

Cash (Asset)	€ 225,000	
Fair Value of Derivative (Asset)		€ 225,000

4) To record the settlement of the sale on 30 June 20X5:

The receivable was revalued at the spot rate prevailing on this date, showing a loss of EUR 1,544,000 (= 100 million/1.2600 − 100 million/1.2850):

FX loss on Accounts Receivable (P&L)	€ 1,544,000	
Accounts Receivable (Asset)		€ 1,544,000

The change in fair value of the range accrual forward since the last valuation was a gain of EUR 1,231,000. This gain was recorded in P&L:

Fair Value of Derivative (Asset)	€ 1,231,000	
Gain on derivative (P&L)		€ 1,231,000

The USD payment from the receivable was exchanged for EUR as soon as it was received using the range accrual forward. The forward rate was 1.23, so the USD 100 million were exchanged for EUR 81,301,000 (= 100 million/1.23):

Cash (Asset)	€ 81,301,000	
Accounts Receivable (Asset)		€ 77,821,000
Fair Value of Derivative (Asset)		€ 3,480,000

APPROACH 2: SPLIT INTO A STANDARD FORWARD AND A RESIDUAL DERIVATIVE

The second approach implied splitting the range accrual forward into two instruments: a standard forward and a "residual" derivative. The standard forward was designated as the hedging instrument in a hedge accounting relationship. The terms of the standard forward were as follows:

Standard Forward Terms	
Instrument	FX Forward
Start date	1 October 20X4
Maturity	30 June 20X5
ABC buys	USD 100,000,000
ABC sells	EUR 81,301,000
Forward Rate	1.2300
Initial fair value	1,263,000

The residual derivative was considered undesignated. As in the first approach, we have performed a prospective test and two retrospective tests. We have assumed the same behaviour of the USD/EUR rate as in the first approach (see Figure 3.24).

Prospective Tests

Let us assume that ABC performed a regression analysis (see Figure 3.25), comparing the changes in fair value of the hedging instrument to the changes in fair value of a hypothetical derivative.

The terms of the hypothetical derivative were such that fair value changes exactly offset the changes in the fair value of the hedged highly expected cash flow for the risk being

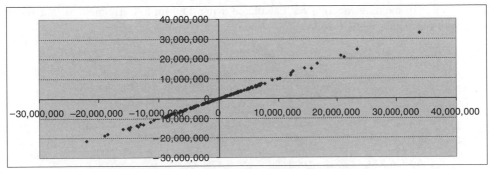

X axis: Cumulative change in fair value of hedging instrument
Y axis: Cumulative change in fair value of theoretical derivative

Figure 3.25   Standard Forward – Regression Analysis.

hedged. The hypothetical derivative in this case was a standard forward with the following terms:

Hypothetical Derivative Terms	
Instrument	FX Forward
Start date	1 October 20X4
Maturity	31 March 20X5
ABC buys	USD 100,000,000
ABC sells	EUR 80,321,000
Forward Rate	1.2450
Initial fair value	Zero

The R-squared of the regression analysis was 99.8 %, so the hedge was deemed to be highly effective on a prospective basis.

Retrospective Tests

A retrospective test was performed at each reporting date and also at the maturity of the hedging relationship. There was no significant deterioration in the credit of the counterparty of the hedging instrument during the life of the hedging relationship. The spot and forward exchange rates at each relevant date were as follows:

Date	Spot rate	Forward to 31-Mar-X5	Forward to 30-Jun-X5
1-Oct-X4	1.2350	1.2450	1.2500
31-Dec-X4	1.2300	1.2350	1.2400
31-Mar-X5	1.2600	1.2600	1.2650
30-Jun-X5	1.2850	—	1.2850

The fair value of the range accrual was calculated using the Monte Carlo method. The results of the split fair values were as follows:

Date	Range Accrual Fair Value (EUR)	Standard Forward Fair Value	Residual Derivative Fair Value
1-Oct-X4	–0–	1,263,000	<1,263,000>
31-Dec-X4	786,000	643,000	143,000
31-Mar-X5	2,474,000	2,227,000	247,000
30-Jun-X5	3,480,000 *(1)*	3,479,000	–0–

(1): Assuming that USD 10 million nominal were sold on 31-Mar-X5, with EUR 225,000 proceeds.

The changes in the fair value of the standard forward were as follows:

Date	Standard Forward Fair Value	Standard Forward Change Fair Value	Standard Forward Cumulative Change Fair Value
1-Oct-X4	1,263,000	—	—
31-Dec-X4	643,000	<620,000>	<620,000>
31-Mar-X5	2,227,000	1,584,000	964,000
30-Jun-X5	3,480,000	1,253,000	Not relevant

The changes in the fair value of the hypothetical derivative were as follows:

Date	Hypothetical Derivative Fair Value (EUR)	Hypothetical Derivative Change in Fair Value	Hypothetical Derivative Cumulative Change in Fair Value
1-Oct-X4	−0−	—	—
31-Dec-X4	<644,000>	<644,000>	<644,000>
31-Mar-X5	956,000	1,600,000	956,000

The results of the retrospective tests are shown in the following table. The retrospective tests showed that the strategy was eligible for hedge accounting.

Date	Standard Forward Cumulative Change in Fair Value	Hypothetical Derivative Cumulative Change in Fair Value	Ratio
1-Oct-X4	—	—	—
31-Dec-X4	<620,000>	<644,000>	96.3 %
31-Mar-X5	964,000	956,000	100.8 %

Accounting Entries

The required journal entries were as follows:

1) To record the forward contract trade on 1 October, 20X4

The standard forward fair value at its inception was EUR 1,263,000. The fair value of the residual derivative was then EUR − 1,263,000:

Fair Value of Derivative-Forward (Asset)	€ 1,263,000	
Cash (Asset)		€ 1,263,000

Cash (Asset)	€ 1,263,000	
Fair Value of Derivative-Residual (Asset)		€ 1,263,000

2) To record the closing of the accounting period on 31 December 20X4:

The change in fair value of the standard forward since the last valuation was a loss of EUR 620,000. As the hedge was completely effective, all this change in fair value was recorded in equity.

Cash Flow Hedges (Equity)	€ 620,000	
Fair Value of Derivative-Forward (Asset)		€ 620,000

The change in fair value of the residual derivative since the last valuation was a gain of EUR 1,406,000 (= 143,000 − (− 1,263,000)). As this derivative was undesignated, all this change in fair value was recorded in P&L.

Fair Value of Derivative-Residual (Asset)	€ 1,406,000	
Other Income and Losses (P&L)		€ 1,406,000

3) To record the closing of the accounting period on 31 March 20X5:

The sale agreement was recorded at the spot rate ruling on the date the sales were recognised (1.2600). Therefore, the sales EUR proceeds were EUR 79,365,000 (= 100 million/1.2600):

Accounts Receivable (Asset)	€ 79,365,000	
Sales (P&L)		€ 79,365,000

The change in fair value of the standard forward since the last valuation was a gain of EUR 1,584,000. As the hedge was completely effective, all this change was recorded in equity:

Fair Value of Derivative-Forward (Asset)	€ 1,584,000	
Cash Flow Hedges (Equity)		€ 1,584,000

The recognition of the sales transaction in P&L caused the release to P&L of the deferred hedge results accumulated in equity, a total of EUR 964,000 (= 1,584,000 − 620,000):

Cash Flow Hedges (Equity)	€ 964,000	
Sales (P&L)		€ 964,000

The change in fair value of the residual derivative since the last valuation was a gain of EUR 104,000 (= 247,000 − 143,000). As this derivative was undesignated, all this change in fair value was recorded in P&L:

| Fair Value of Derivative-Residual (Asset) | € 104,000 | |
| Other Income and Losses (P&L) | | € 104,000 |

The nominal of the range accrual forward was USD 110 million. Because the derivative was hedging the USD 100 million sale, ABC unwinded USD 10 million of the residual derivative, getting EUR 225,000 ($= 10$ million $^{*}(1/1.2300 - 1.2650)$), as the forward rate for 30 June 20X5 was 1.2650 (assuming a discount factor of one):

| Cash (Asset) | € 225,000 | |
| Fair Value of Derivative-Residual (Asset) | | € 225,000 |

4) To record the settlement of the sale on 30 June 20X5:

The receivable was revalued at the spot rate prevailing on this date, showing a loss of EUR 1,544,000 ($= 100$ million$/1.2600 - 100$ million$/1.2850$):

| FX loss on Accounts Receivable (P&L) | € 1,544,000 | |
| Accounts Receivable (Asset) | | € 1,544,000 |

The split of the range accrual ended on 31 March 20X5. The change in fair value of the range accrual forward since the last valuation was a gain of EUR 1,231,000. This gain was recorded in P&L:

| Fair Value of Derivative (Asset) | € 1,231,000 | |
| Gain on derivative (P&L) | | € 1,231,000 |

The USD payment from the receivable was exchanged for EUR as soon as it was received using the range accrual forward. The forward rate was 1.23, so the USD 100 million were exchanged for EUR 81,301,000 ($= 100$ million$/1.23$):

Cash (Asset)	€ 81,301,000	
Accounts Receivable (Asset)		€ 77,821,000
Fair Value of Derivative (Asset)		€ 3,480,000

Final Remarks

The case just covered highlighted the accounting challenge when hedging with range accrual forwards. The strategy worked very well from an economic point of view, however it added volatility to the P&L statement. The increase in P&L volatility was caused by its non-qualification for hedge accounting.

Approach 1: No split of range accrual forward

P&L 31-Dec-X4	P&L 31-Mar-X5	P&L 31-Jun-X5	P&L Total
Deriv: 786,000	Sales: 79,365,000 Deriv: 1,688,000	A/R: <1,544,00> Deriv: 1,231,000	Sales: 79,365,000 A/R: <1,544,000> Deriv: 3,705,000
Total: 786,000	Total: 81,053,000	Total: <313,000>	Total: 81,526,000

Approach 2: Split between standard forward + residual

P&L 31-Dec-X4	P&L 31-Mar-X5	P&L 31-Jun-X5	P&L Total
Deriv: 1,406,000	Sales: 80,329,000 Deriv: 104,000	A/R: <1,544,00> Deriv: 1,231,000	Sales: 80,329,000 A/R: <1,544,000> Deriv: 2,741,000
Total: 1,406,000	Total: 80,433,000	Total: <313,000>	Total: 81,526,000

Figure 3.26   Income Statement Comparisons.

In order to minimise the P&L volatility, two approaches were analysed: a first approach taking the whole range accrual as the hedging instrument, and a second approach splitting the range accrual into a standard forward and a residual derivative. Although the first approach showed a lower P&L volatility than the second, this conclusion is not to be generalised because it is largely dependent on the behaviour of the USD/EUR rate during the life of the hedge.

There is, however, a major difference between both approaches. The objective of the hedging strategy was to diminish the FX exposure of the highly expected sale. The range accrual largely achieved this objective, but only the second approach allowed most of the effect of the hedge to end up in the "sales" line. Therefore, the second approach showed a less volatile "sales" figure, as seen in Figure 3.26.

Finally, ABC expected 70 % of the USD/EUR fixings to fall within the accrual range. A large deviation from this percentage meant that ABC could be either overhedged or underhedged, adding an extra exposure to the USD/EUR rate. In our case, ABC was lucky because it ended up being overhedged and unwinded the excess hedge at favourable market rates. From an economic point of view, the range accrual performed very well. The USD 100 million were exchanged for EUR 81,526,000, implying a 1.2266 USD/EUR rate!!!, much better than the 1.2500 original market rate.

CASE 3.7

The Treasury Centre Challenge

Under IAS 39 treasury centres hedging activity is not effective in accounting terms. The problem is caused by IAS 39's hedge accounting treatment of internal hedges. This case sets out an example in order to analyse the accounting problem faced by treasury centres when managing the whole group's foreign exchange risk, and a potential solution.

It is a well-established practice in most large companies to centralise their financial activities into a group treasury centre. Treasury centres manage a broad range of functions for the group including global cash and liquidity management, bank relationship management, funding of debt and equity, and risk management. Some companies have a single treasury centre that is based at corporate headquarters or a tax-efficient location while others establish several centres, each strategically located to meet the needs of a specific region.

When hedging financial risk, the treasury centre serves as an in-house bank netting off compensating exposures arising across the group. Exposures are identified at the subsidiary level and these subsidiaries then hedge using internal deals with the centre. The treasury centre then lays off the net risk position with external parties. This hedging approach is more efficient than having each subsidiary working independently with banks to hedge their local financial risk.

While the logic of this hedging policy is clear, IAS 39 does not allow a treasury centre to designate the net of its internal contracts as the hedged item and the single offsetting derivative with a external party as the hedging instrument. IAS 39 allows some portfolio hedging for interest rate risk, but unfortunately it cannot be applied to hedges of FX, commodity and equity risk.

A key requirement of IAS 39's hedge accounting is that all hedging derivatives must involve a third party. Intragroup derivatives are not eligible for hedge accounting treatment in the consolidated accounts, causing significant difficulties where a group operates through a treasury centre. In these circumstances and in order to achieve hedge accounting it is usually necessary to identify, on a one-to-one basis, subsidiary exposures with external parties that may be designated as hedged items of the risks being hedged by the derivatives traded by the treasury centre with outside banks. In other words, the treasury centre would need to identify sufficient exposures in each of its various subsidiaries and designate, on a potentially arbitrary basis, some of those exposures on a one to one basis with its external contract.

To illustrate, let us consider a group that comprises a parent company, a treasury centre and three subsidiaries (see Figure 3.27). The group and Subsidiary-A have the EUR as its functional currency. Subsidiary-B and Subsidiary-C have the USD and the JPY as their functional currency, respectively.

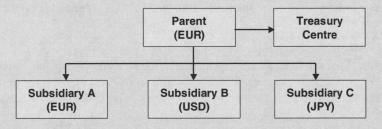

Figure 3.27   Group Entities.

Sub-A's revenues are in EUR and GBP. It forecasts revenues of EUR 60 and GBP 30 (i.e., the equivalent in GBP to EUR 30). It forecasts cost of sales related to those revenues of EUR 70. To keep the case simple, let us assume that all the flows are expected to take place on the same date. To hedge its exposure to GBP risk, Sub-A enters into a FX forward with

Treasury Centre at market rates, under which Sub-A agrees to sell GBP 30 and to buy EUR 30 on the same date that the rest of the cash flows are expected to take place.

Sub-B's revenues are in USD and EUR. It forecasts revenues of USD 70 (i.e., the equivalent in USD to EUR 70) and EUR 30. It forecasts cost of sales related to those revenues of USD 70. To keep the case simple, let us assume that all the flows are expected to take place on the same date. To hedge its exposure to EUR risk, Sub-B enters into a FX forward with Treasury Centre at market rates, under which Sub-B agrees to sell EUR 30 and to buy USD 30 on the same date that the rest of the cash flows are expected to take place.

Sub-C's revenues are in JPY and USD. It forecasts revenues of JPY 70 (i.e., the equivalent in JPY to EUR 70) and USD 30. It forecasts cost of sales related to those revenues of JPY 70. To keep the case simple, let us assume that all the flows are expected to take place on the same date. To hedge its exposure to USD risk, Sub-C enters into a FX forward with Treasury Centre at market rates, under which Sub-C agrees to sell USD 30 and to buy JPY 30 on the same date that the rest of the cash flows are expected to take place.

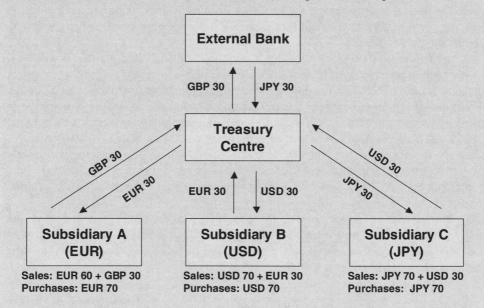

Figure 3.28   Group FX Hedges.

As a result, Treasury Centre's net exposure with the subsidiaries is a long GBP 30 and a short JPY 30 positions (see Figure 3.28). Consequently, Treasury Centre to hedge its exposure must enter into a FX forward with an external bank under which it agrees to sell GBP 30 and to buy JPY 30.

	GBP	EUR	USD	JPY
Subsidiary-A	+ 30	− 30		
Subsidiary-B		+ 30	− 30	
Subsidiary-C			+ 30	− 30
Total	+ 30	−0−	−0−	− 30

Accounting Implications at Subsidiary Level

From the subsidiaries point of view (see Figure 3.29) their hedges pose no accounting problem: each subsidiary can apply hedge accounting in its stand-alone financial statements. They can designate its FX forward as a cash flow hedge of its highly probable revenues of GBP 30 (Sub-A), EUR 30 (Sub-B) and USD 30 (Sub-C). All changes in the fair value of the FX forwards will be recorded in equity and recycled to P&L when the hedged revenues ultimately show-up in P&L.

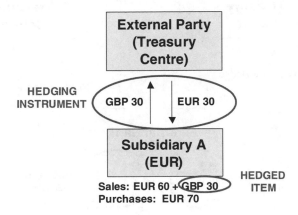

Figure 3.29   Subsidiary – A Hedge.

From the Treasury Centre point of view, all the hedges also have no special implications, although it cannot apply hedge accounting in its stand-alone financial statements. Treasury Centre will measure all the FX forwards at fair value with changes in fair value recorded in P&L. As all the changes in these fair values offset, Treasury Centre will have no profit or loss in its P&L statement.

Accounting Implications at the Consolidated Level

For hedge accounting purposes, only derivatives that involve a party external to the entity can be designated as hedging instruments. On consolidation all internal derivatives eliminate and cannot qualify as a hedging instrument. A potential solution to achieve hedge accounting is to create a link between the external hedging instrument and an external forecast hedged item.

The approach has the following steps:

1) Hedge separately against the EUR each long and short foreign currency positions (see Figure 3.30). In our case, Treasury Centre was long GBP and short JPY. It will need to enter with the external bank into two FX forwards: one to sell GBP and buy EUR, and other to buy JPY and to sell EUR. This step diminishes one of the main advantages of treasury centres: to lower the transaction costs of hedging.
2) Link each hedge to a external cash flow (see Figure 3.31). Treasury Centre will review the documentation already in place at the subsidiary level, and will identify a highly expected external cash flow that could be designated as hedged item of the step 1 derivatives. In our case, the group will identify the highly probable sales of GBP 30 in Sub-A as the hedged item of the GBP-EUR FX forward. Similarly, the highly probable cost of sales of JPY 30 in Sub-C will be identified as the hedged item of the JPY-EUR FX forward.

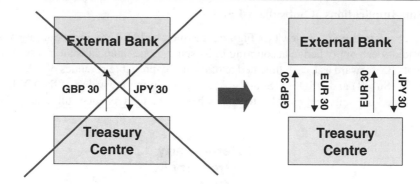

Figure 3.30   Treasury Centre Hedge.

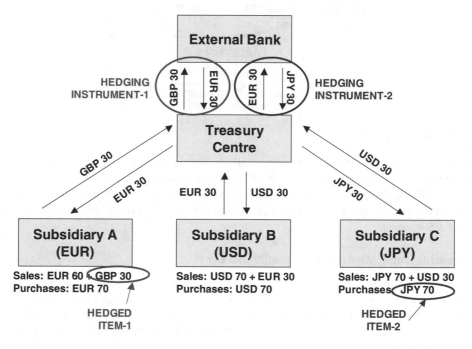

Figure 3.31   Group Hedges.

Conclusions

We have just seen that in order to apply hedge accounting on the consolidated statements a process of arbitrary designation has to be followed. At first sight it looks as if this process only involves an additional administrative burden. In reality the designation process is much more complicated than in our example.

First of all, bear in mind that the above example is highly simplified as all the expected cash flows are expected to take place on the same date. In reality, there is often a time lag between timing of the external hedges and the timing of the identified hedged items. Timing differences may create important hedge ineffectiveness.

Secondly, we are assuming that the treasury centre nets out all its exposure created by the internal derivatives with external derivatives. In reality, the treasury centre may decide keep some residual risk or even hedge using a different currency pair, complicating things further. For example, the exposure may be created by an illiquid currency and the treasury centre may prefer to use a hedge on a different currency that is highly correlated to the illiquid one.

Finally, applying hedge accounting on a consolidated basis may require one to execute more hedging transactions with the external banks than if hedge accounting were not applied, increasing hedging costs and operational risk.

CASE 3.8

Hedging Forecast Intragroup Transactions

In its consolidated financial statements, a group may designate as the hedged item in a foreign currency cash flow hedge, a highly probable forecast transaction with a external party to the group, provided that the transaction is denominated in a currency other than the group's functional currency.

IAS 39 does not permit an intragroup item to be a hedged item, but there is an exception for intragroup monetary items provided that:

1) The transaction is highly probable and meets all other criteria (other than the requirement that it should involve a party external to the group);
2) The hedge is a foreign currency cash flow hedge;
3) The hedged transaction is denominated in a currency other than the functional currency of the entity entering into the hedge (i.e., the entity designating a hedging relationship); and
4) The transaction gives rise to a foreign currency risk exposure that will affect consolidated P&L. In other words, the transaction foreign currency profit and loss does not eliminate fully on consolidation.

Gains and losses on the hedging instrument are recognised in equity, and are reclassified into P&L in the same period or periods during which the foreign currency risk affects consolidated P&L.

Examples of forecast intragroup transactions that could result in the foreign exchange risk affecting consolidated P&L are:

- Forecast sales and purchases of inventories between entities in a group with a subsequent sale of the inventory to a party external to the group. Any hedging gains or losses that are initially recognised in equity are reclassified to P&L in the same period that the foreign currency risk affects consolidated P&L. This would be when the onward sale to the external party occurs (and not when intragroup sales occur) because it is when the hedged transaction affects consolidated P&L.
- A forecast intragroup sale of equipment from a group entity that manufactured it to another group entity that uses the equipment. When the purchasing entity depreciates the equipment, the amount recognised initially in the consolidated financial statements for the equipment may change because the transaction is denominated in a currency other than the functional currency of the purchasing entity. In this example, a related external transaction does not exist and the item affects consolidated P&L.

Examples of forecast intragroup transactions unlikely to result in the foreign exchange risk affecting consolidated P&L are intragroup management fees, interest on intragroup loans or intragroup royalty payments.

IAS 39 does not explicitly consider situations where the intragroup transaction is committed rather than forecast. In our view committed transactions are also eligible for hedge accounting since they have a higher probability of occurrence.

Example of Hedge of Forecast Intragoup Transaction

ABC is a group that comprises operating subsidiaries Sub-A and Sub-B. The group has the EUR as its funtional currency. Sub-A's functional currency is the GBP and Sub-C's functional currency is the USD.

Sub-A incurs most of its production costs in EUR. It sells most of its production to Sub-B and those transactions are denominated in USD. Sub-B sells the product on to external customers, also in USD. Sub-A forecasts in March 20X6 that it will sell in June 20X6 USD 100 million of inventory to Sub-B. These sales are highly probable, and all the other IAS 39 conditions for hedge accounting are met. Sub-B expects to sell this inventory to external customers in early September 20X6.

Sub-A in January 20X6 enters into USD/EUR derivative to hedge the expected sale of USD 100 million to Sub-B in June 20X6.

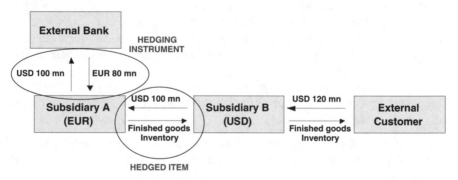

Figure 3.32   Hedging Relationship.

The forecast intragroup sales of USD 100 million can be designated in the consolidated financial statements as a hedged item in a foreign currency cash flow hedge (see Figure 3.32). All four conditions outlined above are met since:

1) The sales are highly probable, and all other conditions for using hedge accounting are met;
2) The hedge is a cash flow hedge of foreign currency risk;
3) The sales are denominated in a currency, the USD, other than Sub-A's functional currency (the EUR); and
4) The existence of the expected onwards sale of the inventory to third parties results in the hedged exposure affecting consolidated P&L.

Gains and losses on the USD/EUR derivative are recognised initially in consolidated equity, to the extent that the hedge is effective. These amounts are reclassified to consolidated P&L in September 20X6 when the external sales occur (i.e., when the transaction affects consolidated P&L).

4

Hedging Foreign Subsidiaries

Very frequently a group carries out foreign activities through foreign operations. Foreign operations must be translated and recorded in the parent entity's financial statements. Additionally, the foreign operation financial statements must be consolidated with the parent using the group functional currency. Consequently, the translation of foreign operations financial statements expose both the parent and the consolidated group to foreign currency risk.

Many companies consider that the FX risk arising from foreign operations is only a translation risk with no impact in cash flows, and thus there is no need to hedge it. This statement is wrong, especially in today's dynamic and competitive environment, as companies frequently buy and sell foreign subsidiaries. This chapter deals with the measurement and hedging of foreign currency exposure caused by foreign operations. Through the cases provided in this chapter, four are the topics that are going to be analysed in detail in this chapter:

1) Measurement and hedge of dividends paid by a foreign operation to the parent company.
2) Measurement and hedge of a foreign operation earnings translation.
3) Measurement and hedge of net investments in a foreign operation. A net investment means the entity's proportionate ownership interest in the net assets of the foreign operation.
4) Interaction of dividends, earnings and net investments, and the hedge of the combined exposure.

It should be noted that these four topics are interdependent, and therefore their joint hedge needs to take into account the total exposure. We will analyse the combined exposure on a parent-only basis as well as on a consolidated basis.

4.1 STAND-ALONE VERSUS CONSOLIDATED FINANCIAL STATEMENTS

For simplicity, in most cases throughout this chapter we have assumed a group formed by two entities: a parent company and its 100%-owned foreign subsidiary. The group functional currency is assumed to the EUR. Since all the subsidiary assets and liabilities are part of the group consolidated statements, any adjustments related to minority interests are avoided. The effect of minority interests is covered in Section 4.5. In our group, the risks and their hedges will be analysed at three different levels: at the subsidiary, at the parent-only and at the consolidated level.

4.1.1 Subsidiary Financial Statements

The purpose of the subsidiary stand-alone financial statements is to present the financial position of the subsidiary as if it were a single business enterprise. The parent company is considered just an outside investor. Normally, the subsidiary financial statements are prepared according to the accounting principles of the country where it operates, principles that may be different to the

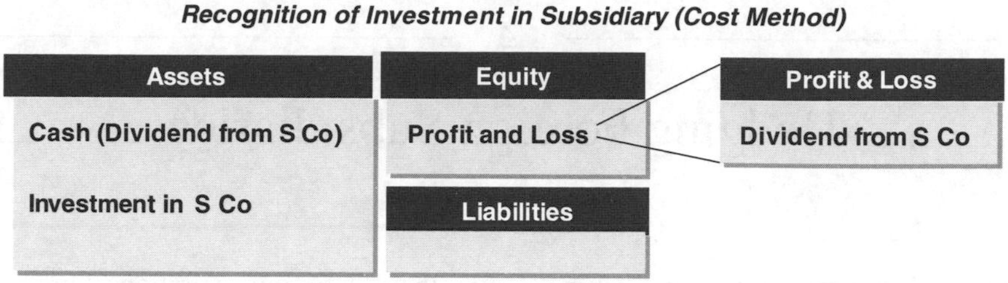

Recognition of Investment in Subsidiary (Cost Method)

Figure 4.1   Parent-only Financial Statements.

IFRS rules. However, the subsidiary statements need to be restated to IFRS upon consolidation. In the cases provided, it is assumed that the subsidiary financial statements are prepared according to IFRS.

4.1.2   Parent-Only Financial Statements

The purpose of the parent stand-alone financial statements is to present the financial position of the parent as if it were a single business enterprise. Its subsidiaries are treated purely as equity investments, ignoring the subsidiaries assets and liabilities.

The parent-only financial statements use the cost method to account for their equity investments in subsidiaries. This is different to the US companies that are required to use the equity method. The general underlying concepts behind the cost method are the following (see Figure 4.1):

1) The original cost of the investment is recognised in the parent financial statements in the "Investment in Subsidiary" account.
2) No adjustments are made to reflect subsequent changes in fair value of the investment, unless serious doubt as to the realisation of the investment exists in which case a permanent write-down is made.
3) Undistributed earnings have no effect on the parent financial statements.
4) When dividends are declared, dividend income is recognised. As just being mentioned, neither the dividend declaration nor the actual dividend payments impact the parent carrying value of the investment.

4.1.3   Consolidated Financial Statements

The consolidated financial statements are prepared using IFRS guidelines, so any subsidiary statements not prepared under IFRS need to be restated to IFRS. The purpose of the consolidated financial statements is to present, primarily for the benefit of the shareholders and creditors of the group, the financial position of the parent company and all of its subsidiaries as if the group were a single economic entity. All the assets and liabilities of the subsidiary are taken into account as assets and liabilities of the group after being translated into the group functional currency. Similarly, the profit and loss statement is also integrated in the group profit and loss, after being translated into the group functional currency.

In consolidation the parent's Investment in Subsidiary account is eliminated. Also upon consolidation, the value of the translation differences must be calculated. The carrying value

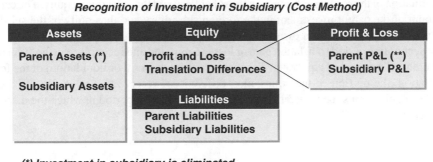

Recognition of Investment in Subsidiary (Cost Method)

(*) Investment in subsidiary is eliminated
(**) Dividend from subsidiary is eliminated

Figure 4.2   Consolidated Financial Statement.

of this account is a "plug" figure that balances all the translated assets and liabilities of the subsidiary. Figure 4.2 summarises the consolidated balance sheet and profit and loss statements, assuming that there are no intragroup transactions.

4.2   THE TRANSLATION PROCESS

The rationale behind the translation of foreign subsidiaries is to preserve the item-to-item relationships (e.g., profitability ratios, liquidity ratios, specific asset to total assets percentages) that exist in the subsidiary foreign currency statements. The only way to maintain these relationships is to translate all the subsidiary assets and liabilities using a single exchange rate.

4.2.1   Basic Procedures before Translation

Certain fundamental procedures must be performed before the financial statements of foreign subsidiaries may be translated into EUR (i.e., the group functional currency).

1) Restatement to IFRS. Operations conducted in a foreign entity must be accounted for using that country's accounting principles. When foreign currency financial statements use accounting principles that differ from IFRS, appropriate restatement adjustments must be made to those statements before translation so that they conform to IFRS.

   When a parent company has significant influence over a subsidiary, a 20 % to 50 % interest, which must be accounted for under the equity method, the investee's foreign statements must also be adjusted to conform to IFRS principles before translation into EUR.

2) Adjustments to the subsidiary receivables and payables. A foreign subsidiary's receivables and payables in a currency other than the subsidiary functional currency must be converted to the subsidiary's functional currency.

3) Reconciliation of intragroup receivable and payable accounts. Inventory and cash are commonly transferred between group entities with different functional currencies. Such transactions are usually recorded in separate intragroup receivable and payable accounts by each accounting entity. Such accounts must be reconciled to each other before translation to ensure that these accounts offset each other after translation.

4) Elimination of the parent investment in the subsidiary and the subsidiary equity. The carrying amount of the parent investment in the foreign subsidiary and the equity of the subsidiary corresponding to the parent ownership are eliminated.
5) The accounting period translation gain or loss is computed and recognised in the "translation differences" account of equity. On disposal (or partial disposal or liquidation) of the foreign operation, the portion of the "translation differences" reserve that relates to the disposal (or liquidation) must be transferred to P&L in the reporting period in which the disposal is recognised.

4.2.2   Specific Translation Procedures

The individual accounts of the foreign operation are translated using the following procedures:

1) All assets and liabilities are translated at the closing exchange rate. The assets and liabilities to be translated include the goodwill and fair value adjustments that arose on the acquisition of the foreign entity.
2) Share capital and share premium are translated at historical exchange rates.
3) Dividend payments, if any, are translated using the exchange rate in effect at the time of its declaration.
4) Income statement accounts are translated at the average exchange rate for the accounting period. The exchange rate existing when each item was recognised in earnings can also be used, but in practice few companies use this alternative.
5) The accounting period translation gain or loss resulting from the previous procedures is included in the "translation differences" account of equity.

The financial statements of a foreign entity that reports in the currency of a hyperinflationary economy should be restated in accordance with IAS 29 *Financial Reporting in Hyperinflationary Economics* before they are translated into the group functional currency.

4.3   THE TRANSLATION DIFFERENCES ACCOUNT

Investments in foreign subsidiaries are exposed to exchange rate fluctuations. The "translation differences" account reports the accumulated translation gains and losses related to a foreign subsidiary net asset position. This account is reported as a separate component of shareholders' equity. The "translation differences adjustment" for the accounting period is the difference between the beginning and the end of the period "translation differences account" amounts. The end of the period amount is calculated in such a way that the sum of all debits match the sum of all credits in the foreign subsidiary translated balance sheet.

The balance of the translation differences account is removed from that component and reported in the consolidated income statement on complete (or substantially complete) sale of the subsidiary, or on liquidation of the investment. On partial divestment of the foreign subsidiary, the proportional part of the translation differences account relating to that subsidiary is recognised in P&L as part of the gain or loss on the divestment.

The translation differences account balance at the end of the accounting period is calculated as follows:

	Calculation of the Accounting Period Translation Differences
	Translated Assets (including goodwill and fair value adjustments)
Less	Translated Liabilities (including fair value adjustments)
Equals	**Shareholders' Equity**
Less	Translated Shared Capital
Less	Translated Share Premium
Equals	**Total Retained Earnings and Translation Differences**
Less	Beginning of accounting period Retained Earnings
Less	Translated Net Income
Plus	Translated Dividends
Equals	**End of Accounting Period Translation Differences**
Less	Beginning of Accounting Period Translation Differences
Equals	**Translation Differences Adjustment**

4.4   SPECIAL ITEMS THAT ARE PART OF THE NET INVESTMENT

Not only is the equity investment in the foreign subsidiary assets and liabilities considered part of the net investment. Some other items, like acquisition goodwill, fair value adjustments and some type of monetary items, can also be part of the net investment in a foreign subsidiary.

4.4.1   Goodwill and Fair Value Adjustments

When a company acquires another company, all the assets and liabilities of the acquiree are fair valued. The fair value adjustments are the difference, at the time of acquisition, between the fair value and the book value of the acquiree assets and liabilities. Goodwill is the difference between what the acquirer paid and the acquiree assets and liabilities fair value. Under IAS 21, goodwill and fair value adjustments arising on the acquisition of a foreign entity are treated as assets and liabilities of the foreign entity and translated at the closing rate.

4.4.2   Special Monetary Items

Some monetary items can be part of an entity's net investment in a foreign operation. This situation takes place when, besides providing capital to the subsidiary in the form of equity, the parent also provides funds through a loan that is similar to an equity investment. The loan is part of the parent's investment in the subsidiary because repayment is neither planned nor likely to occur in the foreseeable future. If the subsidiary's functional currency is different from that of the parent, exchange differences are recognised initially in equity, and recognised in the P&L only on disposal or liquidation of the subsidiary. This recognition in equity is applicable only in the consolidated financial statements. The impacts on the individual financial statements are:

- If the loan is denominated in the functional currency of the subsidiary, exchange differences arising on the loan are recognised in P&L in the parent-only financial statements.
- If the loan is denominated in the functional currency of the parent, exchange differences arising on the loan are recognised in P&L in the subsidiary-only financial statements.

- If the loan is denominated in a currency that is not the functional currency of either the parent or the subsidiary, exchange differences are recognised in P&L in both parent-only and in the subsidiary-only financial statements.

4.5 EFFECT OF MINORITY INTERESTS ON TRANSLATION DIFFERENCES

Where there are minority interests relating to foreign entities, their share of the translation gains and losses should be added to the "minority interests" in the consolidated balance sheet, as highlighted in the following example:

Let us assume that ABC, a EUR based entity, has an 80 % investment in a US subsidiary. The net assets of the foreign subsidiary are USD 1 billion. No activity takes place during the period. The exchange rates were 1.0000 on 1 January and 1.2500 on 31 December. The translation adjustments loss was EUR 200 million (= 1 billion * (1/1.0000 − 1/1.2500)).

As ABC owns 80 % of the subsidiary, EUR 160 million are recorded in the translation differences account and the remaining EUR 40 million are added to minority interests in the consolidated balance sheet.

4.6 HEDGING NET INVESTMENTS IN FOREIGN OPERATIONS

Under IAS 39, for hedging purposes the net investment is viewed as a single asset, as opposed to several individual assets and liabilities that comprise the balance sheet of the foreign subsidiary. The accounting for hedges of net investments in foreign operations follows rules similar to those of cash flow hedges. That is, the effective portion of the change in fair value of the hedging instrument is recognised in equity, in the translation differences account.

The hedging of net investments in foreign operations is usually implemented by one of the group holding companies through the following instruments:

1) Non-derivatives: Usually debt denominated in the subsidiary functional currency; and/or
2) Derivatives: Usually FX forwards, FX options, or cross-currency swaps.

4.6.1 Net Investment Hedge Issuing Foreign Currency Debt

IAS 21 allows the use of non-derivatives, such as foreign currency debt to hedge a net investment. This is the preferred alternative when the acquisition is financed with new debt. All of the hedge accounting requirements of IAS 39 must be met and consequently a high degree of correlation between gains and losses on the net investment and gains and losses on the debt.

The accounting of non-derivatives hedges under IAS 39's hedge accounting is the same as for derivative hedges, except that hedge ineffectiveness is not accounted separately in P&L. Both effective and ineffective portions of the gain or loss on the borrowing are taken to equity.

Conceptually, it does seem possible to use a borrowing in one foreign currency to hedge a net investment in another currency and any hedge ineffectiveness to be deferred in equity. The practical difficulty is that, before hedge accounting is allowed, the prospective test must show that the hedge is highly effective.

4.6.2 Net Investment Hedge Using Derivatives

Sometimes the foreign currency is non-convertible making it impossible for non-resident holding company to issue the foreign currency debt. It may also be that the debt market in the currency concerned is too thin to accommodate the issue of debt. In these cases the group is only left with derivatives to hedge the net investment.

A hedge of a net investment in a foreign subsidiary using derivatives should be accounted as follows:

1) The portion of the gain or loss on the hedging instrument that is determined to be an effective hedge should be recognised directly in equity, in the translation differences account.
2) The ineffective portion should be reported in P&L

CASE 4.1

Hedging Intragroup Foreign Dividends

Generally foreign subsidiaries pay dividends to their shareholders. Dividends are usually paid in the subsidiary local currency, so both the parent company and the group may be exposed to FX risk. In this case, the accounting impact of dividends at the subsidiary, parent and group levels is discussed. Also the potential distortions that hedges may create are discussed in detail. It is worth noting that hedging only dividends (i.e., without taking into account the earnings translation and net investment risk exposures) may end up creating undesirable effects in the consolidated financial statements.

Let us assume that ABC, whose functional currency is the EUR, has a 100% owned US foreign subsidiary. The foreign subsidiary declared, and later paid, a dividend of USD 100 million to ABC. The exchange rates at the relevant dates were as follows:

Date	Spot USD/EUR	USD Dividend (Millions)	Dividend EUR Value (Millions)
Previous Reporting Date: 31-Dec-W9	1.2000		
Declaration Date: 1-Jan-X0	1.2300	100	81.3
Reporting Date: 31-Mar-X0	1.2500	100	80
Dividend Payment Date: 30-Jun-X0	1.2850	100	77.8

In order to analyse the FX exposure of the dividend, let us review the accounting of the dividends from the subsidiary, parent and group perspectives.

Impact on the Subsidiary Financial Statements

On declaration date (1 January 20X0), the subsidiary recorded the declared dividends as follows:

Retained earnings (Equity – Subsidiary)	$ 100,000,000	
Dividends payable (Liability – Subsidiary)		$ 100,000,000

On the first reporting date, 31 March 20X0, no accounting entries were required.

On dividend payment date, 30 June 20X0, the subsidiary recorded the payment as follows:

Dividends payable (Liability – Subsidiary)	$ 100,000,000	
Cash (Asset – Subsidiary)		$ 100,000,000

As a result, it can be seen that the subsidiary was not exposed to any FX risk as all the flows were denominated in its functional currency.

Impact on the Parent-Only Financial Statements

The required accounting entries on the parent book were as follows:

1) Accounting entries on 1 January 20X0

Under the cost method, the parent records dividends declared by a foreign subsidiary as dividend income and as dividend receivable. The exchange rate used to convert it into euros was the exchange rate ruling on the dividend declaration date (1.2300). As a result, on 1 January 20X0 the recorded dividend EUR amount was EUR 81,300,000 (USD 100 million/1.2300).

Dividends receivable (Asset – Parent)	€ 81,300,000	
Dividend income (P&L – Parent)		€ 81,300,000

2) Accounting entries on 31 March 20X0

In the parent stand-alone statements, the dividend receivable constituted a monetary item denominated in a foreign currency (USD) and therefore it was revalued on each balance sheet date. Any changes in the exchange rate from the last revaluation resulted in an FX gain or loss that was recognised in the income statement. The USD 100 million dividend receivable lost EUR 1.3 million (= 80,000,000 − 81,300,000) in value.

FX gains and losses (P&L – Parent)	€ 1,300,000	
Dividends receivable (Asset – Parent)		€ 1,300,000

3) Accounting entries on 30 June 20X0

On 30 June 20X0, the USD dividend was received by the parent. ABC had first to revalue the dividend receivable, recognising a EUR 2,100,000 loss (= 77,800,000 − 80,000,000):

FX gains and losses (P&L – Parent)	€ 2,100,000	
Dividends receivable (Asset – Parent)		€ 2,100,000

The receipt of the USD 100 million from the subsidiary was recorded as follows:

USD cash (Asset – Parent)	€ 77,800,000	
Dividends receivable (Asset – Parent)		€ 77,800,000

Let us assume that to eliminate the USD/EUR FX exposure, ABC converted the USD 100 million cash balance into EUR through a FX spot transaction. As the USD/EUR spot rate on the 30 June 20X0 was 1.2850, ABC delivered USD 100 million in exchange for EUR 77.8 million. The related accounting entry was as follows:

EUR Cash (Asset – Parent)	€ 77,800,000	
USD Cash (Asset – Parent)		€ 77,800,000

It can be seen that the parent was exposed to FX risk in its stand-alone statements. This exposure was caused by the revaluation of a monetary item denominated in a foreign currency.

Impact on the Consolidated Financial Statements

ABC performed the consolidation process at each reporting date.

1) Consolidation adjustments on 31 March 20X0:

On 31 March 20X0, in the subsidiary books there was a USD dividend payable and in the parent books there was a USD dividend receivable. Upon consolidation, intragroup receivables and payables were eliminated and all its effects unwind.

Dividends Payable (Liability – Subsidiary)	$ 100,000,000	
Retained Earnings (Equity – Subsidiary)		$ 100,000,000

Dividend Income (P&L – Parent)	€ 81,300,000	
Dividends Receivable (Asset – Parent)		€ 81,300,000

Dividends Receivable (Asset – Parent)	€ 1,300,000	
FX Gains and Losses (P&L – Parent)		€ 1,300,000

Also when preparing its consolidated statements on 31 March 20X0, ABC had to compute the translation differences adjustment related to its net investment in the US subsidiary. We had only look at the dividend portion of the net investment to isolate the dividend effect from the rest. As the dividend had not being paid yet, the USD 100 million was still part of the net investment. The spot rate prevailing at the previous reporting date (31 December

20X0) was 1.2000. The spot rate prevailing at the current reporting date (31 March 20X0) was 1.2500. Accordingly, the change in the net investment was a EUR 3,333,000 (= 100 million/1.25 − 100 million/1.20) loss. The loss was recorded in the translation differences account of equity:

Translation Differences (Equity – Consolidated)	€ 3,333,000	
USD Cash (Asset – Consolidated)		€ 3,333,000

2) Consolidation adjustments on 30 June 20X0:

On 30 June 20X0 and prior to the recognition of the dividend payment/receipt, the revaluation of the USD 100 million net investment showed a EUR 2,179,000 (= 100 million/1.285 − 100 million/1.25) loss that was recorded in the translation differences account of equity:

Translation Differences (Equity – Consolidated)	€ 2,179,000	
USD Cash (Asset – Consolidated)		€ 2,179,000

Also on 30 June 20X0, the dividend was paid to the parent. As a result, the USD 100 million was now part of the parent monetary assets and not of the net investment in the subsidiary. Upon consolidation, the revaluation of the parent monetary assets performed at the stand-alone parent level also remained at the consolidated level. The net investment exposure also decreased, so the computation of the translation differences adjustment was computed on a smaller net assets amount.

Summary of Impacts in the Financial Statements

On dividend declaration date, 1 January 20X0, the effects on the two individual statements were as follows (see Figure 4.3):

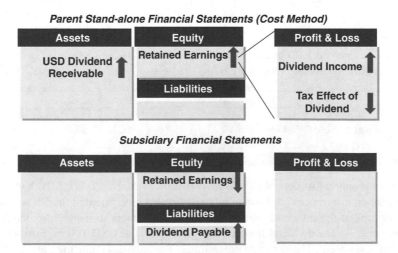

Figure 4.3   Dividend Declaration – Effect on Individual Statements.

Parent Stand-alone Financial Statements (Cost Method)

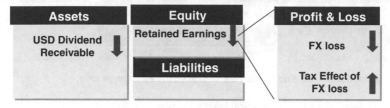

Subsidiary Financial Statements

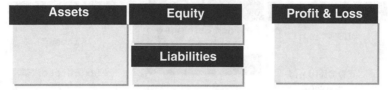

Figure 4.4   Reporting Date (31-Mar-X0) Effect on Individual Statements.

- On the subsidiary books, a dividend payable was recognised coming from undistributed retained earnings from previous years.
- On the parent books, the declared dividend was valued at the prevailing USD/EUR exchange rate and recognised as dividend income and a dividend receivable. The recognition in P&L had a tax impact.
- On the consolidated books, there was still no effect as no consolidation process was performed.

On the first reporting date, 31 March 20X0, the effects on the three different reported statements were as follows:

- On the subsidiary books, there was no effect (see Figure 4.4).
- On the parent books, the declared dividend was revalued at the prevailing USD/EUR exchange rate and recognised as FX gains or losses (a loss in our case) in P&L. The recognition in P&L had a tax impact. Figure 4.4 highlights the effects.
- On the consolidated books, the declared dividend still remained part of the net investment, as it was not been paid yet. Therefore, the FX gains and losses due to the net investment revaluation were recorded in translation differences account in equity (see Figure 4.5). In this case, as the USD depreciated versus the EUR, a translation loss was recorded.

On 30 June 20X0, the USD 100 million dividend was paid. This USD cash moved from the subsidiary USD cash account to the parent USD cash account. The effects on the three different reported statements were as follows:

- On the subsidiary books, the cash account showed a USD 100 million decrease and the dividend payable was cancelled (see Figure 4.6).

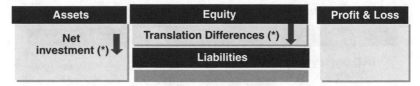

(*) Decrease was due to the rise of USD/EUR exchange rate

Figure 4.5   31-Mar-X0 – Effect on Consolidated Statements.

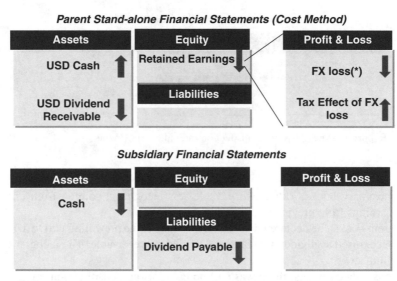

(*) Due to the revaluation of the USD Dividend Receivable

Figure 4.6   Divident Payment Date (30-Jun-X0) Effect on Individual Statements.

- On the parent books, there were several effects (see Figure 4.6). Firstly, there was a FX loss due to the revaluation of the dividend receivable. This loss was recognised in P&L, which also had a tax impact. Secondly, the USD cash account increased by USD 100 million and the dividend receivable was cancelled.
- At first sight, the dividend payment seemed to have no effect on a consolidated basis, as the USD cash accounts are grouped together. However, there was an important effect: the FX gains or losses from the revaluation of the USD 100 million were recognised differently.

Before the dividend was paid, the USD 100 million cash was part of the net investment in the US subsidiary. Thus, foreign exchange gains or losses on the USD 100 million cash remeasurement were recorded in the translation differences account in equity.

After the dividend was paid, the USD 100 million cash was part of a monetary item of a group entity (i.e., the parent) that had the same functional currency as the group. Thus, foreign exchange gains or losses on the USD 100 million cash remeasurement were recorded in P&L.

Consequently, the effect of the dividend payment was a reduction in the net investment in the US subsidiary and an increase in the monetary items of the parent company (see Figure 4.7).

Consolidated Financial Statements

(*) The decline in net investment will cause the translation differences to be less exposed to the USD/EUR FX rate
(**) The USD cash will expose the consolidated P&L to the USD/EUR FX rate

Figure 4.7 Dividend payment and Reporting Date (30-Jun-X0) Effect on Consolidated Statements.

The FX spot transaction that took place on 30 June 20X0 eliminated the exposure to the USD 100 million of the P&L statement.

Hedging Intercompany Foreign Dividends with a FX Forward

Many companies seek to hedge forecast foreign currency dividends paid by their foreign subsidiaries. Next, the implications of hedging foreign intragroup dividends will be discussed in detail.

Let us assume that on 1 January 20X0 ABC (the parent company) hedged the declared dividend through a FX forward with the following terms:

FX Forward Terms	
Trade date	1 January 20X0
Nominal	USD 100,000,000
Maturity	30 June 20X0
Forward Rate	1.2320
Settlement	Cash settlement

Assume further that the fair value of the FX forward at each relevant date was as follows:

Date	Forward to 30-Jun-X0	FX Forward Fair Value
Declaration Date: 1-Jan-X0	1.2320	–0–
Reporting Date: 31-Mar-X0	1.2510	1,222,000
Dividend Payment Date: 30-Jun-X0	1.2850	3,348,000

Subsidiary Accounting Entries Related to the FX Forward

No entries were required as the subsidiary was no party to the FX forward.

Hedge Parent-Only Accounting Entries Related to the FX Forward

The required accounting entries on the parent books relating to the FX forward were as follows:

1) Entries on 1 January 20X0:

No entries were required as the fair value of the forward was zero at its inception.

2) Entries on 31 March 20X0 (reporting date):

The fair value change of the FX forward was a gain of EUR 1,222,000 (= 1,222,000 – 0).

FX forward (Asset – Parent)	€ 1,222,000	
FX gain (P&L – Parent)		€ 1,222,000

3) Entries on 30 June 20X0:

On 30 June 20X0, the FX forward matured. The change in fair value of the forward was EUR 2,126,000 (= 3,348,000 – 1,222,000).

FX forward (Asset – Parent)	€ 2,126,000	
FX gain (P&L – Parent)		€ 2,126,000

Through the forward, ABC delivered the dividend proceeds (USD 100 million) and received EUR 81,169,000:

EUR cash (Asset – Parent)	€ 3,348,000	
FX forward (Asset – Parent)		€ 3,348,000

Consolidated Accounting Entries Related to the FX Forward

No entries were required as no adjustments were necessary to the parent accounting entries.

Summary of Impacts of the Hedge in the Financial Statements

On 31 March 20X0, the effects on the three different reported balance sheet and income statement were as follows:

- On the subsidiary books, there was no effect as the subsidiary was not a party to the FX forward.
- On the parent income statement, the EUR 1,222,000 gain on the hedge largely offset the EUR 1,300,000 loss on the revaluation of the dividend receivable (see Figure 4.8). Therefore, the hedge performed well at the parent level.

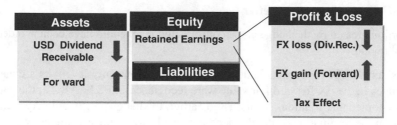

Figure 4.8   Reporting Date (31-Mar-X0) Effect on Parent-only Statements.

- On the consolidated statements, the EUR 1,222,000 gain on the hedge showed up on the P&L statement. This FX gain was no offsetting any FX loss. The only FX loss showed up in the translation differences account, and as a result, the hedge largely eliminated the FX exposure (relating to the USD 100 million portion of the net investment in the subsidiary) of the consolidated equity. Therefore, the FX forward exposed the consolidated P&L to the USD/EUR exchange rate, as shown in Figure 4.9.

On 30 June 20X0, the effects on the three different reported balance sheet and income statement were as follows:

- On the subsidiary books, there was no effect as the subsidiary was not a party to the FX forward.
- On the parent income statement, we had a similar effect to the one on 31 March 20X0. The EUR 2,126,000 (= 3,348,000 − 1,222,000) gain on the hedge largely offset the EUR 2,100,000 loss on the revaluation of the dividend receivable. Therefore, the hedge performed well at the parent level.
- On the consolidated statements, we had a similar effect to the one on 31 March 20X0. The FX forward showed a EUR 2,126,000 gain that was recognised in the consolidated P&L statement, while there was a EUR 2,179,000 gain in the translation differences account. Therefore, the consolidated P&L was exposed to the USD/EUR exchange rate.

In summary, the hedge worked well at the individual financial statements, but created distortions in the consolidated P&L.

Consolidated Financial Statements

Assets	Equity	Profit & Loss
Net investment (*) ⬇	Translation Differences (*) ⬇	FX gain (Forward) ⬆
Forward ⬆	Retained Earnings ⬆	
	Liabilities	

(*) Decrease was due to the rise of the USD/EUR exchange rate

Figure 4.9   Reporting Date (31-Mar-X0) Effect on Consolidated Statements.

What ABC Could Have Done Better

The distortion created by the hedge at the consolidated level could have been avoided if ABC did the following:

- To consider the FX forward as undesignated at the parent-only level. As a consequence, the changes in the FX forward fair value were recognised in P&L. ABC at the parent level already adopted this solution. As discussed earlier, the hedge performed very well because the loss on the revaluation of the dividend receivable was almost completely offset by the gain in the FX forward (see Figure 4.8).
- To designate, at the consolidated level, the FX forward as the hedging instrument in a net investment hedge. As a consequence, the effective part of the changes of the FX forward fair value were recognised in the translation differences account of equity. This way, there will be a natural offset in the translation differences account between the effective part of the changes of the FX forward and the revaluation changes of the net investment. In Case 4.4 there is a detailed discussion of a net investment hedge with a FX forward.

The parent-only accounting entries relating to the FX forward will the same as before. However, the consolidated accounting entries were different.

Consolidated Accounting Entries Related to the FX Forward

The required accounting entries on the parent books relating to the FX forward were as follows:

1) Entries on 1 January 20X0: No entries were required.

2) Entries on 31 March 20X0 (reporting date):

The EUR 1,222,000 gain recognised at the parent level was reversed. At the consolidated level, the FX forward was designated as hedging instrument in a net investment hedge. Assuming that the hedge was completely effective, the changes in the fair value of the FX forward were recognised in the translation differences account.

FX gain (P&L – Parent)	€ 1,222,000	
Translation Differences (Equity – Consolidated)		€ 1,222,000

3) Entries on 30 June 20X0:

Similarly, the EUR 2,126,000 change in fair value of the forward was recorded similarly to the 31 March 20X0 adjustment.

FX gain (P&L – Parent)	€ 2,126,000	
Translation Differences (Equity – Consolidated)		€ 2,126,000

Now the hedge performed very well at both the parent-only and consolidated levels, as shown in Figure 4.10.

Parent-only Financial Statements

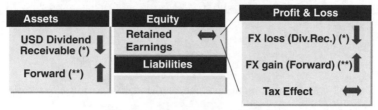

Consolidated Financial Statements

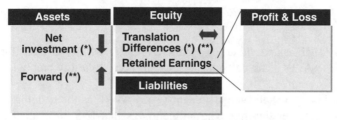

(*) Decrease was due to the rise of the USD/EUR exchange rate
(**) Increase was due to the rise of the USD/EUR exchange rate

Figure 4.10   Hedge Optimised Solution Effect on parent and Consolidated Statements.

CASE 4.2

Hedging Foreign Subsidiary Earnings

This case illustrates a problem presently faced by many multinationals: the hedge of foreign earnings translation risk. Upon consolidation, most multinationals translate foreign subsidiaries' net income at the average exchange rate for the accounting period. As a consequence, corporations are exposed to this average exchange rate. The hedging problem arises because IAS 39 at present does not allow the direct hedging of foreign earnings translation.

Let us assume that ABC had a US subsidiary that is expected to earn USD 400 million evenly during 20X0. Assume further that ABC reported quarterly its consolidated financial statements. To hedge the quarterly translation exposure arising from the US subsidiary, ABC entered into the following four FX average rate forwards ("AVRF"):

	AVRF-1	AVRF-2	AVRF-3	AVRF-4
Trade date	1-Jan-20X0	1 January 20X0	1 January 20X0	1 January 20X0
Nominal	USD 100 Mn	USD 100 Mn	USD 100 Mn	USD 100 Mn
Maturity	31-Mar-20X0	30-Jun-20X0	30-Sep-20X0	31-Dec-20X0
Forward Rate	1.2500	1.2500	1.2500	1.2500
Final Rate	The arithmetic average of the monthly closing USD/EUR spot from 1-Jan-X0 to 31-Mar-X0	The arithmetic average of the monthly closing USD/EUR spot from 1-Apr-X0 to 30-Jun-X0	The arithmetic average of the monthly closing USD/EUR spot from 1-Jul-X0 to 30-Sep-X0	The arithmetic average of the monthly closing USD/EUR spot from 1-Oct-X0 to 31-Dec-X0
Settlement	Cash settlement	Cash settlement	Cash settlement	Cash settlement

The payoff at maturity of each AVRF assured an arithmetic average daily USD/EUR exchange rate during the quarter of 1.2500. For example, the EUR payoff of the first AVRF at maturity was:

$$\text{Payoff} = 100{,}000{,}000 * (1/1.25 - 1/\text{Average})$$

Where "Average" was the arithmetic average of the daily closing USD/EUR spot from 1-Jan-X0 to 31-Mar-X0.

The next thing that ABC had to decide was how to account for each AVRF. ABC had two alternatives:

- To treat each AVRF as undesignated, and therefore, to recognise in P&L the changes in fair value of the AVRF. The potential increase in P&L volatility precluded ABC from adopting this alternative.
- To designate, in the consolidated statements, each AVRF as the hedging instrument in a hedge accounting relationship. The problem was that IAS 39 at that time (as well as currently) did not allow the direct hedging of foreign earnings translation. One way to overcome this problem was to designate the AVRF as the hedging instrument in a cash-flow hedge. The hedged item was a proportion of the foreign subsidiary's USD sales sufficient to equal the foreign subsidiary's forecast profit (USD 100 million) on consolidation for the quarterly accounting period. This was the alternative finally adopted by ABC. As a consequence, changes in the effective part of the AVRF fair value were initially recognised in equity, and recycled to P&L once the hedged cash flow affected P&L.

Hedge Relationship Documentation

ABC documented the first quarter hedging relationship (remember there were four hedging relationships, one for each quarter) as follows:

Hedging Relationship Documentation	
Risk management objective and strategy for undertaking the hedge	The objective of the hedge is to protect the EUR value of the USD 100 million highly expected sales of finished goods against unfavourable movements in the USD/EUR exchange rate. This hedging objective is consistent with ABC's overall FX risk management strategy of reducing the variability of its Profit and Loss statement.
Type of hedge	Cash flow hedge
Risk being hedged	FX risk. The variability in EUR value of the highly expected transaction.
Hedging instrument	The FX average rate forward (AVRF) contract with reference number 017812. The counterparty to the AVRF is XYZ Bank and the credit risk associated with this counterparty is considered to be very low.
Hedged item	USD 100 million sale of finished goods expected to take place between 1 January 20X0 and 30 March 20X0.

Assessment of effectiveness testing	Hedge effectiveness will be assessed by comparing changes in the fair value of the hedging instrument to changes in the fair value of the expected cash flows.
	Hedge effectiveness assessment will be performed on a forward-forward basis. In other words, the forward points of both the hedging instrument and the expected cash flows are included in the assessment.

Prospective test

A prospective test will be performed at each reporting date, using the linear regression method comparing the cumulative change since hedge inception in the fair value of the expected cash flow arising from the forecast sale with the cumulative change since hedge inception in the fair value of the hedging instrument. The credit risk of the counterparty of the hedging instrument will be monitored continuously.

Retrospective test

A retrospective test will be performed at each reporting date using the "ratio analysis method". The ratio will compare the cumulative change since hedge inception in the fair value of the expected cash flow arising from the forecast sale with the cumulative change since hedge inception in the fair value of the hedging instrument. The hedge will be assumed to be highly effective on a retrospective basis if the ratio is between 80 % and 125 %.

Prospective and Retrospective Tests

To keep the case short, the prospective and retrospective tests results are not included. The reader can find a detailed discussion of these tests in the cases provided in Chapter 3. It this case, it is assumed that the hedge was highly effective prospectively and retrospectively at hedge inception and at each reporting date.

The spot USD/EUR exchange rates and the fair value of the AVRFs on the relevant dates were as follows:

Date	Spot Rate	AVRF-1 Fair Value	AVRF-2 Fair Value	AVRF-3 Fair Value	AVRF-4 Fair Value
1-Jan-20X0	**1.2392**	**<475,000>**	**<150,000>**	**160,000**	**465,000**
31-Jan-20X0	1.2400				
28-Feb-20X0	1.2600				
31-Mar-20X0	**1.2800**	**635,000**	**2,057,000**	**2,333,000**	**2,602,000**
30-Apr-20X0	1.3000				
31-May-20X0	1.2900				
30-Jun-20X0	**1.2700**		**2,280,000**	**1,451,000**	**1,738,000**
31-Jul-20X0	1.2800				
31-Aug-20X0	1.2600				
30-Sep-20X0	**1.2500**			**844,000**	**211,000**
31-Oct-20X0	1.2700				
30-Nov-20X0	1.2900				
31-Dec-20X0	**1.3100**				**2,481,000**

Accounting Entries

The required journal entries were as follows:

1) Entries on 1 January 20X0

The following entries were required as the fair value of the AVRFs at their inception were not zero.

Cash (Asset)	€ 475,000	
Fair Value of Derivative (AVRF-1) (Asset)		€ 475,000

Cash (Asset)	€ 150,000	
Fair Value of Derivative (AVRF-2) (Asset)		€ 150,000

Fair Value of Derivative (AVRF-3) (Asset)	€ 160,000	
Cash (Asset)		€ 160,000

Fair Value of Derivative (AVRF-4) (Asset)	€ 465,000	
Cash (Asset)		€ 465,000

2) To record the closing of the accounting period on 31 March 20X0:

The changes in fair value of the AVRFs since the last valuation were as follows: IVRF-1: a gain of EUR 1,110,000 (= 635,000 + 475,000), IVRF-2: a gain of EUR 2,207,000 (= 2,057 + 150,000), IVRF-3: a gain of EUR 2,173,000 (= 2,333,000 − 160,000), and IVRF-4: a gain of EUR 2,137,000 (= 2,602,000 − 465,000). Assuming all the hedges were completely effective, all their changes in fair value were recorded in equity:

Fair Value of Derivative (AVRF-1) (Asset)	€ 1,110,000	
Cash flow Hedges (Equity)		€ 1,110,000

Fair Value of Derivative (AVRF-2) (Asset)	€ 2,207,000	
Cash flow Hedges (Equity)		€ 2,207,000

Fair Value of Derivative (AVRF-3) (Asset)	€ 2,173,000	
Cash flow Hedges (Equity)		€ 2,173,000

| Fair Value of Derivative (AVRF-4) (Asset) | € 2,137,000 | |
| Cash flow Hedges (Equity) | | € 2,137,000 |

All the USD 100 million sales of the US subsidiary, designated as the hedged item in the first hedging relationship, were recorded in the subsidiary's P&L. As a consequence, the amount related to the AVRF-1 recorded in equity (EUR 1,110,000) was recycled to P&L:

| Cash flow Hedges (Equity) | € 1,110,000 | |
| Sales (P&L) | | € 1,110,000 |

Finally, the AVRF-1 matured and ABC received EUR 635,000 ($= 100$ million $*$ $(1/1.25 - 1/\text{Average})$, where "Average" was the average of the spot rates at the end of each month of the first quarter ($= (1.24 + 1.26 + 1.28)/3$).

| Cash (Asset) | € 635,000 | |
| Fair Value of Derivative (AVRF-1) (Asset) | | € 635,000 |

3) To record the closing of the accounting period on 30 June 20X0:

The changes in fair value of the AVRFs since the last valuation were as follows: IVRF-2: a gain of EUR 223,000 ($= 2,280,000 - 2,057,000$), IVRF-3: a loss of EUR 882,000 ($= 1,451,000 - 2,333,000$), and IVRF-4: a loss of EUR 864,000 ($= 1,738,000 - 2,602,000$). As the hedges were completely effective, all these changes in fair value were recorded in equity:

| Fair Value of Derivative (AVRF-2) (Asset) | € 223,000 | |
| Cash flow Hedges (Equity) | | € 223,000 |

| Cash flow Hedges (Equity) | € 882,000 | |
| Fair Value of Derivative (AVRF-3) (Asset) | | € 882,000 |

| Cash flow Hedges (Equity) | € 864,000 | |
| Fair Value of Derivative (AVRF-4) (Asset) | | € 864,000 |

All the USD 100 million sales of the US subsidiary, designated as the hedged item in the second hedging relationship, were recorded in the subsidiary's P&L. As a consequence, the amount related to the AVRF-2 recorded in equity (EUR 2,430,000) was recycled to P&L:

Cash flow Hedges (Equity)	€ 2,430,000	
Sales (P&L)		€ 2,430,000

Finally, the AVRF-2 matured and ABC received EUR 2,280,000 (= 100 million * (1/1.25 − 1/Average), where "Average" was the average of the spot rates at the end of each month of the second quarter (= (1.30 + 1.29 + 1.27)/3).

Cash (Asset)	€ 2,280,000	
Fair Value of Derivative (AVRF-2) (Asset)		€ 2,280,000

4) To record the closing of the accounting period on 30 September 20X0:

The changes in fair value of the AVRFs since the last valuation were as follows: IVRF-3: a loss of EUR 607,000 (= 844,000 − 1,451,000) and IVRF-4: a loss of EUR 1,527,000 (= 211,000 − 1,738,000). As the hedges were completely effective, all these changes in fair value were recorded in equity:

Cash flow Hedges (Equity)	€ 607,000	
Fair Value of Derivative (AVRF-3) (Asset)		€ 607,000

Cash flow Hedges (Equity)	€ 1,527,000	
Fair Value of Derivative (AVRF-4) (Asset)		€ 1,527,000

All the USD 100 million sales of the US subsidiary, designated as the hedged item in the third hedging relationship, were recorded in the subsidiary's P&L. As a consequence, the amount related to the AVRF-3 recorded in equity (EUR 684,000) was recycled to P&L:

Cash flow Hedges (Equity)	€ 684,000	
Sales (P&L)		€ 684,000

Finally, the AVRF-3 matured and ABC received EUR 844,000 (= 100 million * (1/1.25 − 1/Average), where "Average" was the average spot rate at the end of each month of the third quarter (= (1.28 + 1.26 + 1.25)/3).

Cash (Asset)	€ 844,000	
Fair Value of Derivative (AVRF-3) (Asset)		€ 844,000

5) To record the closing of the accounting period on 31 December 20X0:

The change in fair value of the AVRF-4 since the last valuation was a gain of EUR 2,270,000 (= 2,481,000 − 211,000). As the hedge was completely effective, this change in fair value was recorded in equity:

Fair Value of Derivative (AVRF-4) (Asset)	€ 2,270,000	
Cash flow Hedges (Equity)		€ 2,270,000

All the USD 100 million sales of the US subsidiary, designated as the hedged item in the fourth hedging relationship, were recorded in the subsidiary's P&L. As a consequence, the amount related to the AVRF-4 recorded in equity (EUR 2,016,000) was recycled to P&L:

Cash flow Hedges (Equity)	€ 2,016,000	
Sales (P&L)		€ 2,016,000

Finally, the AVRF-4 matured and ABC received EUR 2,481,000 (= 100 million*(1/1.25 − 1/Average), where "Average" was the average spot rate at the end of each month of the third quarter (= (1.27 + 1.29 + 1.31)/3).

Cash (Asset)	€ 2,481,000	
Fair Value of Derivative (AVRF-3) (Asset)		€ 2,481,000

Final Remarks

The hedge worked well as the objective of converting the USD 400 million expected subsidiary's pre-tax income at an exchange rate of 1.2500 (or EUR 320 million) was achieved, as shown in Figure 4.11.

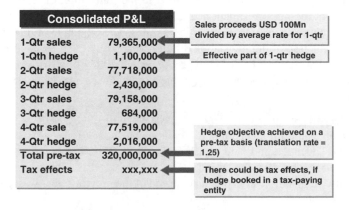

Figure 4.11   Subsidiary Earnings Hedge – Effect on Consolidated P&L.

However, specific issues may arise as a result of implementing this hedging strategy. Five in particular are worth noting:

- Firstly, when deciding the USD nominal of the AVRFs, ABC needed to forecast its foreign subsidiary earnings and may forecast inaccurately.
- Second, ABC needed to track a portion of the subsidiary's USD sales. ABC designated a portion of the subsidiary's external highly probable forecast sales in USD as the hedged item in a cash flow hedge. It required the subsidiary to be also involved, increasing its administrative load.
- Third, there could be undesired P&L and tax effects. If for example the hedge is booked in the parent company, the four AVRFs will most probably be treated as undesignated. As a result the change in fair value of the AVRFs will be recorded in P&L, increasing the volatility of the parent's P&L. There could also be tax effects as losses on the AVRFs will be tax deductible, while gains on the AVRFs will be taxed. In reality, most corporations will execute the consolidation related hedges in a treasury centre, avoiding tax effects on their group hedges.
- Fourth, the hedge may distort EBITDA figures. The results of the hedge went to the same line as the USD sales.
- Finally, the average USD/EUR exchange rate used to translate the subsidiary's P&L may be different to the average rate used in the AVRFs. Often, the subsidiary's P&L is translated using the daily average rate during the accounting period while the group may decide to use monthly average rate in the AVRFs to reduce their administrative load. Average mismatches may create hedge ineffectiveness and result in undesired P&L effects.

CASE 4.3

Accounting for Net Investments in Foreign Operations

Before addressing the hedge on net investments in foreign operations, it is worth giving a quick remainder of the different components behind the translation differences account. A net investment in a foreign operation is the amount of the reporting entity's interest in the net assets of the operation. Any change in the translated value of the net assets of the operation into the group's currency is embodied in the translation differences account of equity. The aim of the net investment hedge is therefore to minimise the exposure of the translation differences account to changes in FX rates. The objective of this case is then to illustrate the calculation of the translation differences.

Let us assume that ABC, a EUR-based group, owned 100 % of a Norwegian subsidiary. The functional currency of the subsidiary was the Norwegian Krona (NOK). Assume further the following:

- The subsidiary was acquired in 1 January 20X0 when the NOK/EUR exchange rate was 7.0. Since then, no additional capital transactions have occurred.
- The subsidiary declared and paid a cash dividend of NOK 171,000,000 on 20 October 20X1, when the exchange rate was 9.5.
- The cumulative translation adjustment at the end of the previous year was a *debit* balance of EUR 51,000,000.

The relevant NOK/EUR exchange rates were as follows:

Date	NOK/EUR FX Rate
31 December 20X0	8.0
Average for year 20X1	9.0
31 December 20X1	10.0

Remember, as mentioned in Section 4.2, that the individual accounts of the foreign operation are translated using the following procedures:

1) All assets and liabilities are translated at the closing exchange rate. The assets and liabilities to be translated include the goodwill and fair value adjustments that arose on the acquisition of the foreign entity.
2) Share capital and share premium are translated at historical exchange rates.
3) Dividend payments, if any, are translated using the exchange rate in effect at the time of its declaration.
4) Income statement accounts are translated at the average exchange rate for the accounting period. The exchange rate existing when each item was recognised in earnings can also be used, but in practice few companies use this alternative.
5) The accounting period translation gain or loss resulting from the previous procedures is included in the "translation differences" account of equity.

ABC subsidiary's NOK denominated and EUR translated financial statements for the year ending 31 December 20X1 are detailed in the table below:

	NOK Amount	Exchange Rate Rate	Exchange Rate Type	Translated Euro Amount
Income Statement				
Sales	2,700,000,000	9,0	**Average**	300,000,000
Cost of Goods Sold	<1,620,000,000>	9,0	**Average**	<180,000,000>
Expenses	<540,000,000>	9,0	**Average**	<60,000,000>
Net Income	540,000,000			60,000
Retained Earnings				
1/1 Retained Earnings	1,680,000,000	8,0	**Closing 20X0**	210,000,000
Net Income (from above)	540,000,000			60,000,000
Dividends Declared	<171,000,000>	9,5	**Declaration date**	<18,000,000>
31/12 Retained Earnings	2,049,000,000			252,000,000
Balance Sheet				
Cash	900,000,000	10,0	**Closing**	90,000,000
Accounts Receivable	800,000,000	10,0	**Closing**	80,000,000
Inventory	900,000,000	10,0	**Closing**	90,000,000
Plant & Equipment (net)	1,300,000,000	10,0	**Closing**	130,000,000
Land	450,000,000	10,0	**Closing**	45,000,000
Total assets	4,350,000,000			435,000,000
Liabilities	341,000,000	10,0	**Closing**	34,000,000
Share Capital	210,000,000	7,0	**Historical**	30,000,000
Share Premium	1,750,000,000	7,0	**Historical**	250,000,000
Retained Earnings (from above)	2,049,000,000			252,000,000
Translation Differences – Prior years				<51,000,000>
Translation Differences – Current year				<80,000,000>
Total liabilities and equity	4,350,000,000			435,000,000

The translation loss was the "plug" figure that balanced the total translated assets and the total translated liabilities and equity. The calculation of the translation differences adjustment for 20X1 is shown in the following table:

	Calculation of Current-year Translation Differences	
	Translated assets	435,000,000
Less	Translated liabilities	<34,000,000>
Equals	**Shareholders' equity**	**401,000,000**
Less	Translated share capital	<30,000,000>
Less	Translated share premium	<250,000,000>
Equals	**Total retained earnings and translation differences**	**121,000,000**
Less	Beginning-of-year retained earnings	<210,000,000>
Less	Translated net income	<60,000,000>
Plus	Translated dividends	18,000,000
Equals	**Total translation differences**	**<131,000,000>**
Less	Beginning-of-year translation differences	51,000,000
Equals	**Current-year translation differences**	**<80,000,000>**

As a result, the investment in the subsidiary experienced a loss of EUR 80 million during the year 20X1. Adding this loss to the previous years' EUR 51 million loss meant an accumulated loss of EUR 131 million. If the group decided to partially or completely sell the subsidiary the corresponding portion of the carrying value of the translation differences account will be recognised as an expense in the same period on which the gain or loss on disposal is recognised. The same is true on liquidation, abandonment or repayment of the subsidiary capital.

CASE 4.4

Net Investment Hedge using a Forward

The objective of this case is to illustrate the hedge of a net investment in a foreign operation through the simplest instrument, an FX forward.

Let us assume that ABC, whose functional currency was the EUR, had a net investment in a US subsidiary. The subsidiary's functional currency was the USD. Let us assume that ABC's net investment in the subsidiary was USD 500 million as of 1 January 20X0. On that date, ABC entered into a FX forward to hedge its net investment in the subsidiary, with the following terms:

FX Forward Terms	
Start date	1 January 20X0
Counterparties	Company ABC and XYZ Bank
Maturity	31 January 20X1
ABC buys	€ 400 million
ABC sells	USD 500 million
Forward Rate	1.2500
Settlement	Cash settlement

The spot and forward FX rates, and the fair value of the forward contract on the relevant dates were:

Date	Spot USD/EUR	Forward USD/EUR	Discount Factor (EUR)	Forward Fair Value (EUR)
1 Jan 20X1	**1.2300**	1.2500	—	-0-
31 Dec 20X1	**1.2850**	1.2900	0.997	12,366,000
31 Jan 20X2	**1.3300**	1.3300	1.000	24,060,000

Forward Fair Value = [(500 million/1.25 − 500 million/(Forward rate)] * Discount Factor

ABC designated the FX forward as the hedging instrument in a net investment hedge. The effectiveness of the hedge was assessed on a forward basis, i.e. the forward points of the FX forward were included in the assessment of hedge effectiveness.

Hedge Relationship Documentation

ABC documented the hedging relationship as follows:

Hedging Relationship Documentation

Risk management objective and strategy for undertaking the hedge	The objective of the hedge is to protect the value of the USD 500 million investment in ABC's US subsidiary XYZ against unfavourable movements in the USD/EUR exchange rate.
	This hedging objective is consistent with ABC's overall FX risk management strategy of reducing the variability of its shareholders' equity.
Type of hedge	Net investment hedge.
Risk being hedged	FX risk. The variability in EUR value of the net investment.
Hedging instrument	The FX forward contract with reference number 012345. The counterparty to the forward is XYZ Bank and the credit risk associated with this counterparty is considered to be very low.
Hedged item	USD 500 million of the net investment in XYZ.
Assessment of effectiveness testing	Hedge effectiveness will be assessed by comparing changes in the fair value of the hedging instrument to changes in the fair value of a hypothetical derivative.
	The terms of the hypothetical derivative are the same as the hedging instrument, but without any exposure to credit risk.
	Hedge effectiveness assessment will be performed on a forward-forward basis. In other words, the forward points of both the hedging instrument and the hypothetical derivative are included in the assessment.

Prospective test
Due to the fact that the terms of the hedging instrument and those of the hypothetical derivative match, the hedge is expected to be highly effective. The credit risk of the counterparty of the hedging instrument will be monitored continuously.

Retrospective test
A retrospective test will be performed at each reporting date using the "ratio analysis method". The ratio will compare the cumulative change since hedge inception in the fair value of the hypothetical derivative with the cumulative change since hedge inception in the fair value of the hedging instrument. The hedge will be assumed to be highly effective on a retrospective basis if the ratio is between 80 % and 125 %.

Retrospective Tests

A retrospective test was performed at each reporting date and also at maturity of the hedging instrument. Because there was no significant deterioration in the credit of the counterparty of the hedging instrument and because the terms of the hedging instrument and those of the hypothetical derivative matched, the hedge relationship was 100 % effective:

Date	Forward Fair Value (EUR)	Cumulative Change in Forward Fair Value	Hypothetical Derivative Fair Value (EUR)	Cumulative Change in Hypothetical Der. Fair Val.	Ratio
1 Jan 20X1	–0–	–0–	–0–	—	—
31 Dec 20X1	12,366,000	12,366,000	12,366,000	12,366,000	100%
31 Jan 20X2	24,060,000	24,060,000	24,060,000	24,060,000	100%

The net investment translation into euros at each relevant date was:

Date	Spot USD/EUR	Net Investment (USD)	Net Investment (€)	Period Change in € Net Investment
1 Jan 20X1	1.2300	500,000,000	**406,504,000**	—
31 Dec 20X1	1.2850	500,000,000	**389,105,000**	<17,399,000>
31 Jan 20X2	1.3300	500,000,000	**375,940,000**	<13,165,000>

Net Investment in Euros = (500 million)/(Spot Rate)

Accounting Entries

Assuming that ABC closed its books annually at year-end, the accounting entries related to the hedge were:

1) To record the forward contract trade on 1 January, 20X1

   No entries in the financial statements were required as the fair value of the forward contract was zero.

2) To record the closing of the accounting period on 31 December 20X1:

   The net investment lost EUR 17,399,000 in value over the period when translated into EUR

Translation Differences (Equity)	€ 17,399,000
Net Investment in Subsidiary (Asset)	€ 17,399,000

The change in the fair value of the FX forward since the last valuation was a gain of EUR 12,366,000. As the hedge had no ineffectiveness, all this change was also recorded in the translation differences account.

| Fair Value of Derivative (Asset) | € 12,366,000 | |
| Translation Differences (Equity) | | € 12,366,000 |

3) To record the settlement of the FX forward on 31 January 20X2:

The net investment lost EUR 13,165,000 in value over the period when translated into EUR.

| Translation Differences (Equity) | € 13,165,000 | |
| Net Investment in Subsidiary (Asset) | | € 13,165,000 |

The change in the fair value of the FX forward since the last valuation was a gain of EUR 11,694,000 (= 24,060,000 − 12,366,000). As the hedge had no ineffectiveness, all this change was also recorded in the translation differences account.

| Fair Value of Derivative (Asset) | € 11,694,000 | |
| Translation Differences (Equity) | | € 11,694,000 |

The settlement of the FX forward resulted in the receipt of EUR 24,060,000.

| Cash (Asset) | € 24,060,000 | |
| Fair Value of Derivative (Asset) | | € 24,060,000 |

Let us analyse next the accounting results of the hedge:

Translation Differences:

Due to net investment translation		< 30,564,000 >
Due to effective part of hedge		24,060,000
	Total	< 6,504,000>

Profit & Loss:

Due to ineffective part of hedge		–0–
	Total	–0–

As we can see, the Translation Differences account showed a deficit, as all the net investment translation loss was not completely offset by the hedge. This deficit was exactly the change in fair value of the FX forward due to the forward points. No part of the hedge was recorded in P&L.

Accounting Entries were the Forward Points Excluded from the Hedge

Let us see what would have been the accounting treatment were the forward points of the FX forward excluded from the hedging relationship. The change in the FX forward fair value would have had two components: one component due to changes in the spot rate and a second component due to changes in the forward points. The following table shows the changes in fair value of the FX forward at each relevant date:

Date	Spot USD/EUR	Forward USD/EUR	Discount Factor (EUR)	Forward Total Fair Value (EUR)	Forward Fair Value due to Spot	Forward Fair Value due to Forward Points
1 Jan 20X1	1.2300	1.2500	—	–0–	–0–	–0–
31 Dec 20X1	1.2850	1.2900	0.997	12,366,000	17,347,000	<4,981,000>
31 Jan 20X2	1.3300	1.3300	1.000	24,060,000	30,564,000	<6,504,000>

Forward Total Fair Value = [(500 million/1.25 − 500 million/(Forward rate)] * Discount Factor
Forward Fair Value due to Spot = [(500 million/1.23 − 500 million/(Spot rate)] * Discount Factor
Fwd. Fair Value due to Forward Points = Fwd. Total Fair Value − Fwd. Fair Value due to Spot

Therefore, the net investment translation amounts and changes in fair value of the FX forward were the following:

Date	Period Change in € Net Investment	Period Change in € Forward due to Spot	Period Change in € Forward due to Forward Points
1 Jan 20X1	—	—	—
31 Dec 20X1	<17,399,000>	17,347,000	<4,981,000>
31 Jan 20X2	<13,165,000>	13,217,000	<1,523,000>

The accounting entries were as follows, assuming that ABC closed its books annually at year-end:

1) To record the forward contract trade on 1 January, 20X1

No entries in the financial statements were required as the fair value of the forward contract was zero.

2) To record the closing of the accounting period on 31 December 20X1:

The net investment lost 17,399,000 in value over the period when translated into EUR:

Translation Differences (Equity)	€ 17,399,000	
Net Investment in Subsidiary (Asset)		€ 17,399,000

The change in the fair value of the FX forward since the last valuation was a gain of EUR 12,366,000. The change in this fair value due to movements in the spot was EUR 17,347,000. All the change due to spot rates was considered effective, as its accumulated change was lower than the accumulated change in fair value of the net investment since hedge inception. The rest of the change in fair value of the FX forward, a loss of EUR

4,981,000, was considered ineffective. The effective part was recorded in the translation differences account. The ineffective part was recorded in P&L.

Fair Value of Derivative (Asset)	€ 12,366,000	
Ineffective Part on Hedge (P&L)	€ 4,981,000	
Translation Differences (Equity)		€ 17,347,000

3) The journal entries on 31 January 20X2:

The net investment lost EUR 13,165,000 in value over the period when translated into EUR:

Translation Differences (Equity)	€ 13,165,000	
Net Investment in Subsidiary (Asset)		€ 13,165,000

The change in the fair value of the FX forward since the last valuation was a gain of EUR 11,694,000 (= 24,060,000 − 12,366,000). The change in this fair value due to movements in the spot was EUR 13,217,000. All the change due to spot rates was considered effective, as its accumulated change is lower than the accumulated change in fair value of the net investment since hedge inception. The rest of the change in fair value of the FX forward, a loss of EUR 1,523,000, was considered ineffective. The effective part was recorded in the translation differences account. The ineffective part was recorded in P&L.

Fair Value of Derivative (Asset)	€ 11,694,000	
Ineffective Part on Hedge (P&L)	€ 1,523,000	
Translation Differences (Equity)		€ 13,217,000

The settlement of the FX forward resulted in the receipt of EUR 24,060,000.

Cash (Asset)	€ 24,060,000	
Fair Value of Derivative (Asset)		€ 24,060,000

Let us analyse the accounting results of the hedge:

Translation Differences:

Due to net investment translation		< 30,564,000 >
Due to effective part of hedge		30,564,000
	Total	–0–

Profit & Loss:

Due to ineffective part of hedge		<6,504,000>
	Total	<6,504,000>

As we can see, the net investment translation loss was completely offset by the hedge. All the forward points value were recorded in P&L.

Effects of the Forward Points

The decision whether to include or exclude the forward points of the FX forward in the hedge may have a strong effect in the financial statements, as has just been seen.

In our case, on 1-January-20X1 the market expected a depreciation of the USD versus the EUR because USD interest rates were higher than the EUR interest rates. This depreciation was represented in the forward points of the FX forward. As a result, at inception of the hedge the FX market expected the value of the investment to be worth on 31 January 20X2 EUR 6,504,000 less than what it was worth on 1 January 20X1. By entering into the FX forward, ABC locked-in this EUR 6,504,000 deterioration, embodied in the forward points of the hedging instrument. The effects of the decision (whether to include the forward points in the hedge) were the following:

1) If ABC decided to include the forward points in the hedge, all the value associated with the forward points (EUR 6,504,000) would have ended up in the translation differences account and not in P&L. The translation differences account would have shown a EUR 6,504,000 deficit because the gain on the hedge (EUR 24,060,000) did not offset completely the loss on the net investment (EUR 30,564,000), as shown in Figure 4.12. Of course, if the interest rate differential implied instead an appreciation of the USD the effect would have been the opposite: the translation differences account would have shown up a surplus.
2) If ABC decided to exclude the forward points from the hedge, all the value associated with the forward points (EUR 6,504,000) would have ended up in P&L, and not in the translation differences account. The translation differences account would have <u>not</u> shown any deficit because the gain on the hedge (EUR 30,564,000) exactly offset the loss on the net investment (EUR 30,564,000), as shown in Figure 4.13.

In a situation in which the functional currency of the subsidiary is expected to depreciate relative to the functional currency of the group, the inclusion of the forward points in the hedge

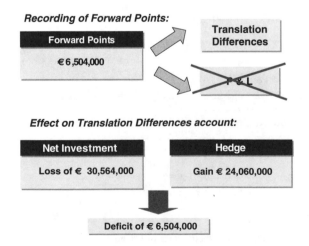

Figure 4.12   Net Investment Hedge with FX Forward Forward Points <u>Included</u> in Hedge.

Recording of Forward Points:

Forward Points
€ 6,504,000

→ ~~Translation Differences~~

→ P&L

Effect on Translation Differences account:

Net Investment	Hedge
Loss of € 30,564,000	Gain € 30,564,000

No Deficit

Figure 4.13   Net Investment Hedge with FX Forward Forward Points <u>Excluded</u> from Hedge.

at first sight looks better because the deterioration in the value of the investment implied in the forward points will not show up in P&L. This, however, is a wrong conclusion. Remember that the amount deferred in the translation differences account will be recycled to P&L on disposal or liquidation of the subsidiary.

Let us imagine that ABC repeated the hedge over several years, the inclusion of the forward points in the hedge could result in a huge loss being deferred in equity. If one day ABC decides to sell the subsidiary, then the huge deficit will show up in P&L immediately. Therefore, when the forward points imply a depreciation of the net investment value, the exclusion of the forward points from the hedge is more conservative as there will be no deficit in the translation differences account. The expected depreciation is gradually being recognised in P&L, as shown in Figure 4.14.

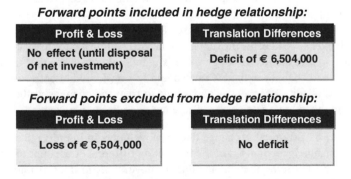

Forward points included in hedge relationship:

Profit & Loss	Translation Differences
No effect (until disposal of net investment)	Deficit of € 6,504,000

Forward points excluded from hedge relationship:

Profit & Loss	Translation Differences
Loss of € 6,504,000	No deficit

Figure 4.14   Net Investment Hedge with FX Forward Summary of Forward Points Effect.

CASE 4.5

Net Investment Hedge using a Cross-Currency Swap

The objective of this case is to illustrate the hedge of a net investment in a foreign operation through a cross-currency swap (CCS). This instrument is commonly used when the hedging horizon is long-term.

Let us assume that ABC, a group with a EUR functional currency, had a net investment in a US subsidiary that had the USD as its functional currency. Assume further that ABC was looking to hedge its net investment in the US subsidiary for the next three years through a CCS. ABC had then four alternatives (see Chapter 2 for a detailed description of CCSs):

1) To enter into a pay-floating receive-floating CCS. Under this CCS, ABC would pay annually USD Libor 12M on a USD nominal and receive annually Euribor 12M on a EUR nominal. At maturity, there would be an exchange of principals, ABC paying the USD nominal and receiving the EUR nominal.
2) To enter into a pay-fixed receive-floating CCS. Under this CCS, ABC would pay annually a fixed-rate on a USD nominal and receive annually Euribor 12M on a EUR nominal. At maturity, there would be an exchange of principals, ABC paying the USD nominal and receiving the EUR nominal.
3) To enter into a pay-floating receive-fixed CCS. Under this CCS, ABC would pay annually USD Libor 12M on a USD nominal and receive annually a fixed-rate on a EUR nominal. At maturity, there would be an exchange of principals, ABC paying the USD nominal and receiving the EUR nominal.
4) To enter into a pay-fixed receive-fixed CCS. Under this CCS, ABC would pay annually a fixed-rate on a USD nominal and receive annually a fixed-rate on a EUR nominal. At maturity, there would be an exchange of principals, ABC paying the USD nominal and receiving the EUR nominal.

Accounting Treatment of CCSs in Net Investment Hedges

Before deciding which CCS to use, ABC analysed the accounting implications of such a decision. Nowadays, the discussion regarding the accounting treatment of CCSs designated as hedging instruments of net investment hedges is a controversial one. Specifically, there is no general consensus as to what part of the change in the fair value of a CCS is considered to be effective and what part is considered to be ineffective.

The fair value of a EUR-USD CCS is exposed to three different market risks: the movement in the USD/EUR exchange rate, the movement of the USD interest rate curve and the movement of the EUR interest rate curve. Although there is a general consensus that the change in the CCS fair value due to changes in the FX rate should be considered effective in net investment hedges, there is as a lack of consensus about how to treat the changes in the CCS fair value due to changes in the interest rate curves. There are two alternative views:

1) To consider the CCS fair value change due to movements in interest rates as effective. As a result, this change is recognised in the translation differences account of equity.
2) To consider the CCS fair value change due to movements in interest rates as ineffective. As a result, this change is recognised in P&L. This alternative is the most conservative, but may cause an undesired increase in P&L volatility.

These two alternatives have different consequences on the four types of CCSs being analysed by ABC:

- In the pay-floating receive-floating CCS, its fair value change due to interest rate movements is usually small relative to its fair value change due to the FX rate movement. As a consequence both alternatives are quite similar. Our suggestion is then to take to equity the changes in the CCS fair value due to movements in interest rates, as any potential restatements due to external auditors having a different understanding of this accounting policy, may result in small restatements. Our suggestion is in line with the equivalent US Gaap rules. Although US Gaap accounting rules are legally irrelevant for an IFRS reporting entity, many auditors accept in particular situations adopting the US Gaap's clearly defined rules when IFRS rules are unclear.
- In the pay-fixed receive-floating CCS, the exposure to the USD interest rate curve can be important. As a result, there could be significant differences between both alternatives. The adoption of one or the other alternative depends on the "particular" understanding of the IFRS by the entity's outside auditors, as not even the US Gaap provides a rule. At the moment, the US Gaap does not consider this type of CCS as an eligible hedging instrument in a net investment hedge.
- In the pay-floating receive-fixed CCS, the exposure to the EUR interest rate curve can be important. Our comments are the same as in the pay-fixed receive-floating CCS.
- In the pay-fixed receive-fixed CCS, the changes in its fair value due to movements in both interest rate curves can be substantial. Many IFRS entities are following the US Gaap guidelines that, at the moment, recognise in equity the whole CCS fair value changes. These entities may be facing the risk of restating their financial statements if their auditors consider that the US guidelines are not appropriate.

Let us assume that ABC decided to enter into a pay-floating receive-floating CCS because the USD interest rate curve was notably steep. When curves are very steep, short-term rates are notably lower than long-term rates. As a result, entities paying a floating-rate initially experience substantial savings relative to paying the fixed-rate in the initial interest periods.

Assume further that ABC's objective was to hedge USD 500 million of its investment in the US subsidiary over the next three years. The terms of the CCS were as follows:

CCS Terms	
Start date	1 January 20X0
Counterparties	Company ABC and XYZ Bank
Maturity	31 December 20X2
EUR notional	€ 400 million
USD notional	USD 500 million
Implied FX rate	1.2500
ABC pays	USD Libor 12M + 10 bps, annually A/360 basis, on the USD nominal
ABC receives	Euribor 12M, annually A/360 basis, on the EUR nominal
Final exchange	On maturity date, there is cash settlement based on the USD/EUR fixing prevailing on than date (instead of the standard ABC receiving the EUR nominal and paying the USD nominal).
	Settlement amount = 500 mn * (1/1.25 − 1/Fixing)
	If "Settlement amount" >0, ABC receives the "settlement amount".
	If "Settlement amount"<0, ABC pays the absolute value of the "settlement amount".

It is important to note that the CCS did not have the usual exchange of principals at maturity. Instead the CCS had a "cash settlement" provision. The reason behind was that since ABC was not planning to sell the US subsidiary on the CCS maturity date, ABC was not hedging a cash-flow risk but an accounting risk. ABC was not interested, at the CCS maturity, in selling USD 500 million and buying EUR 400 million, but instead to receive (or pay) a compensation equivalent to the depreciation (or appreciation) of its investment in the US subsidiary.

ABC designated the CCS as the hedging instrument in a net investment hedge. The whole change in fair value of the CCS was assumed to be effective and, therefore, recorded in the translation differences account of equity.

Hedge Relationship Documentation

ABC documented the hedging relationship as follows:

Hedging Relationship Documentation	
Risk management objective and strategy for undertaking the hedge	The objective of the hedge is to protect the value of the USD 500 million investment in ABC's US subsidiary XYZ against unfavourable movements in the USD/EUR exchange rate. This hedging objective is consistent with ABC's overall FX risk management strategy of reducing the variability of its shareholders' equity.
Type of hedge	Net investment hedge.
Risk being hedged	FX risk. The variability in EUR value of the net investment.
Hedging instrument	The cross-currency swap ("CCS") with reference number 016795. The counterparty to the CCS is XYZ Bank and the credit risk associated with this counterparty is considered to be very low.
Hedged item	USD 500 million of the net investment in XYZ.
Assessment of effectiveness testing	Hedge effectiveness will be assessed by comparing changes in the fair value of the hedging instrument to changes in the fair value of a hypothetical derivative. The terms of the hypothetical derivative are the same as the hedging instrument, but without any exposure to credit risk. Hedge effectiveness assessment will be performed including all the change in fair value of both the hedging instrument and the hypothetical derivative in the assessment. **Prospective test** Due to the fact that the terms of the hedging instrument and those of the hypothetical derivative match, the hedge is expected to be highly effective. The credit risk of the counterparty of the hedging instrument will be monitored continuously. **Retrospective test** A retrospective test will be performed at each reporting date using the "ratio analysis method". The ratio will compare the cumulative change since hedge inception in the fair value of the hypothetical derivative with the cumulative change since hedge inception in the fair value of the hedging instrument. The hedge will be assumed to be highly effective on a retrospective basis if the ratio is between 80 % and 125 %.

Retrospective Tests

A retrospective test was performed at each reporting date and also at maturity of the hedging instrument. Because there was no significant deterioration in the credit of the counterparty of the hedging instrument and because the terms of the hedging instrument and those of the hypothetical derivative matched, the hedge relationship was 100 % effective:

Date	CCS Fair Value (EUR)	Cumulative Change in CCS Fair Value	Hypothetical Derivative Fair Value (EUR)	Cumulative Change in Hypothetical Der. Fair Val.	Ratio
1-Jan-X0	–0–	–0–	–0–	–0–	—
31-Dec-X0	6,299,000	**6,299,000**	6,299,000	**6,299,000**	100 %
31-Dec-X1	18,321,000	**18,321,000**	18,321,000	**18,321,000**	100 %
31-Dec-X2	12,403,000	**12,403,000**	12,403,000	**12,403,000**	100 %

Other Relevant Information

The net investment translation into euros at each relevant date was:

Date	Spot USD/EUR	Net Investment (USD)	Net Investment (€)	Period Change in € Net Investment
1 Jan 20X0	1.2500	500,000,000	400,000,000	—
31 Dec 20X0	1.2700	500,000,000	393,701,000	<6,299,000>
31 Dec 20X1	1.3100	500,000,000	381,679,000	<12,022,000>
31 Dec 20X2	1.2900	500,000,000	387,597,000	5,918,000

In our case, the changes in the fair value of the hedging instrument exactly matched those of the hedged item. This coincidence was due to two facts: (1) that both legs were based on floating rates and (2) that the interest rates were reset at the beginning of each interest period
    The interest flows that ABC paid during the life of the CCS were the following:

Date	Spot USD/EUR	USD Libor Rate	Interest Payments (in USD)	Equivalent EUR Amount
31 Dec 20X0	1.2700	5.20 %	26,868,000 (1)	21,156,000 (2)
31 Dec 20X1	1.3100	5.50 %	28,389,000	21,671,000
31 Dec 20X2	1.2900	5.70 %	29,403,000	22,793,000

Notes:

(1): Interest payment = USD 500 million * (5.20 % + 0.10 %) * 365/360
(2): Equivalent EUR amount = Interest payment/Spot = 26,868,000/1.27

The interest flows that ABC received during the life of the CCS were the following:

Date	EUR Euribor Rate	Interest Received (in EUR)
31 Dec 20X0	4.00 %	16,222,000 (1)
31 Dec 20X1	4.20 %	17,033,000
31 Dec 20X2	4.40 %	17,844,000

Note:

(1): Interest received = EUR 400 million * 4.00% * 365/360

Accounting Entries

Assuming that ABC closed its books annually at year-end, the accounting entries related to the hedge were:

1) To record the CCS trade on 1 January 20X0

   No entries in the financial statements were required as the fair value of the CCS was zero.

2) To record the closing of the accounting period on 31 December 20X0:

   The net investment lost EUR 6,299,000 in value over the period when translated into EUR:

Translation differences (Equity)	€ 6,299,000	
Net investment in subsidiary (Asset)		€ 6,299,000

   The change in the fair value of the CCS since the last valuation was a gain of EUR 6,299,000. As the hedge had no ineffectiveness, all this change was also recorded in the translation differences account:

Fair value of derivative (Asset)	€ 6,299,000	
Translation differences (Equity)		€ 6,299,000

   Under the CCS, ABC paid on 31 December 20X0 a USD interest equivalent to EUR 21,156,000. Simultaneously, ABC received a EUR interest of EUR 16,222,000:

Interest expense (P&L)	€ 21,156,000	
Interest payable (Liability)		€ 21,156,000

Interest payable (Liability)	€ 21,156,000	
Cash (Asset)		€ 21,156,000

Interest receivable (Asset)	€ 16,222,000	
Interest income (P&L)		€ 16,222,000

Cash (Asset)	€ 16,222,000	
Interest receivable (Asset)		€ 16,222,000

3) To record the closing of the accounting period on 31 December 20X1:

The net investment lost EUR 12,022,000 in value over the period when translated into EUR:

Translation differences (Equity)	€ 12,022,000	
Net investment in subsidiary (Asset)		€ 12,022,000

The change in the fair value of the CCS since the last valuation was a gain of EUR 12,022,000. As the hedge had no ineffectiveness, all this change was also recorded in the translation differences account:

Fair value of derivative (Asset)	€ 12,022,000	
Translation differences (Equity)		€ 12,022,000

Under the CCS, ABC paid on 31 December 20X1 a USD interest equivalent to EUR 21,671,000. Simultaneously, ABC received a EUR interest of EUR 17,033,000:

Interest expense (P&L)	€ 21,671,000	
Interest payable (Liability)		€ 21,671,000

Interest payable (Liability)	€ 21,671,000	
Cash (Asset)		€ 21,671,000

Interest receivable (Asset)	€ 17,033,000	
Interest income (P&L)		€ 17,033,000

Cash (Asset)	€ 17,033,000	
Interest receivable (Asset)		€ 17,033,000

4) To record the closing of the accounting period on 31 December 20X2:

The net investment gained EUR 5,918,000 in value over the period when translated into EUR:

Net investment in subsidiary (Asset)	€ 5,918,000	
Translation differences (Equity)		€ 5,918,000

The change in the fair value of the CCS since the last valuation was a loss of EUR 5,918,000. As the hedge had no ineffectiveness, all this change was also recorded in the translation differences account:

Translation differences (Equity)	€ 5,918,000	
Fair value of derivative (Asset)		€ 5,918,000

Under the CCS, ABC paid on 31 December 20X2 a USD interest equivalent to EUR 22,793,000. Simultaneously, ABC received a EUR interest of EUR 17,844,000:

Interest expense (P&L)	€ 22,793,000	
Interest payable (Liability)		€ 22,793,000

Interest payable (Liability)	€ 22,793,000	
Cash (Asset)		€ 22,793,000

Interest receivable (Asset)	€ 17,844,000	
Interest income (P&L)		€ 17,844,000

Cash (Asset)	€ 17,844,000	
Interest receivable (Asset)		€ 17,844,000

At maturity of the CCS, ABC received a settlement amount of EUR 12,403,000:

Cash (Asset)	€ 12,403,000	
Fair value of derivative (Asset)		€ 12,403,000

Final Remarks

In our case the hedge performed very well, as the decline in value of the net investment due to the depreciation of the USD relative to the EUR was completely offset by the change in fair value of the CCS. However, three comments are worth noting:

- The pay-floating receive-floating CCS is an effective way to implement long-term hedges of net investments in foreign operations.
- ABC P&L statement was exposed to increases in USD rates, to declines in EUR rates and to declines in the USD/EUR FX rate. Nevertheless, ABC's translation differences account

was not exposed to changes in the fair value of the CCS due to movements in the USD and EUR interest rate curves because both legs were linked to floating interest rates.
- At CCS maturity, ABC received EUR 12,403,000 cash, a substantial amount. In this case, ABC was lucky because the USD/EUR was greater than 1.25 but it could have been the other way around. In other words, a hedge of a large investment in a foreign operation through a CCS may have strong implications to the entity's cash resources.

CASE 4.6

Net Investment Hedge using Foreign Currency Debt

The objective of this case is to illustrate the hedge of a net investment with a non-derivative denominated in the functional currency of the subsidiary. This instrument is commonly used when the hedging horizon is long-term.

Let us assume that ABC, a group with a EUR functional currency, had a net investment in a US subsidiary that had the USD as its functional currency. Assume further that ABC was looking to hedge USD 500 million net investment in the US subsidiary for the next three years through the issuance of a USD-denominated debt. Thus, on 1 January 20X0, ABC issued a three-year fixed-rate USD denominated bond with the following terms:

USD-Denominated Bond Terms	
Start date	1 January 20X0
Issuer	ABC
Maturity	31 December 20X2
Currency	USD
Notional	USD 500 million
Interest	5.20 %, annually 30/360 basis

ABC designated the USD bond as the hedging instrument in a net investment hedge of its US subsidiary.

Hedge Relationship Documentation

ABC documented the hedging relationship as follows:

Hedging Relationship Documentation	
Risk management objective and strategy for undertaking the hedge	The objective of the hedge is to protect during the next three years the value of the USD 500 million investment in ABC's US subsidiary XYZ against unfavourable movements in the USD/EUR exchange rate. This hedging objective is consistent with ABC's overall FX risk management strategy of reducing the variability of its shareholders' equity.
Type of hedge	Net investment hedge.

(Continued)

Hedging Relationship Documentation	
Risk being hedged	FX risk. The variability in EUR value of the net investment.
Hedging instrument	The USD-denominated 3-year bond with reference number 016135.
Hedged item	USD 500 million of the net investment in XYZ.
Assessment of effectiveness testing	Hedge effectiveness will be assessed by comparing changes in the fair value of the hedging instrument to changes in the fair value of a hypothetical hedging non-derivative instrument. The hypothetical hedging non-derivative instrument is a USD-denominated debt instrument that has a notional that matches the hedged net investment and with a term that matches the targeted hedging horizon.
	Prospective test Due to the fact that the terms of the hedging instrument and those of the hypothetical non-derivative match, the hedge is expected to be highly effective.
	Retrospective test A retrospective test will be performed at each reporting date using the "ratio analysis method". The ratio will compare the cumulative change since hedge inception in the fair value of the hypothetical non-derivative with the cumulative change since hedge inception in the fair value of the hedging instrument. The hedge will be assumed to be highly effective on a retrospective basis if the ratio is between 80 % and 125 %.

Prospective Tests

A prospective test was performed at hedge inception and at each reporting date. Due to the fact that the terms of the hedging instrument and those of the hypothetical non-derivative matched, the hedge was expected to be highly effective prospectively.

Retrospective Tests

A retrospective test was performed at each reporting date and also at maturity of the hedging instrument. Because the terms of the hedging instrument and those of the hypothetical non-derivative matched, the hedge relationship was 100 % effective:

Date	Bond Fair Value (EUR) (Changes due Only to FX)	Cumulative Change in Bond Fair Value	Hypothetical Non-Derivative Fair Value (EUR)	Cumulative Change in Hypothetical Non-Der. Fair Value	Ratio
1-Jan-X0	400,000,000	—	400,000,000	-0-	—
31-Dec-X0	393,701,000	**6,299,000**	393,701,000	**6,299,000**	100 %
31-Dec-X1	381,679,000	**18,321,000**	381,679,000	**18,321,000**	100 %
31-Dec-X2	387,597,000	**12,403,000**	387,597,000	**12,403,000**	100 %

Other Relevant Information

The net investment translation into euros at each relevant date was:

Date	Spot USD/EUR	Net Investment (USD)	Net Investment (€)	Period Change in € Net Investment
1-Jan-X0	1.2500	500,000,000	400,000,000	—
31-Dec-X0	1.2700	500,000,000	393,701,000	<6,299,000>
31-Dec-X1	1.3100	500,000,000	381,679,000	<12,022,000>
31-Dec-X2	1.2900	500,000,000	387,597,000	5,918,000

The interest flows that ABC paid during the life of the bond were the following:

Date	Spot USD/EUR	USD Libor Rate	Interest Payments (in USD)	Equivalent EUR Amount
31 Dec 20X0	1.2700	5.20%	26,000,000 (1)	20,472,000 (2)
31 Dec 20X1	1.3100	5.20%	26,000,000	19,847,000
31 Dec 20X2	1.2900	5.20%	26,000,000	20,155,000

Notes:

(1): Interest payment = USD 500 million*5.20%
(2): Equivalent EUR amount = Interest payment / Spot = 26,000,000/1.27

Accounting Entries

As a result of applying net investment hedge accounting, the bond's carrying amount change due to the movement of the USD/EUR exchange rate was reported in the same manner as the translation adjustment associated with the net investment. In this case, as the functional currency of the subsidiary and the currency denomination of the debt matched, and as the notional amount of the debt did not exceeded the net investment hedged amount, no hedge ineffectiveness was recognised in P&L.

Assuming that ABC closed its books annually at year-end, the accounting entries related to the hedge were:

1) To record the bond issuance on 1 January 20X0

ABC proceeds from the USD bond were USD 500 million. Assuming that ABC immediately converted those USD into EUR at the then prevailing USD/EUR spot rate (1.2500), the EUR proceeds from the bond were EUR 400 million (= 500 million/1.25):

Cash (Asset)	€ 400,000,000
Financial debt (Liability)	€ 400,000,000

2) To record the closing of the accounting period on 31 December 20X0:

The net investment lost EUR 6,299,000 in value over the period when translated into EUR:

Translation differences (Equity)	€ 6,299,000
Net investment in subsidiary (Asset)	€ 6,299,000

The change in the bond's carrying amount due to the movement of the USD/EUR exchange rate was a gain of EUR 6,299,000. As the hedge had no ineffectiveness, all this change was also recorded in the translation differences account:

Financial debt (Liability)	€ 6,299,000	
Translation differences (Equity)		€ 6,299,000

Under the bond, ABC paid on 31 December 20X0 a USD interest equivalent to EUR 20,472,000:

Interest expense (P&L)	€ 20,472,000	
Interest payable (Liability)		€ 20,472,000

Interest payable (Liability)	€ 20,472,000	
Cash (Asset)		€ 20,472,000

3) To record the closing of the accounting period on 31 December 20X1:

The net investment lost EUR 12,022,000 in value over the period when translated into EUR:

Translation differences (Equity)	€ 12,022,000	
Net investment in subsidiary (Asset)		€ 12,022,000

The change in the bond's carrying amount due to the movement of the USD/EUR exchange rate was a gain of EUR 12,022,000. As the hedge had no ineffectiveness, all this change was also recorded in the translation differences account:

Financial debt (Liability)	€ 12,022,000	
Translation differences (Equity)		€ 12,022,000

Under the bond, ABC paid on 31 December 20X1 a USD interest equivalent to EUR 19,847,000:

Interest expense (P&L)	€ 19,847,000	
Interest payable (Liability)		€ 19,847,000

| Interest payable (Liability) | € 19,847,000 | |
| Cash (Asset) | | € 19,847,000 |

4) To record the closing of the accounting period on 31 December 20X2:

The net investment gained EUR 5,918,000 in value over the period when translated into EUR:

| Net investment in subsidiary (Asset) | € 5,918,000 | |
| Translation differences (Equity) | | € 5,918,000 |

The change in the bond's carrying amount due to the movement of the USD/EUR exchange rate was a loss of EUR 5,918,000. As the hedge had no ineffectiveness, all this change was also recorded in the translation differences account:

| Translation differences (Equity) | € 5,918,000 | |
| Financial debt (Liability) | | € 5,918,000 |

Under the bond, ABC paid on 31 December 20X2 a USD interest equivalent to EUR 20,155,000:

| Interest expense (P&L) | € 20,155,000 | |
| Interest payable (Liability) | | € 20,155,000 |

| Interest payable (Liability) | € 20,155,000 | |
| Cash (Asset) | | € 20,155,000 |

On 31 December 20X2, ABC had to repay the USD 500 million. Assuming that ABC exchanged a EUR amount for USD 500 million at the then prevailing USD/EUR spot rate (1.2900), the EUR amount was EUR 387,597,000 (= 500 million/1.29):

| Financial debt (Liability) | € 387,597,000 | |
| Cash (Asset) | | € 387,597,000 |

Final Remarks

In our case the hedge performed very well, as the decline in value of the net investment due to the depreciation of the USD relative to the EUR was completely offset by the change in the carrying value of the USD debt. However, two comments are worth noting:

- ABC's P&L statement was exposed to declines in the USD/EUR FX rate.
- At bond maturity, ABC had to repay the USD 500 million notional. ABC had to exchange in the FX spot market an amount of EUR equivalent to USD 500 million. As a result, a severe decline in the USD/EUR FX rate could have had strong implications to the entity's cash resources.

CASE 4.7

Integral Hedging of an Investment in a Foreign Operation

In our experience advising multinationals on how to hedge their exposure to foreign subsidiaries, we have found an evolution (see Figure 4.15)in their hedging strategies over the years. Usually entities start hedging the exposure stemming from the dividends they receive from the foreign subsidiary. After a few years hedging dividends, multinationals also address the exposure stemming from the translation of the subsidiary's income statement. Finally, after gaining experience hedging earnings and dividends, multinationals also decide to hedge their net investment exposure.

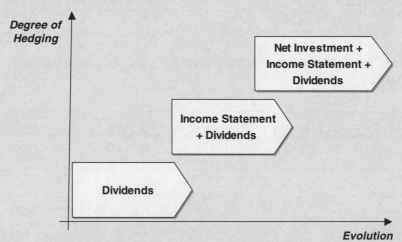

Figure 4.15   Foreign Subsidary Hedging – Common Evolution Pattern.

If an entity hedges these three risks separately – dividends, income statement and net investment – it could experience severe hedging inefficiencies as the three risks are interrelated. A special analysis is then needed when trying to hedge the combined risk. The key to the analysis is to understand how the net assets of the subsidiary change during the accounting year and at what exchange rates these changes show up in the year-end net assets.

The year-end net investment can be thought of four different components (see Figure 4.16):

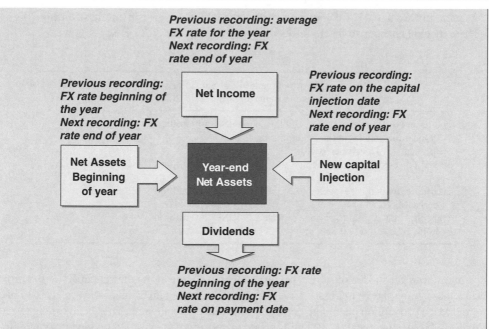

Figure 4.16   Foreign Subsidiary Hedging – Components.

1) The net assets at the beginning of the year. The previous revaluation of this component was performed using the exchange rate prevailing at the closing of the previous year. As this component has to be revalued at the year-end exchange rate, the translation risk is caused by the change in the exchange rate from the closing of the previous year to the closing rate of the current year.

2) The investment of new capital in the subsidiary. Adding new capital increases the net investment in the subsidiary. The capital injection is initially recorded at the FX rate prevailing at the moment of the injection. As this component has to be revalued at the year-end exchange rate, the translation risk is caused by the change in the exchange rate from the capital injection date to the closing rate of the current year.

3) The net income of the subsidiary. Positive earnings for the year increase the net investment in the subsidiary. Recall that the subsidiary's earnings are usually translated at the average exchange rate of the year. As this component has to be revalued at the year-end exchange rate, the translation risk is caused by the change in the exchange rate from the average exchange rate during the year to the closing rate of the current year.

4) Dividends paid by the subsidiary. Dividends decrease the net investment. On the consolidated statements, dividends effectively leave the net investment when they are paid. Once paid, dividends do not affect the net investment risk (they become part of the parent monetary assets). Thus, the translation risk is caused by the change in the exchange rate from the closing of the previous year to the exchange rate prevailing at dividend payment date.

Let us work on a specific example assuming that ABC, a group with a EUR functional currency, had a net investment in a US subsidiary that had the USD as its functional currency.

Assume further that ABC is looking to hedge the whole net investment flows during 20X1. The expected changes to the net investment during the year 20X1 are as follows:

Net Investment in US Subsidiary Expected Changes During Year 20X1	
Net assets (including goodwill and fair value adjustments) at the beginning of the year (31 December 20X0)	USD 500 million
Expected subsidiary's net income	USD 120 million (USD 10 million per month)
Expected dividends (expected to be paid on 31 May 20X1)	USD 100 million
Expected new capital injection (expected to be executed on 30 September 20X1)	USD 200 million

In order to get an idea of ABC's net investment exposure along the year 20X1, ABC produced the graph shown in Figure 4.17. During 20X1, the net investment was expected to increase USD 10 million per month due to the subsidiary's net income. The net investment was expected to decline by USD 100 million due to subsidiary's expected dividend payment to the parent company on 31 May 20X1. Finally, the net investment was expected to increase by USD 200 million as a result of the parent's expected capital injection on 30 September 20X1.

One way to perfectly hedge the profile shown in Figure 4.17 was to execute on 1 January 20X1 a series of FX forwards aimed to hedge the five building blocks shown in

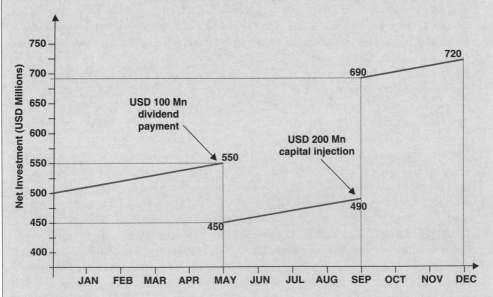

Figure 4.17   Net Investment Profile – Year 20X1.

	Net Assets at Year-end	720 Mn / (Year-end Rate)
Less	Net Assets at Beginning-Year	500 Mn / 1.25 ← *Beginning-of-year Rate*
Less	Translated Net income	120 Mn / Average Rate
Less	Capital Injection	200 Mn / Injection Date Rate
Plus	Dividend paid	100 Mn / Dividend Payment Date Rate
Equals	Exchange Differences	

Figure 4.18   Exchange Differences Calculation Year 20X1.

Figure 4.16: hedging the end-of-year net assets, hedging the subsidiary's expected net income, hedging the expected new capital to be invested in the subsidiary, and hedging the expected dividends paid by the subsidiary (see also Figure 4.18). There was no need to hedge the net assets at the beginning of the year, as its rate was already known (1.25).

Let us assume that the market USD/EUR forward FX rates, as of 1-January 20X1, for the relevant dates were as follows:

Date	Forward rate (as of 1-Jan-X1)
1 January 20X1	1.2500
31 May 20X1	1.2580
30 September 20X1	1.2650
31 December 20X1	1.2700
Average during 20X1	1.2600

Hedge 1: Hedging the End-of-Year Net Assets

The end-of-the-year net investment was USD 720 million, as shown in Figure 4.18. ABC entered into a standard FX forward ("forward-1") with a nominal of USD 720 million and maturity 31 December 20X1, to hedge the year-end revaluation of the USD 720 million. The forward rate for 31 December 20X1 was 1.2700. The forward payoff at maturity compensated ABC from any appreciation of the year-end rate:

Hedge 1: Forward-1 Payoff = USD 720 million * [1/1.2700 − 1/(Year-end rate)]

With this forward, ABC hedged the "Net assets at year-end" part of Figure 4.18 (first line of the formula).

Hedge 1

	Net Assets at Year-end	720 Mn / (Year-end Rate)
Less	Net Assets at Beginning-Year	500 Mn / 1.25
Less	Translated Net income	120 Mn / Average Rate
Less	Capital Injection	200 Mn / Injection Date Rate
Plus	Dividend paid	100 Mn / Dividend Payment Date Rate

Equals	Exchange Differences

Figure 4.18 Exchange Differences Calculation Year 20X1.

Hedge 2: Hedging the Subsidiary's Expected Net Income

The subsidary's expected net income was USD 120 million. This net income was to become part of the net investment at the average rate for 20X1 and was to be revalued at year-end. The revaluation at year-end was already included in hedge 1. Therefore, ABC needed to hedge the translation of the subsidiary's net income at the average rate for the year 20X1.This hedge covered the third line of Figure 4.18:

Hedge 2

	Net Assets at Year-end	720 Mn / (Year-end Rate)
Less	Net Assets at Beginning-Year	500 Mn / 1.25
Less	Translated Net income	120 Mn / Average Rate
Less	Capital Injection	200 Mn / Injection Date Rate
Plus	Dividend paid	100 Mn / Dividend Payment Date Rate

Equals	Exchange Differences

Figure 4.18 Exchange Differences Calculation Year 20X1.

As seen in Case 4.2, the appropriate hedging instrument was an average rate forward (forward-2).

The average rate forward had a USD 120 million nominal amount and 31 December 20X1 maturity. The market expected the average rate to be 1.26. Its payoff at maturity was:

> Hedge 2: Forward-2 Payoff = USD 120 million *[1/(Year average rate) − 1/1.2600]

Hedge 3: Hedging the Expected New Capital Injection into the Subsidiary

ABC's parent company expected to add USD 200 million capital into its US subsidiary. From a "net investment" perspective, ABC was exposed to the year-end appreciation of the USD/EUR rate relative to the rate prevailing on the capital investment date (30 September 20X1). The first part (the year-end revaluation) was already hedged through hedge-1. ABC needed then to hedge ("hedge 3") the exposure to rate prevailing on the capital investment date, which is equivalent to hedge the fourth line of Figure 4.18.

	Net Assets at Year-end	720 Mn / (Year-end Rate)
Less	Net Assets at Beginning-Year	500 Mn / 1.25
Less	Translated Net income	120 Mn / Average Rate
Less	Capital Injection	200 Mn / Injection Date Rate
Plus	Dividend paid	100 Mn / Dividend Payment Date Rate
Equals	Exchange Differences	

Hedge 3

Figure 4.18 Exchange Differences Calculation Year 20X1.

The appropriate instrument was a FX forward (forward-3) with a nominal of USD 200 million, maturity 30 September 20X1, and the following payoff at maturity:

Hedge 3: Forward-3 Payoff = USD 200 million * [1/(30-Sept-X1 rate) − 1/1.2650]

Hedging the Expected Dividends Paid by the Subsidiary

ABC's parent company expected to receive USD 100 million dividends from the US subsidiary on 31 May 20X1. As a result, ABC's parent company was exposed to an appreciation of the USD/EUR FX rate prevailing on the dividend payment date (31 May 20X1).

The appropriate hedge was a FX forward ("forward-4") with a nominal of USD 100 million and maturity 31 May 20X1. This forward payoff at maturity compensated ABC from any appreciation of the 31 May 20X1 rate:

Hedge 4: Forward-4 Payoff = USD 100 million *[1/1.2580 − 1/(31-May-X1 rate)]

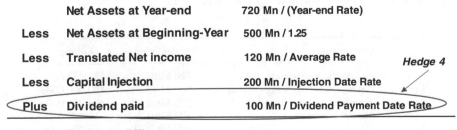

	Net Assets at Year-end	720 Mn / (Year-end Rate)
Less	Net Assets at Beginning-Year	500 Mn / 1.25
Less	Translated Net income	120 Mn / Average Rate
Less	Capital Injection	200 Mn / Injection Date Rate
Plus	Dividend paid	100 Mn / Dividend Payment Date Rate
Equals	Exchange Differences	

Hedge 4

Figure 4.18 Exchange Differences Calculation Year 20X1.

	Net Assets at Year-end	**720 Mn / 1.27 = EUR 566,929,000**
Less	**Net Assets at Beginning-Year**	**500 Mn / 1.25 = EUR 400,000,000**
Less`	**Translated Net income**	**120 Mn / 1.26 = EUR 95,238,000**
Less	**Capital Injection**	**200 Mn / 1.265 = EUR 158,103,000**
Plus	**Dividend paid**	**100 Mn / 1.258 = EUR 79,491,000**
Equals	**Exchange Differences**	**EUR –6,921,000**

Figure 4.19   Exchange Difference Caluclation with Integral Hedge Year 20X1.

Expected Translation Differences Adjustment for the Year 20X1

As a result of these four hedges, ABC expected to recognise a translation differences deficit of EUR 6,921,000, as shown in Figure 4.19.

Analysis of the Hedge Performance

Let us see if the integral hedge worked well in practise. Let us assume that the market USD/EUR FX rates during 20X1 were as follows:

Date	Spot USD/EUR Rate
1 January 20X1	1.2500
31 May 20X1	1.3000
30 September 20X1	1.2000
31 December 20X1	1.3500
Average during 20X1	1.2800

The following table shows the translation exchange differences for the year 20X1, without taking into account the hedge. If ABC did not have the hedge in place, the translation differences account would have included a deficit of EUR 50,161,000.

	Component	Calculation	Amount
	Net assets at year-end	720 Mn/1.35	533,333,000
Less	Net assets at beginning-of-year	500 Mn/1.25	<400,000,000>
Less	Translated net income	120 Mn/1.28	<93,750,000>
Less	Capital injection	200 Mn/1.20	<166,667,000>
Plus	Dividend	100 Mn/1.30	76,923,000
Equals	**Translation exchange differences**		**<50,161,000>**

Fortunately, ABC had a hedge in place. The hedge was implemented through four instruments, each designed to eliminate the exposure to the USD/EUR rate of each component. The following table details the payoffs of each instrument:

	Payoff Calculation	EUR Amount
Hedge 1:	720 Mn * (1/1.27 − 1/1.35)	33,596,000
Hedge 2:	120 Mn * (1/1.28 − 1/1.26)	<1,488,000>
Hedge 3:	200 Mn * (1/1.20 − 1/1.265)	8,564,000
Hedge 4:	100 Mn * (1/1.258 − 1/1.30)	2,568,000
	Total hedge payoff	**43,240,000**

Through the integral hedge, ABC received EUR 43,240,000. Therefore, the translation differences account showed "only" an adjustment of a EUR 6,921,000 deficit (see following table). The hedge worked very well, as this amount was exactly the amount ABC expected (see Figure 4.19).

	EUR Amount
Translation differences adjustment without hedge	<50,161,000>
Hedge payoff	43,240,000
Total translation differences adjustment	**<6,921,000>**

Additional Remarks

A couple of particular issues are worth noting:

- Firstly, hedge 2 was aimed to eliminate the exposure of the translation differences account from a depreciation of the 20X1 USD/EUR average rate. This hedge was exactly the opposite to the net income translation hedge that was discussed in Case 4.2. Therefore, both hedges cancel out so there is no need to implement both hedges simultaneously in the market.
- Secondly, hedge 4 was aimed to eliminate the exposure of the translation differences account from an appreciation of the 31 May 20X1 USD/EUR rate. This hedge was exactly the same as the dividend hedge that was discussed in Case 4.1. Therefore, if ABC implemented the net investment integral hedge, there is no need to implement the dividend hedge mentioned in Case 4.1.

5
Hedging Interest Rate Risk

This chapter focuses on one of the most common financial risks that an entity may hedge: interest rate risk. Interest rate risk arises from entities holding interest-bearing financial assets and/or liabilities, or from forecasted or committed future transactions embodying an interest-bearing element. An entity's ability to manage interest rate exposure can enhance financial exposure, mitigate losses, and reduce funding costs.

The most common interest rate exposures are due to the following situations:

1) An already recognised financial liability (or asset) pays a fixed interest. In this case, the interest rate risk relates to the fair value change of the financial liability (or asset) due to movements in interest rates; or
2) An already recognised financial liability (or asset) pays a floating interest (i.e., future interest payments are linked to a benchmark interest index). In this case, the interest rate risk relates to variations in future cash flows; or
3) Highly probable anticipated future issuance of an interest bearing financial liability (or asset). In this case, the interest rate risk relates to variations in future cash flows.

The objective of this chapter is not to identify the appropriate hedging strategy to mitigate exposure to changes in interest rates. Instead, the objective of this chapter is to provide a practical insight on the accounting implications of a chosen interest rate hedging strategy. In order to emphasise the practical angle of interest rate hedge accounting, several cases are analysed in detail based on our experience.

5.1 COMMON INTEREST RATE HEDGING STRATEGIES

We have summarised the most common hedging strategies used by corporations in the following table:

Hedged Item	Risk	Type of Hedge	Usual Hedging Strategy
Existing fixed-rate debt	Exposure to variability in fair value	Fair value hedge of a recognised liability (or asset)	1) Convert the interest paid (or received) to floating by entering into an interest rate swap. 2) If an asset, lock in a minimum value by buying a put option to sell the asset at a specified price (or buying a payer swaption). 3) If a liability, lock-in a maximum value by buying a call option to repurchase it at a specified price (or buying a receiver swaption).

(Continued)

Hedged Item	Risk	Type of Hedge	Usual Hedging Strategy
Highly expected issuance, or firm commitment to issue, fixed-rate debt	Exposure to variability in interest rate payments due to changes in interest rates to date of issuance	Cash flow hedge of a highly expected issue or of firm commitment	1) Lock-in the future interest to be paid by entering into an pay-fixed receive-floating interest rate swap. 2) Limit the future interest to be paid by buying a cap or by entering into a collar. 3) Participate in declines of interest rates by buying a payer swaption. 4) Participate in declines of interest rates by buying a put option on a bond.
Existing floating-rate debt	Exposure to variability in interest rate payments (or receipts)	Cash flow hedge of a recognised liability (or asset)	1) Convert the interest paid (or received) to fixed by entering into an interest rate swap. 2) Limit the maximum interest paid (or received) by buying a cap (or floor).
Highly expected issuance, or firm commitment to issue, floating-rate debt	Exposure to variability in interest rate payments due to changes in interest rates to date of payment	Cash flow hedge of a highly expected issue or of firm commitment	1) Lock-in the future interest to be paid by entering into an pay-fixed receive-floating interest rate swap. 2) Limit the future interest to be paid by buying a cap or by entering into a collar. 3) Participate in declines of interest rates by buying a payer swaption. Participate in declines of interest rates by buying a put option on a bond.

5.2   SEPARATION OF EMBEDDED DERIVATIVES IN STRUCTURED BONDS

In the fixed income market it is not unusual to find bonds that pay interest that differs considerably from the interest that otherwise would be paid by the issuer, or received by the investor, on a standard bond. A better than market yield is usually achieved by including a derivative in the bond. IAS 39 does not require the separation of the embedded derivative from the rest of the bond (the "host contract") if:

1) the combined instrument is already measured at fair value through P&L; or
2) the economic characteristics and risks of the embedded derivative are clearly and closely related to those of the host contract.

The embedded derivative is assumed to be closely related to the host contract if it satisfies the following three requirements:

1) The embedded derivative could not potentially result in the investor failing to recover substantially all of its initially recorded investment; and

2) The embedded derivative could potentially result in the issuer having to pay a leveraged rate of return. Usually if the debt cannot pay more than twice the market rate, it is assumed that the derivative is not leveraging the interest payments; and

3) The embedded derivative does not extend the maturity date of fixed rate debt, except when interest rates are reset to market rates.

The following are examples of structured bonds and whether or not, in our view, is required the separation of the embedded derivative. They assume that the yield of an equivalent fixed rate bond would be 6 %. The structured bonds that we have chosen are the following:

- An inverse floater. It is a bond that pays a coupon that varies inversely with changes in the interest rate.
- A CMS bond. It is a bond that pays a coupon that is a percentage of a medium-term or long-term interest rate.
- A range floater. It is a bond that pays a coupon that depends on the number of days that an underlying reference interest rate stays within a pre-established range.
- A ratchet floater. It is a bond that pays a floating interest rate whose increase or decrease each period is limited relative to the previous coupon.
- A callable bond. It is a bond that pays an initial above market interest rate and that can be cancelled by the issuer on a specific date (or dates).
- An inflation-linked bond. It is a bond that pays a fixed interest on a principal amount that is indexed to the inflation rate.

Coupon	Investor May not Recover Initial Investment?	Issuer May Pay More Than Twice the the Market Rate?	Option to Extend Fixed Rate Debt at Non-market Rates?	Need to Separate Embedded Derivative?
Inverse floater: 10 % – Euribor12M, with a minimum of 0 %	No	No	No	No
Inverse floater: 14 % – 2*Euribor12M, with a minimum of 2 %	No	Yes	No	Yes
Inverse floater: 10 % – 2*Euribor12M, without a minimum	Yes	No	No	Yes
CMS: 75 % * (10-year swap rate) + 1 %	No	No	No	No
CMS: 200 % * (10-year swap rate)	No	Yes	No	Yes
Range accrual: 6 % * (Number days within range)/(Total days in period) Range is 3 %–4 %	No	No	No	No

(*Continued*)

Coupon	Investor May not Recover Initial Investment?	Issuer May Pay More Than Twice the Market Rate?	Option to Extend Fixed Rate Debt at Non-market Rates?	Need to Separate Embedded Derivative?
Ratchet floater: Euribor12M + 60 bps Coupon cannot increase more than 35 bps relative to previous coupon	No	No	No	No
Callable bond: 6 % annually. Bond can be cancelled after year-3	No	No	Yes	Yes
Inflation-linked bond: 4 % on principal. Principal is adjusted to inflation	No	No	No	Unclear. Most auditors consider separation is required

5.3   DISCOUNTING DEBT

An important question that arises when discounting cash flows, is what yield to use to compute the discount factors. We have seen discussions that vary from using the risk free yield curve (i.e., the curve implied by liquid debt issued by AAA governments), to using the company yield curve (i.e., the curve implied by the company bonds). Our suggestion is to use the curve that best estimates the fair value of the instrument being valued for the risk being hedged.

In order to discuss the relevant yield curve to be used, we have provided two examples of an investor hedging a bond. In one example the investor hedges the bond for all its risks, and in the other example the investor hedges the bond only for interest rate risk.

5.3.1   Hedging a Debt Instrument in Its Entirety

When pricing a specific debt instrument, the financial markets take into account the curve implied by the debt of the issuer, or by the debt of issuers with similar credit risk. The yield curve of a specific issuer trades at a spread over the benchmark interest rate curve (in the case of EUR bonds, the benchmark curve is the Euribor deposits and the Euribor swaps curve). The spread recognises the credit risk of the investment, and it is not constant for a specific issuer, usually the longer the maturity of the bond the larger the spread.

Let us assume that an investor buys a five-year bond issued by company ABC. The bonds are trading at Euribor plus 60 basis points (bps). The 60 bps spread is pricing the credit risk of ABC relative to comparable AA-rated debt (assuming the AA issuers are able to fund themselves at Euribor flat). In order to hedge the whole fair value of the bond, the investor enters into two instruments:

1) An interest rate swap: a 5-year swap rate in which the investor pays 4.34 % and receives Euribor 12-month. This instrument hedges the interest rate risk of the bond.

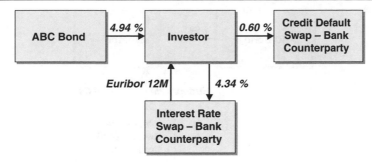

Figure 5.1   Hedging a Bond Invesment in Its Entirety.

2) A credit default swap (CDS): a 5-year CDS in which the investor pays 0.60 % annually for the protection. This instrument hedges the credit risk of the bond.

Figure 5.1 shows the periodic cash flows from the investor point of view. As a result, the whole strategy yields Euribor 12-month flat (i.e., without any credit spread). The investor is not exposed to changes in fair value of the bond due to interest rate and credit risk.

The price of a 5-year ABC bond with an annual coupon of 4.94 % should be trading at par. The following table shows how the price of a 5-year, EUR 100 million nominal, 4.94 % annual coupon issued by ABC, discounting the cash flows using the Euribor + 60 bps curve, is exactly par (EUR 100 million).

	Cash flow	Discount Factor (using Euribor + 60 bps)	Present Value of Cash Flow
Year-1	4,940,000	0.9588	4,736,000
Year-2	4,940,000	0.9140	4,515,000
Year-3	4,940,000	0.8698	4,297,000
Year-4	4,940,000	0.8269	4,085,000
Year-5	104,940,000	0.7849	82,367,000
		Total	**100,000,000**

If instead, the previous cash flows are discounted using the Euribor flat (i.e., without spread) curve, the value of the bond is very different to its market value, as shown in the following table:

	Cash flow	Discount Factor (using Euribor)	Present Value of Cash Flow
Year-1	4,940,000	0.9643	4,764,000
Year-2	4,940,000	0.9246	4,568,000
Year-3	4,940,000	0.8849	4,371,000
Year-4	4,940,000	0.8469	4,184,000
Year-5	104,940,000	0.8078	84,711,000
		Total	**102,598,000**

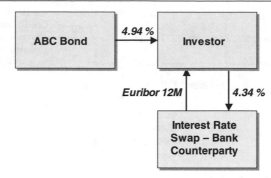

Figure 5.2   Bond Investment Hedging only Interest Rate Risk.

It can be inferred from the previous calculations that, when hedging the fair value of a whole bond, the more meaningful way to compute the fair value of a bond is to discount the bond cash flows including the credit spread of the issuer.

5.3.2   Hedging Only the Euribor Part of the Debt Instrument

A more common strategy is to hedge only the Euribor part of a debt instrument (see Figure 5.2). In this example, the investor would assume the credit risk and would only hedge the interest rate risk of the bond. In order to achieve this objective, the investor enters into a 5-year swap paying 4.34 % and receiving Euribor 12-month. Accordingly, when defining the hedge relationship, the investor would state that the credit spread (60 bps) is excluded from the hedge relationship.

The initial fair value of the hedged part of the bond is calculated by discounting the cash flows using the Euribor flat (i.e., without spread) curve, as shown in the following table:

	Cash Flow	Discount Factor (using Euribor)	Present Value of Cash Flow
Year-1	4,340,000	0.9643	4,185,000
Year-2	4,340,000	0.9246	4,013,000
Year-3	4,340,000	0.8849	3,840,000
Year-4	4,340,000	0.8469	3,676,000
Year-5	104,340,000	0.8078	84,286,000
		Total	**100,000,000**

Therefore, when the risk being hedged excludes the credit spread it makes sense to discount the cash flows at the Euribor flat yield curve. This guideline is especially relevant when assessing hedge effectiveness. If the hedged item cash flows were discounted using the Euribor plus 60 bps yield curve and the hedging instrument cash flows were discounted using the Euribor flat yield curve, their sensitivity to interest rate changes could be quite different, potentially jeopardising the hedge qualification for hedge accounting.

As we will see in some of the cases provided, it is very useful to replace the hedged item for a hypothetical derivative when assessing hedge effectiveness. This way, it is often possible to use the critical terms method for prospective assessment. It also simplifies the discounting problems we have just discussed, as the calculation of the hedged item fair value changes, are computed based on the hypothetical derivative fair value changes.

5.4 DISCOUNTING DERIVATIVES

Similarly, the cash flows of a derivative have to be discounted using the yield curve that best approximates the fair value of the derivative, for the risk being hedged. In theory, when entering into a derivative with a bank, the entity would be quoted a price that takes into account the credit risk of the entity and the bank. Accordingly, in theory ABC's derivative cash flows should be discounted at the equivalent Euribor plus spread of ABC's debt with the same term as the swap, and the bank's derivative cash flows should be discounted at the equivalent Euribor plus spread of the bank's debt with the same term as the swap.

In reality, unless ABC's credit is perceived to be very risky, most derivatives would be priced using the Euribor curve flat. The Euribor curve implies the risk for transactions among banks (or approximately AA-rated entities). In other words, swaps and deposit rates transacted between most banks are priced using the Euribor curve (unless the bank credit is perceived to be very weak). Because the activity of banks with corporations (i.e., non financial institutions) is very competitive for vanilla products, corporations are able to enter into transactions priced without taking into account their credit spreads. Therefore, in calculating most derivatives we will be using the Euribor curve flat (i.e., without any spread). This approach is usually valid unless the entity's credit risk is so weak that financial institutions take it into account when entering into derivatives with this risky entity.

5.5 INTEREST ACCRUALS

When computing the fair values of the hedging instrument and its related debt, the accruals on each instrument have to be excluded from the computation. This exclusion is especially relevant if the swap and the debt interest periods differ. Failure to exclude the accruals may affect the effectiveness of the hedge and may create important distortions in the P&L statement. Case 5.3 of this chapter illustrates the effects of not excluding the accruals from the calculations.

The formulae to compute the appropriate fair value of a swap, assuming that under the swap the entity pays floating rate and receives the fixed rate, are the following

$$\text{Fair value (excluding accruals)} = \text{Fair value of swap (including accruals)} - \text{Fixed-leg accrual} + \text{Floating-leg accrual}$$

$$\text{Fixed-leg accrual} = \text{Next fixed interest amount} \times \frac{\text{Days since last payment date}}{\text{Number of days in current interest period}}$$

$$\text{Floating-leg accrual} = \text{Next floating interest amount} \times \frac{\text{Days since last payment date}}{\text{Number of days in current interest period}}$$

5.6 THE FIXED-BACK-TO-FIXED HEDGING PROBLEM

For efficient funding, entities issue debt in the markets that provide the lowest cost of funding at the time. Often as institutional investors demand fixed rate assets, an entity issues a fixed-rate bond and simultaneously swaps it into floating through a pay-fixed receive-floating interest rate swap. Later, because the entity manages its exposure to interest rate risk through the proportion of fixed and floating rate debt in its total debt portfolio, the entity may enter into an additional pay-floating receive-fixed interest rate swap.

Although this strategy is equivalent from an economic perspective to the IAS 39 friendly cash flow hedge of floating rate debt with a pay-fixed receive-floating interest rate swap, the entity cannot apply IAS 39 hedge accounting for the strategy. The reason behind this problem is that the IAS 39 standard does not allow a derivative to become a hedge item in a hedging relationship. As a consequence, the change in fair value of the pay-floating receive-fixed interest rate swap would be recorded in P&L.

5.7 INTEREST RATE RISK MACROHEDGING

Organisations, especially financial institutions, often manage their interest rate risk positions on a portfolio basis. IAS 39 allows the fair value hedge of the interest rate exposure of a portfolio of financial assets and/or financial liabilities by designating the hedged item in terms of an amount of assets or liabilities in a maturity time period, rather than as individual assets or liabilities. The approach allowed by IAS 39 is as follows:

1) The entity identifies the portfolio of interest-earning assets and/or interest-bearing liabilities whose interest rate risk it wishes to hedge. The selected assets and/or liabilities need to have qualified for fair value hedge accounting under IAS 39 had they been hedged individually.
2) The entity allocates the portfolio into maturity time periods based on expected, rather than contractual, repricing dates (i.e., the date on which the item will be repaid or repriced to market rates). The time periods must be sufficiently narrow to ensure that all assets (or liabilities) in a time period are homogeneous with respect to the hedged risk (i.e., the fair value of each item moves proportionately to changes in the hedged interest rate risk).
3) Based on the previous analysis, the entity then designates:
    a) the hedged item as an amount of assets (or liabilities) from the identified portfolio, in each time period, equal to the amount it wishes to designate as being hedged. For example, if in a time period there are assets of EUR 600 million and liabilities of EUR 500 million, the entity would designate an amount of EUR 100 million as the hedged item. All of the assets from which the hedged amount is drawn must be items (a) whose fair value changes in response to the risk being hedged and (b);
    b) the hedged interest rate risk. This risk could be a portion of the interest rate risk in each of the items in the portfolio, such as a benchmark interest rate like Euribor;
    c) the hedging instrument (or portfolio of instruments) for each time period.
4) The entity measures the change in the fair value of the hedged item that is attributable to the hedged risk and recognises it as a gain or loss in P&L. The result is also recognised as a separate asset or liability in the balance sheet. This separate balance sheet line item is presented on the face of the balance sheet adjacent to the related asset(s) or liability(ies).

5) The entity measures the change in the fair value of the hedging instrument(s) and recognises it as a gain or loss in P&L. It recognises the fair value of the hedging instrument(s) as an asset or liability in the balance sheet.

5.7.1 Demand Deposits

Demand deposits and similar items with a demand feature (such as a bank's current accounts and savings accounts) cannot be designated as the hedged item in a fair value hedge for any period beyond the shortest period in which the counterparty can demand repayment. Thus deposits payable immediately on demand are ineligible for hedge accounting. This is because of IFRS' concern that permitting maturity based on a time period beyond the shortest period in which the counterparty can demand payment would result in a fair value gain on initial recognition as a result of the liability being less than the amount repayable on demand.

As a consequence, a bank with a large demand deposit base is not be able to use fair value hedge accounting for a relevant part of their liabilities. If the bank wants to hedge its demand deposits, it is obliged to adopt cash flow hedging for their demand deposits and thus assume the volatility in equity that it entails.

5.7.2 Asset and Liability Management

Most asset and liability management practices try to reduce the interest rate risk derived from a net portfolio of assets and liabilities. However, under the current version of IAS 39 it is not possible to designate the hedged amount against the net of the assets and the liabilities. A potential improvement of IAS 39 would be to allow the net of the portfolio of assets and liabilities to be the hedged item instead of an amount of the asset or of the liability equal to the net amount. In order to be consistent with other IAS 39 requirements, the group of assets and liabilities being netted will have to have sufficiently similar characteristics such that taken individually they would have met the effectiveness tests to qualify for hedge accounting.

5.8   INFLATION-LINKED BONDS AND SWAPS

An inflation-linked bond (ILB) is an instrument with a principal amount that is indexed to the inflation rate. The coupon rate is fixed and is typically below that of standard fixed-rate bonds.

Inflation-linked swaps allow entities to swap inflation-linked cash flows for fixed cash flows and vice versa. Inflation-linked swaps are usually traded to hedge future inflation-linked revenue swaps or to pre-hedge future ILB issuances.

Currently there is little guidance on the following two topics:

• Whether an entity is permitted to designate inflation risk as the risk being hedged for the purposes of applying IAS 39 hedge accounting.
• Whether the inflation component of an inflation-linked bond should be separated and fair valued.

The US Gaap FAS 133 provides specific guidance on the accounting for inflation-linked debt instruments. It states that the separation of the inflation component from the rest of the bond in non-leveraged ILBs is not required as:

1) it is unlikely that the investor will not recover substantially all of its original investment (it would require a negative inflation over the whole life of the bond); and

2) the interest payments are not leveraged; and
3) the inflation rates are closely related to interest rates.

The ILBs Inconsistency Under US Gaap

Let's assume that a US company is contemplating raising inflation-linked debt. It can either borrow via an ILB or via a fixed rate bond plus an inflation-linked swap (ILS). Both strategies give the same economic effect. However under US Gaap rules, the ILB would not get marked-to-market, whereas the ILS gets marked-to-market.

One solution is to regard the ILS as a natural hedge of a part of the company's revenues that is by its nature very highly correlated to moves in the inflation index. However, the ILS is usually long-dated and often the linkage of the underlying revenues cannot be demonstrated over a long period.

Other potential solution is to assume that the fixed rate on the fixed rate bond is made up of a real rate of interest plus an indexation element, and hence the ILS can be designated as a fair value hedge of the indexation component of the bond. However, this solution is difficult to justify.

5.9 REPOS

Securities sold under agreements to repurchase (repurchase agreements) or securities purchased under agreements to resell (reverse repurchase agreements) are not recognised on or derecognised from the balance sheet, unless the risks and rewards of ownership are obtained or relinquished. Therefore, most repurchase and reverse repurchase agreements represent collateralised financing transactions used to earn net interest income, increase liquidity or facilitate trading activity.

In repurchase agreements, the cash received, including accrued interest, is recognised on the balance sheet with a corresponding obligation to return it. In reverse repurchase agreements, the cash delivered is derecognised and a corresponding receivable, including accrued interest, is recorded, recognising the entity's right to receive it back.

In repurchase agreements where the entity transfers owned securities and where the recipient is granted the right to resell or re-pledge them, the securities are reclassified in the balance sheet to "assets pledged as collateral". Securities received in a reverse repurchase agreement are disclosed as off-balance sheet items if the entity has the right to resell or re-pledge them, with securities that the entity has actually resold or re-pledged also disclosed separately.

Interest earned on reverse repurchase agreements and interest incurred on repurchase agreements is recognised as interest income or interest expense over the life of each agreement.

5.10 STEP-UP/STEP-DOWN PROVISIONS

Sometimes bonds contain step-up provisions whereby the interest rates are increased or decreased when the issuer credit rating is upgraded above or downgraded below certain levels. Under IFRS, when the issuer changes its estimated interest payments as a result of a step-up or step-down in interest rates, the issuer adjusts the carrying value of the debt to reflect the impact of the revised cash flows. The adjustment is recognised as income or expense in P&L.

5.11 SUMMARY OF MOST POPULAR HEDGING DERIVATIVES – INTEREST RATE RISK

Hedging Instrument	Comments
Interest rate swap	Most friendly interest rate instrument to qualify for hedge accounting. Substitution of liability for hypothetical swap is highly recommended. For fair value hedges, exclusion of liability credit spread, often useful to minimise retrospective test failure. Exclude interest accruals when assessing effectiveness and computing fair value changes.
Purchased options (caps or floors)	Treated quite unfavourably by IAS 39. Hedge accounting only includes intrinsic value changes. Time value changes are taken to P&L (can be significant for long-dated caps/floors). Hedge effectiveness assessed using hypothetical derivative. Hypothetical derivative is a cap (or floor).
Collar	Written option subject to stringent conditions to qualify for hedge accounting. Better IAS 39 treatment than stand-alone options. Although time value changes are also taken to P&L, in some rate intervals there may be a big offset between both time value changes. Hedge effectiveness assessed using hypothetical derivative. Hypothetical derivative is a collar.
Swap in-arrears	Effectiveness testing uses a hypothetical derivative. Hypothetical derivative is a standard (vanilla) swap. Significant risk of highly effective test failure in the final periods, if curve remains notably steep.
KIKO Collar	Split into two components: a hedge accounting compliant derivative and a residual derivative. Compliant derivative is a collar. Potential P&L volatility due to residual derivative, specially close to the barriers.
Inflation swaps	Uncertainty regarding whether or not inflation risk can be designated as the hedged risk in a hedge accounting relationship. Uncertainty also regarding whether an embedded inflation derivative in a inflation-linked bond needs to be bifurcated.

CASE 5.1

Hedging a Floating-Rate Liability Using an Interest Rate Swap

This case covers the hedge with an interest rate swap (also called a "IRS" or just a "swap") of the variability in interest payments pertaining to a floating rate debt due to changes in interest rates. When hedging interest rate risk, swaps are the friendliest instruments from an IAS 39 perspective. A particular point addressed in this case is the application of the "critical terms method" to assess effectiveness.

Background Information

On 31 December 20X0, Company ABC issued at par a floating rate bond with the following characteristics:

Bond Terms	
Issue date	31 December 20X0
Maturity	5 years (31 December 20X5)
Notional	€ 100 million
Coupon	Euribor 12m + 1.50 %, annually
Euribor fixing	Euribor is fixed at the beginning of the annual interest period

ABC wanted to hedge against increases in the coupon payments of the bond by locking in the coupon payment at 5.36 % (including the 150 basis points spread). Therefore simultaneously with the issuance of the bond, ABC entered into an interest rate swap (IRS) with the following terms:

Interest Rate Swap Terms	
Start date	31 December 20X0
Counterparties	Company ABC and XYZ Bank
Maturity	5 years (31 December 20X5)
Notional	€ 100 million
ABC pays	3.86 % annually, Actual/360 basis
ABC receives	Euribor 12m, annually, Actual/360 basis
	Euribor is fixed at the beginning of the annual interest period

The IRS was designated as the hedging instrument in a cash flow hedge of the coupon payments on the bond. The credit spread associated with the bond (150 basis points) was not included in the hedging relationship.

Hedging Relationship Documentation

The hedging relationship was documented as follows:

Hedging Relationship Documentation	
Risk management objective and strategy for undertaking the hedge	The objective of the hedge is to fix to 3.86 % the cash outflows related to Euribor 12M of one ABC's bonds. The combination of the swap and the bond will result in a expected net cash outflow equal to 5.36 %.
	This hedging objective is consistent with ABC's overall risk management strategy of managing the exposure to interest rate risk through the proportion of fixed and floating rate net debt in its total debt portfolio.

Type of hedge	Cash flow hedge.
Risk being hedged	Interest rate risk. The variability in the bond cash outflows attributable to changes in the Euribor 12 month rates.
Hedging instrument	The interest rate swap with reference number 012345. The counterparty to the swap is XYZ Bank and the credit risk associated with this counterparty is considered to be very low.
Hedged item	The cash flows of the 5-year floating bond with reference number 678901 that are linked to Euribor 12 month. The fixed spread on the bond (150 basis points) is not part of the hedged cash flows.
Assessment of effectiveness testing	Hedge effectiveness will be assessed by comparing changes in the fair value of the hedging instrument to changes in the fair value of a hypothetical derivative.
	The terms of the hypothetical derivative are such that its fair value changes offset exactly the changes in fair value of the hedged item for the risk being hedged. The hypothetical derivative terms in this hedging relationship are identical to the hedging instrument terms but assuming no counterparty credit exposure.

Prospective test

A prospective test will be performed at inception and at each reporting date using the critical terms method.

Because (i) the critical terms of the hypothetical derivative and the hedging instrument match (i.e., notional amount, currency, underlying and interest periods), and (ii) the credit risk of the counterparty to the hedging instrument is very low, the hedge will be considered to be highly effective prospectively.

The credit risk of the counterparty to the hedging instrument will be monitored continuously.

Retrospective test

A retrospective test will be performed at each reporting date using the "ratio analysis method". The ratio will compare the change since the last assessment in the fair value of the hedging instrument with the change since the last assessment in the fair value of the hypothetical derivative. The hedge will be assumed to be highly effective on a retrospective basis if the ratio is between 80 % and 125 %.

Bond and Swap Valuations

The fair value of the swap was calculated as the present value of all the future floating-rate receipts less the present value of all the future fixed-rate payments, as follows:

1) The different interest periods for the floating leg and for the fixed leg were determined.
2) The expected floating rate for each interest period was determined. The floating rate of a specific interest period was determined as the implied Euribor 12-month rate expected on the day that was two business days prior to the commencement of the interest period.

3) The fixed amount and the floating amounts for each interest period were computed. The fixed amount was calculated as (i)*(ii)*(iii). Where, (i) was the notional, (ii) was the fixed rate and (iii) was the day count fraction. The floating amount was calculated similarly but taking the floating rate of the interest period instead of the fixed rate.
4) Each of the individual fixed and floating amounts was discounted at the corresponding rate along the yield curve.

As an example, the calculation of the fair value of the swap on 31 December 20X1 is illustrated in the following table:

Cash Flow Date	Notional (in Euros)	Euribor Fixing Date	Implied Euribor 12M Rate	Fixed Rate	Swap Expected Amount	Discount Factor	Present Value
		Swap Fair Value on 31 December 20X1					
31-Dec X2	100 million	29-Dec-X1	4.21 %	3.86 %	350,000	0.9588	336,000
31 Dec X3	100 million	29-Dec-X2	4.80 %	3.86 %	940,000	0.9145	860,000
31 Dec X4	100 million	29-Dec-X3	5.00 %	3.86 %	1,140,000	0.8704	992,000
31 Dec X5	100 million	29-Dec-X4	5.12 %	3.86 %	1,260,000	0.8274	1,043,000
					Swap Fair Value		**3,231,000**

Notes:

The Euribor rate was fixed two business days prior to the commencement of the interest period.

The implied Euribor 12M rate was the Euribor 12 month rate expected on each Euribor fixing date, as of 31 December 20X1.

The swap expected amount to be received (or paid) by ABC was calculated as:

Notional * (Euribor12M * Floating Day Factor-Fixed Rate * Fixed Day Factor)

As the basis in the floating leg was Actual/360, the floating day factor was equal to (Number of days in interest period)/360. To keep calculations simple, it was assumed that both the floating day factor and the fixed day factor were equal to one.

The bond interest payments and swap fair values on each relevant date were as follows:

Balance Sheet Date	Period Euribor 12M	Bond Interest (in Euros)	Swap Fixed Rate	Swap Settlement Amount	Swap Fair Value	Change in Swap Fair Value
		Bond Interest Payment and Swap Fair Value on Each Reporting Date				
31-Dec-X0	—	—	—		–0–	—
31-Dec-X1	3.21 %	<4,710,000>	3.86 %	<650,000>	3,231,000	3,231,000
31-Dec-X2	4.21 %	<5,710,000>	3.86 %	350,000	850,000	<2,381,000>
31-Dec-X3	3.71 %	<5,210,000>	3.86 %	<150,000>	276,000	<574,000>
31-Dec-X4	3.80 %	<5,300,000>	3.86 %	<60,000>	<87,000>	<363,000>
31-Dec-X5	3.95 %	<5,450,000>	3.86 %	90,000	–0–	87,000

The bond interest was calculated as:

Notional * [(Euribor12M + 1,50 %) * Floating Day Factor]

As the basis of the bond interest was Actual/360, the floating day factor was equal to (Number of days in interest period)/360. To keep calculations simple the floating day factor was assumed to be equal to one.

The swap settlement amount was calculated as:

Notional * (Euribor12 M * Floating Day Factor − Fixed Rate * Fixed Day Factor)

As the basis in the floating leg was Actual/360, the floating day factor was equal to (Number of days in interest period)/360. To keep calculations simple, the floating day factor and the fixed day factor were assumed to be equal to one.

Hedge Effectiveness Testing – Prospective Tests

The objective of the prospective tests was to demonstrate that ABC had a valid expectation that the hedge will be highly effective. ABC performed a prospective test at hedge inception (31 December 20X0) and at each reporting date. ABC used the critical terms method to assess prospective assessment. The hedged item was substituted by a hypothetical derivative. The terms of the hypothetical derivative were such that the changes in fair value of the hypothetical derivative perfectly offset the changes in fair value of the hedged item for variations in the risk being hedged. In this case, the terms of the hypothetical derivative identically matched those of the hedging instrument (i.e., the swap), but without any credit risk exposure to the counterparty of the derivative. Because (i) the critical terms of hedging instrument matched those of the hypothetical derivative identically and (ii) the credit risk associated with the counterparty to the hedging instrument was considered to be very low, ABC concluded that the hedge was highly effective prospectively.

Hedge Effectiveness Testing – Retrospective Tests

ABC performed a retrospective test at each reporting date and at maturity of the hedging relationship. The retrospective test was expected to be highly effective as the changes in fair value of the hypothetical derivative were identical to the changes in fair value of the hedging instrument. However, ineffectiveness may have arisen if there was a substantial deterioration in the creditworthiness of the swap counterparty or if there was a substantial change in the liquidity of the swap. ABC performed each retrospective test using the ratio analysis method:

$$\text{Effectiveness Ratio} = \frac{\text{Change in fair value of hedging instrument}}{\text{Change in fair value of hypothetical derivative}}$$

In our case the creditworthiness of the swap counterparty (i.e., XYZ Bank) did not experienced a substantial deterioration during any of the retrospective assessment periods, so the result of the retrospective tests using the ratio analysis was always 100 %. The retrospective tests were performed as follows:

				Retrospective Tests Results	
Test Date	Swap Fair Value	Change in Swap Fair Values	Hypothetical Derivative Fair Value	Change in Hypothetical Derivative Fair Value	Ratio
31-Dec-X0	–0–	—	–0–	—	
31-Dec-X1	3,231,000	3,231,000	3,231,000	3,231,000	100 %
31-Dec-X2	850,000	<2,381,000>	850,000	<2,381,000>	100 %
31-Dec-X3	276,000	<574,000>	276,000	<574,000>	100 %
31-Dec-X4	<87,000>	<363,000>	<87,000>	<363,000>	100 %
31-Dec-X5	–0–	87,000	–0–	87,000	100 %

The change in fair value was computed on a period-by-period basis, instead of on a cumulative basis. In this case the alternative chosen was not relevant because of the hedge high effectiveness. However, in more structured hedging strategies it is highly recommended to use the cumulative basis alternative as it improves the chances of effectiveness.

Journal Entries

The following journal entries illustrate the swap and the bond accounting treatment

1) Journal entries on 31 December 20X0

   To record the issuance of the bond:

Cash (Asset)	€ 100,000,000	
Financial Debt (Liability)		€ 100,000,000

No journal entries were required to record the swap since its fair value was zero at inception.

2) Journal entries on 31 December 20X1

   To record the bond coupon payment:

Interest Expense (Income Statement)	€ 4,710,000	
Cash (Asset)		€ 4,710,000

Because the swap was considered to be completely effective, all the change in the swap fair value was recorded in equity. To record the change in fair value of the swap:

Fair Value of Derivative (Asset)	€ 3,231,000	
Cash Flow Hedge (Equity)		€ 3,231,000

To record the swap settlement amount:

Interest Expense (Income Statement)	€ 650,000	
Cash (Asset)		€ 650,000

3) Journal entries on 31 December 20X2

To record the bond coupon payment:

Interest Expense (Income Statement)	€ 5,710,000	
Cash (Asset)		€ 5,710,000

Because the swap was considered to be completely effective, all the change in the swap fair value was recorded in equity. To record the change in fair value of the swap:

Cash Flow Hedge (Equity)	€ 2,381,000	
Fair Value of Derivative (Asset)		€ 2,381,000

To record the swap settlement:

Cash (Asset)	€ 350,000	
Interest Expense (Income Statement)		€ 350,000

4) Journal entries on 31 December 20X3 and 31 December 20X4

The journal entries are similar to the 31 December 20X2 entries.

5) Journal entries on 31 December 20X5
To record the redemption of the bond:

Financial Debt (Liability)	€ 100,000,000	
Cash (Asset)		€ 100,000,000

To record the bond coupon payment:

Interest Expense (Income Statement)	€ 5,450,000	
Cash (Asset)		€ 5,450,000

To record the change in fair value of the swap:

Fair Value of Derivative (Liability)	€ 87,000	
Cash Flow Hedge (Equity)		€ 87,000

To record the swap settlement:

Cash (Asset)	€ 90,000	
Interest Income (Income Statement)		€ 90,000

CASE 5.2

Hedging a Floating-Rate Liability Using a Zero-Cost Collar

The objective of this case is to illustrate the hedge accounting effects when using interest rate options. In order to make the case easier to follow, all interest payments take place at the end of the accounting period. The hedged liability is the same as the previous case.

Background Information

On 31 December 20X0, Company ABC issued at par a floating rate bond with the following characteristics:

Bond Terms	
Issue date	31 December 20X0
Maturity	5 years (31 December 20X5)
Notional	€ 100 million
Coupon	Euribor 12m + 1.50 %, annually
Euribor fixing	Euribor is fixed at the beginning of the annual interest period

ABC wanted to hedge against increases in the coupon payments of the bond by buying an interest rate cap. Simultaneously, to avoid paying an upfront premium, ABC sold an interest rate floor. The combination of a cap and a floor is called a collar. The terms of the collar were as follows:

Interest Rate Cap Terms	
Start date	31 December 20X0
Counterparties	Company ABC and XYZ Bank
Cap buyer	Company ABC
Maturity	5 years (31 December 20X5)
Notional amount	€ 100 million
Premium	95 bps of notional amount (EUR 950,000)
Strike	4.50 % annually, Actual/360 basis
Underlying	Euribor 12-month rate
	Euribor is fixed at the beginning of the annual interest period

Interest Rate Floor Terms	
Start date	31 December 20X0
Counterparties	Company ABC and XYZ Bank
Floor buyer	XYZ Bank
Maturity	5 years (31 December 20X5)
Notional amount	€ 100 million
Premium	95 bps of notional amount (EUR 950,000)
Strike	3.52 % annually, Actual/360 basis
Underlying	Euribor 12-month rate
	Euribor is fixed at the beginning of the annual interest period

The collar was designated as the hedging instrument in a cash flow hedge of the coupon payments on the bond. The bond credit spread (150 basis points) was not included in the hedging relationship.

The combination of cap and the floor (i.e., the collar) could be designated as the hedging instrument because the following conditions were met:

1) No net premium was received; and
2) The underlying of the cap and the floor were the same (i.e., Euribor 12-month); and
3) The cap and the floor had the same maturity; and
4) The notional amount of the written option (i.e., the floor) was not greater than the notional amount of the purchased option (i.e., the cap).

Hedging Relationship Documentation

The hedging relationship was documented as follows:

Hedging Relationship Documentation	
Risk management objective and strategy for undertaking the hedge	The objective of the hedge is to limit to a maximum of 4.50 % the cash outflows related to Euribor 12M of one of ABC's bonds. To achieve this objective and simultaneously not to pay an upfront premium for the hedge, the cash flows related to Euribor 12M are limited to a minimum of 3.52 %. The hedge objective will be obtained by entering into an interest rate collar (a combination of a purchased interest rate cap and a sold interest rate floor). The combination of the collar and the bond will result in an expected net cash outflow between 6.00 % and 5.02 % (including the bond 1.50 % spread).

(Continued)

	This hedging objective is consistent with ABC's overall risk management strategy of managing the exposure to interest rate risk through the proportion of fixed and floating rate net debt in its total debt portfolio, using swaps and interest rate options.
Type of hedge	Cash flow hedge.
Risk being hedged	Interest rate risk. The variability in cash outflows of the bond attributable to changes in the Euribor 12 month rates.
Hedging instrument	The interest rate cap with reference number 012346, and the interest rate floor with reference number 012347. The counterparty to the cap is XYZ Bank and the credit risk associated with this counterparty is considered to be very low.
Hedged item	The cash flows of the 5-year floating bond with reference number 678901 that are linked to Euribor 12 month. The bond spread (150 basis points) is not part of the hedged cash flows.
Assessment of effectiveness testing	Hedge effectiveness will be assessed by comparing changes in the fair value of the hedging instrument to changes in the fair value of a hypothetical derivative.
	The terms of the hypothetical derivative are such that its fair value changes offset exactly the changes in fair value of the hedged item for the risk being hedged. The terms of the hypothetical derivative terms in this hedging relationship match those of the hedging instrument identically, but assuming no counterparty credit exposure.
	The options' time value is excluded from the hedge relationship.

Prospective test

A prospective test will be performed at inception and at each reporting date using the critical terms method.

If (i) the critical terms of the hypothetical derivative and the hedging instrument match (i.e., notional amount, currency, underlying and interest periods), and (ii) the credit risk of the counterparty to the hedging instrument is very low, the hedge will be considered to be highly effective prospectively.

The credit risk of the counterparty to the hedging instrument will be monitored continuously.

Retrospective test

A retrospective test will be performed at each reporting date using the "ratio analysis method" (also called "dollar-offset method). The ratio will compare the cumulative change since hedge inception in the intrinsic value of the hedging instrument with the cumulative change since hedge inception in the intrinsic value of the hypothetical derivative. The hedge will be assumed to be highly effective on a retrospective basis if the ratio is between 80 % and 125 %.

Collar Fair Value Calculations

The total value of each caplet and floorlet were computed using the Black formula. This formula is an adaptation to interest rate options of the Black-Scholes options model. The inputs to price each caplet or floorlet were:

1) the time to expiry of the option;
2) the forward interest rate;
3) the discount factor (the price at today of a risk-free zero-coupon bond paying EUR 1 at the option payoff payment date);

4) the strike rate of the option;
5) the volatility of the forward rate.

The intrinsic value of each option was computed using the same model, but assuming zero volatility. The time value of the option was then computed as the difference between the option total value and the option intrinsic value.

Time value = Total value – Intrinsic value

The cap and floor intrinsic and time values at each balance sheet date were as follows:

Balance Sheet Date	Cap Total Value	Cap Intrinsic Value	Cap Time Value	Floor Total Value	Floor Intrinsic Value	Floor Time value
31-Dec-X0	950,000	–0–	950,000	<950,000>	<300,000>	<650,000>
31-Dec-X1	1.900.000	1,250,000	650,000	<90,000>	–0–	<90,000>
31-Dec-X2	600,000	–0–	600,000	<100,000>	–0–	<100,000>
31-Dec-X3	170,000	–0–	170,000	<50,000>	–0–	<50,000>
31-Dec-X4	20,000	–0–	20,000	<10,000>	–0–	<10,000>
31-Dec-X5	–0–	–0–	–0–	–0–	–0–	–0–

The "cap time value" was computed as: "cap total value"–"cap intrinsic value"
The "floor time value" was computed as: "floor total value"–"floor intrinsic value"

The cumulative and the period changes in the collar intrinsic and time values were as follows:

Balance Sheet Date	Collar Cumulative Change Intrinsic Value	Collar Cumulative Change Time Value	Collar Period Change Intrinsic Value	Collar Period Change Time Value
31-Dec-X0	—	—	—	—
31-Dec-X1	1,550,000	260,000	1,550,000	260,000
31-Dec-X2	300,000	200,000	<1,250,000>	<60,000>
31-Dec-X3	300,000	<180,000>	–0–	<380,000>
31-Dec-X4	300,000	<290,000>	–0–	<110,000>
31-Dec-X5	300,000	<300,000>	–0–	<10,000>

Notes:
The "cumulative change in collar intrinsic value" was computed as:
    "End of period collar intrinsic value – collar intrinsic value at inception"
The "cumulative change in collar time value" was computed as:
    "End of period collar time value – collar time value at inception"
The "period change in collar intrinsic value" was computed as:
    "End of period collar intrinsic value – start of period collar intrinsic value"
The "period change in collar time value" was computed as:
    "End of period collar time value – start of period collar time value"

Hedge Effectiveness Testing – Prospective Test

The objective of the prospective tests was to demonstrate that ABC had a valid expectation that the hedge will be highly effective during the hedging term. ABC performed a prospective test at hedge inception (31 December 20X0) and at each reporting date. Each prospective test was carried out using the critical terms method.

The hedged item was substituted by a hypothetical derivative. The terms of the hypothetical derivative were such that the changes in fair value of the hypothetical derivative offset perfectly the changes in fair value of the hedged item for variations in the risk being hedged. In this case the hedging objective was to limit to a maximum of 4.50 % and to a minimum of 3.52 % the cash outflows related to Euribor 12M of the bond. The derivative that perfectly achieved this objective was a collar with strikes 4.50 % and 3.52 %. Therefore, the terms of the hypothetical derivative identically matched those of the hedging instrument (i.e., the collar), but without any credit risk exposure to the counterparty of the derivative.

Because (i) the critical terms of hedging instrument identically matched those of the hypothetical derivative and (ii) the credit risk associated with the counterparty to the hedging instrument was considered to be very low, ABC concluded that the hedge was highly effective prospectively at each testing date.

Hedge Effectiveness Testing – Retrospective Test

ABC performed a retrospective test at each reporting date and at maturity of the hedging relationship. The retrospective test was expected to be highly effective as the changes in fair value of the hypothetical derivative were identical to the changes in fair value of the hedging instrument. However, ineffectiveness may have arisen if there was a substantial deterioration in the creditworthiness of the swap counterparty or if there was a substantial change in the liquidity of the swap. ABC performed each retrospective test using the ratio analysis method:

$$\text{Effectiveness Ratio} = \frac{\text{Change in fair value of hedging instrument}}{\text{Change in fair value of hypothetical derivative}}$$

In our case, neither the creditworthiness of the swap counterparty (i.e., XYZ Bank) experienced a substantial deterioration nor the liquidity of the swap dried up during any of the retrospective assessment periods, so the result of the retrospective tests using the ratio analysis was always 100 %. The retrospective tests were performed as follows:

Balance Sheet Date	Collar Cumulative Change Intrinsic Value	Hypothetical Derivative Cumulative Change Intrinsic Value	Ratio
	Retrospective Tests		
31-Dec-X0	—	—	—
31-Dec-X1	1,550,000	1,550,000	100 %
31-Dec-X2	300,000	300,000	100 %
31-Dec-X3	300,000	300,000	100 %
31-Dec-X4	300,000	300,000	100 %
31-Dec-X5	300,000	300,000	100 %

Because the ratio was within the 80%–125% range, ABC concluded at each assessment date that the hedge was highly effective retrospectively. Note that the changes in time value of the collar were not included in the hedging relationship, so even if the retrospective tests show no ineffectiveness, the changes in time value of the collar were recorded in P&L.

Journal Entries

In order to produce the required journal entries, we have summarised the cap and floor changes in intrinsic and time values, and the bond and collar payoffs at each balance sheet date in the following tables:

Balance Sheet Date	Cap Total Value	Cap Intrinsic Value	Cap Time Value	Cap Change in Total Value	Cap Change in Intrinsic Val.	Cap Change in Time Value
31-Dec-X0	950,000	–0–	950,000	—	—	—
31-Dec-X1	1.900.000	1,250,000	650,000	950,000	1,250,000	<300,000>
31-Dec-X2	600,000	–0–	600,000	<1,300,000>	<1,250,000>	<50,000>
31-Dec-X3	170,000	–0–	170,000	<430,000>	–0–	<430,000>
31-Dec-X4	20,000	–0–	20,000	<150,000>	–0–	<150,000>
31-Dec-X5	–0–	–0–	–0–	<20,000>	–0–	<20,000>

Balance Sheet Date	Floor Total Value	Floor Intrinsic Value	Floor Time Value	Floor Change in Total Value	Floor Change in Intrinsic Value	Floor Change in Time Value
31-Dec-X0	<950,000>	<300,000>	<650,000>	—	—	—
31-Dec-X1	<90,000>	–0–	<90,000>	860,000	300,000	560,000
31-Dec-X2	<100,000>	–0–	<100,000>	<10,000>	–0–	<10,000>
31-Dec-X3	<50,000>	–0–	<50,000>	50,000	–0–	50,000
31-Dec-X4	<10,000>	–0–	<10,000>	40,000	–0–	40,000
31-Dec-X5	–0–	–0–	–0–	10,000	–0–	10,000

Balance Sheet Date	Period Euribor 12M Rate	Bond interest (in Euros)	Cap Payoff (in Euros)	Floor Payoff (in Euros)	Collar Period Change in Time Value	Collar Period Change in Intrinsic Value
31-Dec-X0	—	—	—	—	—	—
31-Dec-X1	3.21%	<4,710,000>	–0–	<310,000>	260,000	1,550,000
31-Dec-X2	4.21%	<5,710,000>	–0–	–0–	<60,000>	<1,250,000>
31-Dec-X3	3.71%	<5,210,000>	–0–	–0–	<380,000>	–0–
31-Dec-X4	3.80%	<5,300,000>	–0–	–0–	<110,000>	–0–
31-Dec-X5	3.95%	<5,450,000>	–0–	–0–	<10,000>	–0–

1) Journal entries on 31 December 20X0

To record the issuance of the bond:

Cash (Asset)	€ 100,000,000	
Financial Debt (Liability)		€ 100,000,000

The fair value of the purchased cap was EUR 950,000. The fair value of the sold floor was also EUR 950,000. The initial journal entries to record the collar:

Derivative Instrument – Cap (Asset)	€ 950,000	
Cash (Asset)		€ 950,000

Cash (Asset)	€ 950,000	
Derivative Instrument – Floor (Liabil.)		€ 950,000

2) Journal entries on 31 December 20X1

To record the bond coupon payment:

Interest Expense (Income Statement)	€ 4,710,000	
Cash (Asset)		€ 4,710,000

Because the Euribor 12M rate (3.21 %) for the period was below the strike rate of the cap (4.50 %), there was no payment under the cap for the period.

Because the Euribor 12M rate (3.21 %) was below the strike rate of the floor (3.52 %), ABC had to make a payment under the floor for the period. In reality, the payment would have been "nominal"*("strike"−"Euribor12M")*("day count factor"). As the interest basis was Actual/360, the "day count factor" would have been computed as the "number of days in interest period" divided by "360". To keep the calculations simple a "day count factor" equal to one has been assumed. Therefore, the payment was EUR 310,000 (= (3.52 %−3.21 %)*100,000,000) assuming no day count factor adjustment:

Interest Expense (Income Statement)	€ 310,000	
Cash (Asset)		€ 310,000

The change in intrinsic value of the cap was a gain of EUR 1,250,000. The change in time value of the cap was a loss of EUR 300,000. The related journal entries were as follows:

Derivative Instrument — Cap (Asset)	€ 950,000	
Other Income/Expenses (P&L)	€ 300,000	
Cash Flow Hedge (Equity)		€ 1,250,000

The change in time value of the floor was a gain of EUR 560,000. The change in intrinsic value of the floor was a gain of EUR 300,000. The related journal entries were as follows:

Derivative Instrument — Floor (Liability)	€ 860,000	
Other Income/Expenses (P&L)		€ 560,000
Cash Flow Hedge (Equity)		€ 300,000

3) Journal entries on 31 December 20X2

To record the bond coupon payment:

Interest Expense (Income Statement)	€ 5,710,000	
Cash (Asset)		€ 5,710,000

Because the Euribor 12M rate for the period was below the strike rate of the cap, there was no receipt under the cap.

Because the Euribor 12M rate was above the strike rate of the floor, there was no payment under the floor.

The change in intrinsic value of the cap was a loss of EUR 1,250,000. The change in time value of the cap was a loss of EUR 50,000. The related journal entries were as follows:

Cash Flow Hedge (Equity)	€ 1,250,000	
Other Income/Expenses (P&L)	€ 50,000	
Derivative Instrument — Cap (Asset)		€ 1,300,000

The change in time value of the floor was a loss of EUR 10,000. There was no change in intrinsic value of the floor during the period. The related journal entries were as follows:

Other Income/Expenses (P&L)	€ 10,000	
Derivative Instrument — Floor (Liabil.)		€ 10,000

4) Journal entries on 31 December 20X3

To record the bond coupon payment:

Interest Expense (Income Statement)	€ 5,210,000	
Cash (Asset)		€ 5,210,000

Because the Euribor 12M rate for the period was below the strike rate of the cap, there was no receipt under the cap.

Because the Euribor 12M rate was above the strike rate of the floor, there was no payment under the floor.

There was no change in intrinsic value of the cap during the period. The change in time value of the cap was a loss of EUR 430,000. The related journal entries were as follows:

Other Income/Expenses (P&L)	€ 430,000	
Derivative Instrument – Cap (Asset)		€ 430,000

The change in time value of the floor was a gain of EUR 50,000. There was no change in intrinsic value of the floor during the period. The related journal entries were as follows:

Derivative Instrument – Floor (Liability)	€ 50,000	
Other Income/Expenses (P&L)		€ 50,000

5) Journal entries on 31 December 20X4

To record the bond coupon payment:

Interest Expense (Income Statement)	€ 5,300,000	
Cash (Asset)		€ 5,300,000

Because the Euribor 12M rate for the period was below the strike rate of the cap, there was no receipt under the cap.

Because the Euribor 12M rate was above the strike rate of the floor, there was no payment under the floor.

There was no change in intrinsic value of the cap during the period. The change in time value of the cap was a loss of EUR 150,000. The related journal entries were as follows:

Other Income/Expenses (P&L)	€ 150,000	
Derivative Instrument–Cap (Asset)		€ 150,000

The change in time value of the floor was a gain of EUR 40,000. There was no change in intrinsic value of the floor during the period. The related journal entries were as follows:

Derivative Instrument – Floor (Liability)	€ 40,000	
Other Income/Expenses (P&L)		€ 40,000

6) Journal entries on 31 December 20X5

To record the bond coupon payment:

Interest Expense (Income Statement)	€ 5,450,000	
Cash (Asset)		€ 5,450,000

Because the Euribor 12M rate for the period was below the strike rate of the cap, there was no receipt under the cap.

Because the Euribor 12M rate was above the strike rate of the floor, there was no payment under the floor.

There was no change in intrinsic value of the cap during the period. The change in time value of the cap was a loss of EUR 20,000. The related journal entries were as follows:

Other Income/Expenses (P&L)	€ 20,000	
Derivative Instrument – Cap (Asset)		€ 20,000

The change in time value of the floor was a gain of EUR 10,000. There was no change in intrinsic value of the floor during the period. The related journal entries were as follows:

Derivative Instrument – Floor (Liability)	€ 10,000	
Other Income/Expenses (P&L)		€ 10,000

To record the redemption of the bond:

Financial Debt (Liability)	€ 100,000,000	
Cash (Asset)		€ 100,000,000

CASE 5.3

Calculations Implications of Interest Accruals

The objective of this case is to illustrate the importance of excluding interest accrual amounts when computing fair values of derivatives. Inclusion of accruals may cause effectiveness tests to fail and P&L volatility to increase. This case is based in a fair value hedge of a two-year bond to show how to properly take into account interest accruals.

Background Information

On 31 March 20x0, ABC issued at par a EUR 100 million, two-year bond with a 3.78 % annual coupon. ABC's hedging policy was to swap all new issues to floating and at a later stage decide, on a portfolio basis, the proportion of fixed versus floating exposure. Accordingly, on the date on which the bond was issued ABC considered entering into an interest rate swap in which it would receive 3.78 % annually and would pay Euribor 12-month annually. However, because the yield curve on 31 March 20X0 was very steep, ABC preferred instead to enter into a swap in which it will receive 3.78 % annually and pay Euribor 3-month quarterly. The terms of the swap were as follows:

	Interest Rate Swap Terms
Instrument	Interest rate swap
Start date	31 March 20x0
Counterparties	Company ABC and Bank XYZ
Maturity	2 years (31 March 20x2)
Notional	€ 100 million
Initial fair value	Zero
ABC receives (fixed leg)	3.78 % annually, 30/360 basis
ABC pays	Euribor 3m, quarterly, Actual/360 basis
(floating leg)	Euribor is fixed at the beginning of the annual interest period

Figure 5.3 shows the cash flows of the two legs of the swap. Under the floating leg, ABC had to pay Euribor 3-month each quarter. Under the fixed leg, ABC had to receive 3.78 % each year.

Figure 5.4 highlights the strategy's interest flows. Through the swap ABC paid quarterly Euribor 3-month and received 3.78 % annually. ABC used the 3.78 % cash flows it received under the swap to pay the bond interest. As a result, ABC obtained synthetically a EUR floating liability. ABC designated the swap as the hedging instrument in a fair value hedge of the bond. Hedge effectiveness was assessed by comparing changes in the fair value of the hedging instrument to changes in the fair value of a hypothetical derivative.

The hypothetical derivative was a derivative whose changes in fair value perfectly offset the changes in fair value of the hedged item for variations in the risk being hedged. In this hedging

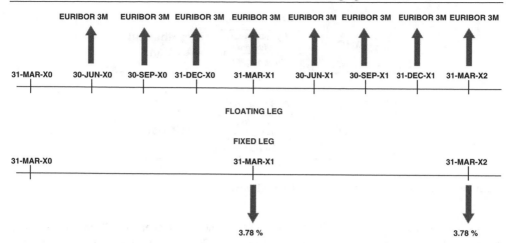

Figure 5.3   Swap Interest Flows.

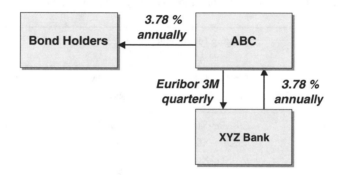

Figure 5.4   Hedging Strategy Interest Flows.

relationship, the hypothetical derivative was a two-year swap with the following economic terms:

Hypothetical Derivative Terms	
Instrument	Interest rate swap
Start date	31 March 20X0
Counterparties	Company ABC and an imaginary AAA counterparty (without credit risk)
Maturity	2 years (31 March 20X2)
Notional	€ 100 million
Fair value at inception	Zero
ABC receives (fixed leg)	3.78 % annually, 30/360 basis
ABC pays (floating leg)	Euribor 12-month, annually, Actual/360 basis

There were only two differences between the hypothetical derivative and the hedging instrument: the counterparty and the floating leg interest rate, as shown in Figure 5.5.

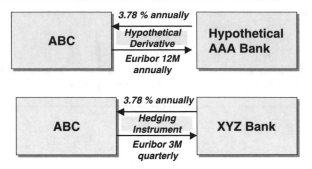

Figure 5.5   Hedging Instrument vs. Hypothetical Derivative.

Let us assume that ABC closed its books annually, each 31 December. Therefore, the first reporting date after hedge inception was 31 December 20X0. By that date and regarding the floating leg of the hedging instrument, four quarterly Euribor 3-month fixings had already been set and interest for three quarters had already being paid, as shown in the following table:

	Hedging Instrument Floating Leg (31 December 20X0)		
Cash Flow Date	Euribor 3M Fixing Date	Euribor 3M Rate	Paid Floating Amount
30-Jun-X0	29-Mar-X0	2.00 %	500,000
30-Sep-X0	28-Jun-X0	2.50 %	625,000
31-Dec-X0	28-Sep-X0	3.00 %	750,000
31-Mar-X1	29-Dec-X0	3.50 %	Not Paid Yet
30-Jun-X1	29-Mar-X1	Not Fixed Yet	Not Paid Yet
30-Sep-X1	28-Jun-X1	Not Fixed Yet	Not Paid Yet
31-Dec-X1	28-Sep-X1	Not Fixed Yet	Not Paid Yet
31-Mar-X2	29-Dec-X1	Not Fixed Yet	Not Paid Yet

Regarding the fixed leg of the hedging instrument, the rates were already known but no interest was paid by 31 December 20X0:

	Hedging Instrument Fixed Leg (31 December 20X0)	
Cash Flow Date	Fixing Date	Paid Floating Amount
31-Mar-X1	3.78 %	Not Paid Yet
31-Mar-X2	3.78 %	Not Paid Yet

The situation of the fixed leg of the hypothetical derivative was identical to situation of the fixed leg of the hedging instrument on 31 December 20X0. Regarding the floating leg of the hypothetical derivative, one Euribor 12-month rate was already fixed but no interest was paid by 31 December 20X0:

Hypothetical Derivative Floating Leg (31 December 20X0)			
Cash Flow Date	Euribor 12M Fixing Date	Euribor 12M Rate	Paid Floating Amount
31-Mar-X1	29-Mar-X0	2.70 %	Not Paid Yet
31-Mar-X2	29-Mar-X1	Not Fixed Yet	Not Paid Yet

The change in fair value of the swap was registered in P&L, and the effective part of this change was recorded as a change in the carrying value of the bond, with an offset in P&L.

The fair value of the hedging instrument and the hypothetical derivative were both zero at inception. On 31 December 20X0, the fair value of each swap was:

- Hedging instrument: EUR 1,882,000. Therefore, the change in its fair value was a gain of EUR 1,882,000.
- Hypothetical derivative: EUR <1,000>. Therefore, the change in its fair value was a loss of EUR 1,000.

Profit and Loss Statement Including the Swap Accruals

There were two major implications form including the swap accruals in the hedge relationship:

- Firstly, the retrospective test failed as the ratio between the change in fair value of the hedging instrument and the change in fair value of the hypothetical derivative was minus 188,200 % (= 1,882,000/(−1,000)), outside the 80–125 % range.
- Secondly, the P&L statement did not achieved the objective of the hedge (to end up paying a floating rate) as shown in the table below:

Profit & Loss Statement – Including Swap Accruals (31 December 20X0)	
Bond interest expense *(1)*	<2,838,000>
Swap floating leg expense *(2)*	<1,875,000>
Swap fixed leg expense *(3)*	2,838,000
Swap fair value change	1,882,000
Less Hypothetical derivative fair value change *(4)*	-0-
Total	**7,000**

Notes:

(1): = 3,780,000 * 274 days/365 days
(2): = − (500,000+625,000+750,000)
(3): = 3,780,000 * 274 days/365 days
(4): As the hedge failed the retrospective test, no amount was reflected as a change in the carrying value of the bond.

The total P&L of EUR 7,000 was equivalent to an equivalent interest rate of 0.0093 % (= 7,000/(100 million*274/365)). This rate was very different to the target interest rate of 2.70 %.

Profit and Loss Statement Excluding the Swap Accruals

The hedging instrument accruals were EUR 2,838,000 (= 2,838,000+0):

- Accrual of the floating leg of the hedging instrument: zero, as the interest was just paid on 31 December 20X0.
- Accrual of the fixed leg of the hedging instrument: EUR 2,838,000 (= 3,780,000 * 274 days/365 days).

The hypothetical derivative accruals were EUR 811,000 (= − 2,027,000 + 2,838,000):

- Accrual of the floating leg of the hypothetical derivative: minus EUR 2,027,000 (= minus 2,700,000 * 274 days/365 days).
- Accrual of the fixed leg of the hypothetical derivative: EUR 2,838,000 (= 3,780,000 * 274 days/365 days).

When the swap accruals were excluded from the hedge relationship, the numbers reflected a more meaningful picture:

- Firstly, the retrospective test passed because the ratio between the change in fair value of the hedging instrument and the change in fair value of the hypothetical derivative was within the 80–125 % range. The change in fair value of the hedging instrument was a loss of EUR 956,000 (= 1,882,000–2,838,000). The change in fair value of the hypothetical derivative was a loss of EUR 812,000 (= −1,000–811,000). Thus the ratio was 117.7 % (= −956,000/ − 812,000)
- Secondly, the P&L statement showed a figure closer to the objective of the hedge, to end up paying a floating rate, as shown in the table below:

Profit & Loss Statement – Including Swap Accruals (31 December 20X0)	
Bond interest expense (1)	<2,838,000>
Swap floating leg expense (2)	<1,875,000>
Swap fixed leg expense (3)	2,838,000
Swap fair value change (4)	<956,000>
Less Hypothetical derivative fair value change (5)	812,000
Total	**<2,019,000>**

Notes:

(1): = 3,780,000* 274 days/365 days
(2): = − (500,000 + 625,000 + 750,000)
(3): = 3,780,000* 274 days/365 days
(4): = change in swap fair value plus accruals = 1,882,000-2,838,000
(5): As the cumulative change in the fair value of the hedging instrument (a loss of 956,000) exceeded the cumulative change in the fair value hypothetical derivative (a loss of 812,000), only the change in fair value of the hypothetical derivative was recorded as a change in the carrying value of the bond (−812,000 = −1,000−811,000).

The total P&L of minus 2,019,000 was equivalent to an interest rate of 2.69 % (= 2,019,000/(100 million*274/365)). If the relationship were 100 % effective, the P&L statement would have shown a total expense of EUR 2,027,000 (an implied interest of 2.70 %). But in our case, there was some inefficiency due to the quarterly interest payments of the floating leg of the hedging instrument.

Concluding Remarks

This case shows that it is necessary to exclude the interest accruals from the fair value calculations of the hedging instrument and the hedged item. Otherwise, effectiveness tests may fail and P&L volatility may increase. Accruals exclusion is especially relevant when the interest periods of the hedging instrument and the hedged item are different.

CASE 5.4

Hedging a Fixed-rate Liability with an Interest Rate Swap

The objective of this case is to illustrate the application of a fair value hedge of a fixed-rate bond using an interest rate swap. This transaction is commonly made by entities that are active in the debt capital markets. Usually a funding department raises and secure funds to attain the entity's funding needs. The funding department has specific funding targets for new issuance of debt. The funding targets are set, for each maturity, as a spread to the corresponding floating rate (for example, a 10 basis points (bps) spread for one-year debt, a 60 bps points spread for five-year debt, etc.). Generally, the funding department is not interested in issuing fixed rate debt, while the investors often require a fixed rate instrument. Accordingly, the funding department issues a fixed-rate bond and simultaneously swaps the bond coupons into floating-rate coupons, effectively funding itself at Euribor plus a spread.

Background Information

On 15 July 20X0, Company ABC issued at par a fixed rate bond with the following characteristics:

Bond Terms	
Issue date	15 July 20X0
Maturity	5 years (15 July 20X5)
Notional	€ 100 million
Coupon	4.94 %, annually 30/360

ABC's policy was to immediately swap to floating all new debt issues and later, as part of its overall hedging policy, decide what fixed-floating mix was the most appropriate for the whole corporation. Accordingly, simultaneously with the issuance of the bond, ABC entered

into a receive-fixed pay-floating interest rate swap with XYZ Bank. As the market five-year €
swap was trading at 4.34 % on 15 July 20X0, the terms of the interest rate swap (IRS) were as
follows:

	Interest Rate Swap Terms
Start date	15 July 20X0
Counterparties	Company ABC and XYZ Bank
Maturity	5 years (15 July 20X5)
Notional	€ 100 million
Fair value at inception	Zero
ABC receives (fixed leg)	4.34 % annually, 30/360 basis
ABC pays (floating leg)	Euribor 12m, annually, Actual/360 basis
	Euribor is fixed two days prior to the beginning of the annual interest period

Although the basis of the floating and the fixed legs were different (A/360 versus 30/360), to
keep calculations simple we have assumed throughout the case that each year had 360 days,
so the day count fraction was always equal to one for each annual period.

Under the swap, ABC paid annually Euribor 12-month and received annually 4.34 %. ABC
then used the 4.34 % received and added 0.60 % to pay the 4.94 % bond interest. The combination of the bond and the swap resulted in ABC paying an interest of Euribor 12M plus 60
bps, as shown in Figure 5.6. The 60 bps spread was the difference between the bond coupon
(4.94 %) and the swap fixed-rate (4.34 %).

The swap was designated as the hedging instrument in a fair value hedge of the
bond.

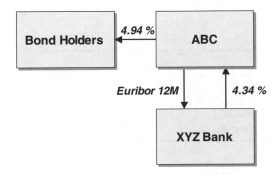

Figure 5.6   Hedging Strategy Interest Flows.

Hedging Relationship Documentation

The hedge relationship was documented as follows:

Hedging Relationship Documentation	
Risk management objective and strategy for undertaking the hedge	The objective of the hedge is to reduce the variability of the fair value of a bond. This hedging objective is consistent with ABC's overall interest rate risk management strategy of transforming all new issued debt into floating rate, and thereafter managing the exposure to interest rate risk through the proportion of fixed and floating rate net debt in its total debt portfolio.
Type of hedge	Fair value hedge.
Risk being hedged	Interest rate risk. The variability in fair value of the bond attributable to changes in the Euribor interest rates. Fair value changes attributable to credit or other risks are not hedged in this relationship. Accordingly, the 60 bps credit spread is excluded from the hedge relationship.
Hedging instrument	The interest rate swap with reference number 012345. The counterparty to the swap is XYZ Bank and the credit risk associated with this counterparty is considered to be very low.
Hedged item	The five-year 4.94 % bond with reference number 678902. The bond credit spread (60 bps) is excluded from the hedging relationship.
Assessment of effectiveness testing	Hedge effectiveness will be assessed by comparing changes in the fair value of the hedging instrument to changes in the fair value of a hypothetical derivative. The terms of the hypothetical derivative are such that its fair value changes offset exactly the changes in fair value of the hedged item for the risk being hedged. The terms of the hypothetical derivative terms in this hedging relationship match identically those of the hedging instrument, but assuming no counterparty credit exposure. **Prospective test** A prospective test will be performed at the inception and at each reporting date, using the critical terms method. If (i) the critical terms of the hypothetical derivative and the hedging instrument match (i.e., notional amount, currency, underlying and interest periods), and (ii) the credit risk of the counterparty to the hedging instrument is very low, the hedge will be considered to be highly effective prospectively. The credit risk of the counterparty to the hedging instrument will be monitored continuously. **Retrospective test** A retrospective test will be performed at each reporting date using the "ratio analysis method". The ratio will compare the change since the last assessment in the fair value of the hypothetical derivative with the change since the last assessment in the fair value of the hedging instrument. The hedge will be assumed to be highly effective on a retrospective basis if the ratio is between 80 % and 125 %. The effective part of the change in fair value of the hedging instrument (excluding the portion attributable to the current period swap accrual) will be recognised in P&L. An equivalent amount will be recorded as a change in the carrying value of the bond, with an offset to P&L.

Fair Value Calculations of the Hedging Instrument

Before performing the prospective and retrospective tests, ABC had to compute the fair values of the hedging instrument (i.e., the swap) and the hypothetical derivative. In our case, because both instruments were identical, only the fair values of one of them had to be calculated. The following two tables show (i) the yield curve prevailing at each reporting date, and (ii) the Euribor 12M prevailing on each 13 July, used in the fixings of the floating leg:

	Yield Curves at Each Reporting Date				
	31-Dec-X0	31-Dec-X1	31-Dec-X2	31-Dec-X3	31-Dec-X4
1 Year	3.95 %	4.01 %	4.15 %	4.33 %	4.39 %
2 Year	4.16 %	4.20 %	4.29 %	4.41 %	4.45 %
3 Year	4.28 %	4.31 %	4.38 %	4.48 %	4.52 %
4 Year	4.37 %	4.39 %	4.45 %	4.55 %	4.59 %
5 Year	4.45 %	4.47 %	4.53 %	4.61 %	4.65 %

Euribor Fixings	
Fixing Date	Euribor 12M Rate
13-Jul-X0	3.70 %
13-Jul-X1	3.85 %
13-Jul-X2	4.05 %
13-Jul-X3	4.25 %
13-Jul-X4	4.35 %

The fair value of the swap was computed summing the present value of each expected future net settlement. The calculation of the fair value of the swap on 31 December 20X0 using the market yield curve on that date was performed as follows:

					Swap Fair Value Calculation on 31 December 20X0		
Cash Flow Date	Notional (Euros)	Euribor Fixing Date (1)	Implied Euribor 12M	Fixed Rate	Period Settlement Amount (2)	Disc. Factor (3)	Present Value
15-Jul-X1	100 Mill.	13-Jul-X0	3.70 %	4.34 %	640,000	0.9801	627,000
15-Jul-X2	100 Mill.	13-Jul-X1	4.24 %	4.34 %	100,000	0.9397	94,000
15-Jul-X3	100 Mill.	13-Jul-X2	4.46 %	4.34 %	<120,000>	0.8990	<108,000>
15-Jul-X4	100 Mill.	13-Jul-X3	4.58 %	4.34 %	<240,000>	0.8591	<206,000>
15-Jul-X5	100 Mill.	13-Jul-X4	4.71 %	4.34 %	<370,000>	0.8200	<303,000>
					Swap Fair Value		**104,000**

Notes:

(1): The Euribor 12 month was fixed two business days prior to the commencement of the interest period.

(2): Period settlement amounts were calculated as:

Notional*(Fixed Rate*Fixed Day Factor − Euribor12M*Floating Day Factor)

As the basis in the floating leg was Actual/360, the floating day factor was equal to (Number of days in interest period)/360. To keep calculations simple, it was assumed to be equal to one. Similarly, the fixed rate factor was assumed to be equal to one.

(3): The discount factors were computed using the Euribor yield curve, without taking into account any credit spread or bid/offers.

Similarly, the calculation of the swap fair value on 31 December 20X1 was performed as follows:

					Swap Fair Value Calculation on 31 December 20X1			
Cash Flow Date	Notional (Euros)	Euribor Fixing Date	Implied Euribor 12M	Fixed Rate	Period Settlement Amount	Disc. Factor	Present Value
15-Jul-X2	100 Mill.	13-Jul-X1	3.85 %	4.34 %	490,000	0.9796	480,000
15-Jul-X3	100 Mill.	13-Jul-X2	4.27 %	4.34 %	70,000	0.9390	66,000
15-Jul-X4	100 Mill.	13-Jul-X3	4.47 %	4.34 %	<130,000>	0.8982	<117,000>
15-Jul-X5	100 Mill.	13-Jul-X4	4.59 %	4.34 %	<250,000>	0.8583	<215,000>
						Swap Fair Value	**214,000**

The calculation of the swap fair value on 31 December 20X2 was performed as follows:

					Swap Fair Value Calculation on 31 December 20X2			
Cash Flow Date	Notional (Euros)	Euribor Fixing Date	Implied Euribor 12M	Fixed Rate	Period Settlement Amount	Disc. Factor	Present Value
15-Jul-X3	100 Mill.	13-Jul-X2	4.05 %	4.34 %	290,000	0.9787	284,000
15-Jul-X4	100 Mill.	13-Jul-X3	4.34 %	4.34 %	0	0.9375	0
15-Jul-X5	100 Mill.	13-Jul-X4	4.50 %	4.34 %	<160,000>	0.8966	<143,000>
						Swap Fair Value	**141,000**

The calculation of the swap fair value on 31 December 20X3 was performed as follows:

					Swap Fair Value Calculation on 31 December 20X3			
Cash Flow Date	Notional (Euros)	Euribor Fixing Date	Implied Euribor 12M	Fixed Rate	Period Settlement Amount	Disc. Factor	Present Value
15-Jul-X4	100 Mill.	13-Jul-X3	4.25 %	4.34 %	90,000	0.9776	88,000
15-Jul-X5	100 Mill.	13-Jul-X4	4.43 %	4.34 %	<90,000>	0.9355	<84,000>
						Swap Fair Value	**4,000**

Finally, the calculation of the swap fair value on 31 December 20X4 was performed as follows:

					Swap Fair Value Calculation on 31 December 20X4			
Cash Flow Date	Notional (Euros)	Euribor Fixing Date	Implied Euribor 12M	Fixed Rate	Period Settlement Amount	Disc. Factor	Present Value
15-Jul-X5	100 Mill.	13-Jul-X4	4.35 %	4.34 %	<10,000>	0.9772	<10,000>
						Swap Fair Value	**<10,000>**

The following table shows the swap fair values and the accruals adjustments at each reporting date:

	Swap Fair Values and Accrual Adjustments					
Balance Sheet Date	Interest Floating Leg	Accrued Floating Leg	Interest Fixed Leg	Accrued Fixed Leg	Swap Fair Value	Swap Fair Value (Excl. Accruals)
15 Jul X0	—	—	—	—	–0–	–0–
31 Dec X0	3,700,000	1,713,000	4,340,000	2,009,000	104,000	<192,000>
31 Dec X1	3,850,000	1,783,000	4,340,000	2,009,000	214,000	<12,000>
31 Dec X2	4,050,000	1,875,000	4,340,000	2,009,000	141,000	7,000
31 Dec X3	4,250,000	1,968,000	4,340,000	2,009,000	4,000	<37,000>
31 Dec X4	4,350,000	2,014,000	4,340,000	2,009,000	<10,000>	<5,000>
15 Jul X5	—	—	—	—	–0–	–0–

The accrued amounts of the floating and the fixed legs were computed as:

Accrued Amount = Leg Interest * (Days in Period)/(Total Days), where

The "Days in Period" were the number of days between the beginning of the interest period (i.e., the previous 15 July to the reporting date) and the reporting date, or 169 days.

The "Total Days" were the number of days in the interest period (i.e., the number of days between the previous 15 July and the next 15 July to the reporting date). We have assumed that all "Days in Period" were 169, and that all the "Total Days" were 365.

The fair value of the swap excluding accruals was computed as:

Swap Fair Value + Accrued Floating Leg − Accrued Fixed Leg

Prospective Tests

The objective of the prospective tests was to demonstrate that ABC had a valid expectation that the hedge will be highly effective during the hedging term. ABC performed a prospective test at hedge inception (15 July 20X0) and at each reporting date. Each prospective test was carried out using the critical terms method.

The hedged item was substituted by a hypothetical derivative. The terms of the hypothetical derivative were such that the changes in fair value of the hypothetical derivative offset perfectly the changes in fair value of the hedged item for variations in the risk being hedged. In this case, the terms of the hypothetical derivative matched identically those of the hedging instrument (i.e., the swap), but without any credit risk exposure to the counterparty of the derivative.

Because (i) the critical terms of hedging instrument matched identically those of the hypothetical derivative and (ii) the credit risk associated with the counterparty to the hedging instrument was considered to be very low, ABC concluded that the hedge was highly effective prospectively at each testing date. The credit risk of the counterparty to the hedging instrument was continuously monitored.

Retrospective Tests

ABC performed a retrospective test at each reporting date and at maturity of the hedging relationship. The retrospective test was expected to be highly effective as the changes in fair value of the hypothetical derivative identically matched those of the hedging instrument. However, ineffectiveness may have arisen if there was a substantial deterioration in the creditworthiness of the swap counterparty or if there was a substantial change in the liquidity of the swap. ABC performed each retrospective test using the ratio analysis method:

$$Ratio = \frac{Change\ in\ fair\ value\ of\ hedging\ instrument\ (*)}{Change\ in\ fair\ value\ of\ hypothetical\ derivative\ (*)}$$

(*) Excluding the period swap accrual

ABC excluded the portion attributable to the current period swap accrual from the retrospective assessments. The retrospective tests were performed as follows:

			Retrospective Tests Results			
Balance Sheet Date	Swap Fair Value (Excl. Accruals)	Change in Swap Fair Value	Change in Hypoth. Derivative Fair Value	Ratio	Hedge Effective Part	Hedge Ineffect. Part
15 Jul X0	–0–	—	—	—	–0–	–0–
31 Dec X0	<192,000>	<192,000>	<192,000>	100 %	<192,000>	–0–
31 Dec X1	<12,000>	180,000	180,000	100 %	180,000	–0–
31 Dec X2	7,000	19,000	19,000	100 %	19,000	–0–
31 Dec X3	<37,000>	<44,000>	<44,000>	100 %	<44,000>	–0–
31 Dec X4	<5,000>	32,000	32,000	100 %	32,000	–0–
15 Jul X5	–0–	5,000	5,000	100 %	5,000	–0–

In our case, neither the creditworthiness of the swap counterparty (i.e., XYZ Bank) experienced a substantial deterioration nor the liquidity of the swap dried up during any of the retrospective assessment periods, so the result of the retrospective tests using the ratio analysis was always 100 %.

Accounting Entries

The required journal entries were as follows:

1) Entries on 15 July 20X0

   To record the bond issuance:

Cash (Asset)	€ 100,000,000	
Financial Debt (Liability)		€ 100,000,000

No journal entries were required for the swap since its fair value was nil at inception.

2) Entries on 31 December 20X0

To record the bond accrued coupon. The bond coupon to be paid on 15 July 20X0 was EUR 4,940,000 (= 100 million*4.94 %). There were 169 days between 15 July 20X0 and 31 December 20X0. Also there were 365 days between 15 July 20X0 and 15 July 20X1. Accordingly, the accrued coupon was EUR 2,287,000 (= 4,940,000*169/365):

Interest Income/Expense (P&L)	€ 2,287,000	
Interest Payable (Liability)		€ 2,287,000

To record the accrued of the swap settlement amount to be paid on 15 July 20X0. The net settlement was EUR 640,000 (= 4,340,000–3,700,000). The accrued amount was EUR 296,000 (= 640,000*169/365):

Interest Receivable (Asset)	€ 296,000	
Interest Income/Expense (P&L)		€ 296,000

The change in fair value of the swap was a loss of EUR 192,000. As this was a fair value hedge, the whole amount was recorded in P&L:

Interest Income/Expense (P&L)	€ 192,000	
Fair Value of Derivative (Liability)		€ 192,000

The effective part of the hedge was a loss of EUR 192,000. Thus, the adjustment to the carrying amount of the bond was a decline of EUR 192,000:

Financial Debt (Liability)	€ 192,000	
Interest Income/Expense (P&L)		€ 192,000

Because the carrying amount of the bond was modified, in theory ABC had to compute the new effective interest of the bond. Instead, ABC's policy was not to re-compute the bond's effective interest each time the bond's carrying amount changed. This policy greatly simplified the accounting process. In our view, this policy did not create important distortions. Because the fair value of the swap were to move toward zero as it moved toward its maturity, the carrying amount of the bond automatically were to return to par.

3) Entries on 15 July 20X1

To record the bond coupon payment:

Interest Payable (Liability)	€ 2,287,000	
Interest Expense (P&L)	€ 2,653,000	
Cash (Asset)		€ 4,940,000

To record the swap settlement:

Cash (Asset)	€ 640,000	
Interest Receivable (Asset)		€ 296,000
Interest Expense (Income Statement)		€ 344,000

4) Entries on 31 December 20X1

To record the bond accrued coupon. The bond coupon to be paid on 15 July 20X2 was EUR 4,940,000. There were 169 days between 15 July 20X1 and 31 December 20X1. Also there were 365 days between 15 July 20X1 and 15 July 20X2. Accordingly, the accrued coupon was EUR 2,287,000 ($= 4,940,000^*169/365$):

Interest Income/Expense (P&L)	€ 2,287,000	
Interest payable (Liability)		€ 2,287,000

The swap net settlement was EUR 490,000 ($= 4,340,000-3,850,000$). The accrued amount was EUR 226,000 ($= 490,000^*169/365$). To record the accrued of the swap settlement amount to be paid on 15 July 20X2:

Interest Receivable (Asset)	€ 226,000	
Interest Income/Expense (P&L)		€ 226,000

The change in fair value of the swap was a gain of EUR 180,000. As this was a fair value hedge, the whole amount was recorded in P&L:

Fair Value of Derivative (Liability)	€ 180,000	
Interest Income/Expense (P&L)		€ 180,000

The effective part of the hedge was a gain of EUR 180,000. Thus, the adjustment to the carrying amount of the bond was an increase of EUR 180,000:

Interest Income/Expense (P&L)	€ 180,000	
Financial Debt (Liability)		€ 180,000

Because the carrying amount of the bond was modified, in theory ABC had to compute the new effective interest of the bond. Instead, ABC's policy was not to re-compute the effective interest each time the bond carrying amount changed.

5) Entries on 15 July 20X2

To record the bond coupon payment:

Interest Payable (Liability)	€ 2,287,000	
Interest Expense (P&L)	€ 2,653,000	
Cash (Asset)		€ 4,940,000

To record the swap settlement:

Cash (Asset)	€ 490,000	
Interest Receivable (Asset)		€ 226,000
Interest Expense (Income Statement)		€ 264,000

6) Entries on 31 December 20X2

The bond coupon to be paid on 15 July 20X3 was EUR 4,940,000. There were 169 days between 15 July 20X2 and 31 December 20X2. Also there were 365 days between 15 July 20X2 and 15 July 20X3. Accordingly, the accrued coupon was EUR 2,287,000 (= 4,940,000*169/365). To record the bond accrued coupon:

Interest Income/Expense (P&L)	€ 2,287,000	
Interest Payable (Liability)		€ 2,287,000

The swap net settlement was EUR 290,000 (= 4,340,000-4,050,000). The accrued amount was EUR 134,000 (= 290,000*169/365). To record the accrued of the swap settlement amount to be paid on 15 July 20X3:

Interest Receivable (Asset)	€ 134,000	
Interest Income/Expense (P&L)		€ 134,000

The change in fair value of the swap was a gain of EUR 19,000. As this was a fair value hedge, the whole amount was recorded in P&L:

Fair Value of Derivative (Asset)	€ 19,000	
Interest Income/Expense (P&L)		€ 19,000

The effective part of the hedge was a gain of EUR 19,000. Thus, the adjustment to the carrying amount of the bond was an increase of EUR 19,000:

Interest Income/Expense (P&L)	€ 19,000	
Financial Debt (Liability)		€ 19,000

Because the carrying amount of the bond was modified, in theory ABC had to compute the new effective interest of the bond. Instead, ABC's policy was not to recompute the effective interest each time the bond carrying amount changed.

7) Entries on 15 July 20X3

To record the bond coupon payment:

Interest Payable (Liability)	€ 2,287,000	
Interest Expense (P&L)	€ 2,653,000	
Cash (Asset)		€ 4,940,000

To record the swap settlement:

Cash (Asset)	€ 290,000	
Interest Receivable (Asset)		€ 134,000
Interest Expense (Income Statement)		€ 156,000

8) Entries on 31 December 20X3

The bond coupon to be paid on 15 July 20X4 was EUR 4,940,000. There were 169 days between 15 July 20X3 and 31 December 20X3. Also there were 365 days between 15 July 20X3 and 15 July 20X4. Accordingly, the accrued coupon was EUR 2,287,000 (= 4,940,000*169/365). To record the bond accrued coupon:

Interest Income/Expense (P&L)	€ 2,287,000	
Interest Payable (Liability)		€ 2,287,000

The swap net settlement was EUR 90,000 (= 4,340,000-4,250,000). The accrued amount was EUR 41,000 (= 90,000*169/365). To record the accrued of the swap settlement amount to be paid on 15 July 20X4:

Interest Receivable (Asset)	€ 41,000	
Interest Income/Expense (P&L)		€ 41,000

The change in fair value of the swap was a loss of EUR 44,000. As this was a fair value hedge, the whole amount was recorded in P&L:

Interest Income/Expense (P&L)	€ 44,000	
Fair Value of Derivative (Liability)		€ 44,000

The effective part of the hedge was a loss of EUR 44,000. Thus, the adjustment to the carrying amount of the bond was a decrease of EUR 44,000:

Financial Debt (Liability)	€ 44,000	
Interest Income/Expense (P&L)		€ 44,000

Because the carrying amount of the bond was modified, in theory ABC had to compute the new effective interest of the bond. Instead, ABC's policy was not to recompute the effective interest each time the bond carrying amount changed.

9) Entries on 15 July 20X4

To record the bond coupon payment:

Interest Payable (Liability)	€ 2,287,000	
Interest Expense (P&L)	€ 2,653,000	
Cash (Asset)		€ 4,940,000

To record the swap settlement:

Cash (Asset)	€ 90,000	
Interest Receivable (Asset)		€ 41,000
Interest Expense (Income Statement)		€ 49,000

10) Entries on 31 December 20X4

The bond coupon to be paid on 15 July 20X5 was EUR 4,940,000. There were 169 days between 15 July 20X4 and 31 December 20X4. Also there were 365 days between 15 July 20X4 and 15 July 20X5. Accordingly, the accrued coupon was EUR 2,287,000 (= 4,940,000*169/365). To record the bond accrued coupon:

Interest Income/Expense (P&L)	€ 2,287,000	
Interest Payable (Liability)		€ 2,287,000

The swap net settlement was EUR -10,000 (= 4,340,000–4,350,000). The accrued amount was EUR −5,000 (= −10,000*169/365). To record the accrued of the swap settlement amount to be paid on 15 July 20X5:

Interest Income/Expense (P&L)	€ 5,000	
Interest Payable (Liability)		€ 5,000

The change in fair value of the swap was a gain of EUR 32,000. As this was a fair value hedge, the whole amount was recorded in P&L:

| Fair Value of Derivative (Liability) | € 32,000 | |
| Interest Income/Expense (P&L) | | € 32,000 |

The effective part of the hedge was a gain of EUR 32,000. Thus, the adjustment to the carrying amount of the bond was an increase of EUR 32,000:

| Interest Income/Expense (P&L) | € 32,000 | |
| Financial Debt (Liability) | | € 32,000 |

Because the carrying amount of the bond was modified, in theory ABC had to compute the new effective interest of the bond. Instead, ABC's policy was not to recompute the effective interest each time the bond carrying amount changed.

11) Entries on 15 July 20X5

To record the bond coupon payment:

Interest Payable (Liability)	€ 2,287,000	
Interest Income/Expense (P&L)	€ 2,653,000	
Cash (Asset)		€ 4,940,000

To record the swap settlement:

Interest Payable (Liability)	€ 5,000	
Interest Income/Expense (P&L)	€ 5,000	
Cash (Asset)		€ 10,000

The change in fair value of the swap was a gain of EUR 5,000. As this was a fair value hedge, the whole amount was recorded in P&L:

| Fair Value of Derivative (Liability) | € 5,000 | |
| Interest Income/Expense (P&L) | | € 5,000 |

The effective part of the hedge was a gain of EUR 5,000. Thus, the adjustment to the carrying amount of the bond was an increase of EUR 5,000:

| Interest Income/Expense (P&L) | € 5,000 | |
| Financial Debt (Liability) | | € 5,000 |

To record the bond redemption:

| Financial Debt (Liability) | € 100,000,000 | |
| Cash (Asset) | | € 100,000,000 |

Summary of Accounting Entries

	Cash	Assets	Liabilities			Profit and Loss
		Interest Receivable	Financial Debt	Interest Payable	Swap Faire Value	
15 July 20X0						
Bond issuance	100,000,000		100,000,000			
31 December 20X0						
Bond accrued coupon				2,287,000		<2,287,000>
Swap accrual		296,000				296,000
Change in fair value of swap					192,000	<192,000>
Bond carrying value adjustment			<192,000>			192,000
15 July 20X1						
Bond coupon payment	<4,940,000>			<2,287,000>		<2,653,000>
Swap settlement	640,000	<296,000>				344,000
31 December 20X1						
Bond accrued coupon				2,287,000		<2,287,000>
Swap accrual		226,000				226,000
Change in fair value of swap					<180,000>	180,000
Bond carrying value adjustment			180,000			<180,000>
15 July 20X2						
Bond coupon payment	<4,940,000>			<2,287,000>		<2,653,000>
Swap settlement	490,000	<226,000>				264,000
31 December 20X2						
Bond accrued coupon				2,287,000		<2,287,000>
Swap accrual		134,000				134,000
Change in fair value of swap					<19,000>	19,000
Bond carrying value adjustment			19,000			<19,000>
15 July 20X3						
Bond coupon payment	<4,940,000>			<2,287,000>		<2,653,000>
Swap settlement	290,000	<134,000>				156,000
31 December 20X3						
Bond accrued coupon				2,287,000		<2,287,000>
Swap accrual		41,000				41,000
Change in fair value of swap					44,000	<44,000>
Bond carrying value adjustment			<44,000>			44,000
15 July 20X4						
Bond coupon payment	<4,940,000>			<2,287,000>		<2,653,000>
Swap settlement	90,000	<41,000>				49,000
31 December 20X4						
Bond accrued coupon				2,287,000		<2,287,000>
Swap accrual				5,000		<5,000>
Change in fair value of swap					<32,000>	32,000
Bond carrying value adjustment			32,000			<32,000>
15 July 20X5						
Bond coupon payment	<4,940,000>			<2,287,000>		<2,653,000>
Swap settlement	<10,000>			<5,000>		<5,000>
Change in fair value of swap					<5,000>	5,000
Bond carrying value adjustment			5,000			<5,000>
Bond redemption	<100,000,000>		<100,000,000>			
TOTAL	–0–	–0–	–0–	–0–	–0–	

Concluding Remarks

By excluding the credit risk from the hedge relationship, ABC could use the critical terms method. The use of this method greatly simplified the accounting process: ABC did not need to compute the change in fair value of the bond as the hedge was completely effective. The carrying amount of the debt was adjusted by an amount that totally offset the change in fair value of the swap.

The hedge perfectly obtained ABC's objective of funding itself at Euribor 12 months plus 60 bps. To demonstrate it, let us take a look at ABC's P&L statement during the first interest period (from 15 July 20X0 until 15 July 20X1).

Profit and Loss From 15-Jul-X0 until 15 Jul-X1	
Entries on 31-Dec-X0:	
Bond accrued coupon	<2,287,000>
Swap accrual	296,000
Change in fair value of swap	<192,000>
Adjustment to carrying value	192,000
Entries on 15-Jul-X1:	
Bond coupon payment	<2,653,000>
Swap settlement	344,000
Total	**<4,300,000>**

The total interest expense for the period was EUR 4,300,000. This expense implied an interest rate of 4.30 %. It meant that ABC funded itself at 3.70 % plus the 0.60 % spread. The 3.70 % rate was exactly the Euribor 12-month rate for the period. Thus, ABC achieved its hedge objective of funding itself at Euribor 12-month plus 0.60 %.

CASE 5.5

Hedging a Future Fixed-rate Bond Issuance with a Swap

The objective of this case is to illustrate the accounting treatment of hedges of highly expected future issuance of fixed-rate debt using a forward starting interest rate swap. A forward starting swap is just a swap that starts some time in the future. With this type of hedge the entity either takes advantage of low interest rates prior to issue the debt, and/or does not want to take the risk of higher rates at issuance date.

Background Information

On 1 January 20X0, Company ABC expected to issue a fixed-rate bond on 15 July 20X0 with the following characteristics:

Bond Terms	
Expected issue date	15 July 20X0
Maturity	5 years (15 July 20X5)
Notional	€ 100 million
Coupon	Fixed, to be paid annually
	The coupon will be set at the 5-year swap rate prevailing at issue date plus 100 bps credit spread

ABC wanted to hedge against potential increases in the 5-year interest rate until issuance date, by locking in the coupon payment at 5.61 % (including the 100 basis points spread). Therefore, ABC entered into a forward starting interest rate swap (IRS) with the following terms:

Interest Rate Swap Terms	
Trade date	1 January 20X0
Start date	15 July 20X0
Counterparties	Company ABC and XYZ Bank
Maturity	5 years (15 July 20X5)
Notional	€ 100 million
ABC pays	4.61 % annually, 30/360 basis
ABC receives	Euribor 12m, annually, Actual/360 basis
	Euribor is fixed at the beginning of the annual interest period

ABC planned to cancel the swap on the bond issue date (15 July 20X0). The fair value of the swap at cancellation would remain in equity on issue date, and thereafter would be gradually recycled to P&L when the bond coupons impact P&L. If the hedge was well constructed, the effective interest rate of the new bond would be close to the sum of the swap fixed-rate and the credit spread, or 5.61 % (= 4.61 % + 1 %).

ABC designated the swap as the hedging instrument in a cash flow hedge of the highly expected issuance of the fixed-rate bond.

Hedging Relationship Documentation

The hedging relationship was documented as follows:

Hedging Relationship Documentation	
Risk management objective and strategy for undertaking the hedge	The objective of the hedge is to fix to 4.61% the Euribor part of the cash outflows of a highly expected issue of a fixed-rate bond. The combination of the swap and the credit spread will result in an expected total cash outflow equivalent to a 5.61 % rate (assuming a 100 bps credit spread at issuance).
	This hedging objective is consistent with ABC's overall risk management strategy of managing the exposure to interest rate risk through the proportion of fixed and floating rate net debt in its total portfolio.
Type of hedge	Cash flow hedge.
Risk being hedged	Interest rate risk. The variability in cash outflows on the bond attributable to changes in the Euribor 5-year rates.
Hedging instrument	The interest rate swap with reference number 012863. The counterparty to the swap is XYZ Bank and the credit risk associated with this counterparty is considered to be very low.
Hedged item	The cash flows of a 5-year fixed-rate bond highly expected to be issued on 15 July 20X0. The credit spread of the bond (expected to be 100 basis points) is excluded from the hedging relationship.

Hedging Relationship Documentation

Assessment of effectiveness testing	**Prospective test**
	A prospective test will be performed at the inception and at each reporting date, using the scenario analysis method.
	Three scenarios will be analysed: (1) a 100 bps parallel shift in the yield curve, (2) a 200 bps yield curve steepening move, and (3) a 200 bps yield curve inversion move. See the documentation of the prospective test performed at hedge inception for a more detailed explanation of the test. The hedge will be assumed to be highly effective on a prospective basis if, under each scenario, the ratio between the fair value change of the hedging instrument and the fair value change of the hedged item is between 80 % and 125 %.
	The credit risk of the counterparty to the hedging instrument will be continuously monitored.
	Retrospective test
	A retrospective test will be performed at each reporting date using the "ratio analysis method". The ratio will compare the cumulative change since hedge inception in the fair value of the hedging instrument with the cumulative change since hedge inception in the fair value of the hedged item. The hedge will be assumed to be highly effective on a retrospective basis if the ratio is between 80 % and 125 %.

Prospective Tests

ABC performed a prospective test at inception of the hedging relationship and at each reporting date. ABC chose the scenario analysis method for prospective assessment. ABC could have chosen the critical terms method, which was notably easier to perform. We preferred instead to use the scenario analysis method to highlight a different method. Readers interested in finding out more about the critical terms method are suggested to read one of the first four cases of this chapter. The scenario analysis method is quite subjective, and its main drawback is that it may not include a potential scenario in which the hedging instrument may behave notably different to the hedged item. In our case, the terms of the hedging instrument and the hedged item were so similar, that an analysis including few scenarios was robust. Let us assume that ABC selected the following scenarios to perform the prospective tests:

1) A parallel shift of 1 % of the par yield curve
2) A 2 % yield curve steepening move: A 2 % upward movement in the 5-year swap rate, no movement in the 1-year rate, and a proportional (to the maturity) movement in the intermediate rates.
3) A 2 % yield curve inversion move: An immediate 2 % downward movement in the 5-year rate, no movement in the 1-year rate, and a proportional (to the maturity) movement of the intermediate rates. A 2 % downward movement would mean 5-year swap rates at 2.62 %, well below its historical minimum.

Let us see the calculations related to the prospective test performed at hedge inception. The first thing ABC calculated were the interest rates to be used in each scenario. Figure 5.7 and

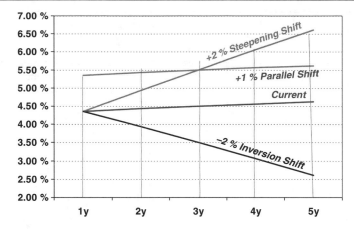

Figure 5.7   Scenario Analysis – Yield Curves.

the following table show the forward yield curve (i.e., starting on 15 July 20X0) as of 1 January 20X0 (hedge inception), and the yield curve of each scenario as of 15 July 20X0 (issue date):

	Forward Yield Curve (start 15-Jul-X0) as of 1-Jan-X0	Spot Yield Curve as of 15-Jul-X0		
		+ 1% Parallel Shift	+ 2% Steepening Shift	− 2 % Inversion Shift
1 Year	4.35 %	5.35 %	4.35 %	4.35 %
2 Years	4.43 %	5.43 %	4.93 %	3.93 %
3 Years	4.50 %	5.50 %	5.50 %	3.50 %
4 Years	4.56 %	5.56 %	6.06 %	3.06 %
5 Years	4.61 %	5.61 %	6.61 %	2.61 %

Once the yield curves were determined, ABC calculated the fair value of the hedging instrument and the hedged item under each scenario, and the changes in their fair value since hedge inception. The following table shows the changes in fair values of the swap and the debt under each scenario. As the ratio between these changes was always within 80 %–125 %, ABC expected the hedge to be highly effective prospectively. The calculations of each fair value have not been included to keep things simple. The pricing mechanics will be covered when performing the retrospective tests.

Prospective Test Results – Scenario Analysis.			
	+ 1% Parallel Shift	+ 2% Steepening Shift	− 2 % Inversion Shift
Swap value at hedge inception	–0–	–0–	–0–
Swap value on issue date	4,270,000	4,063,000	<4,287,000>
Bond value at hedge inception	100,000,000	100,000,000	100,000,000
Bond value on issue date	95,730,000	95,937,000	104,287,000
Change in swap value	4,270,000	4,063,000	<4,287,000>
Change in bond value	<4,270,000>	<4,063,000>	4,287,000
Ratio	**100.0 %**	**100.0 %**	**100.0 %**

The test just described was performed at hedge inception. A similar test was performed at each reporting date, portraying the same conclusions.

Retrospective Tests

A retrospective test was performed on each reporting date (31 March 20X0 and 30 June 20X0) and also at the maturity of the hedge (15 July 20X0). During the term of the hedge, there was no significant deterioration in the credit of the counterparty to the hedging instrument.

To value the hedging instrument and the hedged item, ABC used the forward yield curves (i.e., the rates starting on the issue date) prevailing at each retrospective test date (we will explain later why ABC did not use the spot yield curves instead). The forward yield curves (i.e., the yield curves starting on 15 July 20X0 as of the balance sheet date) were as follows:

	Forward Yield Curves		
	31-Mar-X0	30-Jun-X0	15-Jul-X0
1 yr	4.15 %	4.55 %	4.85 %
2 yr	4.19 %	4.66 %	4.95 %
3 yr	4.22 %	4.77 %	5.04 %
4 yr	4.25 %	4.87 %	5.13 %
5 yr	4.27 %	4.97 %	5.22 %

The fair valuation of the swap on 31-Mar-X0 was performed as follows:

					Swap Fair Value on 31-Mar-X0			
Cash Flow Date	Notional (Euros)	Euribor Fixing Date (1)	Implied Euribor 12M	Fixed Rate	Period Settlement Amount (2)	Disc. Factor (3)	Present Value
15-Jul-X1	100 Mill.	13-Jul-X0	4.15 %	4.61 %	<460,000>	0.9602	<442,000>
15-Jul-X2	100 Mill.	13-Jul-X1	4.23 %	4.61 %	<380,000>	0.9212	<350,000>
15-Jul-X3	100 Mill.	13-Jul-X2	4.28 %	4.61 %	<330,000>	0.8834	<292,000>
15-Jul-X4	100 Mill.	13-Jul-X3	4.33 %	4.61 %	<280,000>	0.8467	<238,000>
15-Jul-X5	100 Mill.	13-Jul-X4	4.38 %	4.61 %	<230,000>	0.8112	<187,000>
						Swap Fair Value	**<1,509,000>**

Notes:

(1) The Euribor 12 month was fixed two business days prior to the commencement of the interest period

(2) Period settlement amounts were calculated as:

Notional*(Euribor12M* Floating Day Factor − Fixed Rate* Fixed Day Factor)

As the basis of the floating leg was Actual/360, the "Floating Day Factor" was equal to (the number of days in the interest period)/360. To keep calculations simple the "Floating Day Factor" was assumed to be equal to one. Similarly the "Fixed Rate Factor" was assumed to be equal to one.

(3) The discount factors represent the present value, as of the issue date, of EUR 1 paid on the cash flow date. The discount factors were computed using the Euribor yield curve, without taking into account any credit spread or bid/offers.

The fair valuation of the highly expected bond on 31 March 20X0 was as follows:

		Bond Fair Value on 31-Mar-X		
Cash Flow Date	Notional (Euros)	Cash flow	Disc. Factor	Present Value
15-Jul-X1	100 Mill.	4,610,000	0.9602	4,427,000
15-Jul-X2	100 Mill.	4,610,000	0.9212	4,247,000
15-Jul-X3	100 Mill.	4,610,000	0.8834	4,072,000
15-Jul-X4	100 Mill.	4,610,000	0.8467	3,903,000
15-Jul-X5	100 Mill.	104,610,000	0.8112	84,860,000
			Bond Fair Value	**101,509,000**

The retrospective test result was a perfect hedge, as the ratio was 100 %:

Retrospective Test on 31 March 20X0 using Forward Fair Values	
Swap fair value change:	
Fair value on 15-Jul-X0 (as of 31-March-20X0)	<1,509,000>
Fair value on 15-Jul-X0 (as of 1-January-20X0)	–0–
Change in fair value	<1,509,000>
Bond fair value change:	
Fair value on 15-Jul-X0 (as of 31-March-20X0)	101,509,000
Fair value on 15-Jul-X0 (as of 1-January-20X0)	100,000,000
Change in fair value	1,509,000
Ratio	**100 %**

One important point we would like to highlight is the following: the fair values calculated are "forward fair values". In other words, the values calculated were the expected fair value of the hedging instrument and the hedged item on the issue date (15 July 20X0). ABC could instead have calculated the "spot fair values" of the bond and swap on the test date. We strongly suggest the use of expected fair values on issue date to make sure that the changes in fair value of the swap and the bond are comparable. Otherwise, inefficiencies may arise due to the different nature of the swap and the bond, as we will see next.

At hedge inception, the forward value (i.e., the expected value on 15 July 20X0) of the swap was zero, as it was entered into at market rates. The spot fair value (i.e., the value on 1 January 20X0) of the swap was also zero. The forward value of the bond was EUR 100 million, as its coupon paid market rates. The spot fair value of the bond was EUR 97,860,000, as the discount factor from 1-Jan-X0 to 15-Jul-X0 was 0.9786. These amounts are highlighted in Figure 5.8.

On the retrospective test date (31 March 20X0), the forward value (i.e., the expected value on 15 July 20X0) of the swap showed a loss of EUR 1,509,000. The spot fair value (i.e., the value on 31 March 20X0) of the swap was a loss of EUR 1,491,000, as the discount factor from 31-Mar-X0 to 15-Jul-X0 was 0.9881. The forward value of the bond was 100 million, as its coupon paid market rates. The spot fair value of the bond was EUR 101,509,000, as the discount factor from 31-Mar-X0 to 15-Jul-X0 was 0.9881. These amounts are highlighted in Figure 5.9.

If instead of using the "forward fair values", ABC used the "spot fair values" the retrospective test would have failed. As shown in the following table, the ratio between the change in the

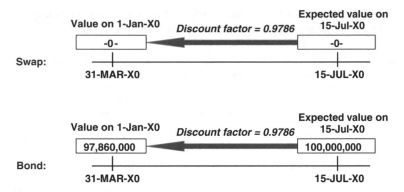

Figure 5.8   Fair Values Calculations at Hedge Inception.

fair value of the hedging instrument and the change in the fair value of the hedged item would
have been 61.1 %, well outside the 80–125 % range.

	Retrospective Test on 31 March 20X0 using Spot Fair Values
Swap fair value change:	
Fair value on 31-Mar-X0 (as of 31-Mar-X0)	<1,491,000>
Fair value on 1-Jan-X0 (as of 1-Jan-X0)	–0–
Change in fair value	<1,491,000>
Bond fair value change:	
Fair value on 31-Mar-X0 (as of 31-Mar-X0)	100,301,000
Fair value on 1-Jan-X0 (as of 1-Jan-X0)	97,860,000
Change in fair value	2,441,000
Ratio	**61.1 %**

One potential solution to this problem is to replace the hedged item by a hypothetical swap.
This way, the fair values of both swaps are directly comparable and the distortions outlined
above disappear. Normally, this is the best way to go, but in our case we preferred not to use
the hypothetical swap alternative to highlight the problem.

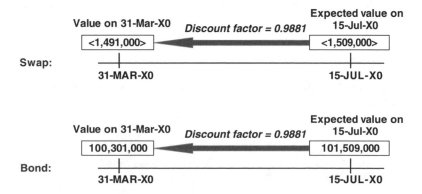

Figure 5.9   Fair Values Calculations on 31-March-X0.

The rest of the retrospective tests were calculated similarly to the 31 March 20X0 test. In the following table we summarise the results of all the retrospective tests:

Retrospective Test using Forward Fair Values			
	31-Mar-X0	30-Jun-X0	15-Jul-X0
Swap fair value change:			
Fair value on 15-Jul-X0 (as of Test Date)	1,509,000	1,485,000	2,573,000
Fair value on 15-Jul-X0 (as of 1-January-20X0)	–0–	–0–	–0–
Change in fair value	1,509,000	1,485,000	2,573,000
Bond fair value change:			
Fair value on 15-Jul-X0 (as of Test Date)	101,509,000	98,515,000	97,427,000
Fair value on 15-Jul-X0 (as of 1-January-20X0)	100,000,000	100,000,000	100,000,000
Change in fair value	1,509,000	<1,485,000>	<2,573,000>
Ratio	**100 %**	**100 %**	**100 %**

Accounting Entries

Assuming that ABC reported quarterly, the required accounting entries were as follows:

1) Entries on 1 January 20X0

   No journal entries were required for the swap since its fair value was zero at inception.

2) Entries on 31 March 20X0
   The change in the fair value of the swap was a loss of EUR 1,509,000:

Cash Flow Hedges (Equity)	€ 1,509,000	
Fair Value of Derivative (Liability)		€ 1,509,000

3) Entries on 30 June 20X0

   The change in the fair value of the swap was a gain of EUR 2,994,000 (= 1,485,000 − (−1,509,000)):

Fair Value of Derivative (Asset)	€ 2,994,000	
Cash Flow Hedges (Equity)		€ 2,994,000

4) Entries on 15 July 20X0 (bond issue date)
The change in the fair value of the swap was a gain of EUR 1,088,000 (= 2,573,000−1,485,000)):

Fair Value of Derivative (Asset)	€ 1,088,000	
Cash Flow Hedges (Equity)		€ 1,088,000

The swap was cancelled. Its fair value was EUR 2,573,000:

Cash (Asset)	€ 2,573,000	
Fair Value of Derivative (Asset)		€ 2,573,000

The bond was issued. The coupon rate was the 5-year swap rate on the issue date (5.22 %) plus a credit spread of 100 bps. Therefore, the bond coupon was 6.22 %, or EUR 6,220,000:

Cash (Asset)	€ 100,000,000	
Financial Debt (Liability)		€ 100,000,000

5) Entries on 30 September 20X0
The number of days between 15 July 20X0 and 30 September 20X0 was 77 days. The accrued interest of the bond was EUR 1,312,000 (= 6,220,000 * 77/365):

Interest Income/Expense (P&L)	€ 1,312,000	
Interest Payable (Liability)		€ 1,312,000

ABC decided that the allocation of the cash flow reserve was going to be assigned to the bond coupons linearly. Therefore each coupon was assigned EUR 515,000 (= 2,573,000/5). The accrued amount of the cash flow reserve assigned to the first coupon was EUR 109,000 (= 515,000 * 77/365):

Cash Flow Hedges (Equity)	€ 109,000	
Interest Income/Expense (P&L)		€ 109,000

6) Entries on 31 December 20X0, 31 March 20X1 and 30 June 20X1

The entries for the next three reporting dates were very similar. We have assumed that each quarterly period had the same number of days.

The accrued interest of the bond was EUR 1,555,000 ($= 6,220,000^*1/4$):

Interest Income/Expense (P&L)	€ 1,555,000	
Interest Payable (Liability)		€ 1,555,000

The allocation of the cash flow reserve was EUR 129,000 ($= 515,000^*1/4$):

Cash Flow Hedges (Equity)	€ 129,000	
Interest Income/Expense (P&L)		€ 129,000

7) Entries on 15 July 20X1

To record the bond coupon payment:

Interest Payable (Liability)	€ 5,977,000	
Interest Income/Expense (P&L)	€ 243,000	
Cash (Asset)		€ 6,220,000

To record the allocation of the cash flow reserve EUR 19,000 ($= 515,000\text{-}109,000\text{-}129,000^*3$):

Cash Flow Hedges (Equity)	€ 19,000	
Interest Income/Expense (P&L)		€ 19,000

8) Entries on each reporting date and coupon payment between on 15 July 20X1 and 15 July 20X5

The entries are similar to the ones described in paragraphs 6) and 7)

9) Entries on 15 July 20X5
To record the bond coupon payment:

Interest Payable (Liability)	€ 5,977,000	
Interest Income/Expense (P&L)	€ 243,000	
Cash (Asset)		€ 6,220,000

To record the bond redemption:

Financial Debt (Liability)	€ 100,000,000	
Cash (asset)		€ 100,000,000

Concluding Remarks

The hedge perfectly obtained ABC's objective of funding itself at 4.61 % plus 100 bps. To demonstrate it, let us have a view of the P&L statement during the first interest period (from 15 July 20X0 until 15 July 20X1).

Profit and Loss From 15-Jul-X0 until 15 Jul-X1	
Entries on 30-Sep-X0:	
Bond accrued coupon	<1,312,000>
Cash flow reserve	109,000
Entries on 31-Dec-X0:	
Bond accrued coupon	<1,555,000>
Cash flow reserve	129,000
Entries on 31-Mar-X1:	
Bond accrued coupon	<1,555,000>
Cash flow reserve	129,000
Entries on 30-Jun-X1:	
Bond accrued coupon	<1,555,000>
Cash flow reserve	129,000
Entries on 15-Jul-X1:	
Bond accrued coupon	<243,000>
Cash flow reserve	19,000
Total	<5,705,000>

The total interest expense for the period was EUR 5,705,000. This expense implied an interest rate of 5.705 %. It meant that ABC funding was at 4.705 % plus the 100 bps spread. The 4.705 % rate was not exactly the swap rate of 4.61 % but was reasonably close. Thus, ABC almost achieved its hedge objective of funding itself at 5.61 %. Without the hedge, ABC would have funded itself at 6.22 %.

Now the reader is probably wondering why ABC did not fund itself exactly at 5.61 %. The answer is that by cancelling the swap and receiving all the fair value of the swap (EUR 2,573,000) on 15 July 20X0, ABC anticipated all the future settlements of the swap. The future settlements were 5.22% − 4.61%. If ABC would have invested the EUR 2,573,000 at Euribor flat, the interest on this investment would have reduced the overall financial expense, and bring it exactly to the 5.61 % target.

CASE 5.6

Hedging a Future Floating-rate Bond Issuance with a Swap

This case illustrates the accounting treatment of hedges of highly expected future issuances of floating-rate debt using a forward starting swap. To synthetically convert to fixed the future floating-rate coupon payments, the entity has two major alternatives:

1) To wait until the bond is issued to enter into a pay-fixed receive-floating swap. Under this alternative the entity will be exposed to rising interest rates, but will benefit if interest rates decline.

2) To lock in current interest rates by entering into a swap that starts on the planned issue date (a forward starting swap). Under this alternative, the entity eliminates the exposure to rising interest rates, but will not benefit if interest rates decline.

Although this strategy is equivalent to the issuance of fixed-rate debt, entities sometimes prefer to issue floating-rate debt to meet specific investor appetite for floating rate debt or to draw down existing bank floating-rate credit lines. This case is very similar to Case 5.5.

Background Information

On 1 January 20X0, Company ABC expected to issue a floating-rate bond on 15 July 20X0 with the following characteristics:

Expected Bond Terms	
Expected issue date	15 July 20X0
Maturity	5 years (15 July 20X5)
Notional	€ 100 million
Coupon	Euribor 12-month plus 100 bps, to be paid annually
Euribor fixing	Euribor to be fixed at the beginning of the annual interest period

ABC wanted to take advantage of the low interest rate environment on 1 January 20X0. At the same time ABC wanted to eliminate the risk of higher rates at issuance date. Therefore, ABC entered into a forward starting interest rate swap with the following terms:

Interest Rate Swap Terms	
Trade date	1 January 20X0
Start date	15 July 20X0
Counterparties	Company ABC and XYZ Bank
Maturity	5 years (15 July 20X5)
Notional	€ 100 million
ABC pays	4.57 % annually, 30/360 basis
ABC receives	Euribor 12m, annually, Actual/360 basis
	Euribor is fixed at the beginning of the annual interest period

ABC planned to keep the swap until its maturity. After the issuance of the bond, the swap will be the hedging instrument in a cash flow hedge of the floating-rate liability. If the hedge was well constructed, the effective yield of the new issuance would be close to the sum of the swap rate and the credit spread, or 5.57 % (= 4.57 % + 1 %).

Hedging Relationship Documentation

The hedging relationship was documented as follows:

Hedging Relationship Documentation	
Risk management objective and strategy for undertaking the hedge	The objective of the hedge is to fix to 4.57 % the interest rate related to the Euribor part of the coupons of a highly expected issue of a floating-rate bond. The combination of the swap and the credit spread will result in an expected interest outflow equivalent to a 5.57 % rate (assuming a 100 bps credit spread at issuance).
	This hedging objective is consistent with ABC's overall risk management strategy of managing the exposure to interest rate risk through the proportion of fixed and floating rate net debt in its total portfolio.

Hedging Relationship Documentation

Type of hedge	Cash flow hedge.
Risk being hedged	Interest rate risk. The variability in cash outflows on the bond attributable to changes in the Euribor 12-month rates.
Hedging instrument	The interest rate swap with reference number 012863. The counterparty to the swap is XYZ Bank and the credit risk associated with this counterparty is considered to be very low.
Hedged item	The cash flows of a 5-year floating-rate bond highly expected to be issued on 15 July 20X0. The credit spread of the bond (expected to be 100 basis points) is excluded from the hedging relationship.
Assessment of effectiveness testing	Hedge effectiveness will be assessed by comparing changes in the fair value of the hedging instrument to changes in the fair value of a hypothetical derivative.
	The terms of the hypothetical derivative are such that its fair value changes offset exactly the changes in fair value of the hedged item for the risk being hedged. The terms of the hypothetical derivative terms in this hedging relationship match identically those of the hedging instrument, but assuming no counterparty credit exposure.

Prospective test

A prospective test will be performed at the inception and at each reporting date, using the critical terms method.

If (i) the critical terms of the portion of the debt designated as being hedged and the hedging instrument match (i.e., notional amount, currency, underlying and interest periods), and (ii) the credit risk of the counterparty to the hedging instrument is very low, the hedge will be considered to be highly effective prospectively.

The credit risk of the counterparty to the hedging instrument will be monitored continuously.

Retrospective test

A retrospective test will be performed at each reporting date using the "ratio analysis method". The ratio will compare the cumulative change since hedge inception in the fair value of the hedging instrument with the cumulative change since hedge inception in the fair value of the hedged item. The hedge will be assumed to be highly effective on a retrospective basis if the ratio is between 80 % and 125 %.

Prospective Tests

The objective of the prospective tests was to demonstrate that ABC had a valid expectation that the hedge will be highly effective during the hedging term. ABC performed a prospective test at hedge inception (1 January 20X0) and at each reporting date. Each prospective test was carried out using the critical terms method.

The hedged item was substituted by a hypothetical derivative. The terms of the hypothetical derivative were such that the changes in fair value of the hypothetical derivative offset perfectly the changes in fair value of the hedged item for variations in the risk being hedged. In this case, the terms of the hypothetical derivative matched identically those of the hedging instrument (i.e., the swap), but without any credit risk exposure to the counterparty of the derivative.

Because (i) the critical terms of hedging instrument matched identically those of the hypothetical derivative and (ii) the credit risk associated with the counterparty to the hedging instrument was considered to be very low, ABC concluded that the hedge was highly effective prospectively at each testing date. The credit risk of the counterparty to the hedging instrument was continuously monitored.

Retrospective Tests

A retrospective test was performed on each reporting date and also at the maturity of the hedge. During the term of the hedge, there was no significant deterioration in the credit of the counterparty to the hedging instrument.

To keep the case short, we have assumed that ABC closed its books annually each 31 December although most firms report on a quarterly basis. The yield curves prevailing at each retrospective test date were as follows:

	1-Year	2-Year	3-Year	4-Year	5-Year	6-Year
1-Jan-X0	4.23 %	4.37 %	4.45 %	4.53 %	4.60 %	4.67 %
31-Dec-X0	4.50 %	4.56 %	4.63 %	4.69 %	4.75 %	4.81 %
31-Dec-X1	4.63 %	4.69 %	4.76 %	4.82 %	4.87 %	4.93 %
31-Dec-X2	4.76 %	4.82 %	4.88 %	4.94 %	4.99 %	5.05 %
31-Dec-X3	4.88 %	4.94 %	5.00 %	5.05 %	5.11 %	5.16 %
31-Dec-X4	5.00 %	5.05 %	5.11 %	5.17 %	5.22 %	5.26 %

The swap valuation on 1 January 20X0 (hedge inception) is shown in the following table:

			Swap Fair Value Calculation on 1-Jan-X0				
Cash Flow Date	Notional (Euros)	Euribor Fixing Date (1)	Implied Euribor 12M	Fixed Rate	Period Settlement Amount (2)	Disc. Factor (3)	Present Value
15-Jul-X1	100 Mill.	13-Jul-X0	4.23 %	4.57 %	<340,000>	0.9370	<319,000>
15-Jul-X2	100 Mill.	13-Jul-X1	4.56 %	4.57 %	<10,000>	0.8961	<9,000>
15-Jul-X3	100 Mill.	13-Jul-X2	4.63 %	4.57 %	50,000	0.8558	43,000
15-Jul-X4	100 Mill.	13-Jul-X3	4.80 %	4.57 %	230,000	0.8161	188,000
15-Jul-X5	100 Mill.	13-Jul-X4	4.70 %	4.57 %	130,000	0.7459	97,000
						Swap Fair Value –0–	

Notes:

(1) The Euribor 12 month was fixed two business days prior to the commencement of the interest period

(2) Period settlement amounts were calculated as:

Notional * (Euribor12M * Floating Day Factor − Fixed RatexFixed Day Factor)

As the basis of the floating leg was Actual/360, the "Floating Day Factor" was in theory equal to (Number of days in interest period)/360. To keep calculations simple, the "Floating Day Factor" was assumed to be equal to one. Similarly, the "Fixed Day Factor" was assumed to be equal to one.

(3) The discount factors represent the present value, as of the valuation date, of EUR 1 paid on the cash flow date. The discount factors were computed using the Euribor yield curve, without taking into account any credit spread or bid/offers.

The floating rate for the first period was fixed on 13 July 20X0 at 4.30 %. The swap valuation on 31 December 20X0 is shown in the following table:

Cash Flow Date	Notional (Euros)	Euribor Fixing Date	Implied Euribor 12M	Fixed Rate	Period Settlement Amount	Disc. Factor	Present Value
\multicolumn{8}{c}{Swap Fair Value Calculation on 31-Dec-X0}
15-Jul-X1	100 Mill.	13-Jul-X0	4.30 %	4.57 %	<270,000>	0.9764	<264,000>
15-Jul-X2	100 Mill.	13-Jul-X1	4.42 %	4.57 %	<150,000>	0.9341	<140,000>
15-Jul-X3	100 Mill.	13-Jul-X2	4.67 %	4.57 %	100,000	0.8921	89,000
15-Jul-X4	100 Mill.	13-Jul-X3	4.77 %	4.57 %	200,000	0.8510	170,000
15-Jul-X5	100 Mill.	13-Jul-X4	4.87 %	4.57 %	300,000	0.8107	243,000
					Swap Fair Value		**98,000**

The floating rate for the second interest period was fixed on 13 July 20X1 at 4.47 %. The swap valuation on 31 December 20X1 is shown in the following table:

Cash Flow Date	Notional (Euros)	Euribor Fixing Date	Implied Euribor 12M	Fixed Rate	Period Settlement Amount	Disc. Factor	Present Value
\multicolumn{8}{c}{Swap Fair Value Calculation on 31-Dec-X1}
15-Jul-X2	100 Mill.	13-Jul-X1	4.47 %	4.57 %	<100,000>	0.9757	<98,000>
15-Jul-X3	100 Mill.	13-Jul-X2	4.55 %	4.57 %	<20,000>	0.9324	<19,000>
15-Jul-X4	100 Mill.	13-Jul-X3	4.80 %	4.57 %	230,000	0.8893	205,000
15-Jul-X5	100 Mill.	13-Jul-X4	4.90 %	4.57 %	330,000	0.8472	280,000
					Swap Fair Value		**368,000**

The swap valuation on the rest of the retrospective test dates followed a pattern similar to the previous valuations. The following table summarises the swap valuations at each relevant date:

Valuation Date	1st Period Euribor Fixing	1st Period Settlement Amount	Swap Fair Value	Interest Accrual	Swap Fair Value (Excluding Accrual)
1-Jan-X0	—	—	-0-	—	-0-
31-Dec-X0	4.30 %	<270,000>	98,000	<125,000>	223,000
31-Dec-X1	4.47 %	<100,000>	368,000	<46,000>	414,000
31-Dec-X2	4.65 %	80,000	472,000	37,000	435,000
31-Dec-X3	4.76 %	190,000	389,000	88,000	301,000
31-Dec-X4	4.80 %	230,000	224,000	106,000	118,000
15-Jul-X5	—	—	-0-	—	-0-

The swap fair value excluding accruals was computed as:

Swap Fair Value (Excl. Accruals) = Swap Fair Value (Incl. Accruals) − Interest Accrual

The retrospective tests were performed using the ratio analysis method, as follows:

$$Ratio = \frac{Change\ in\ fair\ value\ of\ hedging\ instrument\,(*)}{Change\ in\ fair\ value\ of\ hypothetical\ derivative\,(*)}$$

(*) Excluding interest accruals

In our case, the terms of the hypothetical derivative matched identically those of the hedging instrument, except the credit exposure to the counterparty of the derivative and the derivative liquidity. Because neither the creditworthiness of the swap counterparty (i.e., XYZ Bank) experienced a substantial deterioration nor the liquidity of the swap dried up during any of the retrospective assessment periods, the result of the retrospective tests using the ratio analysis was always 100 %, as shown in the table below:

| | Retrospective Tests | | |
Test Date	Swap Cumulative Change Fair Value	Hypothetical Derivative Cumulative Change Fair Value	Ratio
31-Dec-X0	223,000	223,000	100 %
31-Dec-X1	414,000	414,000	100 %
31-Dec-X2	435,000	435,000	100 %
31-Dec-X3	301,000	301,000	100 %
31-Dec-X4	118,000	118,000	100 %
15-Jul-X5	–0–	–0–	100 %

Because the ratio was within the 80 %–125 % range, ABC concluded at each assessment date that the hedge was highly effective retrospectively. Note that the ratio on 15 July 20X5, in theory was undetermined (= 0/0), but in practice the interpretation was that the cumulative change in fair value of the hedging instrument identically matched that of the hypothetical derivative.

Journal Entries

Assuming that ABC reported annually each 31 December, the required journal entries of the transaction were as follows:

1) Entries on 1 January 20X0

No journal entries were required for the swap since its fair value was nil at inception.

2) Entries on 15 July 20X0
   To record the bond issuance:

Cash (Asset)	€ 100,000,000	
Financial Debt (Liability)		€ 100,000,000

3) Entries on 31 December 20X0

The bond coupon to be paid on 15 July 20X1 was EUR 5,300,000 (= 100 million*(4.30 % + 1 %)) The number of days between 15 July 20X0 and 31 December 20X0 was 169 days. The accrued interest of the bond was EUR 2,454,000 (= 5,300,000*169/365):

Interest Income/Expense (P&L)	€ 2,454,000	
Interest Payable (Liability)		€ 2,454,000

The accrued settlement of the swap was minus EUR 125,000:

Interest Income/Expense (P&L)	€ 125,000	
Interest Payable (Liability)		€ 125,000

The change in the fair value of the swap was a gain of EUR 223,000 (= 223,000 − 0):

Fair Value of Derivative (Asset)	€ 223,000	
Cash Flow Hedges (Equity)		€ 223,000

4) Entries on 15 July 20X1

To record the bond coupon payment of EUR 5,300,000:

Interest Payable (Liability)	€ 2,454,000	
Interest Income/Expense (P&L)	€ 2,846,000	
Cash (Asset)		€ 5,300,000

To record the swap settlement:

Interest Payable (Liability)	€ 125,000	
Interest Income/Expense (P&L)	€ 145,000	
Cash (Asset)		€ 270,000

5) Entries on 30 December 20X1

The bond coupon to be paid on 15 July 20X2 was EUR 5,470,000 (= 100 million*(4.47 % + 1 %)) The number of days between 15 July 20X1 and 31 December 20X1 was 169 days. The accrued interest of the bond was EUR 2,533,000 (= 5,470,000*169/365):

Interest Income/Expense (P&L)	€ 2,533,000	
Interest Payable (Liability)		€ 2,533,000

The accrued settlement of the swap was minus EUR 46,000:

Interest Income/Expense (P&L)	€ 46,000	
Interest Payable (Liability)		€ 46,000

The change in the fair value of the swap was a gain of EUR 191,000 (= 414,000-223,000):

Fair Value of Derivative (Asset)	€ 191,000	
Cash Flow Hedges (Equity)		€ 191,000

6) Entries on 15 July 20X2

To record the bond coupon payment of EUR 5,470,000:

Interest Payable (Liability)	€ 2,533,000	
Interest Income/Expense (P&L)	€ 2,937,000	
Cash (Asset)		€ 5,470,000

To record the swap settlement:

Interest Payable (Liability)	€ 46,000	
Interest Income/Expense (P&L)	€ 54,000	
Cash (Asset)		€ 100,000

7) Entries on 30 December 20X2

The bond coupon to be paid on 15 July 20X3 was EUR 5,650,000 (= 100 million*(4.65 %+1 %)) The number of days between 15 July 20X2 and 31 December

20X2 was 169 days. The accrued interest of the bond was EUR 2,616,000 (= 5,650,000*169/365):

Interest Income/Expense (P&L)	€ 2,616,000	
Interest Payable (Liability)		€ 2,616,000

The accrued settlement of the swap was EUR 37,000:

Interest Receivable (Asset)	€ 37,000	
Interest Income/Expense (P&L)		€ 37,000

The change in the fair value of the swap was a gain of EUR 21,000 (= 435,000-414,000):

Fair Value of Derivative (Asset)	€ 21,000	
Cash Flow Hedges (Equity)		€ 21,000

8) Entries on 15 July 20X3

To record the bond coupon payment of EUR 5,650,000:

Interest Payable (Liability)	€ 2,616,000	
Interest Income/Expense (P&L)	€ 3,034,000	
Cash (Asset)		€ 5,650,000

To record the swap settlement:

Cash (Asset)	€ 80,000	
Interest Receivable (Asset)		€ 37,000
Interest Income/Expense (P&L)		€ 43,000

9) Entries on 30 December 20X3

The bond coupon to be paid on 15 July 20X4 was EUR 5,760,000 (= 100 million*(4.76 % + 1 %)) The number of days between 15 July 20X3 and 31 December 20X3 was 169 days. The accrued interest of the bond was EUR 2,667,000 (= 5,760,000*169/365):

Interest Income/Expense (P&L)	€ 2,667,000	
Interest Payable (Liability)		€ 2,667,000

The accrued settlement of the swap was EUR 88,000:

Interest Receivable (Asset)	€ 88,000	
Interest Income/Expense (P&L)		€ 88,000

The change in the fair value of the swap was a loss of EUR 134,000 (= 301,000-435,000):

Cash Flow Hedges (Equity)	€ 134,000	
Fair Value of Derivative (Asset)		€ 134,000

10) Entries on 15 July 20X4

To record the bond coupon payment of EUR 5,760,000:

Interest Payable (Liability)	€ 2,667,000	
Interest Income/Expense (P&L)	€ 3,093,000	
Cash (Asset)		€ 5,760,000

To record the swap settlement:

Cash (Asset)	€ 190,000	
Interest Receivable (Asset)		€ 88,000
Interest Income/Expense (P&L)		€ 102,000

11) Entries on 30 December 20X4

The bond coupon to be paid on 15 July 20X5 was EUR 5,800,000 (= 100 million* (4.80 % + 1 %)) The number of days between 15 July 20X4 and 31 December 20X4 was 169 days. The accrued interest of the bond was EUR 2,685,000 (= 5,800,000*169/365):

Interest Income/Expense (P&L)	€ 2,685,000	
Interest Payable (Liability)		€ 2,685,000

The accrued settlement of the swap was EUR 106,000:

Interest Receivable (Asset)	€ 106,000	
Interest Income/Expense (P&L)		€ 106,000

The change in the fair value of the swap was a loss of EUR 183,000 (= 118,000-301,000):

Cash Flow Hedges (Equity)	€ 183,000	
Fair Value of Derivative (Asset)		€ 183,000

12) Entries on 15 July 20X5

To record the bond coupon payment of EUR 5,800,000:

Interest Payable (Liability)	€ 2,685,000	
Interest Income/Expense (P&L)	€ 3,115,000	
Cash (Asset)		€ 5,800,000

To record the swap settlement:

Cash (Asset)	€ 230,000	
Interest Receivable (Asset)		€ 106,000
Interest Income/Expense (P&L)		€ 124,000

The change in the fair value of the swap was a loss of EUR 118,000 (= 0-118,000):

Cash Flow Hedges (Equity)	€ 118,000	
Fair Value of Derivative (Asset)		€ 118,000

To record the bond redemption:

Financial Debt (Liability)	€ 100,000,000	
Cash (Asset)		€ 100,000,000

Concluding Remarks

The hedge perfectly obtained ABC's objective of funding itself at 5.57 %. To demonstrate it, let us have a view of the P&L statement during the first interest period (from 15 July 20X0 until 15 July 20X1).

Profit and Loss From 15-Jul-X0 until 15 Jul-X1	
Entries on 31-Dec-X0:	
Bond accrued coupon	<2,454,000>
Swap accrued settlement	<125,000>
Entries on 15-Jul-X1:	
Bond accrued coupon	<2,846,000>
Swap accrued settlement	<145,000>
Total	**5,570,000**

The total interest expense for the period was EUR 5,570,000. This expense implied an interest rate of 5.57 %. It meant that ABC funding was at 4.57 % plus the 100 bps spread. The 4.57 % rate was exactly the swap fixed-rate.

CASE 5.7

Hedging a Fixed-Rate Liability with a Swap In-Arrears

This case illustrates the accounting treatment of a hedge of a flixed-rate liability with a swap in-arrears. This hedging strategy takes advantage of a steep yield curve. The fixed-legs of a swap in-arrears and a standard swap are identical. The difference between them lies in the fixings of the floating-leg:

- In a standard swap, the Euribor rate is set at the beginning of the interest period (precisely, two business days prior to the commencement of the period).
- In a swap in-arrears, the Euribor rate is set at the end of the interest period (precisely, two business days prior to the end of the period).

The payment of the floating-leg interest is paid at the end of the interest period. For example, let us assume that the interest period of the floating leg starts on 15 July 20X0 and ends on 15 July 20X1, and that the underlying variable is the Euribor 12-month rate. Under a standard swap, the Euribor 12-month rate will be fixed on the 13 July 20X0 and the floating leg interest will be paid on 15 July 20X1 (see Figure 5.10). Under a swap in-arrears, the Euribor 12-month rate will be fixed on the 13 July 20X1 and the floating leg interest will be paid on 15 July 20X1 (see also Figure 5.10).

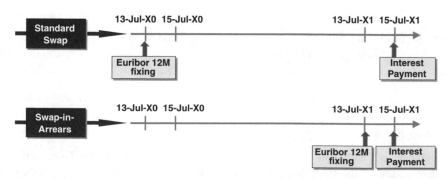

Figure 5.10   Floating Leg Interest Period – Standard Swap vs. Swap-in-Arrears.

Background Information

On 1 January 20X0, Company ABC issued at par a fixed rate bond with the following characteristics:

Bond Terms	
Issue date	1 January 20X0
Maturity	5 years (31 December 20X4)
Notional	€ 100 million
Coupon	6.12 %, annually 30/360

ABC's policy was to immediately swap to floating all new debt issues and later, as part of its overall hedging policy, decide what fixed-floating mix was the most appropriate for the whole corporation. First, ABC considered entering into a standard swap in which ABC would pay Euribor 12-month and receive 5.12 %. Through the standard swap, ABC would be effectively funding itself at Euribor 12M plus 100 bps (= 6.12 %-5.12 %). Because the EUR yield curve was unusually steep, ABC preferred instead to enter into a swap in-arrears with the following terms:

Interest Rate Swap Terms	
Start date	1 January 20X0
Counterparties	Company ABC and XYZ Bank
Maturity	5 years (31 December 20X4)
Notional	€ 100 million
Fair value at inception	Zero
ABC receives (fixed leg)	5.70 % annually, 30/360 basis
ABC pays (floating leg)	Euribor 12m, annually, Actual/360 basis
	Euribor is fixed two days prior to the end
	of the annual interest period

Under the swap in-arrears, ABC paid annually Euribor 12-month in-arrears and received annually 5.70 %. ABC then used the 5.70 % received and added 0.42 % to pay the 6.12 % bond interest. The combination of the bond and the swap resulted in ABC paying an interest of Euribor 12M in-arrears plus 42 bps, as shown in Figure 5.11. The 42 bps spread was the difference between the bond coupon (6.12 %) and the swap fixed-rate (5.70 %).

The swap in-arrears was designated as the hedging instrument in a fair value hedge of the bond.

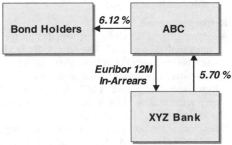

Figure 5.11   Hedging Strategy Interest Flows.

Hedging Relationship Documentation

The hedge relationship was documented as follows:

Hedging Relationship Documentation	
Risk management objective and strategy for undertaking the hedge	The objective of the hedge is to reduce the variability of the fair value of a bond. This hedging objective is consistent with ABC's overall interest rate risk management strategy of transforming all new issued debt into floating rate, and thereafter managing the exposure to interest rate risk through the proportion of fixed and floating rate net debt in its total debt portfolio.
Type of hedge	Fair value hedge.
Risk being hedged	Interest rate risk. The variability in fair value of the bond attributable to changes in the Euribor interest rates. Fair value changes attributable to credit or other risks are not hedged in this relationship. Accordingly, the 100 bps credit spread is excluded from the hedge relationship.
Hedging instrument	The interest rate swap in-arrears with reference number 012349. The counterparty to the swap is XYZ Bank and the credit risk associated with this counterparty is considered to be very low.
Hedged item	The five-year 6.12 % bond with reference number 678907. The bond credit spread (100 bps) is excluded from the hedging relationship.
Assessment of effectiveness testing	Hedge effectiveness will be assessed by comparing changes in the fair value of the hedging instrument to changes in the fair value of a hypothetical derivative. The terms of the hypothetical derivative are such that its fair value changes offset exactly the changes in fair value of the hedged item for the risk being hedged. The hypothetical derivative in this hedging relationship is a swap in which the entity pays annually Euribor 12M (set at the beginning of the interest period) and receives annually 5.12 %, with no counterparty credit exposure.

Prospective test

A prospective test will be performed at the inception and at each reporting date, using the regression analysis method.

The hedge will be considered to be highly effective prospectively if:

1) The R-squared statistic is above 80 %
2) The slope of the regression line is in the range of 0.80 and 1.25
3) The F-statistic indicates statistical significance at the 95 % confidence level

The credit risk of the counterparty to the hedging instrument will be continuously monitored.

Retrospective test

A retrospective test will be performed at each reporting date using the "ratio analysis method". The ratio will compare the cumulative change since hedge inception in fair value of the hedging instrument with the cumulative change since hedge inception in the fair value of the hypothetical derivative. The hedge will be assumed to be highly effective on a retrospective basis if the ratio is between 80 % and 125 %.

The effective part of the change in fair value of the hedging instrument (excluding the portion attributable to the current period swap accrual) will be recognised in P&L. An equivalent amount will be recorded as a change in the carrying value of the bond, with an offset to P&L.

Prospective Tests

The objective of the prospective tests was to demonstrate that ABC had a valid expectation that the hedge will be highly effective during the hedging term. ABC performed a prospective test at hedge inception (1 January 20X0) and at each reporting date. Each prospective test was carried out using the regression analysis method.

The hedged item was substituted by a hypothetical derivative. The terms of the hypothetical derivative were such that the changes in fair value of the hypothetical derivative perfectly offset the changes in fair value of the hedged item for variations in the risk being hedged. In this case, the terms of the hypothetical derivative were a standard swap but without any credit risk exposure to the counterparty of the derivative. as follows:

Hypothetical Derivative Terms	
Start date	1 January 20X0
Counterparties	Company ABC and hypothetical AAA-rated counterparty
Maturity	5 years (31 December 20X4)
Notional	€ 100 million
Fair value at inception	Zero
ABC receives (fixed leg)	5.12 % annually, 30/360 basis
ABC pays (floating leg)	Euribor 12m, annually, Actual/360 basis
	Euribor is fixed two days prior to the beginning of the annual interest period

Figure 5.12 highlights the regression analysis performed at hedge inception (1 January 20X0), comparing the changes in fair value of the hedging instrument to the changes in the fair value of a hypothetical derivative.

Regression analysis assesses the level of correlation between changes in the clean (i.e., excluding accruals) fair value of the hedging instrument and the changes in the clean fair value

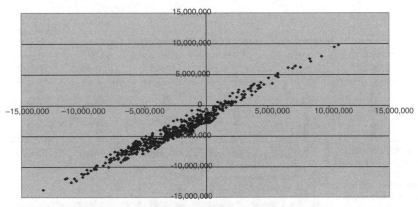

X axis: Cumulative change in fair value of hedging instrument
Y axis: Cumulative change in fair value of theoretical derivative

Figure 5.12   Swap In-Arrears – Regression Analysis.

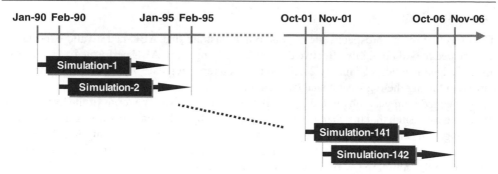

Figure 5.13   Regression Analysis – Simulation Periods.

of the hypothetical derivative, using historical interest rate information. If a high correlation exists, then movements in the fair value of the bond can be reasonably expected to trigger similar offsetting movements in the fair value of the swap. The analysis was based on the historical EUR interest rates from January 1990 until November 2006 (the "historical time horizon"). The historical time horizon was divided into 142 "simulation periods" of five years each, as shown in Figure 5.13.

Each simulation period had an inception date and five subsequent annual balance sheet dates. In each simulation period, the behaviour of an equivalent hedging relationship using the historical data was simulated. At the beginning of the simulation period, the terms of the hedging instrument and hypothetical derivative were determined as if the hedge were entered into on that date. The terms were such that the simulated hedge were equivalent to the actual terms but taking into account the market rates prevailing at the beginning of the simulation period. Each observation pair (X,Y) was generated by computing the cumulative change in the fair value of the simulation hedging instrument (variable X) and the cumulative change in fair value of the simulation hypothetical derivative (observation Y). Figure 5.14 highlights the process for simulation 13.

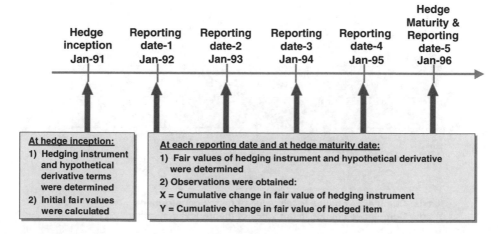

Figure 5.14   Regression Analysis – Observations in Simulation 13.

The results of the regression analysis showed a R-squared of 90.2 %, a slope of the regression line of 1.05 and the F-statistic provided evidence of statistical soundness. ABC concluded that the hedge was highly effective prospectively because:

- the R-squared statistic was above 80 %; and
- the slope of the regression line was in the range between 0.80 and 1.25; and
- the F-statistic indicated statistical significance at the 95 % confidence level.

A similar test was performed at each reporting date, showing similar results. The credit risk of the counterparty to the hedging instrument was continuously monitored and throughout the hedge life this credit risk was considered to be very low.

Retrospective Tests

ABC performed a retrospective test at each reporting date and at maturity of the hedging relationship. During the term of the hedge, there was no significant deterioration in the credit of the counterparty to the hedging instrument and there was no substantial change in the liquidity of the hedging instrument.

Before performing a retrospective test, ABC had to compute the fair values of the hedging instrument (i.e., the swap in-arrears) and the hypothetical derivative. The following two tables show (i) the yield curve prevailing at each reporting date, and (ii) the Euribor 12M fixings:

Yield Curves at Each reporting Date						
	1-Year	2-Year	3-Year	4-Year	5-Year	6-Year
1-Jan-X0	3.60 %	4.37 %	4.70 %	4.90 %	5.20 %	5.30 %
31-Dec-X0	3.70 %	4.20 %	4.50 %	4.70 %	5.05 %	5.15 %
31-Dec-X1	3.80 %	4.30 %	4.60 %	4.80 %	4.90 %	5.00 %
31-Dec-X2	4.76 %	4.82 %	4.88 %	4.94 %	4.99 %	5.05 %
31-Dec-X3	4.88 %	4.94 %	5.00 %	5.05 %	5.11 %	5.16 %

Euribor Fixings	
Fixing Date	Euribor 12M Rate
29-Dec-W9	3.60 %
29-Dec-X0	3.70 %
29-Dec-X1	3.80 %
29-Dec-X2	4.76 %
29-Dec-X3	4.88 %
29-Dec-X4	5.00 %

We will show next the fair value calculations of the hedging instrument and the hypothetical derivative at hedge inception (1 January 20X0) and at the first balance-sheet date (31 December

20X0). The rest of the fair value calculations follow a similar pattern and have not been included to avoid showing too repetitive calculations.

The hedging instrument (i.e., the swap in-arrears) valuation on 1 January 20X0 (hedge inception) is shown in the following table:

Hedging Instrument Fair Value Calculation on 1-Jan-X0							
Cash Flow Date	Notion. (Euros)	Euribor Fixing Date (1)	Fixed Rate	Impl. Eur. 12M	Period Settlement Amount (2)	Disc. factor (3)	Present Value
31-Dec-X0	100 Mill.	29-Dec-X0	5.70 %	5.10 %	600,000	0.9653	579,000
31-Dec-X1	100 Mill.	29-Dec-X1	5.70 %	5.40 %	300,000	0.9177	275,000
31-Dec-X2	100 Mill.	29-Dec-X2	5.70 %	5.80 %	<100,000>	0.8705	<87,000>
31-Dec-X3	100 Mill.	29-Dec-X3	5.70 %	6.00 %	<300,000>	0.8246	<247,000>
31-Dec-X4	100 Mill.	29-Dec-X4	5.70 %	6.37 %	<670,000>	0.7732	<518,000>
				Hedging Instrument Fair Value			**–0–**

Notes:

(1) The Euribor 12 month was to be fixed two business days prior to the end of the interest period

(2) Period settlement amounts were calculated as:

Notional*(Fixed Rate* Fixed Day Factor − Euribor12M* Floating Day Factor)

As the basis of the floating leg was Actual/360, the "Floating Day Factor" was in theory equal to (Number of days in interest period)/360. To keep calculations simple, the "Floating Day Factor" was assumed to be equal to one. Similarly, the "Fixed Day Factor" was assumed to be equal to one.

(3)The discount factors represent the present value, as of the valuation date, of EUR 1 paid on the cash flow date. The discount factors were computed using the Euribor yield curve, without taking into account any credit spread or bid/offers.

The hypothetical derivative (i.e., the standard swap) valuation on 1 January 20X0 (hedge inception) is shown in the following table:

Hypothetical Derivative Fair Value Calculation on 1-Jan-X0							
Cash Flow Date	(Notion. Euros)	Euribor (Fixing Date) (1)	Fixed Rate	Impl. Eur. 12M	Period Settlement Amount (2)	factor Disc. (3)	Present Value
31-Dec-X0	100 Mill.	29-Dec-W9	5.12 %	3.60 %	1,520,000	0.9653	1,467,000
31-Dec-X1	100 Mill.	29-Dec-X0	5.12 %	5.10 %	20,000	0.9177	18,000
31-Dec-X2	100 Mill.	29-Dec-X1	5.12 %	5.40 %	<280,000>	0.8705	<244,000>
31-Dec-X3	100 Mill.	29-Dec-X2	5.12 %	5.80 %	<680,000>	0.8246	<561,000>
31-Dec-X4	100 Mill.	29-Dec-X3	5.12 %	6.00 %	<880,000>	0.7732	<680,000>
				Hedged Item Fair Value			**–0–**

Notes: The notes are the same as in the hedging instrument calculation except that the Euribor 12 month was in this calculation fixed two business days prior to the commencement of the interest period (note-1).

The hedging instrument fair valuation on 31 December 20X0 is shown in the following table:

		Hedging Instrument Swap Fair Value Calculation on 31-Dec-X0					
Cash Flow Date	(Notion. Euros)	Euribor (Fixing Date) (1)	Fixed Rate	Impl. Eur. 12M	Period Settlement Amount (2)	factor Disc. (3)	Present Value
31-Dec-X1	100 Mill.	29-Dec-X1	5.70 %	5.08 %	620,000	0.9643	598,000
31-Dec-X2	100 Mill.	29-Dec-X2	5.70 %	5.28 %	420,000	0.9209	387,000
31-Dec-X3	100 Mill.	29-Dec-X3	5.70 %	5.40 %	300,000	0.8758	263,000
31-Dec-X4	100 Mill.	29-Dec-X4	5.70 %	5.67 %	30,000	0.8313	25,000
					Fair Value		**1,273,000**

The hypothetical derivative fair valuation on 31 December 20X0 is shown in the following table:

		Hypothetical Derivative Swap Fair Value Calculation on 31-Dec-X0					
Cash Flow Date	(Notion. Euros)	Euribor (Fixing Date) (1)	Fixed Rate	Impl. Eur. 12M	Period Settlement Amount (2)	factor Disc. (3)	Present Value
31-Dec-X1	100 Mill.	29-Dec-X0	5.12 %	3.70 %	1,420,000	0.9643	1,369,000
31-Dec-X2	100 Mill.	29-Dec-X1	5.12 %	5.08 %	40,000	0.9209	37,000
31-Dec-X3	100 Mill.	29-Dec-X2	5.12 %	5.28 %	<160,000>	0.8758	<140,000>
31-Dec-X4	100 Mill.	29-Dec-X3	5.12 %	5.40 %	<280,000>	0.8313	<233,000>
					Fair Value		**1,033,000**

The hedging instrument valuation on the rest of the retrospective test dates followed a pattern similar to the previous valuations. The following table summarises the hedging instrument valuations at each relevant date:

		Hedging Instrument Fair Values				
Valuation Date	1st Period Euribor Fixing	1st Period Settlement Amount		Fair Value	Interest Accrual	Fair Value (Excluding Accrual)
1-Jan-X0	—	—		–0–	—	–0–
31-Dec-X0	3.70 %	2,000,000		1,273,000	–0–	1,273,000
31-Dec-X1	3.80 %	1,900,000		1,673,000	–0–	1,673,000
31-Dec-X2	4.76 %	940,000		1,542,000	–0–	1,542,000
31-Dec-X3	4.88 %	820,000		734,000	–0–	734,000
31-Dec-X4	5.00 %	700,000		–0–	–0–	–0–

The following table summarises the hypothetical derivative valuations at each relevant date:

	Hypothetical Derivative Fair Values		
Valuation Date	Fair Value	Interest Accrual	Fair Value (Excluding Accrual)
1-Jan-X0	–0–	—	–0–
31-Dec-X 0	1,033,000	–0–	1,033,000
31-Dec-X1	1,625,000	–0–	1,625,000
31-Dec-X2	692,000	–0–	692,000
31-Dec-X3	296,000	–0–	296,000
31-Dec-X4	–0–	–0–	–0–

The results of the retrospective tests are shown in the table below:

	Retrospective Tests Results				
Test Date	Hedging Instrument Fair Value Change (1)	Hypothetical Derivative Fair Value Change (1)	Ratio	Hedge Effective Part	Fair Value Hedge Ineffective Part
31-Dec-X0	1,273,000	1,033,000	123.2 %	1,033,000	240,000
31-Dec-X1	1,673,000	1,625,000	103.0 %	400,000	–0–
31-Dec-X2	1,542,000	692,000	222.8 %	–0–	<131,000>
31-Dec-X3	734,000	296,000	248.0 %	–0–	<808,000>
31-Dec-X4	–0–	–0–	— (2)	–0– (2)	<734,000>

Notes:
Cumulative change since hedge inception.
There was no test because the hedge was already terminated.

Because the ratio was within the 80 %–125 % range in the first two tests, ABC concluded on 31 December 20X0 and 31 December 20X1 that the hedge was highly effective retrospectively. However, on 31 December 20X2 the retrospective test failed and ABC decided to wait until the next test result before making a decision whether to terminate the hedging relationship. Once the highly effective test also failed on 31 December 20X3, ABC decided to end the hedging relationship on this date. As a result, no retrospective test was performed on 31 December 20X4.

Journal Entries

Assuming that ABC reported annually each 31 December, the required journal entries of the transaction were as follows:

1) Entries on 1 January 20X0

To record the bond issuance:

Cash (Asset)	€ 100,000,000	
Financial Debt (Liability)		€ 100,000,000

No journal entries were required for the swap in-arrears since its fair value was nil at inception.
2) Entries on 31 December 20X0

The bond coupon was EUR 6,120,000 (= 100 million*6.12%):

Interest Income/Expense (P&L)	€ 6,120,000	
Cash (Asset)		€ 6,120,000

The swap settlement was EUR 2,000,000:

Cash (Asset)	€ 2,000,000	
Interest Income/Expense (P&L)		€ 2,000,000

The change in the fair value of the swap was a gain of EUR 1,273,000 (= 1,273,000−0):

Fair Value of Derivative (Asset)	€ 1,273,000	
Interest Income/Expense (P&L)		€ 1,273,000

The effective part of the hedge was EUR 1,033,000. Thus the adjustment to the carrying amount of the bond was an increase of EUR 1,033,000:

Interest Income/Expense (P&L)	€ 1,033,000	
Financial Debt (Liability)		€ 1,033,000

Because the carrying amount of the bond was modified, in theory ABC had to compute the new effective interest of the bond. Instead, ABC's policy was not to re-compute the bond's effective interest each time the bond's carrying amount changed. This policy greatly simplified the accounting process. In our view, this policy did not create important distortions. Because the fair value of the swap to move toward zero as it moved toward its maturity, the carrying amount of the bond was to return automatically to par.

3) Entries on 31 December 20X1

The bond coupon was EUR 6,120,000 (= 100 million*6.12 %):

Interest Income/Expense (P&L)	€ 6,120,000	
Cash (Asset)		€ 6,120,000

The swap settlement was EUR 1,900,000:

Cash (Asset)	€ 1,900,000	
Interest Income/Expense (P&L)		€ 1,900,000

The change in the fair value of the swap was a gain of EUR 400,000 (= 1,673,000-1,273,000):

Fair Value of Derivative (Asset)	€ 400,000	
Interest Income/Expense (P&L)		€ 400,000

The effective part of the hedge was EUR 400,000. Thus the adjustment to the carrying amount of the bond was an increase of EUR 400,000:

Interest Income/Expense (P&L)	€ 400,000	
Financial Debt (Liability)		€ 400,000

Because the carrying amount of the bond was modified, in theory ABC had to compute the new effective interest of the bond. Instead, ABC's policy was not to re-compute the bond's effective interest each time the bond's carrying amount changed. This policy greatly simplified the accounting process. In our view, this policy did not create important distortions. Because the fair value of the swap was to move toward zero as it moved toward its maturity, the carrying amount of the bond was to return automatically to par.

4) Entries on 31 December 20X2

The bond coupon was EUR 6,120,000 (= 100 million*6.12 %):

Interest Income/Expense (P&L)	€ 6,120,000	
Cash (Asset)		€ 6,120,000

The swap settlement was EUR 940,000:

Cash (Asset)	€ 940,000	
Interest Income/Expense (P&L)		€ 940,000

The change in the fair value of the swap was a loss of EUR 131,000 (= 1,542,000-1,673,000):

Interest Income/Expense (P&L)	€ 131,000	
Fair Value of Derivative (Asset)		€ 131,000

The hedge failed the retrospective test. Thus no adjustment to the bond's carrying amount was made.

5) Entries on 31 December 20X3

The bond coupon was EUR 6,120,000 (= 100 million*6.12 %):

Interest Income/Expense (P&L)	€ 6,120,000	
Cash (Asset)		€ 6,120,000

The swap settlement was EUR 820,000:

Cash (Asset)	€ 820,000	
Interest Income/Expense (P&L)		€ 820,000

The change in the fair value of the swap was a loss of EUR 808,000 (= 734,000 − 1,542,000):

Interest Income/Expense (P&L)	€ 808,000	
Fair Value of Derivative (Asset)		€ 808,000

The hedge failed the retrospective test. Thus no adjustment to the bond's carrying amount was made. ABC terminated the hedging relationship.

6) Entries on 31 December 20X4

The bond coupon was EUR 6,120,000 (= 100 million*6.12 %):

Interest Income/Expense (P&L)	€ 6,120,000	
Cash (Asset)		€ 6,120,000

Because the effective interest was not recomputed each time there was an adjustment to the bond carrying value, we need to record the difference between the bond par amount and the carrying value (EUR 100,000,000 − 101,433,000):

Financial Debt (Liability)	€ 1,433,000	
Interest Income/Expense (P&L)		€ 1,433,000

The swap settlement was EUR 700,000:

Cash (Asset)	€ 700,000	
Interest Income/Expense (P&L)		€ 700,000

The change in the fair value of the swap was a loss of EUR 734,000 (= 0-734,000):

Interest Income/Expense (P&L)	€ 734,000	
Fair Value of Derivative (Asset)		€ 734,000

To record the bond redemption:

Financial Debt (Liability)	€ 100,000,000	
Cash (Asset)		€ 100,000,000

Summary of Accounting Entries

	ASSETS		Liabilities	Profit and
	Cash	Swap In-Arrears	Financial Debt	Loss
1 January 20X0				
Bond issuance	100,000,000		100,000,000	
31 December 20X0				
Bond coupon	<6,120,000>			<6,120,000>
Swap settlement	2,000,000			2,000,000
Swap fair value change		1,273,000		1,273,000
Bond value adjustment			1,033,000	<1,033,000>
31 December 20X1				
Bond coupon	<6,120,000>			<6,120,000>
Swap settlement	1,900,000			1,900,000
Swap fair value change		400,000		400,000
Bond value adjustment			400,000	<400,000>
31 December 20X2				
Bond coupon	<6,120,000>			<6,120,000>
Swap settlement	940,000			940,000
Swap fair value change		<131,000>		<131,000>
Bond value adjustment				
31 December 20X3				
Bond coupon	<6,120,000>			<6,120,000>
Swap settlement	820,000			820,000
Swap fair value change		<808,000>		<808,000>
Bond value adjustment				
31 December 20X4				
Bond coupon	<6,120,000>			<6,120,000>
Swap settlement	700,000			700,000
Swap fair value change		<734,000>		<734,000>
Bond value adjustment			<1,433,000>	1,433,000
Bond redemption	<100,000,000>		<100,000,000>	
Totals	**<24,240,000>**	**–0–**	**–0–**	**<24,240,000>**

Concluding Remarks

From an economic point of view the hedge performed very well. ABC's view that the interest rate curve on 1 January 20X0 was too steep (i.e., was discounting too high future Euribor 12M rates) was right. As a consequence, ABC paid an average 4.85 % annual interest (= 24,240,000/5/100,000,000), instead of the 6.12 % bond interest. Also when compared to a standard swap, the hedge performed notably well: the average interest would have been 5.15 % (the sum of the average Euribor 12M during the 5 years + 1 %).

From an accounting perspective, ABC could not apply hedge accounting in the last three years. As a result, ABC's P&L was exposed to the changes in the fair value of the swap in-arrears. Although this accounting difficulty cannot be generalised, a swap in-arrears and a standard swap may show notably different sensitivity to interest rate changes when few interest periods are left.

CASE 5.8

Hedging a Floating-Rate Liability with a European KIKO Collar

The objective of this case is to illustrate the hedge accounting effects when using interest rate exotic options. A quite popular strategy is to hedge a floating rate liability using a European KIKO collar. In Case 3.5 in Chapter 5 we covered the accounting implications when hedging a FX exposure with a FX KIKO forward in which the barriers were continuously observed. The KIKO covered in this case is a European KIKO: the barriers were only observed at expiry of the options. Therefore, it is irrelevant if a barrier was crossed before option expiration. The only event that counted was whether at expiry the barrier was crossed. The hedged liability is the same as in the first two cases of this chapter.

Background Information

On 31 December 20X0, Company ABC issued at par a floating rate bond with the following characteristics:

Bond Terms	
Issue date	31 December 20X0
Maturity	5 years (31 December 20X5)
Notional	€ 100 million
Coupon	Euribor 12M + 1.50 %, annually
Euribor fixing	Euribor is fixed at the beginning of the annual interest period

ABC had the view that the curve was too steep and that the Euribor 12-month rate was not going to reach 5.25 % in the next five years. ABC also believed that it was unlikely that the Euribor 12M rate would reach 2.90 % in the next five years. As a consequence, ABC hedged against increases in the coupon payments of the bond by entering into a European KIKO collar. The KIKO collar was composed of a knock-out cap and a knock-in forward. The terms of the knock-out cap were as follows:

	Knock-out Cap Terms
Start date	31 December 20X0
Counterparties	Company ABC and XYZ Bank
Cap buyer	Company ABC
Maturity	5 years (31 December 20X5)
Notional amount	€ 100 million
Premium	EUR 890,000
Strike	3.75 % annually, Actual/360 basis
Underlying	Euribor 12-month rate
	Euribor is fixed at the beginning of the annual interest period
Barrier	5.25 %
Knock-out event	Caplet ceases to exist if at its expiry
	the Euribor 12M rate is at or above the Barrier

Each caplet could only be exercised if at its expiry date the Euribor 12M rate was below 5.25 %. Thus, if at the beginning of an interest period Euribor 12M was at or above 5.25 %, ABC had no protection for that period. The remaining caplets remained active. Figure 5.15 shows the payoff of each caplet.

The terms of the knock-in floor were as follows:

	Knock-in Floor Terms
Start date	31 December 20X0
Counterparties	Company ABC and XYZ Bank
Floor buyer	XYZ Bank
Maturity	5 years (31 December 20X5)
Notional amount	€ 100 million
Premium	EUR 890,000
Strike	3.52 % annually, Actual/360 basis
Underlying	Euribor 12-month rate
	Euribor is fixed at the beginning of the annual interest period
Barrier	2.90 %
Knock-in event	Floorlet can only be exercised if at its expiry date
	the Euribor 12M rate trades at or below the Barrier

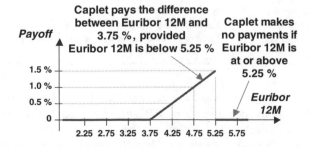

Figure 5.15   K/O Caplet Payoff (Excl. Premium).

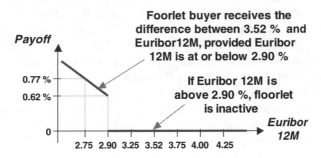

Figure 5.16   K/I Floorlet Payoff (Excl. Premium).

Each floorlet could only be exercised if at its expiry date the Euribor 12M rate was at or below 2.90 %. Thus, if at the beginning of an interest period Euribor 12M was above 2.90 %, ABC needed not to make any payment under that period floorlet. The remaining floorlets could be activated at their corresponding expiry. Figure 5.16 shows the payoff of each floorlet.

Split Between Hedge Accounting Compliant Derivative and Residual Derivative

One of the main issues that ABC faced regarding the KIKO collar was how to split the instrument into two parts, a first part eligible for hedge accounting and a second part treated as undesignated, to minimise the overall impact in P&L volatility. ABC considered the following six choices:

1) Divide the KIKO collar into two parts: (i) a standard collar and (ii) a "residual" derivative. The standard collar would be the combination of a bought 3.75 % cap and a sold 2.90 % floor. The residual derivative would be the rest of the KIKO collar payoffs not included in the standard collar.
2) Divide the KIKO collar into two parts: (i) a standard collar and (ii) a "residual" derivative. The standard collar would be the combination of a bought 3.75 % cap and a sold 3.52 % floor. The residual derivative would be the rest of the KIKO collar payoffs not included in the standard collar.
3) Divide the KIKO collar into two parts: (i) the combination of a standard collar-1 and a standard collar-2, and (ii) a "residual" derivative. The standard collar-1 would be the combination of a bought 3.75 % cap and a sold 2.90 % floor. The standard collar-2 would be a bought very out-of-the money floor (e.g., with a 0.50 % floor rate) and a sold 5.25 % cap. The residual derivative would be the rest of the KIKO collar payoffs not included in the combination of standard collars. This choice is based on a IAS 39 interpretation that the combination of the two standard collars is eligible for hedge accounting because all the sold options nominal and premium do not exceed all the bought options nominal and premium. In our view this is quite an aggressive interpretation of the IAS 39 standard. Therefore, ABC preferred not to select this choice.
4) Consider the whole KIKO collar as undesignated. As a consequence, all changes in fair value of the KIKO would be recorded in P&L. This choice was the simplest, saving the effort required to comply with hedge accounting. However, ABC did not select this choice due to its potential effect in P&L volatility.

5) Consider the whole KIKO as eligible for hedge accounting. The objective of the hedge would be defined as: "To limit to a maximum of 3.75 % the interest payments related to Euribor 12M of the bond, provided that the Euribor 12M rate is not equal or greater than 5.25 %. To achieve this objective and not to pay an upfront premium, the interest payments are limited to a minimum of 3.52 % only if the Euribor 12M rate is below 2.90 %". Hedge effectiveness would be tested using a hypothetical derivative whose terms matched exactly those of the KIKO. As a result, all the changes in the intrinsic value of the KIKO would be recorded in equity until the hedged cash flows impacted P&L. This accounting treatment is, in our view, very controversial and we think that many auditors will question its validity. Therefore, ABC preferred not to select this choice.
6) Consider the whole KIKO as eligible for hedge accounting. The objective of the hedge would be defined as: "To limit to a maximum of 3.75 % the interest payments related to Euribor 12M of the bond. To achieve this objective and not to pay an upfront premium, the interest payments are limited to a minimum of 3.52 %". Hedge effectiveness would be tested replacing the hedged item by a hypothetical derivative. The terms of the hypothetical derivative would be a purchased 3.75 % cap and a sold 3.52 % floor. There are two potential problems with this choice: (i) it is unlikely that it passes the prospective tests and (ii) there is a substantial danger of failing a retrospective test if the Euribor 12M is around 3.52 %. Thus, ABC preferred not to select this alternative.

Therefore, ABC considered only the first two choices. The first was better if ABC decided that it was unlikely that implied Euribor 12M rates would trade around 2.90 %. Otherwise the second would be better. Because ABC had the view that rates would remain notably higher than 2.90 %, it chose the first:

- The designated hedging instrument was a collar that combined a purchased 3.75 % cap and a sold 2.90 %. The changes in the intrinsic value of the collar would be recorded in equity and subsequently recycled to P&L when the hedged cash flows impact P&L. The changes in time value of the collar would be recorded in P&L.
- The residual derivative would have such terms that when combined with the hedging instrument terms, the KIKO collar terms are obtained. The changes in fair value of the residual derivative would be recorded in P&L.

The terms of the collar (i.e., the hedging instrument) were as follows:

3.75% Cap Terms		2.90% Floor Terms	
Start date	31 December 20X0	Start date	31 December 20X0
Counterparties	Company ABC and XYZ Bank	Counterparties	Company ABC and XYZ Bank
Cap buyer	Company ABC	Floor buyer	XYZ Bank
Maturity	5 years (31 December 20X5)	Maturity	5 years (31 December 20X5)
Notional amount	€ 100 million	Notional amount	€ 100 million
Premium	EUR 2,237,000	Premium	EUR 280,000
Strike	3.75 % annually, Actual/360 basis	Strike	2.90 % annually, Actual/360 basis
Underlying	Euribor 12M rate	Underlying	Euribor 12M rate

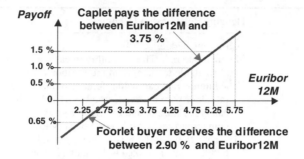

Figure 5.17   Hedge Accounting Compliant Part (Bought 3.75 % Cap – Sold 2.90 % Floor).

Figure 5.17 shows the payoff of each caplet and floorlet combination.

The collar was designated as the hedging instrument in a cash flow hedge of the coupon payments on the bond. The combination of cap and the floor (i.e., the collar) could be designated as the hedging instrument because:

1) No net premium was received; and
2) The underlying of the cap and the floor were the same (i.e., Euribor 12-month); and
3) The cap and the floor had the same maturity; and
4) The notional amount of the written option (i.e., the floor) was not greater than the notional amount of the purchased option (i.e., the cap).

The bond credit spread (150 basis points) was not included in the hedging relationship. The residual derivative comprised the following options:

- A sold knock-in cap with a 3.75 % strike and a 5.25 % barrier
- A sold digital floor with strike 2.90 % and 0.62 % payoff (= 3.52 % − 2.90 %)

5.11.1   Hedging Relationship Documentation

The hedging relationship was documented as follows:

Hedging Relationship Documentation	
Risk management objective and strategy for undertaking the hedge	The objective of the hedge is to limit to a maximum of 3.75 % the cash outflows related to Euribor 12M of one of ABC's bonds. To achieve this objective and simultaneously reduce the upfront premium for the hedge, the cash flows related to Euribor 12M are limited to a minimum of 2.90 %. The hedge objective will be obtained by entering into an interest rate collar (a combination of a purchased interest rate cap and a sold interest rate floor). The combination of the collar and the bond will result in an expected net cash outflow between 5.25 % and 4.40 % (including the bond 1.50 % spread).
	This hedging objective is consistent with ABC's overall risk management strategy of managing the exposure to interest rate risk through the proportion of fixed and floating rate net debt in its total debt portfolio, using swaps and interest rate options.

(Continued)

Hedging Relationship Documentation	
Type of hedge	Cash flow hedge.
Risk being hedged	Interest rate risk. The variability in cash outflows of the bond attributable to changes in the Euribor 12M rates.
Hedging instrument	The interest rate cap with reference number 012376, and the interest rate floor with reference number 012377. The counterparty to the cap is XYZ Bank and the credit risk associated with this counterparty is considered to be very low.
Hedged item	The cash flows of the 5-year floating bond with reference number 678901 that are linked to Euribor 12 month. The bond spread (150 basis points) is not part of the hedged cash flows.
Assessment of effectiveness testing	Hedge effectiveness will be assessed by comparing changes in the fair value of the hedging instrument to changes in the fair value of a hypothetical derivative. The terms of the hypothetical derivative are such that its fair value changes offset exactly the changes in fair value of the hedged item for the risk being hedged. The hypothetical derivative terms in this hedging relationship are identical to the hedging instrument terms but assume no counterparty credit exposure. The options' time value is excluded from the hedge relationship. **Prospective test** A prospective test will be performed at inception and at each reporting date using the critical terms method. If (i) the critical terms of the hypothetical derivative and the hedging instrument match (i.e., notional amount, currency, underlying and interest periods), and (ii) the credit risk of the counterparty to the hedging instrument are very low, the hedge will be considered to be highly effective prospectively. The credit risk of the counterparty to the hedging instrument will be continuously monitored. **Retrospective test** A retrospective test will be performed at each reporting date using the "ratio analysis method" (also called "dollar-offset method). The ratio will compare the cumulative change since hedge inception in the intrinsic value of the hedging instrument with the cumulative change since hedge inception in the intrinsic value of the hypothetical derivative. The hedge will be assumed to be highly effective on a retrospective basis if the ratio is between 80 % and 125 %.

Hedging Instrument and Residual Derivative Fair Values

The total fair value of the KIKO was computed using a variation of the Black-Scholes formula to price barrier options. The fair value of the collar was determined computing the value of each of its caplets and floorlets using the Black formula. This formula is an adaptation to interest rate options of the Black-Scholes options model. The inputs to price each caplet or floorlet were:

1) The time to expiry of the option
2) The forward interest rate

3) The discount factor (the price at today of a risk-free zero-coupon bond paying EUR 1 at the option payoff payment date)
4) The strike rate of the option
5) The volatility of the forward rate

The intrinsic value of the collar was computed similarly to the collar fair value calculation, but assuming zero volatility. The time value of the collar was then computed as the difference between the collar fair value and the collar intrinsic value:

$$\text{Collar time value} = \text{Collar fair value} - \text{Collar Intrinsic value}$$

The fair value of the residual derivative was computed as the difference between the KIKO fair value and the collar fair value:

$$\text{Residual derivative fair value} = \text{KIKO fair value} - \text{Collar fair value}$$

The fair values of the derivatives at each balance sheet date were as follows:

Balance Sheet Date	KIKO Fair Value	Collar Fair Value	Residual Fair Value	Collar Intrinsic Value	Collar Time Value
31-Dec-X0	–0–	1,957,000	<1,957,000>	1,198,000	759,000
31-Dec-X1	1,140,000	3,328,000	<2,188,000>	3,031,000	297,000
31-Dec-X2	333,000	933,000	<600,000>	525,000	408,000
31-Dec-X3	228,000	381,000	<153,000>	167,000	214,000
31-Dec-X4	141,000	141,000	–0–	141,000	–0–
31-Dec-X5	–0–	–0–	–0–	–0–	–0–

Prospective Tests

The objective of the prospective tests was to demonstrate that ABC had a valid expectation that the hedge will be highly effective. ABC performed a prospective test at hedge inception (31 December 20X0) and at each reporting date. Each prospective test was carried out using the critical terms method.

The hedged item was substituted by a hypothetical derivative. The terms of the hypothetical derivative were such that the changes in fair value of the hypothetical derivative perfectly offset the changes in fair value of the hedged item for variations in the risk being hedged. In this case the hedging objective was to limit to a maximum of 3.75 % and to a minimum of 2.90 % the cash outflows related to Euribor 12M of the bond. The derivative that perfectly achieved this objective was a collar with strikes of 3.75 % and 2.90 %. Therefore, the terms of the hypothetical derivative identically matched those of the hedging instrument (i.e., the collar), but without any credit risk exposure to the counterparty of the derivative.

Because (i) the critical terms of hedging instrument matched identically those of the hypothetical derivative and (ii) the credit risk associated with the counterparty to the hedging instrument was considered to be very low, ABC concluded that the hedge was highly effective prospectively at each testing date. The credit risk of the counterparty to the hedging instrument was continuously monitored.

Retrospective Tests

A retrospective test was performed on each reporting date and also at the maturity of the hedge. During the term of the hedge, there was no significant deterioration in the credit of the counterparty to the hedging instrument.

In our case, the terms of the hypothetical derivative matched identically those of the hedging instrument, except the credit exposure to the counterparty of the derivative and the derivative liquidity. Because neither the creditworthiness of the swap counterparty (i.e., XYZ Bank) experienced a substantial deterioration nor the liquidity of the swap dried up during any of the retrospective assessment periods, the result of the retrospective tests using the ratio analysis was always 100 %, as shown in the table below:

Balance Sheet Date	Collar Cumulative Change Intrinsic Value	Hypothetical Derivative Cumulative Change Intrinsic Value	Ratio	Hedge Effective Part
31-Dec-X0	—	—	—	—
31-Dec-X1	1,833,000	1,833,000	100 %	1,833,000
31-Dec-X2	<673,000>	<673,000>	100 %	<2,506,000>
31-Dec-X3	<1,031,000>	<1,031,000>	100 %	<358,000>
31-Dec-X4	<1,057,000>	<1,057,000>	100 %	<26,000>
31-Dec-X5	<1,198,000>	<1,198,000>	100 %	<141,000>

Notes: 1) The "cumulative change in collar intrinsic value" was computed as:

   End of period collar intrinsic value – Collar intrinsic value at inception

2) The cumulative change in intrinsic value of the hedging instrument and the hypothetical derivative coincided because their critical terms were identical and because there was no substantial deterioration of the creditworthiness of the collar counterparty.

At each balance sheet date, the ratio was within the 80 %–125 % range, and thus, the hedging relationship was highly effective retrospectively at each test date. Remember that the time value of the collar was not included in the hedging relationship, so even if each test showed no ineffectiveness, the change in time value of the collar was recorded in P&L.

5.11.2   Journal Entries

In order to produce the corresponding journal entries of this case, we have summarised in the following tables the main figures:

Balance Sheet Date	Period Euribor 12M Rate	Bond Interest	KIKO Payoff	KIKO Fair Value Change
31 Dec X0	—	—	—	—
31 Dec X1	3.21 %	<4,710,000>	-0-	1,140,000
31 Dec X2	4.21 %	<5,710,000>	460,000	<807,000>
31 Dec X3	3.71 %	<5,210,000>	-0-	<105,000>
31 Dec X4	3.80 %	<5,300,000>	50,000	<87,000>
31 Dec X5	3.95 %	<5,450,000>	200,000	<141,000>

Balance Sheet Date	Collar Fair Value Change	Collar Effective Part	Collar Ineffective Value	Residual Derivative Change Fair Value
31 Dec X0	—	—	—	—
31 Dec X1	1,371,000	1,833,000	<462,000>	<231,000>
31 Dec X2	<2,395,000>	<2,506,000>	111,000	1,588,000
31 Dec X3	<552,000>	<358,000>	<194,000>	447,000
31 Dec X4	<240,000>	<26,000>	<214,000>	153,000
31 Dec X5	<141,000>	<141,000>	–0–	–0–

Notes:

Bond interest = 100 million * (Euribor 12M + 1.50 %) * (Day Count Factor).
The Day Count Factor assumed to be equal to one.

KIKO Payoff = 100 million* [Maximum (Euribor 12M – 3.75%; 0)]*(Day Count Factor) + 100 million* [Maximum (2.90 %−Euribor 12M; 0)]*(Day Count Factor), as neither barrier was crossed.

Collar ineffective part = Change in collar fair value −Collar effective part.

Residual derivative fair value change = KIKO fair value change – Collar fair value change.

1) Journal entries on 31 December 20X0

To record the issuance of the bond:

Cash (Asset)	€ 100,000,000	
Financial Debt (Liability)		€ 100,000,000

The initial fair value of the collar (i.e., the hedging instrument) was EUR 1,957,000. The journal entries to record the collar:

Derivative – Collar (Asset)	€ 1,957,000	
Cash (Asset)		€ 1,957,000

The initial fair value of the residual derivative was EUR-1,957,000. The journal entries to record the residual derivative:

Cash (Asset)	€ 1,957,000	
Derivative – Residual (Liability)		€ 1,957,000

2) Journal entries on 31 December 20X1

To record the bond coupon payment:

Interest Expense (Income Statement)	€ 4,710,000	
Cash (Asset)		€ 4,710,000

Because the Euribor 12M rate (3.21 %) for the period was below the strike rate of the cap (3.75 %) and above the strike of the floor (2.90 %), there was no settlement under the KIKO for the period.

The change in fair value of the collar was a gain of EUR 1,371,000. The collar effective part was a gain of EUR 1,833,000 and the ineffective part was a loss of 462,000. The related journal entries were as follows:

Derivative – Collar (Asset)	€ 1,371,000	
Other Income/Expenses (P&L)	€ 462,000	
Cash Flow Hedge (Equity)		€ 1,833,000

The change in fair value of the residual derivative was a loss of EUR 231,000:

Other Income/Expenses (P&L)	€ 231,000	
Derivative – Residual (Liability)		€ 231,000

3) Journal entries on 31 December 20X2

To record the bond coupon payment:

Interest Income/Expense (P&L)	€ 5,710,000	
Cash (Asset)		€ 5,710,000

Because the Euribor 12M rate (4.21 %) for the period was above the strike rate of the cap (3.75 %), there was a EUR 460,000 settlement under the KIKO for the period.

Cash (asset)	€ 460,000	
Interest Income/Expense (P&L)		€ 460,000

The change in fair value of the collar was a loss of EUR 2,395,000. The collar effective part was a loss of EUR 2,506,000 and the ineffective part was a gain of 111,000. The related journal entries were as follows:

Cash Flow Hedge (Equity)	€ 2,506,000	
Other Income/Expenses (P&L)		€ 111,000
Derivative – Collar (Asset)		€ 2,395,000

The change in fair value of the residual derivative was a gain of EUR 1,588,000:

Derivative – Residual (Liability)	€ 1,588,000	
Other Income/Expenses (P&L)		€ 1,588,000

4) Journal entries on 31 December 20X3

To record the bond coupon payment:

Interest Income/Expense (P&L)	€ 5,210,000	
Cash (Asset)		€ 5,210,000

Because the Euribor 12M rate (3.71 %) for the period was below the strike rate of the cap (3.75 %) and above the strike of the floor (2.90 %), there was no settlement under the KIKO for the period.

The change in fair value of the collar was a loss of EUR 552,000. The collar effective part was a loss of EUR 358,000 and the ineffective part was a loss of 194,000. The related journal entries were as follows:

Cash Flow Hedge (Equity)	€ 358,000	
Other Income/Expenses (P&L)	€ 194,000	
Derivative – Collar (Asset)		€ 552,000

The change in fair value of the residual derivative was a gain of EUR 447,000:

Derivative – Residual (Liability)	€ 447,000	
Other Income/Expenses (P&L)		€ 447,000

5) Journal entries on 31 December 20X4

To record the bond coupon payment:

Interest Income/Expense (P&L)	€ 5,300,000	
Cash (Asset)		€ 5,300,000

Because the Euribor 12M rate (3.80 %) for the period was above the strike rate of the cap (3.75 %), there was a EUR 50,000 settlement under the KIKO for the period.

Cash (asset)	€ 50,000	
Interest Income/Expense (P&L)		€ 50,000

The change in fair value of the collar was a loss of EUR 240,000. The collar effective part was a loss of EUR 26,000 and the ineffective part was a loss of 214,000. The related journal entries were as follows:

Cash Flow Hedge (Equity)	€ 26,000	
Other Income/Expenses (P&L)	€ 214,000	
Derivative – Collar (Asset)		€ 240,000

The change in fair value of the residual derivative was a gain of EUR 153,000:

Derivative – Residual (Liability)	€ 153,000	
Other Income/Expenses (P&L)		€ 153,000

6) Journal entries on 31 December 20X5

To record the bond coupon payment:

Interest Income/Expense (P&L)	€ 5,450,000	
Cash (Asset)		€ 5,450,000

Because the Euribor 12M rate (3.95 %) for the period was above the strike rate of the cap (3.75 %), there was a EUR 200,000 settlement under the KIKO for the period.

Cash (Asset)	€ 200,000	
Interest Income/Expense (P&L)		€ 200,000

The change in fair value of the collar was a loss of EUR 141,000. The collar effective part was a loss of EUR 141,000. The collar ineffective part was zero. The related journal entries were as follows:

Cash Flow Hedge (Equity)	€ 141,000	
Derivative – Collar (Asset)		€ 141,000

The change in fair value of the residual derivative was zero. Thus, no accounting entries were required.

To record the bond redemption:

Financial Debt (Liability)	€ 100,000,000	
Cash (Asset)		€ 100,000,000

6

Hedging Foreign Currency Liabilities

The global nature of the capital markets allows many entities to fund in the lowest cost market available to them. Frequently, entities capture lower costs of funds and greater market liquidity by raising capital in currencies other than their functional currency. Because the foreign currency liability is a monetary item, IAS 21 requires the liability to be translated into the entity's functional currency using the exchange rate prevailing at the reporting date, as covered in Chapter 4. The translation gains or losses on the debt are recorded in P&L. Thus, absence of a FX hedging strategy may result in significant P&L volatility. This chapter deals with the hedge accounting treatment of foreign currency borrowings swapped back to the issuer's functional currency.

6.1 HEDGING USING CROSS-CURRENCY SWAPS

The most common technique to hedge foreign debt is through cross-currency swaps (CCS). A CCS converts the debt's foreign cash flows back to the entity's functional currency. Assuming the EUR as the issuer's functional currency and a USD-denominated debt, four are the potential hedging situations:

USD Liability	CCS Characteristics	Resulting EUR Liability	Type of Hedge
Floating	Receive USD floating – Pay EUR floating	Floating	Fair Value
Floating	Receive USD floating – Pay EUR fixed	Fixed	Cash flow
Fixed	Receive USD fixed – Pay EUR floating	Floating	Fair Value
Fixed	Receive USD fixed – Pay EUR fixed	Fixed	Cash flow

The following four cases illustrate the accounting implications of these four hedging strategies.

CASE 6.1

Hedging a Floating-rate Foreign Currency Liability Using a Receive-Floating Pay-Floating Cross-Currency Swap

The objective of this case is to illustrate the hedge accounting implications of a floating-rate cross-border financing hedged with a pay-floating receive-floating CCS. This case is much more complex that it may look. We have made a particular attempt to discuss in detail some of the challenging aspects of the case, specially the selection of the most suitable hedging instrument, the interaction between the translation of the foreign currency liability and the hedge item fair value adjustments, and the calculation of accruals.

Background Information

On 15 July 20X0, Company ABC issued a USD-denominated floating-rate bond. ABC's functional currency was the EUR. The bond had the following characteristics:

Bond Terms	
Expected issue date	15 July 20X0
Maturity	3 years (15 July 20X3)
Notional	USD 100 million
Coupon	USD Libor 12-month plus 50 bps, to be paid annually
USD Libor fixing	Libor is fixed two days prior to the beginning of each annual interest period

Since ABC's objective was to raise EUR funding, on issue date ABC entered into a CCS. Through the CCS, the entity agreed to receive a floating rate equal to the bond coupon and pay a Euribor floating rate plus a spread. The CCS had the following terms:

Cross-currency Swap Terms	
Trade date	15 July 20X0
Start date	15 July 20X0
Counterparties	Company ABC and XYZ Bank
Maturity date	3 years (15 July 20X3)
USD nominal	USD 100 million
EUR nominal	EUR 80 million
Initial exchange	On start date, ABC receives the EUR nominal and pays the USD nominal
ABC pays	Euribor 12m + 49 bps, annually, A/360 basis, on the EUR nominal
	Euribor is fixed two business days prior to the beginning of the annual interest period
ABC receives	USD Libor 12m + 50 bps, annually, A/360 basis, on the USD nominal
	Libor is fixed two business days prior to the beginning of the annual interest period
Final exchange	On maturity date, ABC receives the USD nominal and pays the EUR nominal

The mechanics of the CCS are described next. It can be seen that through the combination of the USD bond and the CCS, ABC synthetically obtained a EUR floating liability.

On issue date and the start of the CCS, there was an initial exchange of principals through the CCS: ABC delivered the USD 100 million proceeds of the issue and received EUR 80 million. The combination of the bond and CCS had the same effect as if ABC issued a EUR-denominated bond, as shown in Figure 6.1.

Annually, there was a periodic exchange of interest payments. ABC received USD Libor interest and paid Euribor interest. ABC used the USD Libor cash flows it received under the CCS to pay the bond interest. Figure 6.2 shows the strategy's intermediate cash flows.

At maturity of the CCS and the debt, ABC re-exchanged the principal, using the USD 100 million it received through the CCS to redeem the bond issue, and delivering EUR 80 million to the CCS counterparty. Note that this final exchange was made at exactly the same rate used in the initial exchange (1.2500). Figure 6.3 shows the strategy's cash flows at maturity.

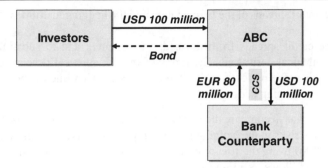

Figure 6.1   Bond with CCS : Initial Cash Flows.

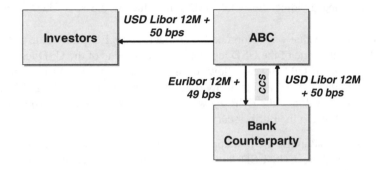

Figure 6.2   Bond with CCS : Intermediate Cash Flows.

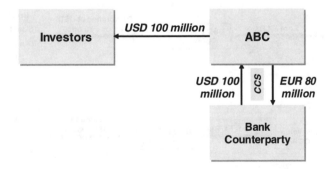

Figure 6.3   Bond with CCS : Cash Flows at Maturity.

Assessing Effectiveness

When assessing effectiveness, a comparison must be made between changes in the fair values of the hedging instrument and the hedged item. Three approaches are usually considered:

1) To directly compare fair values computed taking into account all the risks in their entirety (i.e., without any exclusions from the hedge assessment).

2) To exclude the credit spreads of the hedged item and the hedging instrument from the hedge assessment.
3) To exclude the credit spreads from the hedge assessment and to substitute the hedged item for a hypothetical derivative. The terms of the hypothetical derivative are such that its changes in fair value perfectly offset the changes in fair value of the hedged item for variations in the risk being hedged.

The first approach was to compare the fair values of the hedged item and the hedging instrument including all the risks in the hedging relationship. In our case, the fair value calculations on 31 December-20X0 using the first approach (not excluding any elements from the hedge relationship) were as follows (see Figure 6.4):

1) The bond USD fair value was obtained by discounting the expected USD bond cash flows using the USD Libor curve plus the 50 bps credit spread. The bond EUR fair value was then obtained dividing the bond USD fair value by the spot USD/EUR exchange rate.
2) The CCS EUR fair value was computed by subtracting the EUR fair value of the EUR leg from the EUR fair value of the USD leg. The EUR fair value of the USD leg was obtained discounting the expected USD cash flows of the CCS using the USD Libor curve flat (i.e., without any credit spreads) and then dividing the result by the spot USD/EUR exchange rate. The EUR fair value of the EUR leg was obtained discounting the expected EUR cash flows of the CCS using the Euribor curve flat.

The main problem of adopting the first approach was its high risk of failing the effectiveness tests as the bond and the CCS USD leg cash flows are discounted using different curves. Another potential element of inefficiency was the Euribor 12M rate (plus the credit spread)

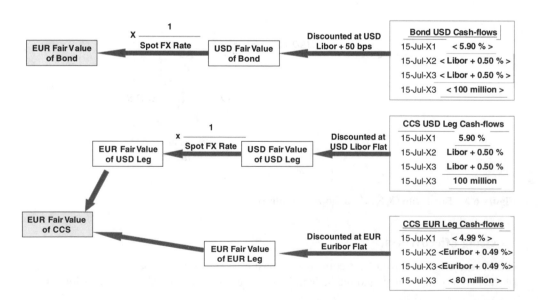

Figure 6.4 Approach 1 – Calculating Fair Values Without Exclusions (31–December–20X0 Fair valuation).

already fixed at 4.99 % on 15 July 20X0. If the Euribor rate plus the 49 bps credit spread from 31 December 20X0 until 15 July 20X1 was significantly different to 4.99 %, the discounting of the cash flow related to this rate may create important distortions. Therefore, we advise not to use this alternative as there is a high likelihood of failing the effectiveness tests.

The second alternative was to exclude the credit spreads of the hedged item and the hedging instrument from the hedge assessment. In our case, the fair value calculation on 31 December-20X0 using this second alternative was as follows (see Figure 6.5):

1) The bond USD fair value is obtained by discounting the expected USD bond cash flows excluding the 50 bps credit spread using the USD Libor curve flat (i.e., without the credit spread). The bond EUR fair value was then obtained by dividing the bond USD fair value by the spot USD/EUR exchange rate.
2) The CCS EUR fair value was computed by subtracting the EUR fair value of the EUR leg from the EUR fair value of the USD leg. The EUR fair value of the USD leg was obtained discounting the expected USD cash flows (excluding the 50 bps credit spread) of the CCS using the USD Libor curve flat and then dividing the result by the spot USD/EUR exchange rate. The EUR fair value of the EUR leg was obtained discounting the expected EUR cash flows (excluding the 49 bps credit spread) of the CCS using the Euribor curve flat.

The only element of potential inefficiency of this second alternative was the Euribor 12M rate already fixed at 4.50 % on 15 July 20X0. If the Euribor rate from 31 December 20X0 until 15 July 20X1 was significantly different to 4.50 %, the discounting of the cash flow related to this rate can create important distortions. However, this alternative was preferable to the first

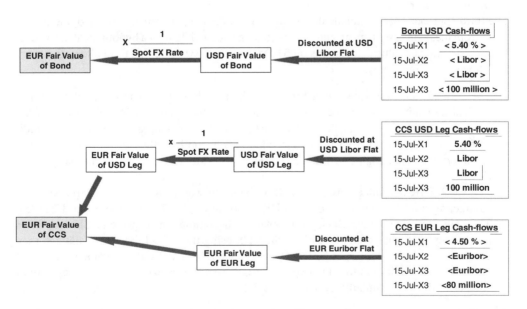

Figure 6.5   Approach 2 – Calculating Fair Values Excluding Credit Spreads (31–December–20X0 Fair valuation).

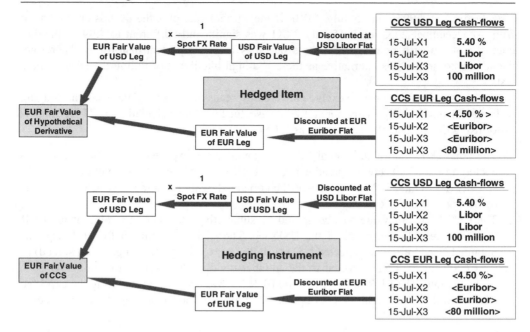

Figure 6.6 Approach – Calculating Fair Values Using Hypothertical Derivative (1–December–20X0 Fair valuation).

alternative, as it eliminated the discounting mismatch on the USD cash flows. Additionally, sometimes short term rates remain stable in periods long enough to not affect the fixings problem just described.

The third approach was to exclude the credit terms of the hedged item and the hedging instrument from the hedge assessment, and to substitute the hedged item by a hypothetical derivative. In our case, the fair value calculations on 31 December 20X0 using this third alternative were as follows (see Figure 6.6):

1) The hedged item was substituted for a hypothetical derivative. The terms of the hypothetical derivative are such that it would fully offset the changes in the fair value of the hedged item attributable to the hedged risks. Under this approach, because the credit spreads were excluded from the hedge relationship, the hypothetical derivative had the same terms as the hedging instrument except that it did not bear any counterparty credit risk.

2) The CCS EUR fair value was computed in the same way as in the second approach: by subtracting the EUR fair value of the EUR leg from the EUR fair value of the USD leg. The EUR fair value of the USD leg was obtained discounting the expected USD cash flows (excluding the 50 bps credit spread) of the CCS using the USD Libor curve flat and then dividing the result by the spot USD/EUR exchange rate. The EUR fair value of the EUR leg was obtained discounting the expected EUR cash flows (excluding the 49 bps credit spread) of the CCS using the Euribor curve flat.

This third approach avoided the inconveniencies of the other two approach as the hedged item and hedging instrument cash flows and discounting coincide. This was the approach that ABC selected to assess the effectiveness of the hedging relationship. The changes in the fair value of the hypothetical derivative were then used to adjust the carrying value of the bond.

Hedge Documentation

ABC documented the hedge relationship as follows:

Hedging Relationship Documentation	
Risk management objective and strategy for undertaking the hedge	The objective of the hedge is to reduce the variability of the fair value of a foreign currency denominated bond. This hedging objective is consistent with ABC's overall interest rate risk management strategy of transforming all new issued foreign-denominated debt into the group functional currency, and thereafter managing the exposure to Euro interest rate risk through the proportion of fixed and floating rate net debt in its total debt portfolio.
Type of hedge	Fair value hedge.
Risk being hedged	Interest rate risk and FX risk. The variability in fair value of the bond attributable to changes in the USD Libor and Euribor interest rates, and the USD/EUR exchange rate. Fair value changes attributable to credit or other risks are not hedged in this relationship. Accordingly, the bond's 50 bps credit spread is excluded from the hedge relationship.
Hedging instrument	The cross-currency swap (CCS) with reference number 005765. The counterparty to the swap is XYZ Bank and the credit risk associated with this counterparty is considered to be very low. The CCS credit spreads (the 50 bps of the USD leg and the 49 bps of the EUR leg) are excluded from the hedge relationship.
Hedged item	The 3-year USD-denominated floating-rate bond with reference number 667902.
Assessment of effectiveness testing	Hedge effectiveness will be assessed by comparing changes in the fair value of the hedging instrument to changes in the fair value of a hypothetical derivative. The terms of the hypothetical derivative are such that the changes in fair value of the hypothetical derivative perfectly offset the changes in fair value of the hedged item for variations in the risk being hedged. In this case, the terms of the hypothetical derivative matched identically those of the hedging instrument (i.e., the CCS), but without any credit risk exposure to the counterparty of the derivative. **Prospective test** A prospective test will be performed at the inception and at each reporting date, using the critical terms method. If (i) the critical terms of the hypothetical derivative and the hedging instrument match (i.e., notional amounts, currencies, underlying and interest periods), and (ii) the credit risk of the counterparty to the hedging instrument is very low, the hedge will be considered to be highly effective prospectively. The credit risk of the counterparty to the hedging instrument will be continuously monitored.

(Continued)

Hedging Relationship Documentation

Retrospective test

A retrospective test will be performed at each reporting date and also at hedge maturity using the "ratio analysis method". The ratio will compare the change since the last assessment in the fair value of the hedging instrument with the change since the last assessment in the fair value of the hypothetical derivative. The hedge will be assumed to be highly effective on a retrospective basis if the ratio is between 80 % and 125 %.

The effective part of the change in fair value of the hedging instrument (excluding the portion attributable to the current period swap accrual) will be recorded as a change in the carrying value of the bond, with an offset in P&L.

Prospective Tests

ABC performed a prospective test at inception of the trade and at each reporting date. On each test date: (i) the critical terms of the hypothetical derivative and the hedging instrument matched (i.e., notional amount, currency, underlying and interest periods), and (ii) the credit risk of the counterparty to the hedging instrument was very low. Accordingly, the hedge was considered to be highly effective prospectively on each test date.

The terms of the hedging instrument were the CCS terms once excluded the credit spreads on both legs. The terms of the hypothetical derivative were the same as those of the hedging instrument but assuming no credit risk on the counterparty, and excluding the initial exchange. The following table shows the terms of the hypothetical derivative for effectiveness assessment:

Hypothetical Derivative Terms	
Trade date	15 July 20X0
Start date	15 July 20X0
Counterparties	Company ABC and a AAA-rated hypothetical counterparty
Maturity date	3 years (15 July 20X3)
USD nominal	USD 100 million
EUR nominal	EUR 80 million
ABC pays	Euribor 12m, annually, A/360 basis, on the EUR nominal
	Euribor is fixed two business days prior to the beginning of the annual interest period
ABC receives	USD Libor 12m, annually, A/360 basis, on the USD nominal
	Libor is fixed two business days prior to the beginning of the annual interest period
Final exchange	On maturity date, ABC receives the USD nominal and pays the EUR nominal

Retrospective Tests

ABC performed a retrospective test at each reporting date and at hedge maturity. The fair value of the hedging instrument and the hypothetical derivative were computed at inception and at each test date. Remember that the terms of the hedging instrument for effectiveness assessment were different to terms of the CCS, because they did not include the credit spreads.

The retrospective test calculations were based on the following USD/EUR spot rate and interest rate curves:

	15-Jul-X0	Test-1 31-Dec-X0	Test-2 31-Dec-X1	Test-3 31-Dec-X2	Test-4 15-Jul-X3
USD/EUR Spot	1.2500	1.2800	1.2200	1.1500	1.1000
USD 1-Year	5.40 %	5.50 %	5.70 %	5.60 %	—
USD 2-Year	5.50 %	5.60 %	5.80 %	5.70 %	—
USD 3-Year	5.59 %	5.69 %	5.89 %	5.79 %	—
EUR 1-Year	4.50 %	4.70 %	4.90 %	5.00 %	—
EUR 2-Year	4.60 %	4.80 %	5.00 %	5.05 %	—
EUR 3-Year	4.70 %	4.89 %	5.09 %	5.10 %	—

Retrospective Test Performed on 31-December-20X0

The following table shows the fair value calculation of the hedging instrument and the hypothetical derivative at hedge inception (15 July 20X0):

Cash Flow Date	Notional	Floating Rate Fixing (1)	Implied Float. Rate (2)	Credit Spread	Period Leg Amount (3)	Disc. Factor (4)	Present Value
Hedging Instrument and Hypothetical Derivative Valuation on 15-Jul-X0							
Cash-flows of USD Leg:							
15-Jul-X1	100 Mill.	13-Jul-X0	5.40 %	Excl.	5,400,000	0.9486	5,122,000
15-Jul-X2	100 Mill.	13-Jul-X1	5.60 %	Excl.	5,600,000	0.8978	5,028,000
15-Jul-X3	100 Mill.	13-Jul-X2	5.78 %	Excl.	5,780,000	0.8494	4,910,000
15-Jul-X3					100 Mill.	0.8494	84,940,000
					Total USD		**100,000,000**
					Total EUR (1.2500)		**80,000,000**
Cash-flows of EUR Leg:							
15-Jul-X1	80 Mill.	13-Jul-X0	4.50 %	Excl.	3,600,000	0.9569	−3,445,000
15-Jul-X2	80 Mill.	13-Jul-X1	4.71 %	Excl.	3,768,000	0.9136	−3,442,000
15-Jul-X3	80 Mill.	13-Jul-X2	4.89 %	Excl.	3,912,000	0.8713	−3,409,000
15-Jul-X3					80 Mill.	0.8713	−69,704,000
					Total EUR		**<80,000,000>**
					Fair Value		**−0−**

Notes:

(1) The USD Libor 12-month and the Euribor 12-month were fixed two business days prior to the commencement of the interest period.

(2) The fixing on 13-Jul-X0 was already known at hedge inception. The fixings of 13-Jul-X1 and 13-Jul-X2 were not known yet, so the valuation used their expected values.

(3) Period settlement amounts were calculated as:

Notional*Floating Rate*Floating Day Factor

As the basis in each leg was Actual/360, the "Floating Day Factor" was equal to (Number of days in interest period)/360, assumed to keep calculations simple to be equal to one.

(4) The discount factors represented the present value, as of the valuation date, of USD 1 (or EUR 1) to be paid on the cash flow date. The discount factors were computed using the mid-market USD Libor (or Euribor) yield curves flat (i.e., without taking into account any credit spread or bid/offers).

The fair value of the hedging instrument and the hypothetical derivative on 31 December 20X0 was calculated as follows:

Hedging Instrument and Hypothetical Derivative Valuation on 31-Dec-X0							
Cash Flow Date	Notional	Floating Rate Fixing	Implied Float. Rate	Credit Spread	Period Leg Amount	Disc. Factor	Present Value
Cash-flows of USD Leg:							
15-Jul-X1	100 Mill.	13-Jul-X0	5.40%	Excl.	5,400,000	0.9720	5,249,000
15-Jul-X2	100 Mill.	13-Jul-X1	5.60%	Excl.	5,600,000	0.9205	5,155,000
15-Jul-X3	100 Mill.	13-Jul-X2	5.80%	Excl.	5,800,000	0.8700	5,046,000
15-Jul-X3					100 Mill.	0.8700	87,000,000
					Total USD		**102,450,000**
					Total EUR (1.2800)		**80,039,000**
Cash-flows of EUR Leg:							
15-Jul-X1	80 Mill.	13-Jul-X0	4.50%	Excl.	3,600,000	0.9759	−3,513,000
15-Jul-X2	80 Mill.	13-Jul-X1	4.81%	Excl.	3,848,000	0.9311	−3,583,000
15-Jul-X3	80 Mill.	13-Jul-X2	5.00%	Excl.	4,000,000	0.8868	−3,547,000
15-Jul-X3					80 Mill.	0.8868	−70,944,000
					Total EUR		**<81,587,000>**
					Fair Value		**<1,548,000>**

The interest accrual of the hedging instrument on 31 December 20X0 was EUR 286,000 (=1,953,000−1,667,000):

- The accrual of the USD leg was EUR 1,953,000 (= 5,400,000*169 days/365 days/1.28)
- The accrual of the EUR leg was EUR −1,667,000 (= −3,600,000*169/365)

Therefore the fair value of the hedging instrument on 31 December 20X0 excluding the accrual was EUR −1,834,000 (= −1,548,000 −286,000). The hypothetical derivative fair value was also EUR −1,834,000. The hedge was then deemed to be effective as the ratio was within the 80%−125% range, as shown in the following table:

Retrospective Test	31-Dec-X0
Hedging instrument fair value change	<1,834,000>
Hypothetical derivative fair value change	<1,834,000>
Ratio	**100,0%**
Hedge effective amount	<1,834,000>
Hedge ineffective amount	−0−

The effective part of the hedge gains or losses was the lesser of the absolute values of the accumulated change in fair value of the hedging instrument and the hypothetical derivative.

In our case, both amounts were identical, and thus, all the change in fair value of the hedging instrument was considered to be effective.

Retrospective Test Performed on 31 December 20X1

The fair value of the hedging instrument and the hypothetical derivative on 31 December 20X1 was calculated as follows:

					Hedging Instrument and Hypothetical Derivative Valuation on 31-Dec-X1		

Cash Flow Date	Notional	Floating Rate Fixing	Implied Float. Rate	Credit Spread	Period Leg Amount	Disc. Factor	Present Value
Cash- flows of USD Leg:							
15-Jul-X2	100 Mill.	13-Jul-X1	5.55 %	Excl.	5,550,000	0.9711	5,390,000
15-Jul-X3	100 Mill.	13-Jul-X2	5.80 %	Excl.	5,800,000	0.9178	5,323,000
15-Jul-X3					100 Mill.	0.9178	91,780,000
					Total USD		**102,493,000**
					Total EUR (1.2200)		**84,011,000**
Cash- flows of EUR Leg:							
15-Jul-X2	80 Mill.	13-Jul-X1	4.75 %	Excl.	3,800,000	0.9749	3,705,000
15-Jul-X3	80 Mill.	13-Jul-X2	5.00 %	Excl.	4,000,000	0.9285	3,714,000
15-Jul-X3					80 Mill.	0.9285	74,280,000
					Total EUR		**<81,699,000>**
					Fair Value		**2,312,000**

The interest accrual of the hedging instrument on 31 December 20X1 was EUR 347,000 (= 2,106,000 − 1,759,000):

- The accrual of the USD leg was EUR 2,106,000 (= 5,550,000*169 days/365 days/1.22)
- The accrual of the EUR leg was EUR −1,759,000 (= −3,800,000*169/365)

Therefore the fair value of the hedging instrument on 31 December 20X1 excluding the accrual was EUR 1,965,000 (= 2,312,000 − 347,000). The hypothetical derivative fair value was also EUR 1,965,000.

The change in fair value of both instruments since the last assessment was a gain of EUR 3,799,000 (= 1,965,000 − (1,834,000)). The hedge was then deemed to be effective as the ratio was within the 80 %−125 % range, as shown in the following table:

Retrospective Test	31-Dec-X1
Hedging instrument fair value change	3,799,000
Hypothetical derivative fair value change	3,799,000
Ratio	**100,0 %**
Hedge effective amount	3,799,000
Hedge ineffective amount	−0−

Retrospective Test Performed on 31 December 20X2

The fair value of the hedging instrument and the hypothetical derivative on 31 December 20X2 was calculated as follows:

Hedging Instrument and Hypothetical Derivative Valuation on 31-Dec-X2							
Cash Flow Date	Notional	Floating Rate Fixing	Implied Float. Rate	Credit Spread	Period Leg Amount	Disc. Factor	Present Value
Cash-flows of USD Leg:							
15-Jul-X3	100 Mill.	13-Jul-X2	5.65 %	Not incl.	5,650,000	0.9715	5,489,000
15-Jul-X3					100 Mill.	0.9715	97,150,000
					Total USD		**102,639,000**
					Total EUR (1.1500)		**89,251,000**
Cash-flows of EUR Leg:							
15-Jul-X3	80 Mill.	13-Jul-X2	4.95 %	Not incl.	3,960,000	0.9744	−3,859,000
15-Jul-X3					80 Mill.	0.9744	−77,952,000
					Total EUR		**<81,811,000>**
					Fair Value		**7,440,000**

The interest accrual of the hedging instrument on 31 December 20X2 was EUR 441,000 (= 2,275,000 − 1,834,000):

- The accrual of the USD leg was EUR 2,275,000 (= 5,650,000*169 days/365 days/1.15)
- The accrual of the EUR leg was EUR -1,834,000 (= −3,960,000*169/365)

Therefore the fair value of the hedging instrument on 31 December 20X2 excluding the accrual was EUR 6,999,000 (= 7,440,000 − 441,000). The hypothetical derivative fair value was also EUR 6,999,000. The change in fair value of both instruments since the last assessment was a gain of EUR 5,034,000 (= 6,999,000 − 1,965,000). The hedge was then deemed to be effective as the ratio was within the 80 %−125 % range, as shown in the following table:

Retrospective Test	31-Dec-X2
Hedging instrument fair value change	5,034,000
Hypothetical derivative fair value change	5,034,000
Ratio	**100,0 %**
Hedge effective amount	5,034,000
Hedge ineffective amount	−0−

Retrospective Test Performed on 15 July 20X3

The final exchange of principals under the hedging instrument meant that ABC had to pay EUR 80 million and receive USD 100 million. The spot exchange rate on 15 July 20X3 was 1.10.

Thus, the fair value of the hedging instrument on 15 July 20X3, after paying the interest settlement but before the final exchange of principals was EUR 10,909,000 (= 100,000,000/1.10 − 80,000,000). The hypothetical derivative fair value was also EUR 10,909,000. The change in fair value of the hedging instrument since the last assessment was a gain of EUR 3,910,000 (= 10,909,000 − 6,999,000). The hedge was then deemed to be effective as the ratio was within the 80 %−125 % range, as shown in the following table:

Retrospective Test	15-Jul-X3
Hedging instrument fair value change	3,910,000
Hypothetical derivative fair value change	3,910,000
Ratio	**100,0 %**
Hedge effective amount	3,910,000
Hedge ineffective amount	−0−

Rest of Relevant Calculations

ABC already computed the fair value of the hedging instrument and the hypothetical derivative when performing the retrospective tests. This computation also provided the effective part of the hedge. Before generating the accounting entries of the transaction, ABC also had to perform other calculations.

Next, ABC has to compute the fair value of the CCS at each of the relevant dates. Remember that the CCS terms were slightly different to those of the hedging instrument (the CCS also included the credit spreads). The fair value of the CCS at hedge inception was zero. The fair value of the CCS on 31 December 20X0 was calculated as follows:

CCS Valuation on 31-Dec-X0							
Cash Flow Date	Notional	Floating Rate Fixing	Implied Float. Rate	Credit Spread	Period Leg Amount	Disc. Factor	Present Value
Cash-flows of USD Leg:							
15-Jul-X1	100 Mill.	13-Jul-X0	5.40 %	0.50 %	5,900,000	0.9720	5,735,000
15-Jul-X2	100 Mill.	13-Jul-X1	5.60 %	0.50 %	6,100,000	0.9205	5,615,000
15-Jul-X3	100 Mill.	13-Jul-X2	5.80 %	0.50 %	6,300,000	0.8700	5,481,000
15-Jul-X3					100 Mill.	0.8700	87,000,000
						Total USD	**103,831,000**
						Total EUR (1.2800)	**81,118,000**
Cash-flows of EUR Leg:							
15-Jul-X1	80 Mill.	13-Jul-X0	4.50 %	0.49 %	3,992,000	0.9759	−3,896,000
15-Jul-X2	80 Mill.	13-Jul-X1	4.81 %	0.49 %	4,240,000	0.9311	−3,948,000
15-Jul-X3	80 Mill.	13-Jul-X2	5.00 %	0.49 %	4,392,000	0.8868	−3,895,000
15-Jul-X3					80 Mill.	0.8868	−70,944,000
						Total EUR	**<82,683,000>**
						Fair Value	**<1,565,000>**

The interest accrual of the hedging instrument on 31 December 20X0 was EUR 286,000
(= 2,134,000 − 1,848,000):

- The accrual of the USD leg was EUR 2,134,000 (= −5,900,000*169 days/365 days/1.28)
- The accrual of the EUR leg was EUR − 1,848,000 (= −3,992,000*169/365)

Therefore the fair value of the hedging instrument on 31 December 20X0 excluding the accrual
was EUR −1,851,000 (= −1,565,000−286,000).

In order not to be too repetitive, we have summarised in the following table the CCS fair
value calculations and the accruals for all the relevant dates.

	31-Dec-X0	31-Dec-X1	31-Dec-X2	15-Jul-X3
CCS fair value (incl. accruals)	<1,565,000>	2,339,000	7,481,000	10,909,000
Accrual amount	286,000 *(1)*	355,000 *(2)*	461,000 *(3)*	−0−
CCS fair value (excl. accruals)	<1,851,000>	1,984,000	7,020,000	10,909,000
Change in CCS fair value (excl. accruals)	<1,851,000>	3,835,000	5,036,000	3,889,000

Notes:

(1) 100,000,000*(5.40 %+0.50 %)*169/365/1.28 − 80,000,000*(4.50 %+0.49 %)*169/365

(2) 100,000,000*(5.55 %+0.50 %)*169/365/1.22 − 80,000,000*(4.75 %+0.49 %)*169/365

(3) 100,000,000*(5.65 %+0.50 %)*169/365/1.15 − 80,000,000*(4.95 %+0.49 %)*169/365

Additionally, ABC had to compute the change in the carrying amount of the bond due to
changes in the spot rate. The translation gains and losses are shown in the following table:

	Issue Date	31-Dec-X0	31-Dec-X1	31-Dec-X2	15-Jul-X3
USD bond amortised cost *(1)*	100,000,000	100,000,000	100,000,000	100,000,000	100,000,000
USD/EUR spot	1.2500	1.2800	1.2200	1.1500	1.1000
Bond re-measured at spot	80,000,000	78,125,000	81,967,000	86,957,000	90,909,000
Translation gain <loss>	—	1,875,000	<3,842,000>	<4,990,000>	<3,952,000>

Note *(1)* As will be explained later, the adjustments to the carrying value due to the fair value hedge were excluded
from the re-measurement at spot.

The adjustments to the carrying value of the USD bond needed also to be calculated. Because
the hedge was a fair value hedge, the carrying amount of the bond had to be adjusted according
to the effective part of the change in fair value of the hedging instrument, once excluding

the re-translation gain. The next table shows the calculations of the adjustments to the bond carrying value performed at each reporting date and at maturity.

	31-Dec-X0	31-Dec-X1	31-Dec-X2	15-Jul-X3
Translation gain <loss>	1,875,000	<3,842,000>	<4,990,000>	<3,952,000>
Hedge effective part (reversed amount)	1,834,000	<3,799,000>	<5,034,000>	<3,910,000>
Difference *(1)*	41,000	<43,000>	44,000	<42,000>
Adjustment to bond carrying amount *(1)*	41,000	<43,000>	44,000	<42,000>

Notes:

(1) The bond carrying amount is adjusted according to the difference between the bond's translation gain or loss and the hedge effective part. In order to clarify it, let us look for example at the 31 December 20X0 adjustment. The bond's re-translation gain (EUR 1,875,000) exceeded the amount of the hedge effective part (EUR 1,834,000) so a EUR 41,000 positive adjustment was made to the carrying value of the bond.

Regarding the adjustments to the carrying value of the bond due to the fair value hedge, ABC had two alternatives:

1) To convert these adjustments into USD, so the carrying amount of the bond was all in USD. Thus, the translation gain or loss was calculated on this total USD carrying value; or
2) To leave the adjustments in EUR, and split the carrying amount of the bond into two sub-accounts, one in USD and other in EUR. The EUR sub-account would contain the adjustments and the USD sub-account will contain the amortised cost of the USD bond without any adjustments. The translation gain or loss was then calculated only on the USD sub-account carrying value.

ABC chose the second alternative because it was simpler to implement.

Accounting Entries

The required journal entries were as follows:

1) Journal entries on 15 July 20X0:

   To record the bond issuance:

Cash (Asset)	€ 80,000,000	
USD Financial Debt (Liability)		€ 80,000,000

No entries were required to record the CCS as its initial fair value was zero.

2) Journal entries on 31 December 20X0:

The accrued interest of the bond was EUR 2,134,000 (= 5,900,000*169 days/365 days/1.28):

Interest Income/Expense (P&L)	€ 2,134,000	
Interest Payable (Liability)		€ 2,134,000

The re-measurement of the bond at spot was a gain of EUR 1,875,000:

USD Financial Debt (Liability)	€ 1,875,000	
Retranslation Gains/Losses (P&L)		€ 1,875,000

The fair value change, excluding accruals, of the CCS was a loss of EUR 1,851,000:

Fair Value Hedge Gain/Loss (P&L)	€ 1,851,000	
Fair Value of Derivative (Liability)		€ 1,851,000

The accrued interest of the CCS was EUR 286,000.

Interest Receivable (Asset)	€ 286,000	
Interest Income/Expense (P&L)		€ 286,000

The effective part of the hedge was a loss of EUR 1,834,000. Because the hedge was a fair value hedge, the carrying amount of the bond had to be adjusted according to the effective part of the change value of the hedging instrument, once excluding the re-translation gain. As the re-translation gain (EUR 1,875,000) exceeded the hedge effective part (EUR 1,834,000), a EUR 41,000 adjustment was made to the carrying value of the bond. In other words, the hedge effective part was indicating ABC to adjust the carrying value of the bond by reducing it in EUR 1,834,000, but as the FX re-measurement already reduced the carrying value of the bond in EUR 1,875,000, a EUR 41,000 increase in its carrying value was needed:

Fair Value Hedge Gain/Loss (P&L)	€ 41,000	
USD Financial Debt (Liability)		€ 41,000

3) Journal entries on 15 July 20X1:

The bond coupon was USD 5,900,000. Assuming a USD/EUR spot rate of 1.2600, ABC had to pay EUR 4,683,000 (= 5,900,000/1.26):

Interest Payable (Liability)	€ 2,134,000	
Interest Income/Expense (P&L)	€ 2,549,000	
Cash		€ 4,683,000

Under the CCS, ABC received EUR 4,683,000 (identical amount to the bond coupon) and paid EUR 3,992,000 (= 80,000,000*(4.50% +0.49%)). Therefore, the CCS settlement amount was EUR 691,000 (= 4,683,000 − 3,992,000):

Cash (Asset)	€ 691,000	
Interest Income/Expense (P&L)		€ 405,000
Interest Receivable (Asset)		€ 286,000

4) Journal entries on 31 December 20X1:

The bond interest to be paid on 15 July 20X2 was USD 6,050,000 (= 100,000,000* (5.55%+0.50%)). The accrued interest of the bond was EUR 2,296,000 (= 6,050,000*169 days/365 days/1.22):

Interest Income/Expense (P&L)	€ 2,296,000	
Interest Payable (Liability)		€ 2,296,000

The re-measurement of the bond at spot was a loss of EUR 3,842,000:

Retranslation Gains/Losses (P&L)	€ 3,842,000	
USD Financial Debt (Liability)		€ 3,842,000

The fair value change, excluding accruals, of the CCS was a gain of EUR 3,835,000:

Fair Value of Derivative (Asset)	€ 3,835,000	
Fair Value Hedge Gain/Loss (P&L)		€ 3,835,000

The accrued interest of the CCS was EUR 355,000:

Interest Receivable (Asset)	€ 355,000	
Interest Income/Expense (P&L)		€ 355,000

The effective part of the hedge was a gain of EUR 3,799,000. Because the hedge was a fair value hedge, the carrying amount of the bond had to be adjusted according to the effective part of the hedge, once excluding the re-translation gain or loss. As the re-translation loss (EUR 3,842,000) exceeded the hedge effective amount (EUR 3,799,000), a EUR 43,000 decrease in the bond's carrying value was needed:

USD Financial Debt (Liability)	€ 43,000	
Fair Value Hedge Gain/Loss (P&L)		€ 43,000

5) Journal entries on 15 July 20X2:

The bond coupon was USD 6,050,000. Assuming a USD/EUR spot rate of 1.1800, ABC had to pay EUR 5,127,000 (= 6,050,000/1.18):

Interest Payable (Liability)	€ 2,296,000	
Interest Income/Expense (P&L)	€ 2,831,000	
Cash		€ 5,127,000

Under the CCS, ABC received EUR 5,127,000 (identical amount to the bond coupon) and paid EUR 4,192,000 (= 80,000,000*(4.75 %+0.49 %)). Therefore, the CCS settlement amount was EUR 935,000 (= 5,127,000 − 4,192,000):

Cash (Asset)	€ 935,000	
Interest Income/Expense (P&L)		€ 580,000
Interest Receivable (Asset)		€ 355,000

6) Journal entries on 31 December 20X2:

The bond interest to be paid on 15 July 20X3 was USD 6,150,000 (= 100,000,000*(5.65 %+0.50 %)). The accrued interest of the bond was EUR 2,476,000 (= 6,150,000*169 days/365 days/1.15):

Interest Income/Expense (P&L)	€ 2,476,000	
Interest Payable (Liability)		€ 2,476,000

The re-measurement of the bond at spot was a loss of EUR 4,990,000:

Retranslation Gains/Losses (P&L)	€ 4,990,000	
USD financial debt (Liability)		€ 4,990,000

The fair value change, excluding accruals, of the CCS was a gain of EUR 5,036,000:

Fair Value of Derivative (Asset)	€ 5,036,000	
Fair Value Hedge Gain/Loss (P&L)		€ 5,036,000

The accrued interest of the CCS was EUR 461,000:

Interest Receivable (Asset)	€ 461,000	
Interest Income/Expense (P&L)		€ 461,000

The effective part of the hedge was a gain of EUR 5,034,000. Because the hedge was a fair value hedge, the carrying amount of the bond had to be adjusted according to the effective part of the hedge, once excluding the re-translation gain or loss. As the re-translation loss (EUR 4,990,000) was lower than the hedge effective amount (EUR 5,034,000), an adjustment of EUR 44,000 (= 5,034,000 − 4,990,000) was made increasing the carrying value of the bond:

Fair Value Hedge Gain/Loss (P&L)	€ 44,000	
USD Financial Debt (Liability)		€ 44,000

7) Journal entries on 15 July 20X3:

Under the CCS, ABC received EUR 5,591,000 (identical amount to the bond coupon) and paid EUR 4,352,000 (= 80,000,000*(4.95 %+0.49 %)). Therefore, the CCS settlement amount was EUR 1,239,000 (= 5,591,000 − 4,352,000):

Cash (Asset)	€ 1,239,000	
Interest Income/Expense (P&L)		€ 778,000
Interest Receivable (Asset)		€ 461,000

The re-measurement of the bond at spot was a loss of EUR 3,952,000:

Retranslation Gains/Losses (P&L)	€ 3,952,000	
USD Financial Debt (Liability)		€ 3,952,000

The fair value change (this time there are no more accruals) of the CCS was a gain of EUR 3,889,000:

Fair Value of Derivative (Asset)	€ 3,889,000	
Fair Value Hedge Gain/Loss (P&L)		€ 3,889,000

The effective part of the hedge was a gain of EUR 3,910,000. Because the hedge was a fair value hedge, the carrying amount of the bond had to be adjusted according to the effective part of the hedge, once excluding the re-translation gain or loss. As the re-translation loss (EUR 3,952,000) was lower than the hedge effective amount (EUR 3,910,000), an adjustment of EUR 42,000 (= 3,910,000 − 3,952,000) was made decreasing the carrying value of the bond:

USD Financial Debt (Liability)	€ 42,000	
Fair Value Hedge Gain/Loss (P&L)		€ 42,000

The bond coupon was USD 6,150,000 (= 100,000,000*(5.65 %+0.50 %)). Assuming a USD/EUR spot rate of 1.1000, ABC had to pay EUR 5,591,000 (= 6,150,000/1.10):

Interest Payable (Liability)	€ 2,476,000	
Interest Income/Expense (P&L)	€ 3,115,000	
Cash		€ 5,591,000

Under the CCS, ABC received USD 100 million (identical to the bond redemption amount) and paid EUR 80,000,000 million. Therefore, the value of this exchange was EUR 10,909,000 (= 100 million/1.10 − 80,000,000):

Cash (Asset)	€ 10,909,000	
Fair Value of Derivative (Asset)		€ 10,909,000

The redemption amount of the bond was EUR 90,909,000 (= USD 100 million/1.10).

USD Financial Debt (Liability)	€ 90,909,000	
Cash (Asset)		€ 90,909,000

Summary of the Journal Entries

	Assets			Liabilities		Profit and Loss
	Cash	Interest Receivable	Derivative Fair Value	Financial Debt	Interest Payable	
15 July 20X0						
Bond issuance	80,000,000			80,000,000		
31 December 20X0						
Bond accrued coupon					2,134,000	<2,134,000>
Bond re-measurement				<1,875,000>		1,875,000
CCS accrual		286,000				286,000
Change in fair value of CCS			<1,851,000>			<1,851,000>
Bond carrying value adjustment				41,000		<41,000>
15 July 20X1						
Bond coupon payment	<4,683,000>				<2,134,000>	<2,549,000>
CCS interest settlement	691,000	<286,000>				405,000
31 December 20X1						
Bond accrued coupon					2,296,000	<2,296,000>
Bond re-measurement				3,842,000		<3,842,000>
CCS accrual		355,000				355,000
Change in fair value of CCS			3,835,000			3,835,000
Bond carrying value adjustment				<43,000>		43,000

(Continued)

Summary of the Journal Entries (Continued)

	Assets			Liabilities		Profit and Loss
	Cash	Interest Receivable	Derivative Fair Value	Financial Debt	Interest Payable	
15 July 20X2						
Bond coupon payment	<5,127,000>				<2,296,000>	<2,831,000>
CCS interest settlement	935,000	<355,000>				580,000
31 December 20X2						
Bond accrued coupon					2,476,000	<2,476,000>
Bond re-measurement				4,990,000		<4,990,000>
CCS accrual		461,000				461,000
Change in fair value of CCS			5,036,000			5,036,000
Bond carrying value adjustment				44,000		<44,000>
15 July 20X3						
Bond coupon payment	<5,591,000>				<2,476,000>	<3,115,000>
CCS interest settlement	1,239,000	<461,000>				778,000
Bond re-measurement				3,952,000		<3,952,000>
Change in fair value of CCS			3,889,000			3,889,000
Bond carrying value adjustment				<42,000>		42,000
Bond redemption	<90,909,000>			<90,909,000>		
CCS final exchange	10,909,000		<10,909,000>			
Totals	**<12,536,000>**	**–0–**	**–0–**	**–0–**	**–0–**	**<12,536,000>**

Concluding Remarks

The CCS allowed ABC to take advantage of opportunities existing outside its home market, broaden its investor base, and preserve its access to domestic capital sources for future use. What we wonder is if it was worth the effort to apply hedge accounting in this case. The re-translation of the bond at the FX spot rate eclipsed most of the advantage of fair value hedging. Therefore, for highly volatile exchange rates it may be worth not to apply hedge accounting, and thus, to treat the CCS as undesignated. However, if the exchange rate is expected to be quite stable, fair value accounting can offer a more stable P&L.

CASE 6.2

Hedging a Fixed-rate Foreign Currency Liability Using a Receive-Fixed Pay-Fixed Cross-Currency Swap

The objective of this case is to illustrate the hedge accounting implications of a fixed-rate cross-border financing hedged with a pay-fixed receive-fixed CCS. This type of hedge of a foreign currency liability, a cash flow hedge, is much friendlier than a fair value hedge.

Background Information

On 15 July 20X0, Company ABC issued a USD-denominated floating-rate bond. ABC functional currency was the EUR. The bond had the following characteristics:

Bond Terms	
Expected issue date	15 July 20X0
Maturity	3 years (15 July 20X3)
Notional	USD 100 million
Coupon	USD 6.09 %, to be paid annually each 15th July

Since ABC's objective was to raise EUR funding, on issue date ABC entered into a CCS. Through the CCS, the entity agreed to receive a fixed-rate equal to the bond coupon and pay a EUR fixed-rate. The CCS had the following terms:

Cross-currency Swap Terms	
Trade date	15 July 20X0
Start date	15 July 20X0
Counterparties	Company ABC and XYZ Bank
Maturity date	3 years (15 July 20X3)
USD nominal	USD 100 million
EUR nominal	EUR 80 million
Initial exchange	On start date, ABC receives the EUR nominal and pays the USD nominal
ABC pays	EUR 5.19 %, annually, 30/360 basis, on the EUR nominal
ABC receives	USD 6.09 %, annually, 30/360 basis, on the USD nominal
Final exchange	On maturity date, ABC receives the USD nominal and pays the EUR nominal

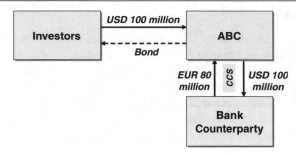

Figure 6.7 Bond with CCS : Initial Cash Flows.

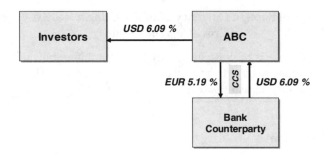

Figure 6.8 Bond with CCS : Intermediate Cash Flows.

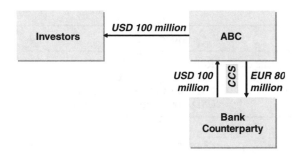

Figure 6.9 Bond with CCS : Cash Flows at Maturity.

The CCS was designated as the hedging instrument in a cash flow hedge of the USD bond. The interaction between the bond and the CCS are described next. It can be seen that with the combination of the USD bond and the CCS, ABC obtained synthetically a EUR fixed-rate liability.

On issue date and the start of the CCS, there was an initial exchange of principals through the CCS: ABC delivered the USD 100 million proceeds of the issue and received EUR 80 million. The combination of the bond and CCS had the same effect as if ABC issued a EUR-denominated bond, as highlighted in Figure 6.7:

Annually, there was a periodic exchange of interest payments. ABC received a USD fixed-rate interest and paid a EUR fixed-rate interest. ABC used the USD fixed-rate cash flows it received from the CCS to pay the bond interest, as shown in Figure 6.8.

At maturity of the CCS and the debt, ABC re-exchanged the principals (see Figure 6.9). ABC used the USD 100 million it received through the CCS to redeem the bond issue, and delivered EUR 80 million to the CCS counterparty. Note that this final exchange was made at exactly the same rate used in the initial exchange (1.2500).

Hedge Documentation

ABC documented the hedge relationship as follows:

Hedging Relationship Documentation	
Risk management objective and strategy for undertaking the hedge	The objective of the hedge is to reduce the variability of the cash flows of a foreign currency denominated bond.
	This hedging objective is consistent with ABC's overall interest rate risk management strategy of transforming all new issued foreign-denominated debt into the group functional currency.
Type of hedge	Cash flow hedge
Risk being hedged	Interest rate risk and FX risk. The variability in the cash flows of the bond attributable to changes in the USD interest rates, EUR interest rates and the USD/EUR exchange rate.
Hedging instrument	The cross-currency swap with reference number 005,767. The counter-party to the swap is XYZ Bank and the credit risk associated with this counterparty is considered to be very low.
Hedged item	The 3-year USD-denominated fixed-rate bond with reference number 667,906.
Assessment of effectiveness testing	Hedge effectiveness will be assessed by comparing changes in the fair value of the hedging instrument to changes in the fair value of the hypothetical instrument.
	The hypothetical derivative is a derivative whose changes in fair value perfectly offset the changes in fair value of the hedged item for variations in the risk being hedged. In this hedging relationship, the terms of the hypothetical derivative coincide exactly with the terms of the hedging instrument but assume no credit risk on the counterparty to the instrument.
	Prospective test
	A prospective test will be performed at hedge inception and at each reporting date, using the critical terms method.
	If (i) the critical terms of the hedging instrument and the hypothetical derivative match (i.e., notional amounts, currencies, underlying and interest periods), and (ii) the credit risk of the counterparty to the hedging instrument is very low, the hedge will be considered to be highly effective prospectively.
	The credit risk of the counterparty to the hedging instrument will be monitored continuously.
	Retrospective test
	A retrospective test will be performed at each reporting date using the "ratio analysis method". The ratio will compare the cumulative change since hedge inception in the fair value of the hedging instrument with the cumulative change since hedge inception in the fair value of the hypothetical derivative. The hedge will be assumed to be highly effective on a retrospective basis if the ratio is between 80 % and 125 %.
	The effective part of the change in fair value of the hedging instrument (excluding the portion attributable to the current period swap accrual and the hedged item translation gains and losses) will be recognised in equity.

Prospective Tests

ABC performed a prospective test at hedge inception (15 July 20X0) and at each reporting date during the hedge relationship (31 December 20X0, 31 December 20X1 and 31 December 20X2). ABC used the critical terms method to assess prospective effectiveness. The terms of the hypothetical derivative were identical to the terms of the CCS.

Because (i) the critical terms of the hypothetical derivative and the hedging instrument matched, and (ii) the credit risk associated with the counterparty to the hedging instrument was considered to be very low, ABC considered that the hedge was highly effective prospectively. The credit risk of the counterparty to the CCS was monitored at each testing date, but it did not experience any significant credit deterioration, so the hedge was considered highly effective prospectively at each test date.

Retrospective Tests

ABC performed a retrospective test at each reporting date and also at hedge maturity. The fair value of the hedging instrument and the hypothetical derivative were computed at inception and at each test date. Remember that in this case, the terms of the hedging instrument (i.e., the derivative designated for effectiveness assessment) were identical to the CCS terms.

The retrospective test calculations were based on the following USD/EUR spot rate and USD Libor and EUR Euribor interest rate curves:

	15-Jul-X0	Test-1 31-Dec-X0	Test-2 31-Dec-X1	Test-3 31-Dec-X2	Test-4 15-Jul-X3
USD/EUR Spot	1.2500	1.2800	1.2200	1.1500	1.1000
USD Libor deposit and swap rates:					
USD 1- Year	5.40 %	5.50 %	5.70 %	5.60 %	—
USD 2–Year	5.50 %	5.60 %	5.80 %	5.70 %	—
USD 3- Year	5.59 %	5.69 %	5.89 %	5.79 %	—
EUR Euribor deposit and swap rates:					
EUR 1- Year	4.50 %	4.70 %	4.90 %	5.00 %	—
EUR 2- Year	4.60 %	4.80 %	5.00 %	5.05 %	—
EUR 3- Year	4.70 %	4.89 %	5.09 %	5.10 %	—

Retrospective Test Performed on 31-December-20X0

The retrospective test on 31 December 20X0 had to compare changes in fair values of the hedging instrument and the hypothetical swap from hedge inception (15 July 20X0) to the test date.

The following table shows the fair value calculation at hedge inception (15 July 20X0) of the CCS. Remember that in this case the economic terms of the CCS, hedging instrument and hypothetical derivative were identical.

CCS Valuation on 15 July 20X0

Cash Flow Date	Notional	Period Rate	Credit Spread	Period Leg Amount (1)	Disc. Factor (2)	Present Value
Cash flows of USD leg:						
15-Jul-X1	100 Mill.	5.59 %	0.50 %	6,090,000	0.9486	5,777,000
15-Jul-X2	100 Mill.	5.59 %	0.50 %	6,090,000	0.8978	5,468,000
15-Jul-X3	100 Mill.	5.59 %	0.50 %	6,090,000	0.8494	5,173,000
15-Jul-X3				100 Mill.	0.8494	84,940,000
				Total USD (3)		**101,360,000**
				Total EUR (1.2500)		**81,088,000**
Cash flows of EUR leg:						
15-Jul-X1	80 Mill.	4.70 %	0.49 %	4,152,000	0.9569	−3,973,000
15-Jul-X2	80 Mill.	4.70 %	0.49 %	4,152,000	0.9136	−3,793,000
15-Jul-X3	80 Mill.	4.70 %	0.49 %	4,152,000	0.8713	−3,618,000
15-Jul-X3				80 Mill.	0.8713	−69,704,000
				Total EUR		**<81,088,000>**
				Fair Value of CCS		**−0−**

Notes:

(1) Period settlement amounts were calculated as:

Notional*Period Rate*Day Factor

As the basis of each fixed leg was 30/360, the "Day Factor" had to assume that each month had 30 days. To keep calculations simple, all "Day Factors" were assumed to be equal to one.

(2) The discount factors represented the present value, as of the valuation date, of USD 1 (or EUR 1) to be paid on the cash flow date. The discount factors were computed using the mid-market USD Libor (or Euribor) yield curves flat (i.e., without taking into account any credit spread or bid/offers).

(3) The sum was USD 101,358,000, but in reality if the rounding of discount factors and present values were not present the sum would have been USD 101,360,000.

Similarly, the fair value on 31 December 20X0 of the CCS was calculated as follows (remember that this was also the calculation of the hedging instrument and hypothetical derivative fair value):

CCS on 31 December 20X0

Cash Flow Date	Notional	Period Rate	Credit Spread	Period Leg Amount	Disc. Factor	Present Value
Cash flows of USD leg:						
15-Jul-X1	100 Mill.	5.59 %	0.50 %	6,090,000	0.9720	5,919,000
15-Jul-X2	100 Mill.	5.59 %	0.50 %	6,090,000	0.9205	5,606,000
15-Jul-X3	100 Mill.	5.59 %	0.50 %	6,090,000	0.8700	5,298,000
15-Jul-X3				100 Mill.	0.8700	87,000,000
				Total USD		**103,823,000**
				Total EUR (1.2800)		**81,112,000**

(Continued)

CCS on 31 December 20X0						
Cash Flow Date	Notional	Period Rate	Credit Spread	Period Leg Amount	Disc. Factor	Present Value
Cash flows of EUR leg:						
15-Jul-X1	80 Mill.	4.70 %	0.49 %	4,152,000	0.9759	−4,052,000
15-Jul-X2	80 Mill.	4.70 %	0.49 %	4,152,000	0.9311	−3,866,000
15-Jul-X3	80 Mill.	4.70 %	0.49 %	4,152,000	0.8868	−3,682,000
15-Jul-X3				80 Mill.	0.8868	−70,944,000
				Total EUR		**<82,544,000>**
				Fair Value of CCS		**<1,432,000>**

The interest accrual of the CCS on 31 December 20X0 was EUR 281,000 ($= -1,922,000 + 2,203,000$):

- The accrual of the USD leg was EUR 2,203,000 ($= 6,090,000^*169$ days/365 days/1.28)
- The accrual of the EUR leg was EUR $-1,922,000$ ($= -4,152,000^*169/365$)

Therefore the fair value of the CCS on 31 December 20X0 excluding the accrual was EUR - 1,713,000 ($= -1,432,000 - 281,000$). The hedging instrument and the hypothetical derivative fair values were also EUR $-1,713,000$. The hedge was then deemed to be effective as the ratio was within the 80 %–125 % range, as shown in the following table:

Retrospective Test	31-Dec-X0
Hedging instrument fair value change	<1,713,000>
Hypothetical derivative fair value change	<1,713,000>
Ratio	**100,0 %**
Hedge effective amount	<1,713,000>
Hedge ineffective amount	−0−

The change in fair value of both instruments since the last assessment was a loss of EUR 1,713,000 ($= -1,713,000$-0). The effective part of the hedge gains or losses was limited by the lesser of the absolute values of the cumulative change in fair value of the hedging instrument and the hypothetical derivative. This condition did not impose this time any limit to the hedge effective amount.

Retrospective Test Performed on 31-December-20X1

The retrospective test on 31 December 20X1 had to compare changes in fair values of the hedging instrument and the hypothetical swap from hedge inception (15 July 20X0) to the test date.

The fair value of the CCS on 31 December 20X1 was calculated as follows (remember that this was also the calculation of the hedging instrument and hypothetical derivative fair values):

CCS on 31 December 20X1

Cash Flow Date	Notional	Period Rate	Credit Spread	Period Leg Amount	Disc. Factor	Present Value
Cash flows of USD leg:						
15-Jul-X2	100 Mill.	5.59 %	0.50 %	6,090,000	0.9711	5,914,000
15-Jul-X3	100 Mill.	5.59 %	0.50 %	6,090,000	0.9178	5,589,000
15-Jul-X3				100 Mill.	0.9178	91,780,000
				Total USD		**103,283,000**
				Total EUR (1.2200)		**84,658,000**
Cash flows of EUR leg:						
15-Jul-X2	80 Mill.	4.70 %	0.49 %	4,152,000	0.9749	−4,048,000
15-Jul-X3	80 Mill.	4.70 %	0.49 %	4,152,000	0.9285	−3,855,000
15-Jul-X3				80 Mill.	0.9285	−74,280,000
				Total EUR		**<82,183,000>**
				Fair Value of CCS		**2,475,000**

The interest accrual of the CCS on 31 December 20X1 was EUR 389,000 (= 2,311,000 − 1,922,000):

- The accrual of the USD leg was EUR 2,311,000 (= 6,090,000*169 days/365 days/1.22)
- The accrual of the EUR leg was EUR -1,922,000 (= − 4,152,000*169/365)

Therefore the fair value of the CCS on 31 December 20X1 excluding the accrual was EUR 2,086,000 (= 2,475,000-389,000). The hedging instrument and the hypothetical derivative fair values were also EUR 2,086,000. The hedge was then deemed to be effective as the ratio was within the 80 %–125 % range, as shown in the following table:

Retrospective Test	31-Dec-X1
Hedging instrument fair value change since hedge inception	2,086,000
Hypothetical derivative fair value change since hedge inception	2,086,000
Retrospective Test	31-Dec-X1
Ratio	**100,0 %**
Hedge effective amount	3,799,000
Hedge ineffective amount	−0−

The change in fair value of both instruments since the last assessment was a gain of EUR 3,799,000 (= 2,086,000−(−1,713,000)). The effective part of the hedge gains or losses was limited by the lesser of the absolute values of the cumulative change in fair value of the hedging instrument and the hypothetical derivative. This condition did not impose this time any limit to the hedge effective amount.

Retrospective Test Performed on 31-December-20X2

The retrospective test on 31 December 20X2 had to compare changes in fair values of the hedging instrument and the hypothetical swap from hedge inception (15 July 20X0) to the test date.

The fair value of the CCS on 31 December 20X2 was calculated as follows (remember that this was also the calculation of the hedging instrument and the hypothetical derivative fair values):

					CCS on 31 December 20X2		
Cash Flow Date	Notional	Period Rate	Credit Spread	Period Leg Amount	Disc. Factor	Present Value
Cash flows of USD leg:						
15-Jul-X3	100 Mill.	5.59 %	0.50 %	6,090,000	0.9715	5,916,000
15-Jul-X3				100 Mill.	0.9715	97,150,000
					Total USD	**103,066,000**
					Total EUR (1.1500)	**89,623,000**
Cash flows of EUR leg:						
15-Jul-X3	80 Mill.	4.70 %	0.49 %	4,152,000	0.9744	−4,046,000
15-Jul-X3				80 Mill.	0.9744	−77,952,000
					Total EUR	**<81,998,000>**
					Total CCS	**7,625,000**

The interest accrual of the CCS on 31 December 20X2 was EUR 530,000 (= 2,452,000-1,922,000):

- The accrual of the USD leg was EUR 2,452,000 (= 6,090,000*169 days/365 days/1.15)
- The accrual of the EUR leg was EUR −1,922,000 (= −4,152,000*169/365)

Therefore the fair value of the CCS on 31 December 20X2 excluding the accrual was EUR 7,095,000 (= 7,625,000-530,000). The hedging instrument and the hypothetical derivative fair values were also EUR 7,095,000. The hedge was then deemed to be effective as the ratio was within the 80 %–125 % range, as shown in the following table:

Retrospective Test	31-Dec-X2
Hedging instrument fair value change since hedge inception	7,095,000
Hypothetical derivative fair value change since hedge inception	7,095,000
Ratio	**100,0 %**
Hedge effective amount	5,009,000
Hedge ineffective amount	−0−

The change in fair value of both instruments since the last assessment was a gain of EUR 5,009,000 (= 7,095,000 − 2,086,000). The effective part of the hedge gains or losses was limited by the lesser of the absolute values of the cumulative change in fair value of the hedging instrument and the hypothetical derivative. This condition did not impose this time any limit to the hedge effective amount.

Retrospective Test Performed on 15 July 20X3

The final exchange of principals under the CCS meant that ABC had to pay EUR 80 million and receive USD 100 million. The spot exchange rate on 15 July 20X3 was 1.10. Thus, the fair value of the CCS on 15 July 20X3, after paying the interest settlement but before the final exchange of principals was EUR 10,909,000 (= 100,000,000/1.10−80,000,000). The hedging instrument and the hypothetical derivative fair values were also EUR 10,909,000.

The change in fair value of the hedging instrument since hedge inception was EUR 10,090,000. The hedge was then deemed to be effective as the ratio was within the 80 %−125 % range, as shown in the following table:

Retrospective Test	15-Jul-X3
Hedging instrument fair value change since hedge inception	10,090,000
Hypothetical derivative fair value change since hedge inception	10,090,000
Ratio	**100,0 %**
Hedge effective amount	3,814,000
Hedge ineffective amount	−0−

The change in fair value of the hedging instrument and the hypothetical derivative since the last assessment was a gain of EUR 3,814,000 (= 10,909,000−7,095,000). The effective part of the hedge gains or losses was limited by the lesser of the absolute values of the cumulative change in fair value of the hedging instrument and the hypothetical derivative. This condition did not impose this time any limit to the hedge effective amount.

Other relevant calculations

In order to generate the transaction accounting entries, let us summarise the CCS fair value calculations at each reporting date and at hedge maturity:

Summary of CCS Fair Values				
	31-Dec-X0	31-Dec-X1	31-Dec-X2	15-Jul-X3
CCS fair value (incl. accruals)	<1,432,000>	2,475,000	7,625,000	10,909,000
Accrual amount	281,000	389,000	530,000	−0−
CCS fair value (excl. accruals)	<1,713,000>	2,086,000	7,095,000	10,909,000
Change in CCS fair value (excl. accruals)	<1,713,000>	3,799,000	5,009,000	3,814,000

Additionally, ABC had to compute the change in the carrying amount of the bond due to changes in the spot rate. The translation gains and losses are shown in the following table:

Bond Translation Gains and Losses					
	Issue Date	31-Dec-X0	31-Dec-X1	31-Dec-X2	15-Jul-X3
USD bond amortised cost	100,000,000	100,000,000	100,000,000	100,000,000	100,000,000
USD/EUR spot	1.2500	1.2800	1.2200	1.1500	1.1000
Bond re-measured at spot	80,000,000	78,125,000	81,967,000	86,957,000	90,909,000
Translation gain <loss>	—	1,875,000	<3,842,000>	<4,990,000>	<3,952,000>

The adjustments to the cash flow equity reserve needed also to be calculated. Because the hedge was a cash flow hedge, the effective part of the hedge had to be recognised in equity, excluding the retranslation gain/loss. The next table shows the calculations of the amounts that were recognised in equity at each reporting date and at maturity.

Cash Flow Hedge Reserve Amounts				
	31-Dec-X0	31-Dec-X1	31-Dec-X2	15-Jul-X3
Translation gain <loss>	1,875,000	<3,842,000>	<4,990,000>	<3,952,000>
Hedge effective part (reversed amount)	1,713,000	<3,799,000>	<5,009,000>	<3,814,000>
Difference	162,000	<43,000>	19,000	<138,000>
Amount recognised in the cash flow reserve (equity)	162,000	<43,000>	19,000	<138,000>
End of period carrying amount of the cash flow reserve	162,000	119,000	138,000	−0−

In order to clarify it, let us look at the 31 December 20X0 figures. In theory, the cash flow hedge indicated that EUR −1,713,000 had to be initially recognised in equity. However, -1,875,000 were reclassified from equity to P&L to offset the FX re-measurement gain of EUR 1,875,000. As a result EUR 162,000 was recognised in the cash flow hedges reserve in equity in that period.

Accounting Entries

The required journal entries were as follows:

1) Journal entries on 15 July 20X0:

To record the bond issuance:

Cash (Asset)	€ 80,000,000	
USD Financial Debt (Liability)		€ 80,000,000

No entries were required to record the CCS as its initial fair value was zero.

2) Journal entries on 31 December 20X0:

The accrued interest of the bond was EUR 2,203,000 (= 6,090,000*169 days/365 days/1.28):

Interest Income/Expense (P&L)	€ 2,203,000	
Interest Payable (Liability)		€ 2,203,000

The re-measurement of the bond at spot was a gain of EUR 1,875,000:

USD Financial Debt (Liability)	€ 1,875,000	
Retranslation Gains/Losses (P&L)		€ 1,875,000

The fair value change, excluding accruals, of the CCS was a loss of EUR 1,713,000.

Retranslation Gains/Losses (P&L)	€ 1,875,000	
Fair Value of Derivative (Liability)		€ 1,713,000
Cash Flow Hedges (Equity)		€ 162,000

The accrued interest of the CCS was EUR 281,000:

Interest Receivable (Asset)	€ 281,000	
Interest Income/Expense (P&L)		€ 281,000

3) Journal entries on 15 July 20X1:

The bond coupon was USD 6,090,000. Assuming a USD/EUR spot rate of 1.2600, ABC had to pay EUR 4,833,000 (= 6,090,000(1.26):

Interest Payable (Liability)	€ 2,203,000	
Interest Income/Expense (P&L)	€ 2,630,000	
Cash		€ 4,833,000

Under the CCS, ABC received EUR 4,833,000 (identical amount to the bond coupon) and paid EUR 4,152,000. Therefore, the CCS settlement amount was EUR 681,000 (= 4,833,000 − 4,152,000):

Cash (Asset)	€ 681,000	
Interest Income/Expense (P&L)		€ 400,000
Interest Receivable (Asset)		€ 281,000

4) Journal entries on 31 December 20X1:

The bond interest to be paid on 15 July 20X2 was USD 6,090,000. The accrued interest of the bond was EUR 2,311,000 (= 6,090,000*169 days/365 days/1.22):

Interest Income/Expense (P&L)	€ 2,311,000	
Interest Payable (Liability)		€ 2,311,000

The re-measurement of the bond at spot was a loss of EUR 3,842,000:

Retranslation Gains/Losses (P&L)	€ 3,842,000	
USD Financial Debt (Liability)		€ 3,842,000

The fair value change, excluding accruals, of the CCS was a gain of EUR 3,799,000:

Fair Value of Derivative (Asset)	€ 3,799,000	
Cash Flow Hedges (Equity)	€ 43,000	
Retranslation Gains/Losses (P&L)		€ 3,842,000

The accrued interest of the CCS was EUR 389,000:

Interest Receivable (Asset)	€ 389,000	
Interest Income/Expense (P&L)		€ 389,000

5) Journal entries on 15 July 20X2:

The bond coupon was USD 6,090,000. Assuming a USD/EUR spot rate of 1.1800, ABC had to pay EUR 5,161,000 (= 6,090,000/1.18):

Interest Payable (Liability)	€ 2,311,000	
Interest Income/Expense (P&L)	€ 2,850,000	
Cash		€ 5,161,000

Under the CCS, ABC received EUR 5,161,000 (identical amount to the bond coupon) and paid EUR 4,152,000. Therefore, the CCS settlement amount was EUR 1,009,000 (= 5,161,000–4,152,000):

Cash (Asset)	€ 1,009,000	
Interest Income/Expense (P&L)		€ 620,000
Interest Receivable (Asset)		€ 389,000

6) Journal entries on 31 December 20X2:

The bond interest to be paid on 15 July 20X3 was USD 6,090,000. The accrued interest of the bond was EUR 2,452,000 (= 6,090,000*169 days/365 days/1.15):

Interest Income/Expense (P&L)	€ 2,452,000	
Interest Payable (Liability)		€ 2,452,000

The re-measurement of the bond at spot was a loss of EUR 4,990,000:

Retranslation Gains/Losses (P&L)	€ 4,990,000	
USD Financial Debt (Liability)		€ 4,990,000

The fair value change, excluding accruals, of the CCS was a gain of EUR 5,009,000:

Fair value of Derivative (Asset)	€ 5,009,000	
Retranslation Gains/Losses (P&L)		€ 4,990,000
Cash Flow Hedges (Equity)		€ 19,000

The accrued interest of the CCS was EUR 530,000:

Interest Receivable (Asset)	€ 530,000	
Interest Income/Expense (P&L)		€ 530,000

7) Journal entries on 15 July 20X3:

The bond coupon was USD 6,090,000. Assuming a USD/EUR spot rate of 1.1000, ABC had to pay EUR 5,536,000 (= 6,090,000/1.10):

Interest Payable (Liability)	€ 2,452,000	
Interest Income/Expense (P&L)	€ 3,084,000	
Cash		€ 5,536,000

Under the CCS, ABC received EUR 5,536,000 (identical amount to the bond coupon) and paid EUR 4,152,000. Therefore, the CCS settlement amount was EUR 1,384,000 (= 5,536,000 − 4,152,000):

Cash (Asset)	€ 1,384,000	
Interest Income/Expense (P&L)		€ 854,000
Interest Receivable (Asset)		€ 530,000

Summary of the Journal Entries

	Assets			Liabilities		Equity	
	Cash	Interest Receivable	Derivative Fair Value	Financial Debt	Interest Payable	Cash flow Hedges	Profit and Loss
15 July 20X0							
Bond issuance	80,000,000			80,000,000			
31 December 20X0							
Bond accrued coupon					2,203,000		<2,203,000>
Bond re-measurement				<1,875,000>			1,875,000
CCS accrual		281,000					281,000
Change in fair value of CCS			<1,713,000>			162,000	<1,875,000>
15 July 20X1							
Bond coupon payment	<4,833,000>				<2,203,000>		<2,630,000>
CCS interest settlement	681,000	<281,000>					400,000
31 December 20X1							
Bond accrued coupon					2,311,000		<2,311,000>
Bond re-measurement				3,842,000			<3,842,000>
CCS accrual		389,000					389,000
Change in fair value of CCS			3,799,000			<43,000>	3,842,000
15 July 20X2							
Bond coupon payment	<5,161,000>				<2,311,000>		<2,850,000>
CCS interest settlement	1,009,000	<389,000>					620,000
31 December 20X2							
Bond accrued coupon					2,452,000		<2,452,000>
Bond re-measurement				4,990,000			<4,990,000>
CCS accrual		530,000					530,000
Change in fair value of CCS			5,009,000			19,000	4,990,000
15 July 20X3							
Bond coupon payment	<5,536,000>				<2,452,000>		<3,084,000>
CCS interest settlement	1,384,000	<530,000>					854,000
Bond re-measurement				3,952,000			<3,952,000>
Change in fair value of CCS			3,814,000			<138,000>	3,952,000
Bond redemption	<90,909,000>			<90,909,000>			
CCS final exchange	10,909,000		<10,909,000>				
Totals	<12,456,000>	–0–	–0–	–0–	–0–		<12,456,000>

The re-measurement of the bond at spot was a loss of EUR 3,952,000:

Retranslation Gains/Losses (P&L)	€ 3,952,000	
USD Financial Debt (Liability)		€ 3,952,000

The fair value change (this time there were no more accruals) of the CCS was a gain of EUR 3,814,000:

Fair Value of Derivative (Asset)	€ 3,814,000	
Cash Flow Hedges (Equity)	€ 138,000	
Retranslation Gains/Losses (P&L)		€ 3,952,000

Under the CCS, ABC received USD 100 million (identical to the bond redemption amount) and paid EUR 80,000,000 million. Therefore, the value of this exchange was EUR 10,909,000 (= 100 million/1.10−80,000,000):

Cash (Asset)	€ 10,909,000	
Fair Value of Derivative (Asset)		€ 10,909,000

The redemption amount of the bond was EUR 90,909,000 (= USD 100 million/1.10):

USD Financial Debt (Liability)	€ 90,909,000	
Cash (Asset)		€ 90,909,000

Concluding Remarks

In this case, most of the potential benefit of applying cash flow hedging was eclipsed by the re-translation of the USD liability. We are not at all advising the reader to forget about applying hedge accounting. In our case, the maturity of the liability was rather short (only three years), and therefore the impact of interest rate moves was much lower than the impact of the USD/EUR rate movements. It is not unusual that corporates issue long-term debt (e.g., 15 years) for which the impact of interest rate movements can be very significant, making hedge accounting valuable.

CASE 6.3
Hedging a Fixed-rate Foreign Currency Liability Using a Receive-Fixed Pay-Floating Cross-Currency Swap
The objective of this case is to illustrate the hedge accounting implications of a fixed-rate cross-border financing hedged with a receive-fixed pay-floating CCS. The hedge covered

in this case is a fair value hedge of a foreign currency denominated liability. It is assumed that the reader has already been through Case 6.1, so many calculations are summarised in this case because they were covered in detail in case 6.1.

Background Information

On 15 July 20X0, Company ABC issued a USD-denominated fixed-rate bond. ABC functional currency was the EUR. The bond had the following characteristics:

Bond Terms	
Expected issue date	15 July 20X0
Maturity	3 years (15 July 20X3)
Notional	USD 100 million
Coupon	USD 6.09 %, 30/360 basis, to be paid annually

Since ABC's objective was to raise EUR funding, on issue date ABC entered into a CCS. In the CCS, the entity agreed to receive a USD fixed-rate equal to the bond coupon and pay a EUR floating-rate. The CCS had the following terms:

Cross-currency Swap Terms	
Trade date	15 July 20X0
Start date	15 July 20X0
Counterparties	Company ABC and XYZ Bank
Maturity date	3 years (15 July 20X3)
USD nominal	USD 100 million
EUR nominal	EUR 80 million
Initial exchange	On start date, ABC receives the EUR nominal and pays the USD nominal
ABC pays	EUR Euribor 12-month plus 49 bps, annually, A/360 basis, on the EUR nominal. Euribor 12M to be fixed two business days prior to the commencement of the interest period
ABC receives	USD 6.09 %, annually, 30/360 basis, on the USD nominal
Final exchange	On maturity date, ABC receives the USD nominal and pays the EUR nominal

The interaction between the bond and the CCS is described next. It can be seen that with the combination of the USD bond and the CCS, ABC obtained synthetically a EUR floating-rate liability.

On issue date and the start of the CCS, there was an initial exchange of principals through the CCS: ABC delivered the USD 100 million proceeds of the issue and received EUR 80 million. The combination of the bond and CCS had the same effect as if ABC issued a EUR-denominated bond, as highlighted in Figure 6.10.

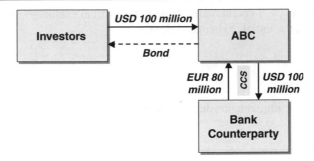

Figure 6.10   Bond with CCS : Initial Cash Flows.

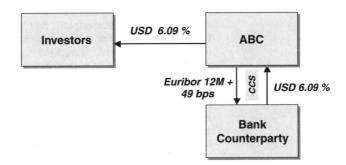

Figure 6.11   Bond with CCS : Intermediate cash-flows.

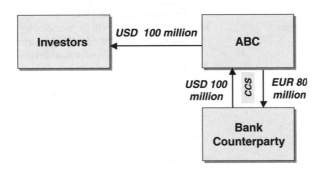

Figure 6.12   Bond with CCS : Cash Flows at Maturity.

Annually, there was a periodic exchange of interest payments. ABC received a USD fixed-rate interest and paid a EUR floating-rate interest. ABC used the USD fixed-rate cash flows it received from the CCS to pay the bond interest, as shown in Figure 6.11 .

At maturity of the CCS and of the debt, ABC re-exchanged the principals (see Figure 6.12), using the USD 100 million it received under the CCS to redeem the bond issue, and delivered

EUR 80 million to the CCS counterparty. Note that this final exchange was made at exactly the same rate used in the initial exchange (1.2500).

Hedge Documentation

ABC documented the hedge relationship as follows:

Hedging Relationship Documentation	
Risk management objective and strategy for undertaking the hedge	The objective of the hedge is to reduce the variability of the fair value of a foreign currency denominated bond.
	This hedging objective is consistent with ABC's overall interest rate risk management strategy of transforming all new issued foreign- denominated debt into the group functional currency, and thereafter managing the exposure to Euro interest rate risk through the proportion of fixed and floating rate net debt in its total debt portfolio.
Type of hedge	Fair value hedge.
Risk being hedged	Interest rate risk and FX risk. The variability in fair value of the bond attributable to changes in the USD Libor and Euribor interest rates, and the USD/EUR exchange rate.
	Fair value changes attributable to credit or other risks are not hedged in this relationship. Accordingly, the CCS 49 bps credit spread is excluded from the hedge relationship.
Hedging instrument	The cross-currency swap with reference number 005769. The counterparty to the swap is XYZ Bank and the credit risk associated with this counterparty is considered to be very low.
Hedged item	The 3-year USD-denominated floating-rate bond with reference number 667904.
Assessment of effectiveness testing	Hedge effectiveness will be assessed by comparing changes in the fair value of the hedging instrument to changes in the fair value of a hypothetical derivative.
	The hypothetical derivative is a derivative whose changes in fair value perfectly offset the changes in fair value of the hedged item for variations in the risk being hedged. In this hedging relationship, the terms of the hypothetical derivative coincide exactly with the terms of the hedging instrument but assume no credit risk on the counterparty to the instrument.
	Prospective test
	A prospective test will be performed at the inception and at each reporting date, using the critical terms method.
	If (i) the critical terms of the hypothetical derivative and the hedging instrument match (i.e., notional amounts, currencies, underlying and interest periods), and (ii) the credit risk of the counterparty to the hedging instrument is very low, the hedge will be considered to be highly effective prospectively.
	The credit risk of the counterparty to the hedging instrument will be monitored continuously.

Hedging Relationship Documentation

Retrospective test

A retrospective test will be performed at each reporting date and also at hedge maturity using the "ratio analysis method". The ratio will compare the change since the last assessment in the fair value of the hedging instrument with the change since the last assessment in the fair value of the hypothetical derivative. The hedge will be assumed to be highly effective on a retrospective basis if the ratio is between 80 % and 125 %.

The effective part of the change in fair value of the hedging instrument (excluding the portion attributable to the current period swap accrual) will be recorded as a change in the carrying value of the bond, with an offset to P&L.

Prospective Tests

ABC performed a prospective test at inception (15 July 20X0) and at each reporting date during the hedge relationship (31 December 20X0, 31 December 20X1 and 31 December 20X2). On each test date: (i) the critical terms of the hypothetical derivative and the hedging instrument matched (i.e., notional amount, currency, underlying and interest periods), and (ii) the credit risk of the counterparty to the hedging instrument was very low. Accordingly, the hedge was considered to be highly effective prospectively on each test date.

The terms of the hedging instrument were the CCS terms once excluded the credit spreads on both legs. The terms of the hedging instrument and the hypothetical derivative were the same except that the hypothetical derivative assumed no counterparty credit risk. The following table shows the terms of the hypothetical derivative for effectiveness assessment:

	Hypothetical Derivative	Hedging Instrument
Trade date	15 July 20X0	——
Start date	15 July 20X0	Same as hypothetical deriv.
Counterparties	ABC and a AAA-rated hypothetical counterparty	ABC and XYZ Bank
Maturity date	3 years (15 July 20X3)	Same as hypothetical deriv.
USD nominal	USD 100 million	Same as hypothetical deriv.
EUR nominal	EUR 80 million	Same as hypothetical deriv.
ABC pays	Euribor 12m, annually, A/360 basis, on the EUR nominal	Same as hypothetical deriv.
	Euribor is fixed two business days prior to the beginning of the annual interest period	
ABC receives	USD 5.59 %, 30/360 basis, on the USD nominal	Same as hypothetical deriv.
Final exchang	On maturity date, ABC receives the USD nominal and pays the EUR nominal	Same as hypothetical deriv.

Retrospective Tests

ABC performed a retrospective test at each reporting date and at hedge maturity. The fair values of the hedging instrument and the hypothetical derivative were computed at inception and at each test date. Remember that the terms of the hedging instrument for effectiveness assessment were different to the CCS terms, because it excluded the credit spreads.

The retrospective test calculations were based on the following USD/EUR spot rate and USD Libor and EUR Euribor interest rate curves:

	15-Jul-X0	Test-1 31-Dec-X0	Test-2 31-Dec-X1	Test-3 31-Dec-X2	Test-4 15-Jul-X3
USD/EUR Spot	1.2500	1.2800	1.2200	1.1500	1.1000
USD Libor deposit and swap rates:					
USD 1- Year	5.40 %	5.50 %	5.70 %	5.60 %	—
USD 2–Year	5.50 %	5.60 %	5.80 %	5.70 %	—
USD 3- Year	5.59 %	5.69 %	5.89 %	5.79 %	—
EUR Euribor deposit and swap rates:					
EUR 1- Year	4.50 %	4.70 %	4.90 %	5.00 %	—
EUR 2- Year	4.60 %	4.80 %	5.00 %	5.05 %	—
EUR 3- Year	4.70 %	4.89 %	5.09 %	5.10 %	—

Retrospective Test Performed on 31-December-20X0

The following table shows the fair value calculation, at hedge inception, of the hedging instrument and the hypothetical derivative:

Hedging Instrument and Hypothetical Derivative Valuation on 15-Jul-X0							
Cash Flow Date	Notional	Floating Rate Fixing *(1)*	Period Rate *(2)*	Credit Spread	Period Leg Amount *(3)*	Disc. Factor *(4)*	Present Value
Cash- flows of USD Leg:							
15-Jul-X1	100 Mill.		5.59 %	Not incl.	5,590,000	0.9486	5,303,000
15-Jul-X2	100 Mill.		5.59 %	Not incl.	5,590,000	0.8978	5,019,000
15-Jul-X3	100 Mill.		5.59 %	Not incl.	5,590,000	0.8494	4,748,000
15-Jul-X3					100 Mill.	0.8494	84,940,000
					Total USD *(5)*		**100,000,000**
					Total EUR (1.2500)		**80,000,000**
Cash- flows of EUR Leg:							
15-Jul-X1	80 Mill.	13-Jul-X0	4.50 %	Not incl.	3,600,000	0.9569	−3,445,000
15-Jul-X2	80 Mill.	13-Jul-X1	4.71 %	Not incl.	3,768,000	0.9136	−3,442,000
15-Jul-X3	80 Mill.	13-Jul-X2	4.89 %	Not incl.	3,912,000	0.8713	−3,409,000
15-Jul-X3					80 Mill.	0.8713	−69,704,000
					Total EUR		**<80,000,000>**
					Fair Value		**−0−**

Notes:

(1) The Euribor 12-month was fixed two business days prior to the commencement of the interest period.

(2) The fixing dates are only relevant to the floating leg. The fixing at 13-Jul-X0 was already known at hedge inception. The fixings of 13-Jul-X1 and 13-Jul-X2 were not known yet, so the valuation used their expected values.

(3) Period settlement amounts were calculated as:

   Notional*Period Rate*Day Factor

The basis of the floating leg was Actual/360. The basis of the fixed leg was 30/360. To keep calculations simple both "Day Factors" were assumed to be equal to one.

*(4)*The discount factors represented the present value, as of the valuation date, of USD 1 (or EUR 1) to be paid on the cash flow date. The discount factors were computed using the mid-market USD Libor (or Euribor) yield curves flat (i.e., without taking into account any credit spread or bid/offers).

(5) The sum is USD 100,010,000, but in reality if the rounding were not present the sum would have been USD 100,000,000

The fair value of the hedging instrument and the hypothetical derivative on 31 December 20X0 was calculated as follows:

Hedging Instrument and Hypothetical Derivative Valuation on 31-Dec-X0							
Cash Flow Date	Notional	Floating Rate Fixing	Period Rate	Credit Spread	Period Leg Amount	Disc. Factor	Present Value
Cash- flows of USD Leg:							
15-Jul-X1	100 Mill.		5.59 %	Not incl.	5,590,000	0.9720	5,433,000
15-Jul-X2	100 Mill.		5.59 %	Not incl.	5,590,000	0.9205	5,146,000
15-Jul-X3	100 Mill.		5.59 %	Not incl.	5,590,000	0.8700	4,863,000
15-Jul-X3					100 Mill.	0.8700	87,000,000
						Total USD	**102,442,000**
						Total EUR (1.2800)	**80,033,000**
Cash- flows of EUR Leg:							
15-Jul-X1	80 Mill.	13-Jul-X0	4.50 %	Not incl.	3,600,000	0.9759	−3,513,000
15-Jul-X2	80 Mill.	13-Jul-X1	4.81 %	Not incl.	3,848,000	0.9311	−3,583,000
15-Jul-X3	80 Mill.	13-Jul-X2	5.00 %	Not incl.	4,000,000	0.8868	−3,547,000
15-Jul-X3					80 Mill.	0.8868	−70,944,000
						Total EUR	**<81,587,000>**
						Fair Value	**<1,554,000>**

The interest accrual of the hedging instrument on 31 December 20X0 was EUR 355,000 (= 2,022,000 − 1,667,000):

- The accrual of the USD leg was EUR 2,022,000 (= 5,590,000*169 days/365 days/1.28)
- The accrual of the EUR leg was EUR −1,667,000 (= −3,600,000*169/365)

Therefore the fair value of the hedging instrument on 31 December 20X0 excluding the accrual was EUR -1,909,000 (= −1,554,000−355,000). The hypothetical derivative fair value was also EUR -1,909,000. The hedge was then deemed to be effective as the ratio was within the 80 %–125 % range, as shown in the following table:

Retrospective Test	31-Dec-X0
Hedging instrument fair value change	<1,909,000>
Hypothetical derivative fair value change	<1,909,000>
Ratio	**100,0 %**
Hedge effective amount	<1,909,000>
Hedge ineffective amount	−0−

The effective part of the hedge gains or losses was the lesser of the absolute values of the accumulated change in fair value of the hedging instrument and the hypothetical derivative. Because both amounts were identical, no ineffectiveness was recognised in the period.

Retrospective Test Performed on 31 December 20X1

The fair value of the hedging instrument and the hypothetical derivative on 31 December 20X1 was calculated as follows:

Hedging Instrument and Hypothetical Derivative Valuation on 31-Dec-X1							
Cash Flow Date	Notional	Floating Rate Fixing	Period Rate	Credit Spread	Period Leg Amount	Disc. Factor	Present Value
Cash-flows of USD Leg:							
15-Jul-X2	100 Mill.		5.59 %	Not incl.	5,590,000	0.9711	5,428,000
15-Jul-X3	100 Mill.		5.59 %	Not incl.	5,590,000	0.9178	5,131,000
15-Jul-X3					100 Mill.	0.9178	91,780,000
					Total USD		**102,339,000**
					Total EUR (1.2200)		**83,884,000**
Cash-flows of EUR Leg:							
15-Jul-X2	80 Mill.	13-Jul-X1	4.75 %	Not incl.	3,800,000	0.9749	3,705,000
15-Jul-X3	80 Mill.	13-Jul-X2	5.00 %	Not incl.	4,000,000	0.9285	3,714,000
15-Jul-X3					80 Mill.	0.9285	74,280,000
					Total EUR		**<81,699,000>**
					Fair Value		**2,185,000**

The interest accrual of the hedging instrument on 31 December 20X1 was EUR 363,000 (= 2,122,000-1,759,000):

- The accrual of the USD leg was EUR 2,122,000 (= 5,590,000*169 days/365 days/1.22)
- The accrual of the EUR leg was EUR −1,759,000 (= −3,800,000*169/365)

Therefore the fair value of the hedging instrument on 31 December 20X1 excluding the accrual was EUR 1,822,000 (= 2,185,000−363,000). The hypothetical derivative fair value was also EUR 1,822,000.

The change in fair value of both instruments since the last assessment was a gain of EUR 3,731,000 (= 1,822,000−(−1,909,000)). The hedge was then deemed to be highly effective retrospectively because the ratio was within the 80 %–125 % range, as shown in the following table:

Retrospective Test	31-Dec-X1
Hedging instrument fair value change	3,731,000
Hypothetical derivative fair value change	3,731,000
Ratio	100,0 %
Hedge effective amount	3,731,000
Hedge ineffective amount	−0−

Retrospective Test Performed on 31 December 20X2

The fair value of the hedging instrument and the hypothetical derivative on 31 December 20X2 was calculated as follows:

	Hedging Instrument and Hypothetical Derivative Valuation on 31-Dec-X2						
Cash Flow Date	Notional	Floating Rate Fixing	Period Rate	Credit Spread	Period Leg Amount	Disc. Factor	Present Value
Cash- flows of USD Leg:							
15-Jul-X3	100 Mill.		5.59 %	Not incl.	5,590,000	0.9715	5,431,000
15-Jul-X3					100 Mill.	0.9715	97,150,000
						Total USD	**102,581,000**
						Total EUR (1.1500)	**89,201,000**
Cash- flows of EUR Leg:							
15-Jul-X3	80 Mill.	13-Jul-X2	4.95 %	Not incl.	3,960,000	0.9744	−3,859,000
15-Jul-X3					80 Mill.	0.9744	−77,952,000
						Total EUR	**<81,811,000>**
						Fair Value	**7,390,000**

The interest accrual of the hedging instrument on 31 December 20X2 was EUR 417,000 (= 2,251,000-1,834,000):

- The accrual of the USD leg was EUR 2,251,000 (= 5,590,000*169 days/365 days/1.15)
- The accrual of the EUR leg was EUR -1,834,000 (= −3,960,000*169/365)

Therefore the fair value of the hedging instrument on 31 December 20X2 excluding the accrual was EUR 6,973,000 (= 7,390,000 − 417,000). The hypothetical derivative fair value was also EUR 6,973,000. The change in fair value of both instruments since the last assessment was a gain of EUR 5,151,000 (= 6,973,000 − 1,822,000). The hedge was then deemed to be highly effective retrospectively as the ratio was within the 80 %–125 % range, as shown in the following table:

Retrospective Test	31-Dec-X2
Hedging instrument fair value change	5,151,000
Hypothetical derivative fair value change	5,151,000
Ratio	**100,0 %**
Hedge effective amount	5,151,000
Hedge ineffective amount	−0−

Retrospective Test Performed on 15 July 20X3

The final exchange of principals under the hedging instrument meant that ABC had to pay EUR 80 million and receive USD 100 million. The spot exchange rate on 15 July 20X3 was 1.10. Thus, the fair value of the hedging instrument and the hypothetical derivative on 15 July

20X3, after paying the interest settlement but before the final exchange of principals was EUR 10,909,000 (= 100,000,000/1.10−80,000,000). The hypothetical derivative fair value was also EUR 10,909,000. The change in fair value of the hedging instrument and the hypothetical derivative since the last assessment was a gain of EUR 3,936,000 (= 10,909,000 − 6,973,000). The hedge was then deemed to be highly effective retrospectively because the ratio was within the 80 %–125 % range, as shown in the following table:

Retrospective Test	15-Jul-X3
Hedging instrument fair value change	3,936,000
Hypothetical derivative fair value change	3,936,000
Ratio	**100,0 %**
Hedge effective amount	3,936,000
Hedge ineffective amount	−0−

Rest of Relevant Calculations

After calculating the fair value of the hedging instrument and the hedge effective part, ABC computed the fair value of the CCS at each of the relevant dates. Remember that the CCS terms were slightly different to those of the hedging instrument (the CCS also included the credit spreads). The fair value of the CCS at hedge inception was zero. The fair value of the CCS on 31 December 20X0 was calculated as follows:

CCS, valuation on 31-Dec-X0							
Cash Flow Date	Notional	Floating Rate Fixing	Period Rate	Credit Spread	Period Leg Amount	Disc. Factor	Present Value
Cash- flows of USD Leg:							
15-Jul-X1	100 Mill.		5.59 %	0.50 %	6,090,000	0.9720	5,919,000
15-Jul-X2	100 Mill.		5.59 %	0.50 %	6,090,000	0.9205	5,606,000
15-Jul-X3	100 Mill.		5.59 %	0.50 %	6,090,000	0.8700	5,298,000
15-Jul-X3					100 Mill.	0.8700	87,000,000
					Total USD		**103,823,000**
					Total EUR (1.2800)		**81,112,000**
Cash- flows of EUR Leg:							
15-Jul-X1	80 Mill.	13-Jul-X0	4.50 %	0.49 %	3,992,000	0.9759	−3,896,000
15-Jul-X2	80 Mill.	13-Jul-X1	4.81 %	0.49 %	4,240,000	0.9311	−3,948,000
15-Jul-X3	80 Mill.	13-Jul-X2	5.00 %	0.49 %	4,392,000	0.8868	−3,895,000
15-Jul-X3					80 Mill.	0.8868	−70,944,000
					Total EUR		**<82,683,000>**
					CCS Fair Value		**<1,571,000>**

The interest accrual of the hedging instrument on 31 December 20X0 was EUR + 355,000 (= 2,203,000−1,848,000):

- The accrual of the USD leg was EUR 2,203,000 (= 6,090,000*169 days/365 days/1.28)
- The accrual of the EUR leg was EUR −1,848,000 (= −3,992,000*169/365)

Therefore the fair value of the hedging instrument on 31 December 20X0 excluding the accrual was EUR $-1,926,000$ $(= -1,571,000-355,000)$.

In order not to be too repetitive, we have summarised in the following table the CCS fair value calculations and their accruals for all the relevant dates.

	31-Dec-X0	31-Dec-X1	31-Dec-X2	15-Jul-X3
CCS fair value (incl. accruals)	<1,571,000>	2,213,000	7,430,000	10,909,000
Accrual amount	355,000	370,000 (1)	437,000 (2)	-0-
CCS fair value (excl. accruals)	<1,926,000>	1,843,000	6,993,000	10,909,000
Change in CCS fair value (excl. accruals)	<1,926,000>	3,769,000	5,150,000	3,916,000

Notes:

(1) $6,090,000*169/365/1.22-80,000,000*(4.75\%+0.49\%)*169/365$

(2) $6,090,000*169/365/1.15-80,000,000*(4.95\%+0.49\%)*169/365$

Additionally, ABC had to compute the change in the carrying amount of the bond due to changes in the spot rate. The translation gains and losses are shown in the following table:

	Issue Date	31-Dec-X0	31-Dec-X1	31-Dec-X2	15-Jul-X3
USD bond amortised cost (1)	100,000,000	100,000,000	100,000,000	100,000,000	100,000,000
USD/EUR spot	1.2500	1.2800	1.2200	1.1500	1.1000
Bond re-measured at spot	80,000,000	78,125,000	81,967,000	86,957,000	90,909,000
Translation gain <loss>	—	1,875,000	<3,842,000>	<4,990,000>	<3,952,000>

Note (1) As will be explained later, the adjustments to the carrying value due to the fair value hedge were excluded from the re-measurement at spot. Thus, the amount subject to translation was USD 100 million.

The adjustments to the carrying value of the USD bond also needed to be calculated. Because the hedge was a fair value hedge, the carrying amount of the bond had to be adjusted according to the effective part of the change in fair value of the hedging instrument, once excluding the re-translation gain. The next table shows the calculations of the adjustments to the bond carrying value performed at each reporting date and at maturity.

	31-Dec-X0	31-Dec-X1	31-Dec-X2	15-Jul-X3
Translation gain <loss>	1,875,000	<3,842,000>	<4,990,000>	<3,952,000>
Hedge effective part (reversed amount)	1,909,000	<3,731,000>	<5,151,000>	<3,936,000>
Difference	<34,000>	<111,000>	161,000	<16,000>
Adjustment to bond carrying amount	<34,000>	<111,000>	161,000	<16,000>

In order to clarify it, let us look at the 31 December 20X0 figures. The bond's re-translation gain (EUR 1,875,000) was lower than the hedge effective part (EUR 1,909,000) so an adjustment of EUR $-34,000$ $(= 1,875,000-1,909,000)$ was made to the carrying value of the bond.

Regarding the adjustments to the carrying value of the bond due to the fair value hedge, ABC had two alternatives:

1) To convert these adjustments into USD, so the carrying amount of the bond was all in USD. Thus, the translation gain or loss was calculated on this total USD carrying value; or
2) To leave the adjustments in EUR, and split the carrying amount of the bond into two sub-accounts, one in USD and other in EUR. The EUR sub-account will contain the adjustments and the USD sub-account will contain the amortised cost of the USD bond without any adjustments. The translation gain or loss was then calculated only on the USD sub-account carrying value. ABC chose this second alternative because it was simpler to implement.

Accounting Entries

The required journal entries were as follows:

1) Journal entries on 15 July 20X0:
   To record the bond issuance:

Cash (Asset)	€ 80,000,000	
USD Financial Debt (Liability)		€ 80,000,000

No entries were required to record the CCS as its initial fair value was nil.
2) Journal entries on 31 December 20X0:
   The accrued interest of the bond was EUR 2,203,000 (= 6,090,000*169 days/365 days/1.28):

Interest Income/Expense (P&L)	€ 2,203,000	
Interest Payable (Liability)		€ 2,203,000

The re-measurement of the bond at spot was a gain of EUR 1,875,000:

USD Financial Debt (Liability)	€ 1,875,000	
Retranslation Gains/Losses (P&L)		€ 1,875,000

The fair value change, excluding accruals, of the CCS was a loss of EUR 1,926,000:

Fair Value Hedge Gain/Loss (P&L)	€ 1,926,000	
Fair Value of Derivative (Liability)		€ 1,926,000

The accrued interest of the CCS was EUR 355,000:

Interest Receivable (Asset)	€ 355,000	
Interest Income/Expense (P&L)		€ 355,000

The effective part of the hedge was a loss of EUR 1,909,000. Because the hedge was a fair value hedge, the carrying amount of the bond had to be adjusted according to the effective part of the change value of the hedging instrument, once excluding the re-translation gain. As the re-translation gain was EUR 1,875,000, a EUR −34,000 (= 1,875,000−1,909,000) adjustment was made, reducing the carrying value of the bond:

USD Financial Debt (Liability)	€ 34,000	
Fair Value Hedge Gain/Loss (P&L)		€ 34,000

3) Journal entries on 15 July 20X1:

The bond coupon was USD 6,090,000. Assuming a USD/EUR spot rate of 1.2600, ABC had to pay EUR 4,833,000 (= 6,090,000/1.26):

Interest Payable (Liability)	€ 2,203,000	
Interest Income/Expense (P&L)	€ 2,630,000	
Cash		€ 4,833,000

Under the CCS, ABC received EUR 4,833,000 (identical amount to the bond coupon) and paid EUR 3,992,000 (= 80,000,000*(4.50 % + 0.49 %)). Therefore, the CCS settlement amount was EUR 841,000 (= 4,833,000−3,992,000):

Cash (Asset)	€ 841,000	
Interest Income/Expense (P&L)		€ 486,000
Interest Receivable (Asset)		€ 355,000

4) Journal entries on 31 December 20X1:

The bond interest to be paid on 15 July 20X2 was USD 6,090,000. The accrued interest of the bond was EUR 2,311,000 (= 6,090,000*169 days/365 days/1.22). In theory, ABC had to re-compute the interest as the carrying value of the bond has changed. Because the adjustment made to the bond carrying amount due to the fair value hedge was small, ABC preferred not to re-compute the effective interest.

Interest Income/Expense (P&L)	€ 2,311,000	
Interest Payable (Liability)		€ 2,311,000

The re-measurement of the bond at spot was a loss of EUR 3,842,000:

Re-translation Gains/Losses (P&L)	€ 3,842,000	
USD Financial Debt (Liability)		€ 3,842,000

The fair value change, excluding accruals, of the CCS was a gain of EUR 3,769,000:

Fair Value of Derivative (Asset)	€ 3,769,000	
Fair Value Hedge Gain/Loss (P&L)		€ 3,769,000

The accrued interest of the CCS was EUR 370,000:

Interest Receivable (Asset)	€ 370,000	
Interest Income/Expense (P&L)		€ 370,000

The effective part of the hedge was a gain of EUR 3,731,000. Because the hedge was a fair value hedge, the carrying amount of the bond had to be adjusted according to the effective part of the change value of the hedging instrument, once excluding the re-translation gain. As the re-translation loss was EUR 3,842,000, a EUR $-111,000 (= -3,842,000 + 3,731,000)$ adjustment was made, reducing the carrying value of the bond:

USD Financial Debt (Liability)	€ 111,000	
Fair Value Hedge Gain/Loss (P&L)		€ 111,000

5) Journal entries on 15 July 20X2:

The bond coupon was USD 6,090,000. Assuming a USD/EUR spot rate of 1.1800, ABC had to pay EUR 5,161,000 (= 6,090,000/1.18):

Interest Payable (Liability)	€ 2,311,000	
Interest Income/Expense (P&L)	€ 2,850,000	
Cash		€ 5,161,000

Under the CCS, ABC received EUR 5,161,000 (identical amount to the bond coupon) and paid EUR 4,192,000 (= 80,000,000*(4.75 % + 0.49 %)). Therefore, the CCS settlement amount was EUR 969,000 (= 5,161,000−4,192,000):

Cash (Asset)	€ 969,000	
Interest Income/Expense (P&L)		€ 599,000
Interest Receivable (Asset)		€ 370,000

6) Journal entries on 31 December 20X2:

The bond interest to be paid on 15 July 20X3 was USD 6,090,000. The accrued interest of the bond was EUR 2,452,000 (= 6,090,000*169 days/365 days/1.15).

Interest Income/Expense (P&L)	€ 2,452,000	
Interest Payable (Liability)		€ 2,452,000

The re-measurement of the bond at spot was a loss of EUR 4,990,000:

Re-translation Gains/Losses (P&L)	€ 4,990,000	
USD Financial Debt (Liability)		€ 4,990,000

The fair value change, excluding accruals, of the CCS was a gain of EUR 5,150,000:

Fair Value of Derivative (Asset)	€ 5,150,000	
Fair Value Hedge Gain/Loss (P&L)		€ 5,150,000

The accrued interest of the CCS was EUR 437,000:

Interest Receivable (Asset)	€ 437,000	
Interest Income/Expense (P&L)		€ 437,000

The effective part of the hedge was a gain of EUR 5,151,000. Because the hedge was a fair value hedge, the carrying amount of the bond had to be adjusted according to the effective part of the change value of the hedging instrument, once excluding the re-translation gain. As the re-translation loss was EUR 4,990,000, an adjustment of EUR 161,000 (= 5,151,000−4,990,000) was made increasing the carrying value of the bond:

Fair Value Hedge Gain/Loss (P&L)	€ 161,000	
USD Financial Debt (Liability)		€ 161,000

7) Journal entries on 15 July 20X3:

The bond coupon was USD 6,090,000. Assuming a USD/EUR spot rate of 1.1000, ABC had to pay EUR 5,536,000 (= 6,090,000(1.10). Additionally, as the final carrying value of the bond was EUR 90,090,000 (= 100,000,000/1.10), EUR 16,000 had to be taken into account when computing the interest expense:

Interest Payable (Liability)	€ 2,452,000	
USD Financial Debt (Liability)	€ 16,000	
Interest Income/Expense (P&L)	€ 3,068,000	
Cash		€ 5,536,000

Under the CCS, ABC received EUR 5,536,000 (identical amount to the bond coupon) and paid EUR 4,352,000 ($= 80,000,000^*(4.95\% + 0.49\%)$). Therefore, the CCS settlement amount was EUR 1,184,000 ($= 5,536,000-4,352,000$):

Cash (Asset)	€ 1,184,000	
Interest Income/Expense (P&L)		€ 747,000
Interest Receivable (Asset)		€ 437,000

The re-measurement of the bond at spot was a loss of EUR 3,952,000:

Retranslation Gains/Losses (P&L)	€ 3,952,000	
USD Financial Debt (Liability)		€ 3,952,000

The fair value change (this time there are no more accruals) of the CCS was a gain of EUR 3,916,000:

Fair Value of Derivative (Asset)	€ 3,916,000	
Fair Value Hedge Gain/Loss (P&L)		€ 3,916,000

Under the CCS, ABC received USD 100 million (identical to the bond redemption amount) and paid EUR 80,000,000 million. Therefore, the value of this exchange was EUR 10,909,000 ($= 100$ million$/1.10 - 80,000,000$):

Cash (Asset)	€ 10,909,000	
Fair Value of Derivative (Asset)		€ 10,909,000

The redemption amount of the bond was EUR 90,909,000 ($=$ USD 100 million$/1.10$).

USD Financial Debt (Liability)	€ 90,909,000	
Cash (Asset)		€ 90,909,000

Summary of the Journal Entries

	Assets			Liabilities		Profit and Loss
	Cash	Interest Receivable	Derivative Fair Value	Financial Debt	Interest Payable	
15 July 20X0						
Bond issuance	80,000,000			80,000,000		
31 December 20X0						
Bond accrued coupon					2,203,000	<2,203,000>
Bond re-measurement				<1,875,000>		1,875,000
CCS accrual		355,000				355,000
Change in fair value of CCS			<1,926,000>			<1,926,000>
Bond carrying value adjustment				<34,000>		34,000
15 July 20X1						
Bond coupon payment	<4,833,000>				<2,203,000>	<2,630,000>
CCS interest settlement	841,000	<355,000>				486,000
31 December 20X1						
Bond accrued coupon					2,311,000	<2,311,000>
Bond re-measurement				3,842,000		<3,842,000>
CCS accrual		370,000				370,000
Change in fair value of CCS			3,769,000			3,769,000
Bond carrying value adjustment				<111,000>		111,000
15 July 20X2						
Bond coupon payment	<5,161,000>				<2,311,000>	<2,850,000>
CCS interest settlement	969,000	<370,000>				599,000

(Continued)

Summary of the Journal Entries (Continued)

	Assets			Liabilities		Profit and Loss
	Cash	Interest Receivable	Derivative Fair Value	Financial Debt	Interest Payable	
31 December 20X2						
Bond accrued coupon					2,452,000	<2,452,000>
Bond re-measurement				4,990,000		<4,990,000>
CCS accrual		437,000				437,000
Change in fair value of CCS			5,150,000			5,150,000
Bond carrying value adjustment				161,000		<161,000>
15 July 20X3						
Bond coupon payment	<5,536,000>					<3,068,000>
CCS interest settlement	1,184,000	<437,000>		<16,000>	<2,452,000>	747,000
Bond re-measurement				3,952,000		<3,952,000>
Change in fair value of CCS			3,916,000			3,916,000
Bond redemption	<90,909,000>			<90,909,000>		
CCS final exchange	10,909,000		<10,909,000>			
Totals	**<12,536,000>**	–0–	–0–	–0–	–0–	**<12,536,000>**

Concluding Remarks

The CCS allowed ABC to take advantage of opportunities existing outside its home market, broaden its investor base, and preserve its access to domestic capital sources for future use. What we wonder is if it was worth the effort to apply hedge accounting in this case. What happened was that the re-translation of the bond at the FX spot rate eclipsed the advantage of fair value hedging.

Therefore, for highly volatile exchange rates and short-term debt it may be worth not to apply hedge accounting. In these situations, the CCS is treated as undesignated. However, if the exchange rate is expected to be quite stable, fair value accounting can be a valuable way to obtain a more stable P&L.

CASE 6.4

Hedging a Floating-rate Foreign Currency Liability Using a Receive-Floating Pay-Fixed Cross-Currency Swap

The objective of this case is to illustrate the hedge accounting implications of a floating-rate cross-border financing hedged with a receive-floating pay-fixed CCS. This type of hedge, a cash flow hedge, is much friendlier than a fair value hedge of a foreign currency liability.

Background Information

On 15 July 20X0, Company ABC issued a USD-denominated fixed-rate bond. ABC functional currency is the Euro. The bond had the following characteristics:

Bond Terms	
Expected issue date	15 July 20X0
Maturity	3 years (15 July 20X3)
Notional	USD 100 million
Coupon	USD Libor 12-month plus 50 bps, A/360 basis, to be paid annually

Since ABC's objective was to raise EUR funding, on issue date ABC entered into CCS. In the CCS, the entity agreed to receive a USD floating-rate equal to the bond coupon and pay a EUR fixed-rate. The CCS had the following terms:

Cross-currency Swap Terms	
Trade date	15 July 20X0
Start date	15 July 20X0
Counterparties	Company ABC and XYZ Bank
Maturity date	3 years (15 July 20X3)
USD nominal	USD 100 million
EUR nominal	EUR 80 million
Initial exchange	On start date, ABC receives the EUR nominal and pays the USD nominal

(Continued)

Cross-currency Swap Terms	
ABC pays	EUR 5.19 %, annually, 30/360 basis, on the EUR nominal
ABC receives	USD Libor 12-month plus 50 bps, annually, A/360 basis, on the USD nominal
	USD Libor 12-month to be fixed two business days prior to the commencement of the interest period
Final exchange	On maturity date, ABC receives the USD nominal and pays the EUR nominal

The CCS was designated as the hedging instrument in a cash flow hedge of the USD bond. The interaction between the bond and the CCS is described next. It can be seen that with the combination of the USD bond and the CCS, ABC obtained synthetically a EUR fixed-rate liability.

On issue date and the start of the CCS, there was an initial exchange of principals through the CCS: ABC delivered the USD 100 million proceeds of the issue and received EUR 80 million. The combination of the bond and CCS had the same effect as if ABC issued a EUR-denominated bond, as highlighted in Figure 6.13.

Annually, there was a periodic exchange of interest payments. ABC received a USD floating-rate interest and paid a EUR fixed-rate interest. ABC used the USD floating-rate cash flows it received from the CCS to pay the bond interest, as shown in Figure 6.14.

At maturity of the CCS and the debt, ABC re-exchanged the principals (see Figure 6.15), using the USD 100 million it received under the CCS to redeem the bond issue, and delivering EUR 80 million to the CCS counterparty. Note that this final exchange was made at exactly the same rate used in the initial exchange (1.2500).

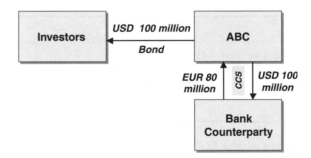

Figure 6.13   Bond with CCS : Initial Cash Flows.

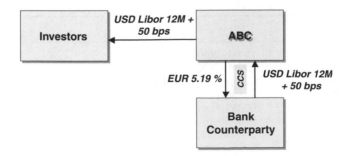

Figure 6.14   Bond with CCS : Intermediate cash-flows.

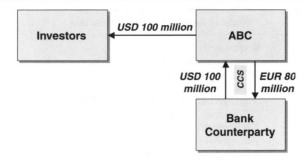

Figure 6.15   Bond with CCS : Cash Flows at Maturity.

Hedge Documentation

ABC documented the hedge relationship as follows:

	Hedging Relationship Documentation
Risk management objective and strategy for undertaking the hedge	The objective of the hedge is to reduce the variability of the cash flows of a foreign currency denominated bond. This hedging objective is consistent with ABC's overall interest rate risk management strategy of transforming all new issued foreign-denominated debt into the group functional currency.
Type of hedge	Cash flow hedge.
Risk being hedged	Interest rate risk and FX risk. The variability in the cash flows of the bond attributable to changes in (i) USD interest rates, (ii) EUR interest rates and (iii) the USD/EUR exchange rate.
Hedging instrument	The cross-currency swap with reference number 005,768. The counterparty to the swap is XYZ Bank and the credit risk associated with this counterparty is considered to be very low.
Hedged item	The 3-year USD-denominated floating-rate bond with reference number 667907.
Assessment of effectiveness testing	Hedge effectiveness will be assessed by comparing changes in the fair value of the hedging instrument to changes in the fair value of the hypothetical instrument.
	The hypothetical derivative is a derivative whose changes in fair value offset perfectly the changes in fair value of the hedged item for variations in the risk being hedged. In this hedging relationship, the terms of the hypothetical derivative coincide exactly with the terms of the hedging instrument but assume no credit risk on the counterparty to the hypothetical derivative.
	Prospective test
	A prospective test will be performed at the inception and at each reporting date, using the critical terms method.
	If (i) the critical terms of the portion of the debt designated as being hedged and the hedging instrument match (i.e., notional amounts, currencies, underlying and interest periods), and (ii) the credit risk of the counterparty to the hedging instrument is very low, the hedge will be considered to be highly effective prospectively.
	The credit risk of the counterparty to the hedging instrument will be monitored continuously.

Hedging Relationship Documentation

Retrospective test

A retrospective test will be performed at each reporting date using the "ratio analysis method". The ratio will compare the change since the last assessment in the fair value of the hedging instrument with the change since the last assessment in the fair value of the hypothetical derivative. The hedge will be assumed to be highly effective on a retrospective basis if the ratio is between 80 % and 125 %.

The effective part of the change in fair value of the hedging instrument (excluding the portion attributable to the current period swap accrual and the hedged item translation gains or losses) will be recognised in equity.

Prospective Tests

ABC performed a prospective test at inception (15 July 20X0) and at each reporting date during the hedge relationship (31 December 20X0, 31 December 20X1 and 31 December 20X2). ABC used the critical terms method to assess prospective effectiveness.

Because (i) the critical terms of the hypothetical derivative and the hedging instrument, and (ii) the credit risk associated with the counterparty to the hedging instrument was considered to be very low, ABC expected that the hedge would be highly effective prospectively. The credit risk of the counterparty to the hedging instrument was monitored at each testing date, but the hedging instrument counterparty did not experience any significant credit deterioration. Thus, the hedge was considered to be highly effective prospectively at each test date.

Retrospective Tests

ABC performed a retrospective test at each reporting date and also at hedge maturity. The fair value of the hedging instrument and the hypothetical derivative were computed at inception and at each test date. Remember that in this case, the terms of the hedging instrument (i.e., the one used for effectiveness assessment) were identical to the CCS terms.

The retrospective test calculations were based on the following USD/EUR spot rate and USD Libor and EUR Euribor interest rate curves:

	15-Jul-X0	Test-1 31-Dec-X0	Test-2 31-Dec-X1	Test-3 31-Dec-X2	Test-4 15-Jul-X3
USD/EUR Spot	1.2500	1.2800	1.2200	1.1500	1.1000
USD Libor deposit and swap rates:					
USD 1-Year	5.40 %	5.50 %	5.70 %	5.60 %	—
USD 2-Year	5.50 %	5.60 %	5.80 %	5.70 %	—
USD 3-Year	5.59 %	5.69 %	5.89 %	5.79 %	—
EUR Euribor deposit and swap rates:					
EUR 1-Year	4.50 %	4.70 %	4.90 %	5.00 %	—
EUR 2-Year	4.60 %	4.80 %	5.00 %	5.05 %	—
EUR 3-Year	4.70 %	4.89 %	5.09 %	5.10 %	—

Retrospective Test Performed on 31 December 20X0

The retrospective test on 31 December 20X0 had to compare changes in fair values of the hedging instrument and the hypothetical derivative from hedge inception (15 July 20X0) until this test date.

The following table shows the CCS fair value calculation, at hedge inception (15 July 20X0). Remember that in this case the economic terms of the CCS, hedging instrument and hypothetical derivative were identical.

CCS Valuation 15 July 20X0						
Cash Flow Date	Notional	Period Rate	Credit Spread	Period Leg Amount *(1)*	Disc. Factor *(2)*	Present Value
Cash flows of USD leg:						
15-Jul-X1	100 Mill.	5.40 %	0.50 %	5,900,000	0.9486	5,597,000
15-Jul-X2	100 Mill.	5.60 %	0.50 %	6,100,000	0.8978	5,477,000
15-Jul-X3	100 Mill.	5.78 %	0.50 %	6,280,000	0.8494	5,334,000
15-Jul-X3				100 Mill.	0.8494	84,940,000
				Total USD *(3)*		**101,348,000**
				Total EUR (1.2500)		**81,088,000**
Cash flows of EUR leg:						
15-Jul-X1	80 Mill.	4.70 %	0.49 %	4,152,000	0.9569	−3,973,000
15-Jul-X2	80 Mill.	4.70 %	0.49 %	4,152,000	0.9136	−3,793,000
15-Jul-X3	80 Mill.	4.70 %	0.49 %	4,152,000	0.8713	−3,618,000
15-Jul-X3				80 Mill.	0.8713	−69,704,000
				Total EUR		**<81,088,000>**
				Fair Value of CCS		**−0−**

Notes:

(1) Period settlement amounts were calculated as:

Notional*Period Rate*Day Factor

The basis of the fixed leg was 30/360 and the basis of the floating leg was A/360. To keep calculations simple, all "Day Factors" were assumed to be equal to one.

(2) The discount factors represented the present value, as of the valuation date, of USD 1 (or EUR 1) to be paid on the cash flow date. The discount factors were computed using the mid-market USD Libor (or Euribor) yield curves flat (i.e., without taking into account any credit spread or bid/offers).

(3) The sum was USD 101,348,000, but in reality if the rounding of discount factors and present values were not made the sum would have been USD 101,360,000

Similarly, the fair value on 31 December 20X0 of the CCS was calculated as shown in the next table. Remember that in this case the terms of the CCS, hedging instrument and hypothetical derivative were identical.

CCS Valuation on 31 December 20X0						
Cash Flow Date	Notional	Period Rate	Credit Spread	Period Leg Amount	Disc. Factor	Present Value
Cash flows of USD leg:						
15-Jul-X1	100 Mill.	5.40 %	0.50 %	5,900,000	0.9720	5,735,000
15-Jul-X2	100 Mill.	5.60 %	0.50 %	6,100,000	0.9205	5,615,000
15-Jul-X3	100 Mill.	5.80 %	0.50 %	6,300,000	0.8700	5,481,000
15-Jul-X3				100 Mill.	0.8700	87,000,000
				Total USD		**103,831,000**
				Total EUR (1.2800)		**81,118,000**
Cash flows of EUR leg:						
15-Jul-X1	80 Mill.	4.70 %	0.49 %	4,152,000	0.9759	−4,052,000
15-Jul-X2	80 Mill.	4.70 %	0.49 %	4,152,000	0.9311	−3,866,000
15-Jul-X3	80 Mill.	4.70 %	0.49 %	4,152,000	0.8868	−3,682,000
15-Jul-X3				80 Mill.	0.8868	−70,944,000
				Total EUR		**<82,544,000>**
				Fair Value of CCS		**<1,426,000>**

The interest accrual of the CCS on 31 December 20X0 was EUR 212,000 (= 2,134,000−1,922,000):

- The accrual of the USD leg was EUR 2,134,000 (= 5,900,000*169 days/365 days/1.28)
- The accrual of the EUR leg was EUR −1,922,000 (= −4,152,000*169/365)

Therefore the fair value of the CCS, the hedging instrument and the hypothetical derivative on 31 December 20X0 excluding the accrual was EUR −1,638,000 (= −1,426,000−212,000). The change in fair value of these instruments since the last assessment was a loss of EUR 1,638,000 (= −1,638,000−0). The hedge was then deemed to be highly effective retrospectively as the ratio was within the 80 %–125 % range, as shown in the following table:

Retrospective Test	31-Dec-X0
Hedging instrument fair value change	<1,638,000>
Hypothetical derivative fair value change	<1,638,000>
Ratio	**100,0 %**
Hedge effective amount	<1,638,000>
Hedge ineffective amount	−0−

The effective part of the hedge gains or losses was limited by the lesser of the absolute values of the cumulative change in fair value of the hedging instrument and the hypothetical derivative. This condition did not impose this time any limit to the hedge effective amount.

Retrospective Test Performed on 31 December 20X1

The retrospective test on 31 December 20X1 had to compare changes in fair values of the hedging instrument and the hypothetical derivative since the last assessment (31 December 20X0) until this test date.

The fair value of the CCS on 31 December 20X1 was calculated as follows (remember that this value was also the fair value of the hedging instrument and the hypothetical derivative):

CCS Valuation on 31 December 20X1						
Cash Flow Date	Notional	Period Rate	Credit Spread	Period Leg Amount	Disc. Factor	Present Value
Cash flows of USD leg:						
15-Jul-X2	100 Mill.	5.55 %	0.50 %	6,050,000	0.9711	5,875,000
15-Jul-X3	100 Mill.	5.80 %	0.50 %	6,300,000	0.9178	5,782,000
15-Jul-X3				100 Mill.	0.9178	91,780,000
				Total USD		**103,437,000**
				Total EUR (1.2200)		**84,784,000**
Cash flows of EUR leg:						
15-Jul-X2	80 Mill.	4.70 %	0.49 %	4,152,000	0.9749	−4,048,000
15-Jul-X3	80 Mill.	4.70 %	0.49 %	4,152,000	0.9285	−3,855,000
15-Jul-X3				80 Mill.	0.9285	−74,280,000
				Total EUR		**<82,183,000>**
				Fair Value of CCS		**2,601,000**

The interest accrual of the CCS on 31 December 20X1 was EUR 374,000 (= 2,296,000–1,922,000):

- The accrual of the USD leg was EUR 2,296,000 (= 6,050,000*169 days/365 days/1.22)
- The accrual of the EUR leg was EUR −1,922,000 (= −4,152,000*169/365)

Therefore the fair value of the CCS, the hedging instrument and the hypothetical derivative on 31 December 20X1 excluding the accrual was EUR 2,227,000 (= 2,601,000–374,000). The change in fair value of these instruments since the last assessment was a gain of EUR 3,865,000 (= 2,227,000−(−1,638,000)). The hedge was then deemed to be highly effective retrospectively as the ratio was within the 80 %–125 % range, as shown in the following table:

Retrospective Test	31-Dec-X1
Hedging instrument fair value change since the last assessment	3,865,000
Hypothetical derivative fair value change since the last assessment	3,865,000
Ratio	**100,0 %**
Hedge effective amount	3,865,000
Hedge ineffective amount	−0−

The effective part of the hedge gains or losses was limited by the lesser of the absolute values of the cumulative change in fair value of the hedging instrument and the hypothetical derivative. This condition did not impose this time any limit to the hedge effective amount.

Retrospective Test Performed on 31 December 20X2

The retrospective test on 31 December 20X2 had to compare changes in fair values of the hedging instrument and the hypothetical derivative since the last assessment (31 December 20X1) until this test date.

The fair value of the CCS on 31 December 20X2 was calculated as follows (remember that this value was also the fair value of the hedging instrument and the hypothetical derivative):

				CCS Valuation on 31 December 20X2		
Cash Flow Date	Notional	Period Rate	Credit Spread	Period Leg Amount	Disc. Factor	Present Value
Cash flows of USD leg:						
15-Jul-X3	100 Mill.	5.65 %	0.50 %	6,150,000	0.9715	5,975,000
15-Jul-X3				100 Mill.	0.9715	97,150,000
				Total USD		**103,125,000**
				Total EUR (1.1500)		**89,674,000**
Cash flows of EUR leg:						
15-Jul-X3	80 Mill.	4.70 %	0.49 %	4,152,000	0.9744	−4,046,000
15-Jul-X3				80 Mill.	0.9744	−77,952,000
				Total EUR		**<81,998,000>**
				Fair Value of CCS		**7,676,000**

The interest accrual of the CCS on 31 December 20X2 was EUR 554,000 (= 2,476,000 − 1,922,000):

- The accrual of the USD leg was EUR 2,476,000 (= 6,150,000*169 days/365 days/1.15)
- The accrual of the EUR leg was EUR −1,922,000 (= −4,152,000*169/365)

Therefore the fair value of the CCS, the hedging instrument and the hypothetical derivative on 31 December 20X2 excluding the accrual was EUR 7,122,000 (= 7,676,000−554,000). The change in fair value of these instruments since the last assessment was a gain of EUR 4,895,000 (= 7,122,000−2,227,000). The hedge was then deemed to be highly effective retrospectively as the ratio was within the 80 %–125 % range, as shown in the following table:

Retrospective Test	31-Dec-X1
Hedging instrument fair value change since the last assessment	4,895,000
Hypothetical derivative fair value change since the last assessment	4,895,000
Ratio	**100,0 %**
Hedge effective amount	4,895,000
Hedge ineffective amount	−0−

The effective part of the hedge gains or losses was limited by the lesser of the absolute values of the cumulative change in fair value of the hedging instrument and the hypothetical derivative. This condition did not impose this time any limit to the hedge effective amount.

Retrospective Test Performed on 15 July 20X3

The final exchange of principals under the hedging instrument meant that ABC had to pay EUR 80 million and receive USD 100 million. The spot exchange rate on 15 July 20X3 was 1.10. Thus, the fair value of the CCS, the hedging instrument and the hypothetical derivative on

15 July 20X3, after paying the interest settlement but before the final exchange of principals, was EUR 10,909,000 (= 100,000,000/1.10−80,000,000).

The change in fair value of the CCS, the hedging instrument and the hypothetical derivative since the last assessment was a gain of EUR 3,787,000 (= 10,909,000−7,122,000). The hedge was then deemed to be highly effective retrospectively as the ratio was within the 80 %–125 % range, as shown in the following table:

Retrospective Test	15-Jul-X3
Hedging instrument fair value change since the last assessment	3,787,000
Hypothetical derivative fair value change since the last assessment	3,787,000
Ratio	**100,0 %**
Hedge effective amount	3,787,000
Hedge ineffective amount	−0−

The effective part of the hedge gains or losses was limited by the lesser of the absolute values of the cumulative change in fair value of the hedging instrument and the hypothetical derivative. This condition did not impose this time any limit to the hedge effective amount.

Other Relevant Calculations

In order to generate the transaction accounting entries, let us summarise the CCS fair value calculations at each deporting date and at hedge maturity:

Summary of CCS Fair Values				
	31-Dec-X0	31-Dec-X1	31-Dec-X2	15-Jul-X3
CCS fair value (incl. accruals)	<1,426,000>	2,601,000	7,676,000	10,909,000
Accrual amount	212,000	374,000	554,000	−0−
CCS fair value (excl. accruals)	<1,638,000>	2,227,000	7,122,000	10,909,000
Change in CCS fair value (excl. accruals)	<1,638,000>	3,865,000	4,895,000	3,787,000

Additionally, ABC had to compute the change in the carrying amount of the bond due to changes in the spot rate. The re-translation gains and losses are shown in the following table:

Bond Re-translation Gains and Losses					
	Issue Date	31-Dec-X0	31-Dec-X1	31-Dec-X2	15-Jul-X3
USD bond amortised cost	100,000,000	100,000,000	100,000,000	100,000,000	100,000,000
USD/EUR spot	1.2500	1.2800	1.2200	1.1500	1.1000
Bond re-measured at spot	80,000,000	78,125,000	81,967,000	86,957,000	90,909,000
Translation gain <loss>	—	1,875,000	<3,842,000>	<4,990,000>	<3,952,000>

The adjustments to the cash flow equity reserve also needed to be calculated. Because the hedge was a cash flow hedge, the effective part of the hedge had to be recognised in equity, once excluding the re-translation gain. The next table shows the calculations of the amounts that were recognised in equity at each reporting date and at maturity.

	Cash Flow Hedge Reserve Amounts			
	31-Dec-X0	31-Dec-X1	31-Dec-X2	15-Jul-X3
Translation gain <loss>	1,875,000	<3,842,000>	<4,990,000>	<3,952,000>
Hedge effective part (reversed amount)	1,638,000	<3,865,000>	<4,895,000>	<3,787,000>
Difference	237,000	23,000	<95,000>	<165,000>
Amount recognised in the cash flow reserve (equity)	237,000	23,000	<95,000>	<165,000>
End of period carrying amount of the cash flow reserve	237,000	260,000	165,000	–0–

In order to clarify it, let us look at the 31 December 20X0 figures. In theory, the cash flow hedge indicated that EUR −1,638,000 had to be initially recognised in equity. However, −1,875,000 was reclassified from equity to P&L to offset the bond re-measurement gain of EUR 1,875,000. As a result EUR 237,000 was recognised in the cash flow equity reserve in that period.

Accounting Entries

The required journal entries were as follows:

1) Journal entries on 15 July 20X0:

   To record the bond issuance:

Cash (Asset)	€ 80,000,000	
USD Financial Debt (Liability)		€ 80,000,000

   No entries were required to record the CCS as its initial fair value was nil.

2) Journal entries on 31 December 20X0:

   The accrued interest of the bond was EUR 2,134,000 (= 5,900,000*169 days/365 days/1.28):

Interest Income/Expense (P&L)	€ 2,134,000	
Interest Payable (Liability)		€ 2,134,000

The re-measurement of the bond at spot was a gain of EUR 1,875,000:

USD Financial Debt (Liability)	€ 1,875,000	
Re-translation Gains/Losses (P&L)		€ 1,875,000

The fair value change, excluding accruals, of the CCS was a loss of EUR 1,638,000:

Re-translation Gains/Losses (P&L)	€ 1,875,000	
Fair Value of Derivative (Liability)		€ 1,638,000
Cash Flow Hedges (Equity)		€ 237,000

The accrued interest of the CCS was EUR 212,000:

Interest Receivable (Asset)	€ 212,000	
Interest Income/Expense (P&L)		€ 212,000

3) Journal entries on 15 July 20X1:

The bond coupon was USD 5,900,000. Assuming a USD/EUR spot rate of 1.2600, ABC had to pay EUR 4,683,000 (= 5,900,000/1.26):

Interest Payable (Liability)	€ 2,134,000	
Interest Income/Expense (P&L)	€ 2,549,000	
Cash		€ 4,683,000

Under the CCS, ABC received EUR 4,683,000 (identical amount to the bond coupon) and paid EUR 4,152,000. Therefore, the CCS settlement amount was EUR 531,000 (= 4,683,000−4,152,000):

Cash (Asset)	€ 531,000	
Interest Income/Expense (P&L)		€ 319,000
Interest Receivable (Asset)		€ 212,000

4) Journal entries on 31 December 20X1:

The bond interest to be paid on 15 July 20X2 was USD 6,050,000. The accrued interest of the bond was EUR 2,296,000 (= 6,050,000*169 days/365 days/1.22):

Interest Income/Expense (P&L)	€ 2,296,000	
Interest Payable (Liability)		€ 2,296,000

The re-measurement of the bond at spot was a loss of EUR 3,842,000:

Re-translation Gains/Losses (P&L)	€ 3,842,000	
USD Financial Debt (Liability)		€ 3,842,000

The fair value change, excluding accruals, of the CCS was a gain of EUR 3,865,000:

Fair Value of Derivative (Asset)	€ 3,865,000	
Cash Flow Hedges (Equity)		€ 23,000
Re-translation Gains/Losses (P&L)		€ 3,842,000

The accrued interest of the CCS was EUR 374,000:

Interest Receivable (Asset)	€ 374,000	
Interest Income/Expense (P&L)		€ 374,000

5) Journal entries on 15 July 20X2:

The bond coupon was USD 6,050,000. Assuming a USD/EUR spot rate of 1.1800, ABC had to pay EUR 5,127,000 (= 6,050,000/1.18):

Interest Payable (Liability)	€ 2,296,000	
Interest Income/Expense (P&L)	€ 2,831,000	
Cash		€ 5,127,000

Under the CCS, ABC received EUR 5,127,000 (identical amount to the bond coupon) and paid EUR 4,152,000. Therefore, the CCS settlement amount was EUR 975,000 (= 5,127,000−4,152,000):

Cash (Asset)	€ 975,000	
Interest Income/Expense (P&L)		€ 601,000
Interest Receivable (Asset)		€ 374,000

6) Journal entries on 31 December 20X2:

The bond interest to be paid on 15 July 20X3 was USD 6,150,000. The accrued interest of the bond was EUR 2,476,000 (= 6,150,000*169 days/365 days/1.15):

Interest Income/Expense (P&L)	€ 2,476,000	
Interest Payable (Liability)		€ 2,476,000

The re-measurement of the bond at spot was a loss of EUR 4,990,000:

Re-translation Gains/Losses (P&L)	€ 4,990,000	
USD Financial Debt (Liability)		€ 4,990,000

The fair value change, excluding accruals, of the CCS was a gain of EUR 4,895,000:

Fair Value of Derivative (Asset)	€ 4,895,000	
Cash Flow Hedges (Equity)	€ 95,000	
Re-translation Gains/Losses (P&L)		€ 4,990,000

The accrued interest of the CCS was EUR 554,000:

Interest Receivable (Asset)	€ 554,000	
Interest Income/Expense (P&L)		€ 554,000

7) Journal entries on 15 July 20X3:

The bond coupon was USD 6,150,000. Assuming a USD/EUR spot rate of 1.1000, ABC had to pay EUR 5,591,000 (= 6,150,000/1.10):

Interest Payable (Liability)	€ 2,476,000	
Interest Income/Expense (P&L)	€ 3,115,000	
Cash		€ 5,591,000

Under the CCS, ABC received EUR 5,591,000 (identical amount to the bond coupon) and paid EUR 4,152,000. Therefore, the CCS settlement amount was EUR 1,439,000 (= 5,591,000−4,152,000):

Cash (Asset)	€ 1,439,000	
Interest Income/Expense (P&L)		€ 885,000
Interest Receivable (Asset)		€ 554,000

The re-measurement of the bond at spot was a loss of EUR 3,952,000:

Re-translation Gains/Losses (P&L)	€ 3,952,000	
USD Financial Debt (Liability)		€ 3,952,000

The fair value change (this time there are no more accruals) of the CCS was a gain of EUR 3,787,000:

Fair Value of Derivative (Asset)	€ 3,787,000	
Cash Flow Hedges (Equity)	€ 165,000	
Re-translation Gains/Losses (P&L)		€ 3,952,000

Under the CCS, ABC received USD 100 million (identical to the bond redemption amount) and paid EUR 80,000,000 million. Therefore, the value of this exchange was EUR 10,909,000 ($= 100$ million/$1.10 - 80,000,000$):

Cash (Asset)	€ 10,909,000	
Fair Value of Derivative (Asset)		€ 10,909,000

The redemption amount of the bond was EUR 90,909,000 ($=$ USD 100 million/1.10):

USD Financial Debt (Liability)	€ 90,909,000	
Cash (Asset)		€ 90,909,000

Concluding Remarks

Most of the potential benefit of applying cash flow hedging was eclipsed by the re-translation of the USD liability. We are not advising the reader to forget about applying hedge accounting. In our case, the maturity of the liability was rather short (only three years), and therefore the impact of interest rate moves was much lower than the impact of the USD/EUR rate movements. It is not unusual for corporates to issue long-term debt (e.g., 10 years) and then the impact of interest rate movements can be very significant, making hedge accounting valuable.

Summary of the Journal Entries

	Assets			Liabilities		Equity	
	Cash	Interest Receivable	Derivative Fair Value	Financial Debt	Interest Payable	Cash flow Hedge	Profit and Loss
15 July 20X0							
Bond issuance	80,000,000			80,000,000			
31 December 20X0							
Bond accrued coupon					2,134,000		<2,134,000>
Bond re-measurement				<1,875,000>			1,875,000
CCS accrual		212,000					212,000
Change in fair value of CCS			<1,638,000>			237,000	<1,875,000>
15 July 20X1							
Bond coupon payment	<4,683,000>				<2,134,000>		<2,549,000>
CCS interest settlement	531,000	<212,000>					319,000
31 December 20X1							
Bond accrued coupon					2,296,000		<2,296,000>
Bond re-measurement				3,842,000			<3,842,000>
CCS accrual		374,000					374,000
Change in fair value of CCS			3,865,000			23,000	3,842,000
15 July 20X2							
Bond coupon payment	<5,127,000>				<2,296,000>		<2,831,000>
CCS interest settlement	975,000	<374,000>					601,000
31 December 20X2							
Bond accrued coupon					2,476,000		<2,476,000>
Bond re-measurement				4,990,000			<4,990,000>
CCS accrual		554,000					554,000
Change in fair value of CCS			4,895,000			<95,000>	4,990,000
15 July 20X3							
Bond coupon payment	<5,591,000>				<2,476,000>		<3,115,000>
CCS interest settlement	1,439,000	<554,000>					885,000
Bond re-measurement				3,952,000			<3,952,000>
Change in fair value of CCS			3,787,000			<165,000>	3,952,000
Bond redemption	<90,909,000>			<90,909,000>			
CCS final exchange	10,909,000		<10,909,000>				
Totals	<12,456,000>	–0–	–0–	–0–	–0–	–0–	<12,456,000>

7
Hedging Equity Risk

This chapter focuses on the issues affecting equity recognition and hedging. Many of the concepts outlined herein are within the scope of IAS 32 *Financial Instruments: Disclosure and Presentation*. Besides the hedging of equity risk of investments in other companies, this chapter also covers the accounting treatment of preference shares and convertibles.

7.1 RECOGNITION OF EQUITY INVESTMENTS IN OTHER COMPANIES

An investment in equity securities of another company is recognised according to the degree of control over the investee (see Figure 7.1) as follows:

1) The group has control over the investee. Control is regarded as the power to govern the operating and financial policies of the investee so as to obtain benefits from its activities. Usually, control is presumed if the investor holds more than 50 % of the voting rights of the investee. The existence and effect of potential voting rights are also considered when assessing whether the group controls the investee. Companies that are controlled by the group are usually called subsidiaries. Subsidiaries are fully consolidated.
2) The group has interests in a joint venture. A joint venture is a contractual arrangement whereby the group and other parties undertake an economic activity that is subject to joint control, that is when the strategic operating and financial policies require the unanimous consent of the parties sharing control. Usually the joint venture is accounted for using the proportionate consolidation method. Under this method, the financial statements of the group include its share of the financial statements of the joint venture it controls.
3) The group has significant influence in an investee and it is neither a subsidiary nor a joint venture. In this case, the investee is called an associate. Significant influence is the power to participate in the operating and financial policies of the investee, but is not control or joint control over those decisions. Usually significant influence is presumed when the group holds at least 20 %, but no more than 50 %, of the actual and potential voting rights of the investee. An associate is accounted for in the consolidated financial statements using the equity method. Under the equity method the investment is originally accounted for at cost. The investment carrying amount increases (decreases) by the proportion of profits (losses) of the associate and decreases by the dividends received from the associate.
4) The group does not exercise significant influence or control over the investee. Usually this is the case when the group holds less than 20 % of the actual and potential voting rights of the investee. The investment is then classified as either held at fair value through profit and loss or available-for-sale.
   (a) The equity investment is classified at fair value through profit and loss if it is acquired for the purpose of selling it in the near term. The investment is measured at fair value. Gains and losses arising from changes in fair value are included in P&L.

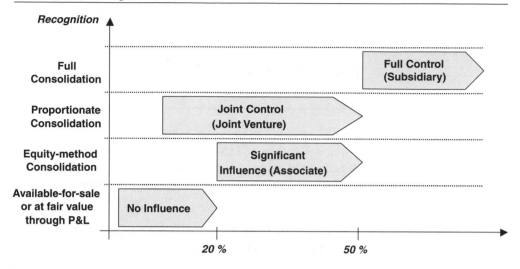

Figure 7.1   Recognition of Equity Investments.

(b) The equity investment is classified as available-for-sale (AFS) if it has not been classified in any of the previous categories. Gains and losses arising from changes in fair value of an AFS equity investment are recognised directly in equity until the security is disposed of or is determined to be impaired, at which time those cumulative gains or losses previously recognised in equity are included in P&L for the period. An investment in an equity instrument which do not have a quoted market price and whose value cannot reliably measured is held at cost.

7.1.1   Impairment of Equity Investments

An entity is required to assess investments in equity instruments for impairment at least at every balance sheet date. A significant and prolonged decline in the fair value of an equity instrument is symptom of impairment. IAS 39 does not give quantitative guidance on "significant and prolonged". Usually, no impairment loss is recognised if the decrease in fair value of the equity investment is attributable to a general decrease in market prices.

When there is objective evidence that the equity instrument is impaired, a loss is recorded in P&L at that date. The loss is measured as the difference between the carrying amount and the estimated fair value of the investment. If the equity investment is classified as available-for-sale, the cumulative loss that has been recognised in equity is removed from equity and recognised in P&L. Impairment losses recognised in P&L for equity investments classified as available-for-sale cannot be reversed through P&L.

7.2   DEBT VERSUS EQUITY CLASSIFICATION OF OWN INSTRUMENTS

IAS 32 establishes the principles for distinguishing between liabilities and equity. The classification of financial instruments issued by the entity as debt or equity can be complex. The economic substance of a financial instrument, rather than its legal form, governs its classification. Liabilities within the scope of IAS 39 are those that arise from contractual present obligations. Conversely, IAS 32 identifies a critical feature of an equity instrument as including no present contractual obligation to pay cash or to transfer another financial asset.

7.2.1 Recognition As a Liability

A fundamental characteristic of a financial liability is a contractual present obligation to transfer assets to the holder of the instrument, over which the issuer has no discretion. A financial instrument is a liability if there is a contractual obligation:

- To deliver cash or another financial asset to another entity; or
- To exchange financial assets or financial liabilities with another entity under conditions that are potentially unfavourable to the entity.

7.2.2 Recognition As Equity

An equity instrument represents a residual interest in the net assets of the issuer. More precisely, a financial instrument is considered an equity instrument if conditions (i) or (ii) are met:

(i) There is no contractual obligation:
  - To deliver cash or another financial asset to another entity; or
  - To exchange financial assets or liabilities under conditions that are potentially unfavourable to the issuer.
(ii) The instrument will or may be settled in the issuer's own equity shares:
  - A non-derivative that includes no contractual obligation for the issuer to deliver a variable number of its own equity instruments; or
  - A derivative that will be settled by the issuer exchanging a fixed amount of cash or another financial asset for a fixed number of its own equity instruments.

Not all instruments are classified as either only debt or only equity. The following table summarises the classification of the most common hybrid and equity instruments:

Instrument	Classification
Ordinary shares	Equity
Redeemable preference shares with non-discretionary dividends	Liability
Redeemable preference shares with discretionary dividends	Liability for principal, and equity for dividends
Non-redeemable preference shares with discretionary dividends	Equity
Convertible bond which converts into a fixed number of shares	Liability for bond and equity for conversion option
Convertible bond which converts into a variable number of shares to the value of the liability	Liability

7.3 HYBRID SECURITIES – PREFERENCE SHARES

The financial capital markets have witnessed in the last decades the strong development of different types of securities. Because some of these securities have simultaneously debt and equity elements, they are called "hybrid securities". In general, there are two types of hybrid securities: preference shares and convertible debt. The aim of preference shares is to optimise their equity treatment by the rating agencies, their dividends tax deductibility, their investor demand and their IFRS accounting impact. It is critical to understand all the terms and conditions of the preference shares in order to ensure its appropriate classification as debt or equity.

7.3.1 Contractual Discretion

An instrument will be considered as equity if the entity has a contractual "discretion" over whether to make any cash payments. A strong economic incentive to make payments does not amount to a contractual obligation and is therefore not sufficient for liability classification. Anything outside the contractual terms is not considered when classifying an instrument under IAS 32. Therefore, contractual discretion is not affected by the following:

- A history of making distributions or an intention or ability to make distributions in the future.
- The amount of the issuer's reserves.
- The entity's expectation of a profit or loss for the period.
- The ability or inability of the issuer to influence the amount of its profit or loss for the period, any economic compulsion to make distribution or the ranking of the instrument on the liquidation of the entity.
- A possible negative impact on the price of ordinary shares of the issuer if dividends are not paid to ordinary shares (because of restrictions on paying dividends on the ordinary shares if dividends are not paid on the preference shares).

7.3.2 Economic Compulsion

Economic compulsion takes place when the entity has an economic motivation, but is not obliged, to make a specific decision. For example, the issuer of a callable bond may have a strong motivation to call the bond if after the call date the bond pays a much higher than market interest rate.

In general, economic compulsion does not play a role in the classification decision under IAS 32. However, once a financial obligation has been established through the terms and conditions, economic compulsion may be relevant in special circumstances. For example, a sold call option on the entity's own shares can have a classification as equity or liability depending on its form of settlement. The option will be considered as equity if the issuer of the shares can choose between physical delivery and cash settlement. The option will be considered as a liability if the option can only be settled in cash. Even though the issuer can choose between physical delivery and cash settlement, if there is a strong economic compulsion to settle the options in cash, the option should be classified as a liability.

Another example in which economic compulsion may play a role in the classification decision was provided in an example in an earlier version of IAS 32. The example was an undated preference shares issue with a contractually accelerating dividend, whereby in the foreseeable future the dividend yield was scheduled to be so large that the issuer would be economically compelled to redeem the instrument. In these circumstances, classification as a financial liability was appropriate because the issuer had little, if any, discretion to avoid redeeming the instrument.

7.3.3 Degree of Subordination

IAS 32 does not take into account the level of seniority of payment of the instrument when classifying it as equity or liability. For example, an instrument can be *pari passu* with all the senior debt and be classified as equity. Similarly, an instrument can be *pari passu* with all other preference shares and be classified as liability. The seniority of payment is only relevant on liquidation of the entity and does not play a role in indicating whether the issuer has or not discretion to make payments under the instrument.

7.3.4 Legal Form

In classifying an instrument as a liability or equity attention should be paid to the underlying substance and economic reality of the contractual obligation and not merely its legal form. For example, just because a financial instrument has the legal title of "shares" does not mean that the instrument should be classified as equity.

In general, the rule of thumb regarding preference shares classification as a liability or as equity is the following:

• Preference shares which are redeemable mandatorily on a specific date or at the option of the holder: the principal is classified as liability.
• Preference shares which carry non-discretionary dividend obligations: the dividends are classified as liabilities and are taken to P&L as finance expense.
• Non-redeemable preference shares are classified based on the other rights attached to them. Non-redeemable preference shares with discretionary dividends, whether cumulative or non-cumulative, are classified as equity. Non-redeemable preference shares with non-discretionary dividends are classified as a liability.

7.4 HYBRID SECURITIES – CONVERTIBLE BONDS

7.4.1 Convertible Bonds Denominated in the Entity's Functional Currency

If a convertible bond allows the holder to convert the bond into a fixed number of the entity's equity instruments in exchange for a fixed amount of cash, the written option is an equity instrument.

Convertible bonds are split into a liability component and an equity component. On issue date, the fair value of the liability component is determined using a market interest rate for an equivalent non-convertible bond. This amount is recorded as a liability on an amortised cost basis until extinguished on conversion or redemption of the bonds. The remainder of the proceeds of the issue is allocated to the equity component (see Figure 7.2). No gain or loss arises from recognising initially the components of the instrument separately. The equity part is recognised in shareholders' equity, net of income tax effects.

While, in general, convertible bonds are treated under IFRS as a hybrid instrument, containing both a debt and an equity component, many convertible bonds are far more complicated. For instance, many convertible bonds contain a clause in the agreement allowing the issuer to net settle the change in value of its equity, in the event that a holder exercises his option to

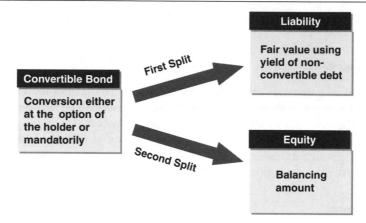

Figure 7.2   Split of Convertible Debt.

convert the bond. This clause would mean that the issuer is not permitted to treat the conversion option as part of its equity, but instead is required to fair value the option and take any gains or losses to the income statement.

On conversion at maturity, the entity derecognises the liability component and recognises it as equity. The original equity component remains as equity (although it may be transferred from one line item within equity to another).

7.4.2   Convertible Bonds Denominated in Foreign Currency

For example, an entity whose functional currency is the Euro issues a US dollar denominated convertible bond that can be converted into a fixed number of the entity's shares for a fixed amount of US dollars.

IAS 32 states that a contract that will be settled by the entity delivering a fixed number of its own equity instruments in exchange for a variable amount of cash is a financial liability. Consequently, the written option should be classified as a liability.

This treatment would result in reporting gains and losses arising from the entity's own equity through P&L, along with the currency gains and losses. Therefore, IAS 39 permits cash flow hedges of such exposures.

7.5   DERIVATIVES ON OWN EQUITY INSTRUMENTS

The term "own equity instruments" usually refers to equity instruments issued by the parent company. However, the term also refers to equity instruments issued by its fully-consolidated subsidiaries, as these instruments are in substance equivalent to equity instruments of the parent company. A derivative on own equity instrument may be accounted for as a derivative instrument or an equity instrument, depending on the type of derivative and method of settlement.

- Derivatives on own equity that result in the delivery of a fixed amount of cash or other financial assets for a fixed number of the entity's own equity instruments are classified as equity instruments. All other derivatives on the entity's own equity are treated as derivatives and accounted for as such under IAS 39.

- Derivatives on own equity which gives the counterparty a choice over their settlement (cash settlement or physical delivery) are treated as a derivative and accounted for as such under IAS 39.

The following table illustrates whether a derivative on own shares is a financial liability or an equity instrument.

	Physical delivery (1)	Physical delivery or cash settlement (at entity option)	Physical delivery or cash settlement (at counterparty option)	Cash settlement
Forward contract to buy own shares	Equity plus recognition of a financial liability	Equity plus recognition of a financial liability	Derivative	Derivative
Forward contract to sell own shares	Equity	Equity	Derivative	Derivative
Purchased call on own shares	Equity	Equity	Derivative	Derivative
Written call on own shares	Equity	Equity	Derivative	Derivative
Purchased put on own shares	Equity	Equity	Derivative	Derivative
Written put on own shares	Equity plus recognition of a financial liability	Equity plus recognition of a financial liability	Derivative	Derivative

Notes:
(1) Assuming the settlement is made by exchanging a fixed amount of cash for a fixed number of the entity's own shares.

CASE 7.1

Accounting for a Stock Lending Transaction

This case covers the accounting of securities lending transactions. Sometimes, entities have large investments in equity instruments of other companies. If an entity wants to earn additional income, or to lower its cost of funding, it might lend some equity instruments to a financial institution. The financial institution may need to borrow those instruments to cover a short position or to meet delivery obligations. Securities lending is a transaction where a lender (the entity) transfers legal title to securities to a borrower (the financial institution) and the borrower is obliged to return the same type of securities to the lender at the end of the lending period.

Securities lending transactions are usually collateralised by receiving cash or low-risk securities. In the event of the financial institution default, the securities lending agreement provides the entity with the right to liquidate the collateral held.

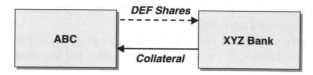

Figure 7.3   Lending Agreement – Initial Flows.

Let us assume that, on 1 April 20X0, ABC Corporation had 40 million shares of DEF Corporation and that it lent those shares to XYZ Bank. The shares were trading at EUR 10.00 on that date. ABC received EUR 400 million cash from XYZ Bank as collateral at the beginning of the transaction. The lending agreement matured on 1 August 20X0 (usually, there is no maturity to the agreement, and either the lender or the borrower can terminate the agreement at any time). Figure 7.3 highlights the initial components of the transaction.

ABC derived income by investment of the cash collateral: ABC invested the EUR 400 million collateral in a deposit yielding 5 %. Normally, as it was ABC's case, this income was paid over to the borrower, less a margin to represent a stock lending fee for providing securities to the financial institution. In our case, this interest was to be received (and passed to the borrower) at maturity of the lending agreement. The margin was 50 basis points, or 0.50 %. Figure 7.4 shows these interest cash-flows.

Let us also assume, that the DEF shares paid a EUR 0.50 dividend per share on 15 July 20X0. Under the lending agreement, XYZ Bank was required to pass the dividend to ABC on the dividend payment date, as shown in Figure 7.5.

At maturity of the transaction, the initial flows were reversed as shown in Figure 7.6: XYZ Bank returned the shares to ABC in exchange for the EUR 400 million collateral.

Accounting Entries

Let us assume that ABC closed its books quarterly. The required journal entries were as follows:

1) To record the DEF shares lending and the collateral received on 1 April 20X0:

The DEF shares were classified as available-for-sale. The 40 million DEF shares were fair valued by ABC on the previous closing date (31 March 20X0) at EUR 9.00 per share. When

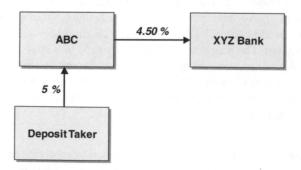

Figure 7.4   Lending Agreement – Interest Flows.

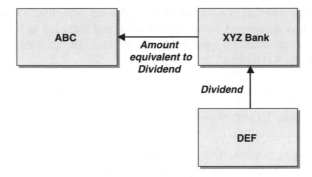

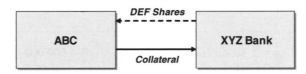

Figure 7.5   Lending Agreement – Dividend Flows.

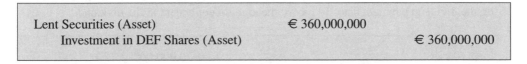

Figure 7.6   Lending Agreement – Final Flows.

an entity lends its securities, it reports these securities as pledged assets in its balance sheet. To record the shares lent:

Lent Securities (Asset)	€ 360,000,000	
Investment in DEF Shares (Asset)		€ 360,000,000

The cash collateral that ABC received on the securities lending transaction was reported as an asset in the balance sheet. Because the collateral must be returned in the future, ABC also recognised a liability.

Cash (Asset)	€ 400,000,000	
Collateral on Securities Lent (Liability)		€ 400,000,000

2) To record the fair valuation and the accrued interest on 30 June 20X0:

The DEF shares were trading at EUR 11.00 on 30 June 20X0. ABC classified the investment in DEF shares as available-for-sale. On the previous balance sheet date (30 March 20X0), the shares were fair valued at EUR 9.00 per share. The change in fair value of the shares was then EUR 80 million ($= 40$ million$^*(11-9)$)To record the change in fair value of the 40 million DEF shares:

Lent Securities (Asset)	€ 80,000,000	
Available-for-sale Gains/Losses (Equity)		€ 80,000,000

The collateral was invested in a deposit yielding 5 % on an Actual/360 basis. The interest to be received was recognised on an accrual basis and recorded as interest income. The number of days elapsed since 1 April 20X0 was 90 days. The accrued interest amount was EUR 5,000,000 (= 400 million*5 %*90/360).

Interest Receivable (Asset)	€ 5,000,000	
Interest Income (Income Statement)		€ 5,000,000

Under the lending agreement, ABC was obliged to pass the interest received less a margin of 50 basis points. The interest to be paid to the financial institution was recognised on an accrual basis and recorded as interest expense. The number of days elapsed since 1 April 20X0 was 90 days. The accrued interest amount was EUR 4,500,000 (= 400 million*(5 %- 0.50 %)*90/360).

Interest Expense (Income Statement)	€ 4,500,000	
Interest Payable (Liability)		€ 4,500,000

3) To record the amount equivalent to the dividend received on 15 July 20X0:

The DEF 40 million shares paid a EUR 20 million dividend (EUR 0.50 per share) on 15 July 20X0. Under the lending agreement, XYZ Bank was required to pass the dividend to ABC on the dividend payment date. To record the amount equivalent to the dividend:

Cash (Asset)	€ 20,000,000	
Interest Income (Income Statement)		€ 20,000,000

4) To record the end of the lending agreement on 1 August 20X0:

The number of days elapsed since 30 June 20X0 was 32 days. Thus, the deposit accrued interest amount was EUR 1,778,000 (= 400 million*5 %*32/360). To record the interest accrued:

Interest Receivable (Asset)	€ 1,778,000	
Interest Income (Income Statement)		€ 1,778,000

On 1 August 20X0, the deposit paid a 5% interest on 122 days (the days elapsed since 1 April 20X0). The interest amount was EUR 6,778,000 (= 400 million*5 %*122/360). To record the interest received:

Cash (Asset)	€ 6,778,000	
Interest Receivable (Asset)		€ 6,778,000

The number of days elapsed since 30 June 20X0 was 32 days. Thus, the accrued amount of the interest to be paid by ABC to the shares borrower was EUR 1,600,000 (= 400 million*(5 %–0.50 %)*32/360). To record the accrued interest:

Interest Expense (Income Statement)	€ 1,600,000	
Interest Payable (Liability)		€ 1,600,000

On 1 August 20X0, ABC had to pay a 4.50 % interest to the shares borrower on 122 days (the days elapsed since 1 April 20X0). The interest amount was EUR 6,100,000 (= 400 million*(5 %-0.50 %)*122/360). To record the interest payment:

Interest Payable (Liability)	€ 6,100,000	
Cash (Asset)		€ 6,100,000

XYZ bank returned to ABC the borrowed 40 million DEF shares. To record the return of the lent shares:

Investment in DEF Shares (Asset)	€ 440,000,000	
Lent Securities (Asset)		€ 440,000,000

ABC returned the EUR 400 million cash collateral. To record the return of the collateral:

Collateral on Securities Lent (Liability)	€ 400,000,000	
Cash (Asset)		€ 400,000,000

Final Remarks

Looking at the income statement during the life of the lending agreement, it can be noted that the rationale behind the lending of DEF shares was to enhance the yield on the investment. ABC obtained a 50 basis points for lending DEF shares (or EUR 678,000). Figure 7.7 compares the pre-tax income statements of ABC without and with the lending agreement in place.

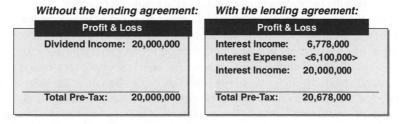

Figure 7.7 Comparison of Income Statements.

The transaction, however, had two major disadvantages. Firstly, ABC lost the voting rights on the lent DEF shares during the life of the transaction. Secondly, ABC received an interest amount equivalent to the gross dividend of DEF shares, but could not claim any tax deductions related to the dividend.

Finally, two particular comments are worth noting. Firstly, in our case the amount of collateral was based on the market value of the DEF shares at the beginning of the lending agreement and this amount remained unchanged during the life of the agreement. Frequently, the collateral amount changes in order to eliminate the lender's (ABC) credit exposure to the borrower (XYZ Bank). The lender monitors the market value of the shares lent on a daily basis and requests additional collateral or returns surplus collateral in accordance with the value of the shares. The corresponding accounting entries are then produced on a daily basis to record the additional collateral received or returned. Secondly, usually lending agreements do not have a fixed maturity. At any time, either the lender or the borrower can terminate the agreement by providing notice to the other party.

CASE 7.2

Measurement of a Mandatory Convertible Bond

This case covers the accounting of a mandatory convertible. A mandatory convertible bond is an instrument that embodies an unconditional obligation requiring the issuer to redeem the bond by transferring a specified number of shares of the issuer (or a third party) at a specified date (or dates).

Let us assume that, on 1 January 20X0, ABC issued a mandatory convertible bond on its own shares with the following terms:

Mandatory Convertible Bond Terms	
Issue date	1 January 20X0
Issuer	ABC Corporation
Issue proceeds	EUR 99.5 million
Principal	EUR 100 million
Maturity	3 years
Interest	5 %, annually payable each 31 December
Conversion	Convertible into new 10 million shares of ABC, to be issued at maturity

Let us also assume that, at bond maturity, ABC issued 10 million ordinary shares with a par value of EUR 1.00 each. The issue value was EUR 10.00 per share. Therefore, the share premium was EUR 9.00 per share.

There are two potential accounting treatments of mandatory convertibles depending upon whether the holders of the bond have the right, or not, to receive the redemption in cash.

Mandatory convertibles, in which the issuer has the right or the obligation to deliver shares, are hybrid instruments that have both debt and equity characteristics. Under IFRS, the components of a mandatory convertible are bifurcated at the time of issuance into a debt component and an equity component. The initial carrying amount of the debt component is calculated as the present value of the bond cash-flows assuming that the bond does not have the equity conversion feature. The cash-flows are discounted using the prevailing yield of similar debt without the conversion feature. The equity component represents the requirement to convert the mandatory convertible into ABC shares. It is the difference

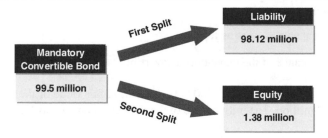

Figure 7.8   Split of Mandatory Convertible.

between the issue proceeds and the debt component. There is no subsequent fair valuation for either component. This is the situation in our case.

Mandatory convertibles, in which the holder has the right or the obligation to receive cash, are compound instruments. At the time of issuance the instrument is split into a debt component (the host contract) and a derivative component. The initial carrying amount of the debt component is calculated as the present value of the bond cash-flows assuming that the bond does not have the equity conversion feature. The cash-flows are discounted using the prevailing yield of similar debt without the conversion feature. The derivative component represents the potential requirement by the holder to receive the principal amount plus (minus) the appreciation (depreciation) of the shares. The derivative component is calculated as the difference between the issue proceeds and the debt component. There is subsequent fair valuation of the derivative component.

Let us assume that when the bond was issued, the prevailing yield of similar debt without the conversion feature was 5.70 %. The debt component was EUR 98.12 million. The calculation of the carrying amount of the debt component as the present value of the bond cash-flows, assuming that the bond does not have the equity conversion feature, was performed as follows:

$$98.12 = \frac{5}{1 + 5.7\,\%} + \frac{5}{(1 + 5.7\,\%)^2} + \frac{105}{(1 + 5.7\,\%)^3}$$

As the proceeds of the mandatory convertible issue were EUR 99.5 million, the equity component was EUR 1.38 million (= 99.5 million − 98.12 million), as shown in Figure 7.8. Therefore, the bifurcation resulted in a positive value being ascribed to the equity component and a lower value (discount) to the debt component. This discount was amortised as an adjustment (increase) to interest expense over the term of the mandatory convertible.

The amortised cost and interest expense of the liability at each accounting date was then computed then as follows:

Year	Amortised Cost beginning Year (a)	Interest Expense (b) = (a)*5.7%	Cash Payment (c)	Amortised Cost End of Year (d) = (a) + (b) − (c)
1	98,120,000	5,593,000	5,000,000	98,713,000
2	98,713,000	5,627,000	5,000,000	99,340,000
3	99,340,000	5,660,000 (*1*)	5,000,000	100,000,000

Note *(1)*
The calculation is in reality 5,662,000, but the figure was adjusted to achieve the amortised cost 100 million final value.

Accounting Entries

The required journal entries were as follows:

1) To record the issuance of the mandatory convertible on 1 January 20X0:

The issue proceeds were EUR 99,500,000. The initial fair value of the equity component was EUR 1.38 million. The initial value of the debt component was EUR 98.12 million.

Cash (Asset)	€ 99,500,000	
Mandatory Convertible (Liability)		€ 98,120,000
Share Premium (Equity)		€ 1,380,000

2) To record the interest expense and payment on 31 December 20X0:

Interest Expense (Income Statement)	€ 5,593,000	
Mandatory Convertible (Liability)		€ 593,000
Cash (Asset)		€ 5,000,000

3) To record the interest expense and payment on 31 December 20X1:

Interest Expense (Income Statement)	€ 5,627,000	
Mandatory Convertible (Liability)		€ 627,000
Cash (Asset)		€ 5,000,000

4) Entries on 31 December 20X2:

To record the interest expense and payment:

Interest Expense (Income Statement)	€ 5,660,000	
Mandatory Convertible (Liability)		€ 660,000
Cash (Asset)		€ 5,000,000

To record conversion of the mandatory convertible and the issuance of 10 million new shares with a par value of EUR 1.00 each:

Mandatory Convertible (Liability)	€ 100,000,000	
Share Capital (Equity)		€ 10,000,000
Share Premium (Equity)		€ 90,000,000

CASE 7.3

Measurement of a Convertible Bond

This case covers the accounting of convertibles. A convertible bond is an instrument which can be converted into shares of the bond issuer at the holder option. At specific dates (usually at any time during the life of the instrument), the holder can exercise its conversion right.

Let us assume that, on 1 January 20X0, ABC issued a convertible bond on its own shares with the following terms:

Mandatory Convertible Bond Terms	
Issue date	1 January 20X0
Issuer	ABC Corporation
Issue proceeds	EUR 99.5 million
Principal	EUR 100 million
Maturity	3 years (31 December 20X2)
Interest	2 %, annually payable each 31 December
Conversion	At the holder option at maturity. Convertible into new 10 million shares of ABC, to be issued at maturity
Conversion rate	EUR 10 per share
Current price of ABC shares	EUR 7 per share

Let us also assume that, when the bond was issued, the prevailing yield for similar debt without the conversion option was 5 %. Assume further that at bond maturity, ABC shares were trading at EUR 13, above the EUR 10 conversion rate. As a consequence, the bond holders exercised their conversion right and ABC issued 10 million ordinary shares with a par value of EUR 1.00 each. The share issue value was EUR 10.00 per share. Therefore, the share premium was EUR 9.00 per share.

There are two potential accounting treatments of convertibles, depending upon whether the holders of the bond have the right, or not, to receive the redemption in cash.

Convertibles that, when exercised by the holder, the issuer has the right or the obligation to deliver shares, are hybrid instruments that have both debt and equity characteristics. Under IFRS, the components of a convertible are bifurcated at the time of issuance into a debt component and an equity component. The initial carrying amount of the debt component is calculated as the present value of the bond cash-flows assuming that the bond does not have the equity conversion feature. The cash-flows are discounted using the prevailing yield of similar debt without the conversion feature. The equity component represents the option to convert the bond into ABC shares. It is calculated as the difference between the issue proceeds and the debt component. There is no subsequent fair valuation for either component. This is the situation in our case.

Convertibles that, when exercised, the holder has the right or the obligation to receive cash, are compound instruments. At the time of issuance the instrument is split into a debt component (the host contract) and a derivative component. The initial carrying amount of the debt component is calculated as the present value of the bond cash-flows assuming that the bond does not have the equity conversion feature. The cash-flows are discounted using the prevailing yield of similar debt without the conversion feature. The derivative component represents the option by the holder to receive the principal amount plus the appreciation of the shares above the conversion rate. The derivative component is calculated as the difference between the issue proceeds and the debt component. There is subsequent fair valuation of the derivative component.

Let us assume that when the bond was issued, the prevailing yield of similar debt without the conversion feature was 5 %. The debt component was EUR 91.83 million. The calculation of the carrying amount of the debt component as the present value of the bond cash-flows, assuming that the bond does not have the equity conversion feature, was performed as follows:

$$91.83 = \frac{2}{1+5\%} + \frac{2}{(1+5\%)^2} + \frac{102}{(1+5\%)^2}$$

As the proceeds of the mandatory convertible issue were EUR 99.5 million, the equity component was EUR 7.67 million (= 99.5 million −91.83 million), as shown in Figure 7.9. Therefore, the bifurcation resulted in a positive value being ascribed to the equity component and a lower value (discount) to the debt component. This discount was amortised as an adjustment (increase) to interest expense over the term of the mandatory convertible.

The amortised cost and interest expense of the liability at each accounting date was computed then as follows:

Year	Amortised Cost beginning Year (a)	Interest Expense (b) = (a)*5%	Cash Payment (c)	Amortised Cost End of Year (d) = (a) + (b) − (c)
1	91,830,000	4,592,000	2,000,000	94,422,000
2	94,422,000	4,721,000	2,000,000	97,143,000
3	97,143,000	4,857,000	2,000,000	100,000,000

Accounting Entries

The required journal entries were as follows:

1) To record the issuance of the convertible on 1 January 20X0:

The issue proceeds were EUR 99,500,000. The initial value of the debt component was EUR 91.83 million. The initial fair value of the equity component was EUR 7.67 million.

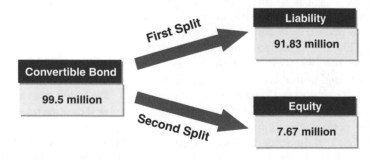

Figure 7.9   Split of Convertible Bond.

Cash (Asset)	€ 99,500,000	
Convertible Bond (Liability)		€ 91,830,000
Share Premium (Equity)		€ 7,670,000

2) To record the interest expense and payment on 31 December 20X0:

Interest Expense (Income Statement)	€ 4,592,000	
Convertible Bond (Liability)		€ 2,592,000
Cash (Asset)		€ 2,000,000

3) To record the interest expense and payment on 31 December 20X1:

Interest Expense (Income Statement)	€ 4,721,000	
Convertible Bond (Liability)		€ 2,721,000
Cash (Asset)		€ 2,000,000

4) Entries on 31 December 20X2:

To record the interest expense and payment:

Interest Expense (Income Statement)	€ 4,857,000	
Convertible Bond (Liability)		€ 2,857,000
Cash (Asset)		€ 2,000,000

As ABC shares were trading above the conversion rate, the bond holders exercised their conversion right. To record conversion of the convertible and the issuance of 10 million new shares with a par value of EUR 1.00 each:

Convertible Bond (Liability)	€ 100,000,000	
Share Capital (Equity)		€ 10,000,000
Share Premium (Equity)		€ 90,000,000

CASE 7.4

Hedging Step-up Perpetual Callable Preference Shares

The objective of this case is to illustrate the process of deciding if an instrument, a set-up callable perpetual preference share, is classified as equity or as a liability. It also highlights the challenge of hedging equity instruments.

A perpetual set-up instrument is an irredeemable callable financial instrument with fixed or floating dividend payments. The instrument includes a "step-up" dividend clause that would increase the dividend at a pre-determined date in the future unless the instrument had previously been called by the issuer. Let us assume that on 1 January 20X0, ABC issued the following step-up perpetual callable preference shares:

Step-up Callable Preference Shares - Terms	
Issue date	1 January 20X0
Issuer	ABC Corporation
Principal	EUR 200 million
Maturity	Perpetual, subject to Call Right
Call Right	The issuer has the right, but not the obligation to redeem the shares on 1-January-20X3
Dividend (annually)	Euribor 12M + 100 bps until and including 31-Dec-X2 Euribor 12M + 500 bps, thereafter
Dividend payment	Payment of dividend is mandatory only if dividends are paid on ABC's ordinary shares
Seniority	On liquidation of the issuer, principal is paid out ahead of ordinary shares, but subordinated to other senior and subordinated claims

First of all, let us analyse whether the elements of the instrument were classified as debt or equity. In our preference shares, ABC had potentially two types of payments to the holder of the preference shares: the principal and the dividends.

- Regarding the principal, ABC had no contractual obligation to redeem the instrument. The fact that ABC was expected to call the instrument in 20X3 so as to avoid the above market payments (this is commonly referred to as "economic compulsion") was not considered relevant in the classification. Therefore, the principal was not considered a liability as ABC had no contractual obligation to deliver cash, or another financial asset, to the holder under conditions that were potentially unfavourable to the entity. Thus, the principal was classified as equity.
- Regarding the dividends, they were payable only if dividends were paid on ordinary shares (which themselves were payable at the discretion of ABC). As a consequence, ABC had no contractual obligation to ever pay a dividend. Thus, the dividends were classified as equity.

IAS 32 considers that the seniority of payment of an obligation, which arises only on liquidation of the entity, does not play a part in the classification of the financial instrument. So in our case, the seniority of the preference shares between subordinated debt and ordinary shares did not affect the liability/equity classification. Similarly, the legal definition of the instrument as "shares" had no impact in the classification. Substance rather than legal form rules the liability/equity classification.

The instrument should be classified as equity under IAS 32, as the entity could choose in perpetuity not to redeem the instrument and not to pay distributions on it. Whilst a payment of a dividend to the ordinary shares obliges the company to pay a dividend to the preference shares, it is not considered a contractual obligation.

Accounting Versus Credit Impact

By issuing the step-up callable preference shares, ABC strengthened its capital base as the issue was considered an equity instrument by the credit rating agencies. The accounting consideration of an instrument as equity or debt is not relevant for the rating agencies when assessing the impact of the instrument on the issuer's credit rating. Conversely, factors that are relevant for the credit rating agencies, like, for example, the seniority of the instrument relative to other claims, may be irrelevant from the accounting viewpoint.

The Hedging Problem

The classification of the dividends as equity may create a problem: dividends cannot be considered a hedged item under IAS 39. The fundamental principle under IAS 39 is that, in a hedging relationship, the hedged item creates an exposure to risk that could affect the income statement. In our case, any paid dividends were considered a distribution of profits, and thus, were be recorded in P&L. As a consequence, the dividends of ABC's step-up callable preference shares were not eligible for hedge accounting.

If ABC wanted to hedge the dividends exposure to Euribor rates by entering into a floating-to-fixed interest rate swap, ABC was left with three options:

1) To consider the swap as undesignated. ABC will have to recognise the changes in fair value of the swap in P&L, probably increasing P&L volatility; or
2) To designate the swap as hedging instrument of a floating rate liability that ABC has already issued and has not yet hedged. Of course this second option does not make much sense, as probably ABC is better off just hedging the liability instead of the preference shares; or
3) To include the swap into an instrument that does not require the mark-to-market of the swap.

Let us assume that ABC decided to pursue the third option. The idea is to include a floating-to-fixed interest rate swap in an asset or liability that does not require the bifurcation of the swap from the host contract. One way to implement this idea is the following:

Simultaneously to the preference shares issue, ABC issued a fixed-rate bond. The bond was accounted for at amortised cost, and therefore, no fair valuing of the bond was required. The bond had the following terms:

Fixed-rate Bond Terms	
Issue date	1 January 20X0
Issuer	ABC Corporation
Principal	EUR 200 million
Maturity	3 years (31-December-20X2)
Interest (annually)	4 %, paid each 31-December

The proceeds of the bond were invested in a floating-rate deposit. The deposit was classified within the "loans and receivables" category, and therefore, it was accounted for at amortised cost. The deposit had the following terms:

Floating-Rate Deposit Terms	
Issue date	1 January 20X0
Issuer	XYZ Bank
Investor	ABC Corporation
Principal	EUR 200 million
Maturity	3 years (31-December-20X2)
Interest (annually)	Euribor 12-month minus 0.10 %, paid each 31-December

In order to generate the appropriate accounting entries, let us assume that the Euribor 12-month rates and the interest/dividend payments were as follows:

Payment Date	Euribor 12-month	Pref. Shares Dividend Rate	Deposit Rate	Bond Rate	Resulting Rate
31-Dec-X0	3.0 %	4.00 %	2.90 %	4.00 %	5.10 %
31-Dec-X1	3.4 %	4.40 %	3.30 %	4.00 %	5.10 %
31-Dec-X2	3.7 %	4.70 %	3.60 %	4.00 %	5.10 %

Accounting Entries

The required journal entries were as follows:

1) To record the issuance of the three instruments on 1 January 20X0:

The proceeds of the preference shares issue were EUR 200 million.

Cash (Asset)	€ 200,000,000	
Preference Shares (Equity)		€ 200,000,000

The proceeds of the fixed-rate bond issue were EUR 200 million.

Cash (Asset)	€ 200,000,000	
Financial Debt (Liability)		€ 200,000,000

The investment in the bank deposit was EUR 200 million.

Bank Deposits (Asset)	€ 200,000,000	
Cash (Asset)		€ 200,000,000

2) To record the interest and dividends on 31 December 20X0:

Let us assume that the ordinary shares paid a dividend, so the holders of the preference shares were entitled to receive a dividend payment. As the rate was 4 %, the dividend was EUR 8 million (= 4 % * 200 million). The accounting entry shown below is simplified. In reality, and previously to 31 December 20X0, ABC would have declared a dividend. The declaration would have recognised a payable that would be eliminated on dividend payment.

Retained Earnings (Equity)	€ 8,000,000	
Cash (Asset)		€ 8,000,000

The interest expense and payment on the fixed-rate bond was EUR 8 million (= 4 % * 200 million).

Interest Expense (Income Statement)	€ 8,000,000	
Cash (Asset)		€ 8,000,000

The interest income from the bank deposit was EUR 5.8 million (= 2.90 % * 200 million).

Cash (Asset)	€ 5,800,000	
Interest Income (Income Statement)		€ 5,800,000

3) To record the interest and dividends on 31 December 20X1:

Let us assume that the ordinary shares paid a dividend, so the holders of the preference shares were entitled to receive a dividend payment. The preference shares dividend payment was EUR 8.8 million (= 4.40 % * 200 million).

Retained Earnings (Equity)	€ 8,800,000	
Cash (Asset)		€ 8,800,000

The interest expense and payment on the fixed-rate bond was EUR 8 million (= 4 % * 200 million).

Interest Expense (Income Statement)	€ 8,000,000	
Cash (Asset)		€ 8,000,000

The interest income from the bank deposit was EUR 6.6 million (= 3.3 % * 200 million).

Cash (Asset)	€ 6,600,000	
Interest Income (Income Statement)		€ 6,600,000

4) To record the interest and dividends on 31 December 20X2:

Let us assume that the ordinary shares paid a dividend, so the holders of the preference shares were entitled to receive a dividend payment. The preference shares dividend payment was EUR 9.4 million (= 4.70 % * 200 million).

Retained Earnings (Equity)	€ 9,400,000	
Cash (Asset)		€ 9,400,000

The interest expense and payment on the fixed-rate bond was EUR 8 million (= 4 % * 200 million).

Interest Expense (Income Statement)	€ 8,000,000	
Cash (Asset)		€ 8,000,000

The interest income from the bank deposit was EUR 7.2 million (= 3.6 % * 200 million).

Cash (Asset)	€ 7,200,000	
Interest Income (Income Statement)		€ 7,200,000

5) To record the redemption of the three instruments on 31 December 20X2:

ABC exercised its call right on 31 December 20X2 to avoid paying the step-up dividend rate. The redemption amount was EUR 200 million.

Preference Shares (Equity)	€ 200,000,000	
Cash (Asset)		€ 200,000,000

The redemption amount of the fixed-rate bond issue was EUR 200 million.

Cash (Asset)	€ 200,000,000	
Financial Debt (Liability)		€ 200,000,000

The redemption amount of the bank deposit was EUR 200 million.

Cash (Asset)	€ 200,000,000	
Bank Deposits (Asset)		€ 200,000,000

Concluding Remarks

The main objective of the hedge was to lock-in the expected cash-flow to be paid each year. The following figure shows the resulting cash-flow from the transaction. It can be seen in Figure 7.10 that ABC paid a fixed amount, or EUR 10.2 million (a yield of 5.1 %), annually on the three instruments.

The secondary objective was to avoid recording the mark-to-market of the hedging strategy in P&L. This objective was also achieved as none of the three instruments had to be marked-to-market.

Although these two primary objectives were achieved, there were some secondary effects that made the hedging strategy far from optimal. Firstly, the balance sheet was notably enlarged

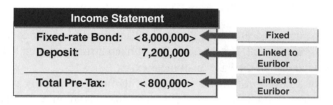

Cash-Flows

Preference Shares:	<9,400,000>
Fixed-rate Bond:	<8,000,000>
Deposit:	7,200,000
Total Pre-Tax:	10,200,000

Figure 7.10   Cash-Flows on 31-Dec-X2.

Income Statement

Fixed-rate Bond:	<8,000,000>	←	Fixed
Deposit:	7,200,000	←	Linked to Euribor
Total Pre-Tax:	<800,000>	←	Linked to Euribor

Figure 7.11   Income Statement on 31-Dec-X2.

and some ratios deteriorated because of the hedge (i.e., ABC's return on assets). Secondly, there was an additional cost because the funding level of the bond was higher than the yield on the deposit. Thirdly, there could be a potential mismatch of cash-flows as the dividend payment may not be paid (e.g., because the ordinary shares did not pay a dividend) while the deposit and bond cash-flows always took place. Finally, the income statement showed an exposure to interest rate risk: it can be seen in Figure 7.11 that the income statement was exposed to rising Euribor 12-month rates.

In summary, ABC hedged the cash-flows of the preference shares, but at the same time introduced additional P&L volatility.

CASE 7.5

Base Instruments Linked to Debt Instruments

The "base" instrument is an irredeemable (i.e., perpetual) callable financial instrument (usually preference shares) with dividends (fixed or variable) that must be paid if interest is paid on another (the "linked") instrument, as shown in Figure 7.12. The terms of the "linked" instrument oblige the issuer to make interest payments and hence the "linked" instrument is classified as a liability.

Although the base instrument does not have a contractual obligation to deliver cash (or another financial asset), the linkage to the linked instrument creates an <u>implicit</u> contractual obligation for the entity to pay dividends on the base instrument. Accordingly, the base instrument is also a liability.

The linked instrument frequently has a small face amount compared to the base instrument. This insignificant value does not impact the liability classification. It does not eliminate the fact that the issuer has no discretion over the payment of the dividend on the base instrument (i.e., the linking has created a contractual obligation with regard to the base instrument).

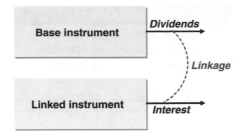

Figure 7.12   Base Preference Shares.

If the linked instrument is callable by the issuer at any time, the issuer could avoid paying interest on the base instrument. However, until the linked instrument is called, a contractual obligation to pay interest on the base instrument exists.

The addition of a linked instrument was one of the most commonly used practices to achieve liability classification for a base instrument that would otherwise be classified as equity. One advantage of the liability classification was the possibility of applying hedge accounting to the hedges of the cash-flows of the transaction, as hedge accounting cannot be used if the hedged base instrument is classified as equity. This loophole was closed after the IFRIC commented on this instrument (the IFRIC's comments have been included in the above discussion of this case).

CASE 7.6

Hedging an Available-for-sale Investment with a Put Option

The objective of this case is to illustrate hedging the equity risk of an available-for-sale equity investment using a purchased call option.

On 31 January 20X7, ABC purchased 10 million shares of DEF Corporation at a price of EUR 10 per share. ABC classified this investment as available-for-sale. To protect the investment from a decline in the share price of DEF in the next four months, ABC hedged its position by purchasing a put option on 31 January 20X7. The terms of the put option were as follows:

Put Option Terms	
Start date	31 January 20X7
Option type	Put option
Counterparties	ABC and XYZ Bank
Option buyer	ABC
Maturity	31 May 20X7
Strike	EUR 9.00
Nominal	10 million shares
Underlying	Ordinary shares of DEF
Premium	EUR 6 million
Settlement	Cash settlement

ABC designated the put option as the hedging instrument in a fair value hedge of its AFS investment.

Hedge Relationship Documentation

ABC documented the hedging relationship as follows:

Hedging Relationship Documentation	
Risk management objective and strategy for undertaking the hedge	The objective of the hedge is to protect the EUR value of 10 million shares of DEF against unfavourable movements in DEF share price below EUR 9.00. This hedging objective is consistent with ABC's overall risk management strategy of reducing the variability of its Profit and Loss statement.
Type of hedge	Fair value hedge
Risk being hedged	Equity risk
Hedging instrument	The put option contract with reference number 023547. The counterparty to the option is XYZ Bank and the credit risk associated with this counterparty is considered to be very low.
Hedged item	10 million shares of DEF Corporation.
Assessment of effectiveness testing	Hedge effectiveness will be assessed by comparing changes in the intrinsic value of the hedging instrument to changes in the intrinsic value of a hypothetical derivative. The intrinsic value of the options will be measured as the difference between the spot share price and the strike price. Effectiveness will be assessed only during those periods in which the options have intrinsic value. Changes in the time value of the options will be excluded from the assessment of effectiveness and will be recognised directly in P&L in each period. The terms hypothetical derivative are such that its fair value changes exactly offset the changes in fair value of the hedged item for the risk being hedged. In this hedging relationship, the terms of the hypothetical derivative coincide exactly with the terms of the hedging instrument but assume no credit risk. **Prospective test** A prospective test will be performed at each reporting date, using the critical terms method. Due to the fact that the terms of the hedging instrument and those of the hypothetical derivative match and that the credit risk to the counterparty to the hedging instrument is very low, the hedge is expected to be highly effective. The credit risk of the counterparty of the hedging instrument will be monitored continuously. **Retrospective test** A retrospective test will be performed at each reporting date using the "ratio analysis method". The ratio will compare the cumulative change since hedge inception in the fair value of the hypothetical derivative with the cumulative change since hedge inception in the fair value of the hedging instrument. The hedge will be assumed to be highly effective on a retrospective basis if the ratio is between 80 % and 125 %.

Fair Valuations of The Hedging Instrument and the Hedged Item

The spot share prices in EUR per share on the relevant dates were as follows:

Date	Share price at indicated date
31 January 20X7	10
31 March 20X7	8
31 May 20X7	6

The fair value calculation of the hedging instrument was calculated using the Back-Scholes model. The option intrinsic value was calculated using spot share prices. The time value of the option was calculated as the difference between the option fair value and the option instrinsic value.

Option Fair Values (EUR)	31-Jan-X7	31-Mar-X7	31-May-X7
Share price	10	8	6
Option fair value	6,000,000	15,000,000	30,000,000
Intrinsic value	-0-(1)	10,000,000(2)	30,000,000 (3)
Time value	6,000,000	5,000,000 (4)	-0-
Change in intrinsic value	—	**10,000,000** (5)	**20,000,000**
Change in time value	—	**<1,000,000>**	**<5,000,000>**(6)

Notes:
(1) = 10 million shares*Max [0; Strike-Spot] = 10 million*Max [0; 9-10]
(2) = 10 million shares*Max [0; Strike-Spot] = 10 million*Max [0; 9-8]
(3) = 10 million shares*Max [0; Strike-Spot] = 10 million*Max [0; 9-6]
(4) = Fair value − Intrinsic value = 15,000,000 − 10,000,000
(5) = Intrinsic value$_{Current}$−Intrinsic value$_{Previous}$ = 10,000,000-0
(6) = Time value$_{Current}$−Time value$_{Previous}$ = 0-5,000,000

The shares fair value calculation was as follows:

Shares Fair Value	31-Jan-X7	31-Mar-X7	31-May-X7
Spot price	10	8	6
Number of shares	10,000,000	10,000,000	10,000,000
Fair value	100,000,000	80,000,000 (1)	60,000,000
Change in fair value	—	<20,000,000>	<20,000,000> (2)

Notes:
(1) = 10,000,000 shares * EUR 8 per share
(2) = Fair value$_{Current}$ − Fair value$_{Previous}$ = 60,000,000 − 80,000,000

Prospective Tests

ABC performed a prospective test at inception (31 January 20X7) and at each reporting date during the hedge relationship (31 March 20X7). ABC used the critical terms method to assess prospective effectiveness. Because (i) the terms of the hypothetical derivative and the hedging instrument, and (ii) the credit risk associated with the counterparty to the hedging instrument was considered to be very low, ABC expected changes in fair value of the shares 9.00 to be completely offset by changes in the intrinsic value of the put option. The credit risk of the counterparty to the hedging instrument was monitored at each testing date.

Retrospective Tests

ABC performed two retrospective tests: one on the reporting date (on 31 March 20X7) and other at maturity of the hedging relationship on 31 May 20X7.

Retrospective Tests	31-Mar-X7	31-May-X7
Hedging instrument intrinsic value change	10,000,000	20,000,000
Hypothetical derivative intrinsic value change	10,000,000	20,000,000
Ratio	100,0 %	100,0 %
Hedge effective amount	10,000,000	20,000,000
Hedge ineffective amount (option time value change)	<1,000,000>	<5,000,000>

As the result of each test was within the 80 %–125 % range, each test was considered to be highly effective retrospectively. Because the option time value was not included in the hedge relationship, it was part of the ineffective amount.

Accounting Entries

The required journal entries were as follows:

1) To record the shares and the option purchases on 31 January 20X7:

   To record the purchase of the shares for EUR 100,000,000 in cash.

Investment in DEF shares (Asset)	€ 100,000,000	
Cash (Asset)		€ 100,000,000

   To record the purchase of the put option for EUR 6,000,000 in cash.

Put option (Asset)	€ 6,000,000	
Cash (Asset)		€ 6,000,000

2) To record the closing of the accounting period on 31 March 20X7:

   The change in fair value of the option was a gain EUR 9 million. Of this amount, a gain of EUR 10 million was effective and a loss of EUR 1 million was ineffective. As it was a fair value hedge, the AFS investment was also adjusted for the effective amount.

Put option (Asset)	€ 9,000,000	
Other income/expense (P&L)		€ 9,000,000

| Other income/expense (P&L) | € 10,000,000 | |
| Investment in DEF shares (Asset) | | € 10,000,000 |

The change in the shares fair value was a loss of EUR 20,000,000. ABC already recognised a loss of EUR 10 million, so there was another EUR 10,000,000 to be recorded in equity as the investment was classified as available-for-sale.

| Available-for-sale gains/losses (Equity) | € 10,000,000 | |
| Investment in DEF shares (Asset) | | € 10,000,000 |

3) To record the expiry of the option and the end of the hedging relationship on 31 May 20X7:

The change in fair value of the option was a gain of EUR 15 million. Of this amount, a gain of EUR 20 million was effective and a loss of EUR 5 million was ineffective. As it was a fair value hedge, the AFS investment was also adjusted for the effective amount.

| Put option (Asset) | € 15,000,000 | |
| Other income/expense (P&L) | | € 15,000,000 |

| Other income/expense (P&L) | € 20,000,000 | |
| Investment in DEF shares (Asset) | | € 20,000,000 |

The change in the shares fair value was a loss of EUR 20,000,000. ABC already recognised a loss of EUR 20 million, so there was no amount to be recorded in equity.

As the hedge relationship finished on 31 May 20X7, any subsequent changes in the fair value of DEF shares would have been recognised in equity.

Concluding Remarks

The problem that ABC faced was that the accumulated amount in equity would be recycled into P&L when the DEF shares were sold. If the shares had a prolonged decline, ABC income statement could suffer a severe hit when the shares are sold.

In our example, if ABC would not have hedged its investment the reserve account would have shown a EUR 40 million deficit. This amount would translate into a loss in P&L when the shares are sold (see Figure 7.13).

Fortunately, ABC was cautious and hedged its investment. At the end of the hedging term, the reserve account showed a EUR 10 million deficit, an amount notably lower than EUR 40 million. However, because ABC wanted to benefit from full appreciation of the shares, the EUR 6 million cost of the protection ended up recorded in P&L.

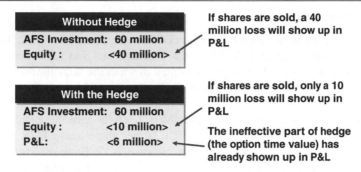

Figure 7.13   Summary of Effects.

CASE 7.7

Parking Shares Through a Total Return Swap

A total return swap (TRS) on shares is a special type of equity swap. It is a cash settled equity swap (i.e., it does not provide for physical settlement). A TRS involves swapping the total return on a specified reference asset in exchange for a string of interest payments. The total return is the capital gain or loss on the reference asset, plus any interim dividends. The TRS allows entities to derive the economic benefit of owning an asset without having to own it.

TRSs are primarily used by corporations to monetise investments in equity instruments of other companies. For example, through a TRS an entity may postpone a monetary gain, may comply with ownership regulations, or may raise collateralised debt. A TRS can also be used as an investment tool to get exposure to the appreciation (and depreciation) of a group of shares. This last use of TRSs is quite uncommon by corporations.

Let us assume that ABC was highly leveraged and did not want to use the debt capital markets to raise new financing. ABC had an investment in DEF and decided to raise financing by monetising the investment. The investment was classified as available-for-sale. As part of the strategy, ABC entered into the following total return swap:

Total Return Swap Terms	
Trade date	1 January 20X0
Counterparties	ABC Corporation and XYZ Bank
Number shares	20 million shares of DEF Corporation
Initial price	EUR 10 per share
Notional amount	EUR 200 million
Maturity	2 years (31-December-20X1)
ABC receives on dividend payment date	An amount equal to the gross dividend paid to the shares. This amount is received on the date that the dividend is paid
ABC pays annually	Euribor 12-month plus 50 basis points, on the Notional, paid annually each 31-December
Final amount at maturity	Final Amount = Number shares * (Final price − Initial price)
Final price	The closing price of the Shares at Maturity

Asset Monetisation Strategy

At the beginning of the transaction, the 20 million DEF shares were sold to XYZ Bank at market value. The shares were trading at EUR 10 per share on that date, thus ABC received EUR 200 million for the sale. Figure 7.14 highlights the initial flows of the monetisation strategy.

During the term of the TRS, ABC paid annually Euribor plus 50 bps on the notional amount of the TRS, as shown in Figure 7.15.

DEF paid periodically a dividend to its shareholders. Let us assume that each 31st December ABC declared and simultaneously paid a EUR 0.10 per share and a EUR 0.12 per share dividends, respectively in 20X0 and in 20X1. In our case, XYZ Bank was the legal owner of the shares and therefore received those dividends. Through the TRS, ABC was obliged to pay ABC an amount equal to the dividends received on the underlying DEF shares. Figure 7.16 shows the cash flows related to the dividends.

At the end of the transaction, ABC had two alternatives: (1) to buy back the shares, or (2) to do nothing. In our case, ABC chose the second alternative, as ABC was not interested in buying back the DEF shares. At the end of the TRS, the closing price of the DEF shares on maturity date (the "final price") was determined and:

1) If the final price was greater than the initial price, XYZ Bank paid ABC the appreciation of the shares. The appreciation was calculated as:

$$\text{Appreciation} = \text{Number Shares} * (\text{Final price} - \text{Initial Price})$$

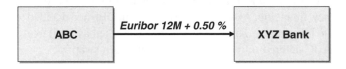

Figure 7.14   Monetisation Strategy – Initial Flows.

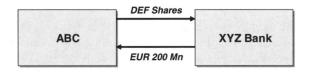

Figure 7.15   Monetisation Strategy – Interest Flows.

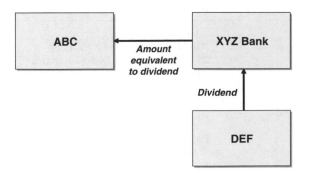

Figure 7.16   Monetisation Strategy – Dividend Flows.

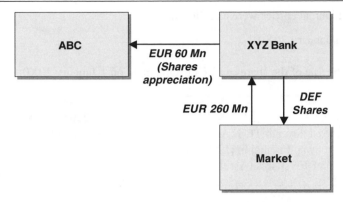

Figure 7.17   Monetisation Strategy – Final Flows.

2) If the final price was lower than the initial price, ABC paid XYZ Bank the depreciation of the shares. The depreciation was calculated as:

$$\text{Depreciation} = \text{Number Shares} * (\text{Initial price} - \text{Final Price})$$

Let us assume that the closing price of the DEF shares on 31 December 20X1 was EUR 13.00. As a consequence, XYZ Bank was obliged to pay ABC the appreciation of the DEF shares, or EUR 60 million (= 20 million shares*(13–10)). In reality, and in order not to be exposed to the price of the DEF shares, XYZ Bank would have sold the shares in the market near the closing of the trading session. As a consequence, XYZ Bank would have received EUR 260 million (= 20 million shares*13) for selling the shares in the market. Figure 7.17 shows the different flows taking place at the TRS maturity.

Accounting Entries

At the beginning of the strategy, the key point for ABC was whether or not it made a disposal of the DEF shares. ABC entered into the TRS where it transferred the DEF shares recognised on its balance sheet but retained all risks and rewards of the transferred DEF shares, even though at the TRS maturity ABC had no obligation to repurchase the DEF shares. As a result, ABC continued to recognise the DEF shares in the balance sheet. In essence, the TRS replicated the position of a secured financing transaction in which ABC borrowed EUR 200 million at Euribor + 50 bps and posted the DEF shares as collateral.

The opinion just stated was based on our interpretation of IAS 39's de-recognition rules. Some accountants may argue that ABC has no continuing involvement in the shares because the transferee (i.e., XYZ Bank) has the ability to transfer the DEF shares to a third party, and therefore ABC should derecognise the asset. In our view, this interpretation is inaccurate as XYZ Bank maintains through the TRS its exposure to DEF shares.

The required journal entries were as follows:

1) Entries on 1 January 20X0:

To record the sale of the shares and TRS agreement on 1 January 20X0:

Cash (Asset)	€ 200,000,000	
Shares transferred through TRS (Asset)	€ 200,000,000	
Total Return Swap Financing (Liability)		€ 200,000,000
Investment in DEF shares (Asset)		€ 200,000,000

2) Entries on 31 December 20X0

Let us assume that the DEF shares were trading at EUR 12 per share. Thus the change in their fair value since the last valuation was a gain of EUR 40 million. To record the fair valuation sale of the shares:

Shares transferred through TRS (Asset)	€ 40,000,000	
Available-for-sale gains/losses (Equity)		€ 40,000,000

Assuming that the Euribor 12-month fixing for the interest period was 4.20 %, ABC paid EUR 9,531,000 interest (= 200 million*(4.20 %+0.50 %)*365/360):

Interest expense (P&L)	€ 9,531,000	
Cash (Asset)		€ 9,531,000

Assuming that the DEF shares paid a EUR 0.10 per share dividend, ABC received EUR 2,000,000 (= 20 million shares*0.10) through the TRS:

Cash (Asset)	€ 2,000,000	
Interest income (P&L)		€ 2,000,000

3) Entries on 31 December 20X1

Let us assume that the DEF shares were trading at EUR 13 per share. Thus the change in their fair value since the last valuation was a gain of EUR 20 million. To record the fair valuation sale of the shares:

Shares transferred through TRS (Asset)	€ 20,000,000	
Available-for-sale gains/losses (Equity)		€ 20,000,000

Assuming that the Euribor 12-month fixing for the interest period was 4.40 %, ABC paid EUR 9,936,000 interest (= 200 million*(4.40 %+0.50 %)*365/360) under the TRS:

Interest expense (P&L)	€ 9,936,000	
Cash (Asset)		€ 9,936,000

Assuming that the DEF shares paid a EUR 0.12 per share dividend, ABC received EUR 2,400,000 (= 20 million shares*0.12) through the TRS:

Cash (Asset)	€ 2,400,000	
Interest income (P&L)		€ 2,400,000

To record the maturity of the TRS, let us address the two alternatives that ABC had at TRS maturity in the entries 4.1) and 4.2) entries.

4.1 If ABC decided not to buy back the shares at TRS maturity:

At the TRS maturity, ABC received EUR 60 million and unwinded the entries related to the TRS. Also, the DEF shares were derecognised from ABC's balance sheet:

Total Return Swap Financing (Liability)	€ 200,000,000	
Cash (Asset)	€ 60,000,000	
Shares transferred through TRS (Asset)		€ 260,000,000

As the DEF shares were derecognised, the amount accumulated in equity was recycled to P&L:

Available-for-sale gains/losses (Equity)	€ 60,000,000	
Other income/expense (P&L)		€ 60,000,000

4.2 If ABC decided to buy back the shares at TRS maturity:

At the TRS maturity, ABC received EUR 60 million and unwinded the entries related to the TRS:

Total Return Swap Financing (Liability)	€ 200,000,000	
Cash (Asset)	€ 60,000,000	
Shares transferred through TRS (Asset)		€ 260,000,000

ABC bought back the shares in the market at EUR 1.30 per share:

Investment in DEF shares (Asset)	€ 260,000,000	
Cash (Asset)		€ 260,000,000

In this second alternative, the amount accumulated in equity (EUR 60 million) remained in equity until future derecognition of the asset.

CASE 7.8

Hedging an Equity-Settled Options Plan with an Equity Swap

It is quite common that corporations motivate key employees by granting them options, called "employee share options plans" or "ESOPs", linked to the entity's own shares. As a result, effective hedging of ESOPs has taken on significance importance among corporate financiers. This case provides an overview of the measurement and recognition of ESOPs, and discusses the hedging of equity-settled ESOPs with equity swaps.

IFRS 2 Terminology

ESOPs are accounted for in accordance with IFRS 2 *Shared-based Payment*. Before addressing the accounting of ESOPs, let us review some of the key terms used by the IFRS 2 standard.

IFRS 2 characterises two types of share-based option transactions:

- Equity-settled share-based options. On exercise date, the entity issues or delivers the employee its own equity instruments.
- Cash-settled options. On exercise date, the entity pays the employee cash. The amount of cash is calculated as a function of the entity's share price.

IFRS 2 defines the following dates and periods (see Figure 7.18).

- Grant date is the date on which the option plan award is agreed between the entity and the participants, and both the entity and the participants have obtained an understanding of all the terms and conditions of the plan.
- Usually before the participant owns the options, certain conditions (called "vesting conditions") have to be satisfied. The vesting period is the period during which the vesting conditions are monitored.
- Vesting date is the date on which the participants are entitled to the options, if the vesting conditions have been met. It is the end date of the vesting period.
- Exercise period is the period in which the participants can, at their discretion, exercise their options.

Under IFRS 2, a vesting condition is classified as either a market condition or a non-market condition, depending on whether it is dependent upon the market price of the entity's shares.

Figure 7.18   ESOP – Key Dates.

- Examples of market conditions are the accomplishment of a specified share price, the attainment of a specified performance of the entity's shares relative to a group of competitors' shares, etc.
- Examples of non-market conditions are continual employment for a specific period, the attainment of a specified EBITDA, etc.

Equity Versus Liability Recognition

Under IFRS 2, shared-based payment transactions are classified as either as equity instruments or as liability instruments.

- Equity instruments are ESOPs in which the settlement is in shares, or ESOPs in which the entity has the choice of settlement in shares or in cash.
- Liability instruments are ESOPs in which the settlement is in cash, or ESOPs in which the participants have the choice of settlement in shares or in cash.

Accounting Treatment of ESOPs Classified as Equity Instruments

Stock options plans that are settled in shares, or that the entity can choose whether they are settled by physical delivery of the shares or in cash, are treated as equity instruments. At grant date, the estimated fair value of the options granted is calculated by multiplying the fair value of all the options with the number of options expected to vest, as follows:

1) The fair value of the options excluding the non-market conditions is determined using generally accepted option valuations models. The most commonly accepted models are the Black-Scholes model, the binomial model and the Monte-Carlo model. This fair value is not recomputed during the ESOP's life.
2) The fair value calculated in 1) is adjusted to include the estimate of the number options that eventually will vest. The non-market vesting conditions are taken into account in the assumptions about the number of options that are expected to become exercisable. The estimation of the options that eventually will vest is revised at each balance sheet date.

The estimated fair value, at the date of grant, of the options is recognised on a straight-line basis as personnel expense in the income statement during the instruments' vesting period, and a corresponding increase in retained earnings.

At each balance sheet date, the entity revises its estimates of the number of options that are expected to become exercisable. It recognises the impact of the revision in the original estimates, if any, in the income statement, and a corresponding adjustment to equity.

Upon the options exercise, the exercise proceeds received net of any directly attributable transaction costs are credited to equity.

If the options lapsed or are cancelled, the expense previously charged to the income statement is not reversed. However, the entity may choose to make transfers between the different classes of equity.

Accounting Treatment of ESOPs Classified as Liability Instruments

Stock options plans that are settled in cash, or that the employee can choose as to whether they are settled by physical delivery of the shares or in cash, are treated as liability instruments.

<u>At each balance sheet date and on the exercise date</u>, the estimated fair value of the options granted is determined in two steps:

1) The fair value of the options excluding the non-market conditions is determined using generally accepted option valuations models. The most commonly accepted models are the Black-Scholes model, the binomial model and the Monte-Carlo model.
2) The fair value calculated in 1) is adjusted to include the estimated number of options that eventually will vest. The non-market vesting conditions are taken into account in the assumptions about the number of options that are expected to become exercisable.

The estimated fair value, at each balance sheet date and at exercise date, of the options is recognised on a straight-line basis as personnel expenses in the income statement during the instruments' vesting period, with a corresponding credit to liabilities.

When options are exercised, the corresponding liability is debited and the cash account is credited.

Hedging an ESOP Treated As an Equity Instrument

Let us assume that ABC Corporation issued on 1 January 20X0 to a group of its executives a stock options plan (the "Plan") with the following terms:

Stock Options Plan Terms	
Grant date	1 January 20X0
Vesting period	3 years (from 1 January 20X0 until 31 December 20X3)
Exercise date	31 December 20X3
Strike	EUR 10.00
Number of options	10 million (each option is on one ABC share)
Settlement	Physical delivery
Non-market condition	Vesting is conditional on the participant's continual employment and achievement of a 50 % growth of ABC's EBITDA during the term of the Plan
Other	ABC is committed to meet the potential Plan exercises by delivering its own treasury shares (i.e., by not issuing new shares)

In order to hedge future exercises under the Plan, ABC considered the following alternatives:

1) Not to hedge the Plan. As ABC committed itself to deliver existing shares, it meant that upon exercise of the options ABC would have to buy 10 million shares in the market. From a cash-flow perspective, ABC would be then exposed to rises in its share price: the higher the share price, the larger the disbursement to buy back its own shares. This approach was not acceptable to ABC.
2) To buy a call option. The terms of the call option were to be identical to the terms of the Plan underlying option. The premium of the call option was EUR 14 million. This approach was the best hedge possible: if the Plan was exercised then ABC would exercise the hedging call option, if the Plan was not exercised then ABC would not exercise the hedging call option. However, ABC discarded this approach as being too expensive.
3) To hold the underlying shares. Under this alternative, ABC would buy 10 million shares in the market at the beginning of the Plan. If the Plan was exercised, ABC would deliver the

shares to the Plan participants. If the Plan were not exercised, ABC would sell the shares in the market. This approach was discarded by ABC as it was not willing to finance the purchase of the shares.

4) To enter into an equity swap. Under this approach, ABC would buy through the equity swap the shares to be delivered potentially on exercise date. Through the equity swap ABC is obliged to buy 10 million of its own shares at maturity. The main disadvantage of this approach is that if the participants do not exercise their options, ABC would end up owning 10 million of its own shares and probably would have to sell them in the market. In other words, this is a hedge only if the options become exercised. ABC decided to pursue this approach, as it would not need to finance the purchase of the shares until the options expiry. The terms of the equity swap were as follows:

Equity Swap Terms	
Start date	1 January 20X0
Counterparties	ABC and XYZ Bank
Maturity date	31 December 20X3
Reference price	EUR 10.00
Number of shares	10 million shares
Nominal amount	EUR 100 million
Underlying	ABC ordinary shares
Settlement	Physical delivery (ABC is obliged to buy on maturity date the number of shares at the reference price)
ABC pays	Euribor 12-month plus 0.50 %, annually A/360 basis, on the nominal amount
ABC receives	100 % of the gross dividend paid to the underlying shares. ABC receives this amount on the dividend payment date

Fair Valuation of The ESOP at Each Reporting Date

On the ESOP grant date, ABC had to value the options granted, excluding the non-market conditions. ABC used the Back-Scholes valuation model with the following inputs: a 3-year time-to-expiry, a EUR 10 strike, a 20 % volatility, a 10 million shares nominal, a 4.50 % interest rate and a 3 % dividend yield. The value of the Plan using this model, excluding the non-market conditions, was EUR 14 million.

At each balance sheet date, ABC had to compute the adjusted fair value of the Plan (i.e., also including the non-market conditions). The Plan EUR 14 million value had to be adjusted to include only the expected number of options that would vest. Vesting was conditional on the participant's continual employment and achievement of a 50 % growth of ABC's EBITDA during the Plan term. ABC estimations at each reporting date are shown in the following table:

Date	Expected Number of Options to Vest	Adjusted Fair Value of Plan	Annual Expense
31-Dec-X0	8.5 million	EUR 11.9 million (= 8.5 mn/10 mn * 14 mn)	EUR 3,967,000
31-Dec-X1	8 million	EUR 11.2 million (= 8 mn/10 mn * 14 mn)	EUR 3,733,000
31-Dec-X2	8.2 million	EUR 11.48 million (= 8.2 mn/10 mn * 14 mn)	EUR 3,827,000

On 31 December 20X3, ABC had an obligation to pay EUR 100 million to XYZ Bank, and XYZ Bank had an obligation to deliver 10 million shares to ABC. Assuming that the 3-year zero-coupon interest rate was 4.50 % at the beginning of the transaction, the present value of the EUR 100 million was EUR 87,630,000. ABC had to recognise a liability whose carrying value at each reporting date was as follows:

Date	Interest expense	Liability Carrying Value
1-Jan-X0		87,630,000
31-Dec-X0	3,943,000	91,573,000
31-Dec-X1	4,121,000	95,694,000
31-Dec-X2	4,306,000	100,000,000

Accounting Entries

The required journal entries were as follows:

1) Entries on 1 January 20X0

   ABC had to recognise a liability recording the present value of ABC's commitment to pay EUR 100 million, or EUR 87,630,000:

Treasury Shares Forward Purchase (Equity)	€ 87,630,000	
Forward obligation (Liability)		€ 87,630,000

2) Entries on 31 December 20X0

   The estimated fair value of the Plan on 31 December 20X0 was EUR 11.9 million to be spread over the 3-year vesting period (or EUR 3,967,000 per annum). To recognise the EUR 3,967,000 employee benefits annual expense:

Employee benefits expense (P&L)	€ 3,967,000	
Retained earnings (Equity)		€ 3,967,000

   Through the equity swap, ABC was obliged to pay an annual interest of Euribor 12-month plus 50 bps. Let us assume that the Euribor 12-month rate was 4.00 % and that there was 365 days in the interest period. The interest expense for the period was EUR 4,563,000 (= 100 million*(4 %+0.50 %)*365/360). To recognise the equity swap interest expense:

Interest expense (P&L)	€ 4,563,000	
Interest payable (Liability)		€ 4,563,000

To recognise the equity swap interest payment:

Interest payable (Liability)	€ 4,563,000	
Cash (Asset)		€ 4,563,000

Through the equity swap, ABC received an amount equivalent to the dividends paid to the underlying shares. Let us assume that ABC distributed a EUR 0.3 dividend per share. For simplicity, assume further that the dividend was paid on 31 December 20X0. To recognise the EUR 3,000,000 amount equivalent to the dividends received through the equity swap:

Cash (Asset)	€ 3,000,000	
Interest income (P&L)		€ 3,000,000

To recognise the liability interest accrual:

Interest expense (Liability)	€ 3,943,000	
Forward obligation (Liability)		€ 3,943,000

3) Entries on 31 December 20X1

The estimated fair value of the Plan on 31 December 20X1 was EUR 11.2 million to be spread over the 3-year vesting period (or EUR 3,733,000 per annum). As EUR 3,967,000 was already recognised on 31 December 20X0, a EUR 3,500,000 (= 3,733,000*2−3,967,000) was to be recognised as employee benefits annual expense:

Employee benefits expense (P&L)	€ 3,500,000	
Retained earnings (Equity)		€ 3,500,000

Through the equity swap, ABC was obliged to pay an annual interest of Euribor 12-month plus 50 bps. Let us assume that the Euribor 12-month rate was 4.20 % and that there was 365 days in the interest period. The interest expense for the period was EUR 4,765,000 (= 100 million*(4.2 %+0.50 %)*365/360). To recognise the equity swap interest expense:

Interest expense (P&L)	€ 4,765,000	
Interest payable (Liability)		€ 4,765,000

To recognise the equity swap interest payment:

Interest payable (Liability)	€ 4,765,000	
Cash (Asset)		€ 4,765,000

Through the equity swap, ABC received an amount equivalent to the dividends paid to the underlying shares. Let us assume that ABC distributed a EUR 0.32 dividend per share. For simplicity, assume further that the dividend was paid on 31 December 20X1. To recognise the EUR 3,200,000 amount equivalent to the dividends received through the equity swap:

Cash (Asset)	€ 3,200,000	
Interest income (P&L)		€ 3,200,000

To recognise the liability interest accrual:

Interest expense (Liability)	€ 4,121,000	
Forward obligation (Liability)		€ 4,121,000

4) Entries on 31 December 20X2

The estimated fair value of the Plan on 31 December 20X2 was EUR 11.48 million to be spread over the 3-year vesting period. As a total of EUR 7,467,000 was already recognised, EUR 4,013,000 (= 11,480,000 − 7,467,000) was to be recognised as employee benefits annual expense:

Employee benefits expense (P&L)	€ 4,013,000	
Retained earnings (Equity)		€ 4,013,000

Through the equity swap, ABC was obliged to pay an annual interest of Euribor 12-month plus 50 bps. Let us assume that the Euribor 12-month rate was 4.40 % and that there was 365 days in the interest period. The interest expense for the period was EUR 4,968,000 (= 100 million*(4.4 %+0.50 %)*365/360):

Interest expense (P&L)	€ 4,968,000	
Interest payable (Liability)		€ 4,968,000

To recognise the equity swap interest payment:

Interest payable (Liability)	€ 4,968,000	
Cash (Asset)		€ 4,968,000

Through the equity swap, ABC received an amount equivalent to the dividends paid to the underlying shares. Let us assume that ABC paid a EUR 0.34 dividend per share on

31 December 20X2. To recognise the EUR 3,400,000 amount equivalent to the dividends received through the equity swap:

Cash (Asset)	€ 3,400,000	
Interest income (P&L)		€ 3,400,000

To recognise the liability interest accrual:

Interest expense (Liability)	€ 4,306,000	
Forward obligation (Liability)		€ 4,306,000

Additionally, through the equity swap ABC was obliged to purchase 10 million of its own shares at a EUR 10.00 per share:

Forward obligation (Liability)	€ 100,000,000	
Treasury Shares (Equity)	€ 87,630,000	
Cash (Asset)		€ 100,000,000
Treasury Shares Forward Purchase (Equity)		€ 87,630,000

Let us assume that all the participants exercised their options. They paid the Plan's EUR 10 strike price per option and received 1 share per option. Thus, they paid EUR 100 million and received 10 million ABC shares.

Cash (Asset)	€ 100,000,000	
Treasury Shares (Equity)		€ 100,000,000

Final Remarks

The hedge via the equity swap worked very well because the options ended up being exercised. The combined effect on the financial statements of the Plan and the equity swap during the three years was as follows:

- ABC's income statement showed the fair value of the Plan, the equity swap interest payments, and the equity swap interest income due to the dividends. The equity swap increased the overall expense as its interest rate exceeded ABC's shares dividend yield (see Figure 7.19).
- ABC's cash showed the difference between the equity swap interest and dividend flows. Thanks to hedge, ABC paid for the shares the same amount it received from the participants. At the same time, ABC's equity showed an increase in share premium equal to the fair value of the Plan plus the difference between (i) the liability final value and (ii) the liability initial value (see Figure 7.20).

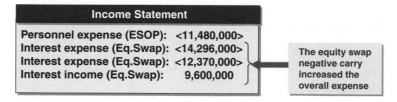

Figure 7.19   Plan + Equity Swap: Income Statement Effect.

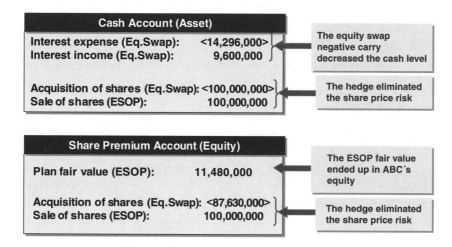

Figure 7.20   Plan + Equity Swap: Balance Sheet Effect.

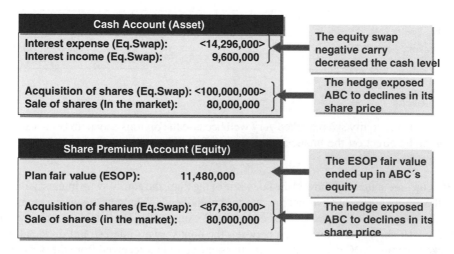

Figure 7.21   Plan + Equity Swap: Balance Sheet Effect.

Nevertheless, the hedge was imperfect and exposed ABC from a cash-flow perspective (although not from a P&L perspective) to a decline in its share price. Let us assume that on exercise date the shares were trading at EUR 8.00 per share and, as a consequence, that the ESOP participants did not exercise their options. Assume further that ABC decided to sell in the market (at EUR 8.00 per share) the shares it acquired through the equity swap.

The effects on ABC's financial statements would have been as shown in Figure 7.21.

- ABC's income statement would have been the same as if the beneficiaries exercised their options (see Figure 7.19).
- However, ABC's cash and equity would have been exposed to a decline in ABC's share price. The difference between the shares acquisition price and sale price affected negatively both the cash and equity levels, as shown in Figure 7.21.

8

Hedging Commodity Risk

This chapter covers the hedge accounting implications when hedging commodity risk. There are many industries that are heavily exposed to commodities. For example, for oil, gas, utilities, mining, and airline companies, prices of certain commodities may have a significant impact in their competitive position.

The accounting treatment of commodities is a delicate area. Some of the most important collapses have been caused by an extensive speculation involving commodities. To complicate things, many commodity contracts are used by companies as an integral part of their day-to-day business.

8.1 OWN-USE VERSUS IAS 39 COMMODITY CONTRACTS

The main issue regarding a contract to buy or sell a non-financial item is whether or not the contract is under IAS 39 scope. Contracts outside IAS 39 scope are called "own-use" contracts.

- Commodity contracts that fall within the scope of IAS 39 are recognised at fair value. The fair value changes are recognised in P&L.
- Own-use contracts. These contracts are not fair valued.

A commodity contract is treated as an IAS 39 instrument if any of the following three conditions is met:

1) The entity has a practice of settling similar contracts net in cash, or by entering in offsetting contracts, or by selling the contracts; or
2) The entity has a practice of taking delivery and selling shortly after so as to profit from short-term fluctuations in price or a dealer's margin; or
3) Where the contract permits either party to settle net in cash, or another financial instrument, or by exchanging financial instruments, or by selling the contracts, or where the non-financial item that is the subject of the contract is readily convertible to cash; unless the contract was entered into, and continues to be held, for the purpose of receipt or delivery in accordance with the entity's normal purchase, sale or usage requirements.

Although at first sight it seems that the contract can be treated as an own-use contract only if the entity intends to take delivery of the underlying to meet its purchase, sale or usage requirements, in practice the three conditions set above are difficult to interpret. Entities that have a practice of entering into contracts both for physical delivery and also for trading purposes may interpret that the contracts for physical delivery should be considered as "own-use" contracts but a rigid application of the first condition may invalidate this consideration. For example a gas company may manage its gas on an integral basis, buying, storing and selling gas as to optimise its overall portfolio. Gas is an asset that flows through the organisation, and it is extraordinarily complex to track the flow of gas from a particular contract. To decide which contracts need

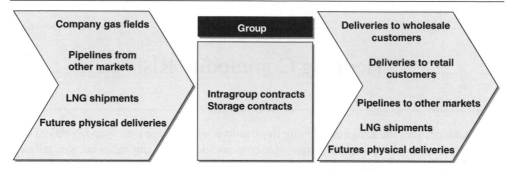

Figure 8.1   Gas Group – Contracts.

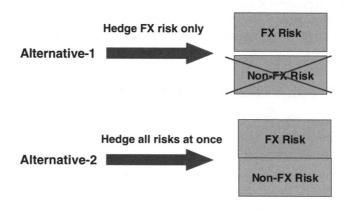

Figure 8.2   Hedging Non-Financial Assets/Liabilities.

to be fair valued and which contracts can be considered own-use can be very challenging, as shown in Figure 8.1. The entity has to understand the spirit of the IFRS rules and try to apply it accordingly.

8.2   HEDGING COMMODITY RISK

Commodity risk is usually linked to non-financial assets or liabilities. IAS 39 only allows non-financial assets or liabilities to be hedged in its entirety or for FX risk only (see Figure 8.2). Therefore, hedging non-financial assets or liabilities that have exposure to several commodities may become difficult as IAS 39 does not allow one to hedge only one commodity risk component.

CASE 8.1

Hedging a Commodity Firm Commitment with a Forward

This case is an example of a fair value hedge of a commodity firm commitment using a forward.

ABC is a European wholesaler of silver. ABC buys the silver from mining companies and sells it to silver users in the electronics industry. On 1 February 20X7, ABC signed a contract to sell to a customer 10 million troy ounces of silver at a price of EUR 5.00 per ounce to be delivered and paid on 31 May 20X7. ABC was expecting to meet this delivery with an agreed purchase from a mining company to be priced at the prevailing spot rate on the purchase delivery date. Accordingly, the sale at a fixed price exposed ABC to rising silver prices. ABC's hedging policy was to pay and receive market prices in all its contracts, so it was not exposed to changes in silver prices.

To protect the sale from rising silver prices, on 1 February 20X7 ABC entered into a forward with the following terms:

Silver Forward Terms	
Start date	1 February 20X7
Counterparties	Company ABC and XYZ Bank
Maturity	31 May 20X7
ABC receives	EUR 45 million
ABC delivers	10 million try ounces of silver
Forward Rate	4.50 EUR/ounce
Settlement	Cash settlement

The forward rate 4.50 was the current forward rate for 31 May 20X7 prevailing on 1 February 20X7. Thus, ABC did not have to pay any premium for entering into the hedge. In other words, the forward had a fair value of zero at inception.

The first question that ABC asked itself was if it was necessary to apply hedge accounting to avoid mismatches in P&L recognition.

- If the firm commitment was classified as a derivative contract, a hedge relationship would not be needed as both the firm commitment and the forward would be fair valued with changes in their fair value recognised in P&L.
- However, in our case ABC classified the firm commitment as an "own-use" contract. Therefore, the firm commitment would not be fair valued unless it was designated as hedged item in a fair value hedge. Thus, ABC designated the forward in a fair value hedge of the firm commitment.

Hedge Relationship Documentation

ABC documented the hedging relationship as follows:

Hedging Relationship Documentation	
Risk management objective and strategy for undertaking the hedge	The objective of the hedge is to protect the EUR value of the firm commitment to sell 10 million silver to ounces against unfavourable movements in the silver price in EUR.
	This hedging objective is consistent with ABC's overall risk management strategy of fair valuing all its purchase and sales to reduce the variability of its Profit and Loss statement.
Type of hedge	Fair value hedge.

(Continued)

Hedging Relationship Documentation	
Risk being hedged	All the risks in their entirety. The variability in EUR value of the firm commitment.
Hedging instrument	The forward contract with reference number 011895. The counterparty to the forward is XYZ Bank and the credit risk associated with this counterparty is considered to be very low.
Hedged item	Firm commitment to sell 10 million ounces of silver.
Assessment of effectiveness testing	Hedge effectiveness will be assessed by comparing changes in the fair value of the hedging instrument to changes in the fair value of a hypothetical derivative. Effectiveness will be assessed based on changes in forward prices (i.e., the forward points will be included in the assessment of effectiveness).
	The terms of the hypothetical derivative are such that its fair value changes exactly offset the changes in fair value of the hedged highly expected cash flow for the risk being hedged. In this hedging relationship, the terms of the hypothetical derivative coincide exactly with the terms of the hedging instrument but assume no credit risk.
	Prospective test
	A prospective test will be performed at each reporting date, using the critical terms method. Due to the fact that the terms of the hedging instrument and those of the hypothetical derivative match and that the credit risk to the counterparty to the hedging instrument are very low, the hedge is expected to be highly effective. The credit risk of the counterparty of the hedging instrument will be monitored continuously.
	Retrospective test
	A retrospective test will be performed at each reporting date using the "ratio analysis method". The ratio will compare the cumulative change since hedge inception in the fair value of the hypothetical derivative with the cumulative change since hedge inception in the fair value of the hedging instrument. The hedge will be assumed to be highly effective on a retrospective basis if the ratio is between 80 % and 125 %.

Fair Valuations of the Hedging Instrument and the Hypothetical Derivative

The forward silver prices and the discount factor on the relevant dates were as follows:

Date	Forward rate for 31 May 20X7	Discount factor for 31 May 20X7
1 February 20X7	4.50	0.9900
31 March 20X7	4.60	0.9950
31 May 20X7	4.80	1.0000

The following table outlines the fair value calculation of the hedging instrument and the hypothetical derivative. Both fair values coincided because the terms of the hypothetical derivative matched those of the hedging instrument (except in their credit risk exposure) and no significant credit deterioration was perceived in the counterparty to the hedging instrument.

Fair Values (EUR)	1-Feb-X7	31-Mar-X7	31-May-X7
Silver forward price to 31-May-X7	4.50	4.60	4.80
Discount factor	0.9900	0.9950	1.0000
Forward fair value	–0– *(1)*	995,000 *(2)*	3,000,000 *(3)*
Change in forward fair value	—	**995,000**	**2,005,000** *(4)*
Hypothetical derivative fair value	–0– *(1)*	995,000 *(2)*	3,000,000 *(3)*
Change in hypothetical derivative fair value	—	**995,000**	**2,005,000** *(4)*

Notes:
(1) = 10 million ounces * (forward price − 4.50) * Discount factor = 10 million * (4.50-4.50) * 0.9900
(2) = 10 million ounces * (forward price − 4.50) * Discount factor = 10 million * (4.60-4.50) * 0.9950
(3) = 10 million ounces * (forward price − 4.50) * Discount factor = 10 million * (4.80-4.50) * 1.0000
(4) = 3,000,000 − 995,000

Prospective Tests

ABC performed a prospective test at hedge inception (1 February 20X7) and at each reporting date during the hedge relationship (31 March 20X7). ABC used the critical terms method to assess prospective effectiveness. Because (i) the terms of the hypothetical derivative and the hedging instrument, and (ii) the credit risk associated with the counterparty to the hedging instrument was considered to be very low, ABC expected that changes in expected fair values from the firm commitment to be completely offset by changes in the fair value of the forward. As a result, ABC concluded that the hedge was highly effective prospectively. The credit risk of the counterparty to the hedging instrument was monitored at each testing date.

Retrospective tests

ABC performed two retrospective tests: one on the reporting date (31 March 20X7) and other at maturity of the hedging relationship (31 May 20X7). Because there was no significant deterioration in the credit of the counterparty of the hedging instrument and because the terms of the hedging instrument and those of the expected cash flow matched, the hedge relationship was 100 % effective:

Retrospective Tests	31-Mar-X7	31-May-X7
Hedging instrument fair value change (since hedge inception)	995,000	3,000,000
Hypothetical derivative fair value change (since hedge inception)	995,000	3,000,000
Ratio	**100.0 %**	**100.0 %**
Hedge effective amount	995,000	2,005,000
Hedge ineffective amount	–0–	–0–

As the result of each test was within the 80 %–125 % range, ABC considered the hedge to be highly effective retrospectively at each test date.

Accounting Entries

The required journal entries were as follows:

1) To record the forward contract on 1 February 20X7:

    No journal entries were required as the fair value of the forward contract was zero.

2) To record the closing of the accounting period on 31 March 20X7:

    The change in fair value of the forward contract was EUR 995,000.

Forward contract (Asset)	€ 995,000	
Fair value hedge gain/loss (P&L)		€ 995,000

The hedge was 100 % effective, so all the change in fair value of the forward contract (EUR 995,000) was recognised as change in fair value of the firm commitment:

Fair value hedge gain/loss (P&L)	€ 995,000	
Firm commitment (Liability)		€ 995,000

3) To record the end of the hedging relationship and the sale of the silver on 31 May 20X7:

    To recognise the change in fair value of the forward (EUR 2,005,000):

Forward contract (Asset)	€ 2,005,000	
Fair value hedge gain/loss (P&L)		€ 2,005,000

To recognise the change in fair value of the firm commitment (EUR 2,005,000):

Fair value hedge gain/loss (P&L)	€ 2,005,000	
Firm commitment (Liability)		€ 2,005,000

To recognise the cash settlement of the forward contract (EUR 3,000,000):

Cash (Asset)	€ 3,000,000	
Forward contract (Asset)		€ 3,000,000

Without the hedge:	With the hedge:
Profit & Loss	**Profit & Loss**
Sales: 50,000,000	Sales: 53,000,000
COGS: 48,000,000	COGS: 48,000,000
EBITDA: 2,000,000	EBITDA: 5,000,000

Figure 8.3   Summary of P&L Effects.

To record the sale of the 10 million silver ounces at EUR 5.00 per ounce, and derecognise the firm commitment.

Cash (Asset)	€ 50,000,000	
Firm commitment (Liability)	€ 3,000,000	
Sales (P&L)		53,000,000

To record the delivery of the silver inventory, assuming that it was valued at the spot on 31 May 20X7, or EUR 4.80 per ounce:

Cost of goods sold (P&L)	€ 48,000,000	
Inventory (Asset)		€ 48,000,000

In this case, the loss on the firm commitment was offset by the gain on the forward contract. The sales proceeds were the original EUR 50 million from the firm commitment to the customer plus EUR 3 million provided by the forward. The effect of the hedge on ABC's EBITDA was to preserve the original EUR 5 million margin, as shown in Figure 8.3.

ABC effectively sold the silver at the spot price prevailing on 31 May 20X7, even though the sales price was fixed on 1 February 20X7.

CASE 8.2

Hedging a Commodity Inventory with Futures

The objective of this case is to illustrate the application of a commodity hedge using futures contracts. Futures contracts are settled daily and any daily gain (or loss) is deposited (or withdrawn) in the entity's margin account at the exchange. As a consequence, the futures position is reset each day so its fair value at the end of the day is zero.

On 1 February 20X7, ABC a gold mining company had 100,000 ounces of gold of inventory carried at an average cost of EUR 600 per ounce. To protect the inventory from a decline in gold prices, ABC hedged its position by selling 100 gold June futures contracts on the futures exchange on 1 February 20X7. Each contract was for 1,000 ounces of gold at EUR 700 per ounce. The futures contracts matured on 21 June 20X7. ABC scheduled delivery of the gold to a metal refining customer external to the ABC group on 31 May 20X7, at the spot price on that date. ABC designated the futures contract as the hedging instrument in a fair value hedge of its gold inventory.

Hedge Relationship Documentation

ABC documented the hedging relationship as follows:

Hedging Relationship Documentation	
Risk management objective and strategy for undertaking the hedge	The objective of the hedge is to protect the EUR value of 100,000 gold ounces of inventory against unfavourable movements of the gold price in EUR. This hedging objective is consistent with ABC's overall risk management strategy of reducing the variability of its Profit and Loss statement.
Type of hedge	Fair value hedge.
Risk being hedged	All the risks in their entirety. The variability in EUR value of the gold inventory.
Hedging instrument	The short 100 future contracts position for delivery on 21 June 20X7 at a price of EUR 700 per troy ounce. Because it is an exchange traded instrument, the credit risk associated with the instrument is considered to be very low.
Hedged item	100,000 ounces of gold of inventory.
Assessment of effectiveness testing	Hedge effectiveness will be assessed by comparing changes in the fair value of the hedging instrument to changes in the fair value of the hedged item. The hedged item will be valued at the spot rate. **Prospective test** A prospective test will be performed at inception and at each reporting date using the regression analysis method. The hedge will be expected to be highly effective if all the following three conditions are met: (i) the R-squared of the regression is equal or greater than 80 %, (ii) the slope of the regression line is between −0.80 and −1.25, and (iii) the F-statistic is statistically significant at the 95 % confidence level. The credit risk of the futures exchange will be continuously monitored. **Retrospective test** A retrospective test will be performed at each reporting date using the "ratio analysis method". The ratio will compare the cumulative change since hedge inception in the fair value of the inventory with the cumulative change since hedge inception in the fair value of the hedging instrument. The hedge will be assumed to be highly effective on a retrospective basis if the ratio is between 80 % and 125 %.

Fair Valuations of the Hedging Instrument and the Hedged Item

The spot and futures gold prices in EUR per ounce on the relevant dates were as follows:

Date	Spot price at indicated date	Futures price for 21 June 20X7	Discount Factor for 21 June 20X7
1 February 20X7	690	700	0.9880
31 March 20X7	644	650	0.9930
31 May 20X7	607	610	0.9980

The fair value calculation of the hedging instrument was as follows:

Futures Contracts Fair Values	1-Feb-X7	31-Mar-X7	31-May-X7
Futures Price on 1-Feb-X7	700	700	700
Futures Price	700	650	610
Futures fair value	–0– (1)	4,965,000 (2)	8,982,000 (3)
Change in futures fair value	—	4,965,000 (4)	4,017,000 (5)

Notes:
(1) = 100 contracts * 1,000 ounces * (700-700) * 0.9880
(2) = 100 contracts * 1,000 ounces * (700-650) * 0.9930
(3) = 100 contracts * 1,000 ounces * (700-610) * 0.9980
(4) = 4,965,000-0
(5) = 8,982,000-4,965,000

The inventory fair value calculation was as follows:

Inventory Fair Value	1-Feb-X7	31-Mar-X7	31-May-X7
Spot price	690	644	607
Inventory theoretical value	69,000,000 (1)	64,400,000	60,700,000
Storing costs (2)	—	100,000	200,000
Inventory fair value	69,000,000	64,300,000 (3)	60,500,000
Change in inventory fair value	—	<4,700,000> (4)	<3,800,000>

Notes:
(1) = 100,000 ounces*690
(2) Storing costs incurred since 1-Feb-X7
(3) = Inventory theoretical value−storing costs = 64,400,000-100,000
(4) = 64,300,000-69,000,000

Prospective Tests

ABC performed a prospective test at inception (1 February 20X7) and at each reporting date during the hedge relationship (31 March 20X7). ABC used the regression analysis test to assess prospective effectiveness. We have not included the regression analysis to keep the case simple. Case 3.6 and Case 5.7 covered in detail the regression analysis method. Let us assume that as a result of the analysis, ABC concluded that the hedge was highly effective prospectively.

Retrospective Tests

ABC performed two retrospective tests: one on the reporting date (31 March 20X7) and other at maturity of the hedging relationship (31 May 20X7).

Retrospective Tests	31-Mar-X7	31-May-X7
Hedging instrument cumulative fair value change	4,965,000	8,982,000
Hedged item cumulative fair value change	<4,700,000>	<8,500,000>
Ratio	**105.6 %**	**105.7 %**
Hedge effective amount	4,700,000	3,800,000
Hedge ineffective amount	265,000	217,000

As the result of each test was within the 80 %–125 % range, the hedge was considered to be highly effective retrospectively. Because the accumulated change in the fair value of the hedging instrument exceeded the accumulated change in the fair value of the hedged item, the excess was considered ineffective.

Accounting Entries

The required journal entries were as follows:

1) To record the futures contracts trade on 1 February 20X7:

In theory, no entries in the financial statements were required as the fair value of the futures contracts were zero. However, ABC had to post a margin in the futures exchange to guarantee the futures position. Let us assume that the initial margin was 10 % of the position, or EUR 7,000,000 in cash.

Futures contracts margin (Asset)	€ 7,000,000	
Cash (Asset)		€ 7,000,000

2) To record the closing of the accounting period on 31 March 20X7:

The futures contracts were revalued daily. If the futures position showed a gain from the previous day, the gain was posted in ABC's margin account at the futures exchange. On the contrary, if the futures position showed a loss, ABC had to post the lost amount in ABC's margin account at the futures exchange. Therefore, at the end of each day the futures position was reset so its fair value was zero.

To keep the case simple, we will summarise all the daily journal entries since 1 February 20X7 in one. The change in fair value of the futures contracts since 1 February 20X7 was a gain of EUR 4,965,000. Of this amount, EUR 4,700,000 was considered effective and recorded in P&L. The remaining amount, EUR 265,000, was considered ineffective and also recorded in P&L. Therefore, because it was a fair value hedge we can see that both the effective and ineffective amounts were recorded in P&L, making the split between effective and ineffective parts irrelevant from the hedging instrument standpoint. We will see later that the split affects the revaluation of the hedged item.

Futures contracts margin (Asset)	€ 4,965,000	
Fair value hedge gain/loss (P&L)		€ 4,965,000

We just mentioned that the margin account was updated daily to take into account the daily profit or loss of the futures position. Let us assume that ABC maintained a EUR

7,000,000 initial margin at all times and withdrew any excess (or deposited any deficit). As the futures position showed a gain of EUR 4,965,000, the exchange would have deposited this amount in ABC's margin account at the exchange and ABC would have withdrawn it immediately:

Cash (Asset)	€ 4,965,000	
Futures contracts margin (Asset)		€ 4,965,000

We saw earlier that the split between effective (EUR 4,700,000) and ineffective parts (EUR 265,000) was irrelevant from the hedging instrument standpoint. However, the effective part affected the revaluation of the hedged item. An extreme situation would be a large amount of ineffectiveness, large enough so the hedge fails the retrospective test. In this extreme situation, the futures contracts would be fair valued through income with no offset for changes in the fair value of the hedged item. In our case, the gold inventory was revalued according to the hedge effective portion (EUR 4,700,000):

Fair value hedge gain/loss (P&L)	€ 4,700,000	
Gold inventory (Asset)		€ 4,700,000

3) To record the end of the hedging relationship and the sale of inventory on 31 May 20X7:

To keep they case simple, we will summarise all the daily journal entries since 31 March 20X7 in one. The change in fair value of the futures contracts since 31 March 20X7 was a gain of EUR 4,017,000. Of this amount, EUR 3,800,000 was considered effective and recorded in P&L. The remaining amount, EUR 217,000, was considered ineffective and also recorded in P&L:

Futures contracts margin (Asset)	€ 4,017,000	
Fair value hedge gain/loss (P&L)		€ 4,017,000

Let us assume that ABC bought back it's futures position, effectively closing its position. The margin account showed a balance of EUR 11,017,000 (= 7,000,000 + 4,017,000) and ABC closed it withdrawing the balance:

Cash (Asset)	€ 11,017,000	
Futures contracts margin (Asset)		€ 11,017,000

We saw that the hedging instrument showed a gain of EUR 4,017,000. Of this amount, EUR 3,800,000 was considered effective. The inventory was revalued according to the hedge effective part:

Fair value hedge gain/loss (P&L)	€ 3,800,000	
Gold inventory (Asset)		€ 3,800,000

The inventory was sold at the spot rate ruling on the date, EUR 607. Therefore, the sales proceeds were EUR 60,700,000 (= 100,000 ounces * 607).

Cash (Asset)	€ 60,700,000	
Sales (P&L)		€ 60,700,000

The inventory was valued at EUR 51,500,000 (= 60,000,000 − 4,700,000 − 3,800,000). To record its removal:

Cost of sales (P&L)	€ 51,500,000	
Gold inventory (Asset)		€ 51,500,000

This case shows how crucial it was for ABC to hedge its gold exposure (see Figure 8.4). Gold prices can be notably volatile. The hedge protected the EBITDA expected value at the beginning of the hedge. Because there was some ineffectiveness, there was an unexpected additional gain of EUR 482,000.

Frequently, the ineffectiveness caused by the futures contracts can be substantial, as the futures price relates to a commodity with specific characteristics and for delivery in specific locations, that may differ notably from the inventory being hedged. Similarly, the actively

Figure 8.4   Summary of P&L Effects.

traded ("liquid") futures contracts can be denominated in USD, creating additional hedging challenges for European based entities.

CASE 8.3

Hedging a Highly Expected Purchase with Futures

The objective of this case is to illustrate the commodity hedge of a highly expected purchase using a futures contract. If the reader went through the cases in Chapter 3, he will find that this case is similar to any foreign currency highly expected cash flow hedge. Remember, from Case 8.2, that futures contracts are settled daily and any daily gain (or loss) is deposited (withdrawn) in the entity's margin account at the exchange. As a consequence, the futures position is reset each day so its fair value at the end of the day is zero.

A second point to take into account is that the hedging instrument may not be accounted as an IAS 39 derivative, and instead be considered as an "own-use" instrument. In this case, because the entity was looking to unwind its futures position when the purchase price was set, the futures contract was under the scope of IAS 39.

On 1 February 20X7, ABC an oil refining company forecasted the purchase of 2 million barrels of WTI oil expected to be agreed on 31 May 20X7 at the spot price prevailing at this date. Delivery and payment were going to take place simultaneously on 7 June 20X7. ABC's functional currency was the EUR. ABC was worried that the EUR value of the oil purchase may increase. To hedge its exposure, ABC entered into a long June futures position for 2 million barrels at a price of USD 50 per barrel. The futures contracts were to expire on 21 June 20X7. Simultaneously, ABC entered into a FX forward to buy USD 100 million at an exchange rate of 1.2500 on 31 May 20X7, and to be settled by cash settlement.

ABC designated the combination of the oil futures contracts and the FX forward as the hedging instrument in a cash flow hedge of its highly expected purchase.

Hedge Relationship Documentation

ABC documented the hedging relationship as follows:

Hedging Relationship Documentation	
Risk management objective and strategy for undertaking the hedge	The objective of the hedge is to protect the EUR value of a highly expected purchase of 2 million barrels of WTI oil against unfavourable movements of the oil price in EUR.
	This hedging objective is consistent with ABC's overall risk management strategy of reducing the variability of its Profit and Loss statement.
Type of hedge	Cash flow hedge.

(Continued)

Hedging Relationship Documentation	
Risk being hedged	All the risks in their entirety. The variability in EUR value of the highly expected cash flow.
Hedging instrument	The combination of
	1) A long future contracts position of 2 million barrels for delivery on 21 June 20X7 at a price of USD 50 per barrel. Because it is an exchange traded instrument, the credit risk associated with the instrument is considered to be very low. 2) The contract number 145679: a FX forward to buy USD 100 million and sell EUR at an exchange rate of 1.2500, value date 31 May 20X7, and cash settlement. The credit risk associated with the counterparty to the FX forward is considered to be very low.
Hedged item	Highly expected purchase of 2 million barrels on 31 May 20X7, at the spot price of WTI oil on that date.
Assessment of effectiveness testing	Hedge effectiveness will be assessed by comparing changes in the fair value of the hedging instrument to changes in the fair value of the hedged item. The FX forward will be valued at the forward rate.
	The hedged item will be valued at the forward price of oil in EUR.
	Prospective test
	A prospective test will be performed at inception and at each reporting date using the regression analysis method. The hedge will be expected to be highly effective all the following three conditions are met: (i) the R-squared of the regression is equal or greater than 80%, (ii) the slope of the regression line is between -0.80 and -1.25, and (iii) the F-statistic is statistically significant at the 95 % confidence level.
	The credit risk of the futures exchange and of the counterparty to the FX contract will be monitored continuously.
	Retrospective test
	A retrospective test will be performed at each reporting date using the "ratio analysis method". The ratio will compare the cumulative change since hedge inception in the fair value of the firm commitment with the cumulative change since hedge inception in the fair value of the hedging instrument. The hedge will be assumed to be highly effective on a retrospective basis if the ratio is between 80 % and 125 %.

Fair Valuations of the Hedging Instrument and the Hedged Item

This part performs all the fair value calculations needed for the prospective tests and for the generation of the accounting entries.

The futures oil prices in USD per barrel on the relevant dates were as follows:

Date	Futures price for 21 June 20X7	USD/EUR Forward to 21 June 20X7
1 February 20X7	50	1.2520
31 March 20X7	55	1.2820
31 May 20X7	60	1.3020

The fair value calculation of the futures contracts was as follows:

Futures Contracts Fair Values	1-Feb-X7	31-Mar-X7	31-May-X7
Futures Price (on 1-Feb-X7)	50	50	50
Futures Price (on specified date)	50	55	60
USD/EUR forward to 21-Jun-X7	1.2520	1.2820	1.3020
Discount factor to 21-Jun-X7	0.9880	0.9900	0.9980
EUR Futures fair value	-0- *(1)*	7,722,000 *(2)*	15,330,000 *(3)*
Change in futures fair value	—	7,722,000 *(4)*	7,608,000 *(5)*

Notes:

(1) = 2,000,000 barrels * (50 − 50)/1.2520 * 0.9880
(2) = 2,000,000 barrels * (55 − 50)/1.2820 * 0.9900
(3) = 2,000,000 barrels * (60 − 50)/1.3020 * 0.9980
(4) = 7,722,000 − 0
(5) = 15,330,000 − 7,722,000

The spot and forward USD/EUR rates on the relevant dates were as follows:

Date	Spot USD/EUR	Forward for 31 May 20X7	Discount Factor for 31 May 20X7
1 February 20X7	1.2400	1.2500	0.9900
31 March 20X7	1.2750	1.2800	0.9930
31 May 20X7	1.3000	1.3000	1.0000

The fair value calculation of the FX forward was as follows:

FX Forward Fair Values	1-Feb-X7	31-Mar-X7	31-May-X7
Forward rate to 31May X7 (on 1-Feb-X7)	1.2500	1.2500	1.2500
Forward rate to 31May X7 (on specified date)	1.2500	1.2800	1.3000
FX forward fair value	-0- *(1)*	<1,862,000> *(2)*	<3,077,000> *(3)*
Change in forward fair value	—	<1,862,000> *(4)*	<1,215,000> *(5)*

Notes:

(1) = 100,000,000 USD * (1/1.2500 − 1/1.2500) * 0.9900
(2) = 100,000,000 USD * (1/1.2500 − 1/1.2800) * 0.9930
(3) = 100,000,000 USD * (1/1.2500 − 1/1.3000) * 1.0000
(4) = 1,862,000 − 0
(5) = 3,077,000 − 1,862,000

The highly expected purchase fair value calculation was as follows:

Forecasted Cash flow Fair Value	1-Feb-X7	31-Mar-X7	31-May-X7
Oil USD forward price to 31-May- X7	49	54	59
USD/EUR forward to 31-May-X7	1.2500	1.2800	1.3000
Discount factor to 31-May-X7	0.9900	0.9930	1.0000
Firm commitment fair value	<77,616,000> *(1)*	<83,784,000> *(2)*	<90,769,000>
Change in firm commitment fair value	—	<6,168,000> *(3)*	<6,985,000>

Notes:

(1) = −2,000,000 barrels * 49/1.25 * 0.9900
(2) = −2,000,000 barrels * 54/1.28 * 0.9930
(3) = −83,784,000 − (−77,616,000)

Prospective Tests

ABC performed a prospective test at inception (1 February 20X7) and at each reporting date during the hedge relationship (31 March 20X7). ABC used the regression analysis test to assess prospective effectiveness. To keep the case simple, we have not included this regression analysis. Case 3.6 and Case 5.7 covered in detail the regression analysis method. Let us assume that as a result of the analysis, ABC concluded that the hedge was highly effective prospectively.

Retrospective Tests

ABC performed two retrospective tests: one on the reporting date (on 31 March 20X7) and other at maturity of the hedging relationship on 31 May 20X7.

Retrospective Tests	31-Mar-X7	31-May-X7
Futures contracts cumulative fair value change	7,722,000	15,330,000
FX forward cumulative fair value change	<1,862,000>	<3,077,000>
Hedging instrument cumulative fair value change	5,860,000	12,253,000
Hedged item cumulative fair value change	<6,168,000>	<13,153,000>
Ratio	**95.0 %**	**93.2 %**
Hedge effective amount	5,860,000	6,393,000
Hedge ineffective amount	-0-	-0-

As the result of each test was within the 80 %–125 % range, ABC considered the hedge to be highly effective retrospectively. Because the accumulated change in the fair value of the hedging instrument did not exceed the accumulated change in the fair value of the hedged item, there was no ineffectiveness in the hedge.

Accounting Entries

The required journal entries were as follows:

1) To record the futures contracts on 1 February 20X7:

ABC had to post a margin in the futures exchange to guarantee the futures position. Let us assume that the initial margin was 10 % of the position, or USD 10,000,000 in cash. As the spot exchange rate on that date was 1.2400, the equivalent EUR amount was EUR 8,065,000 (= 10 million/1.2400).

Futures contracts margin (Asset)	€ 8,065,000	
Cash (Asset)		€ 8,065,000

2) To record the closing of the accounting period on 31 March 20X7:

The futures contracts were revalued daily. If the futures position showed a gain from the previous day, the gain was posted in ABC's margin account at the futures exchange. If on the contrary, the futures position showed a loss, ABC had to post the lost amount in ABC's margin account at the futures exchange. Therefore, at the end of each day the futures position was reset so its fair value was zero.

To keep the case simple, we will summarise all the daily journal entries since 1 February 20X7 in one entry. The change in fair value of the futures contracts since 1 February 20X7 was a gain of EUR 7,722,000. All this amount was considered effective and recorded in equity.

Futures contracts margin (Asset)	€ 7,722,000	
Cash flow hedges (Equity)		€ 7,722,000

We just mentioned that the margin account was updated daily to take into account the daily profit or loss of the futures position. Let us assume that ABC maintained the USD 7,000,000 initial margin at all times and withdrew any excess (or deposited any deficit). As the futures position showed a gain of EUR 7,722,000, the exchange would have deposited the USD equivalent of this amount in ABC's margin account at the exchange and ABC would have withdrawn it immediately:

Cash (Asset)	€ 7,722,000	
Futures contracts margin (Asset)		€ 7,722,000

The initial margin of USD 10,000,000 in cash, had a value of EUR 8,065,000. This is a monetary item and, therefore, had to be revalued at the spot rate on 31 March 20X7 (1.2750).

The margin new value was EUR 7,843,000 (= USD 10 million/1.2750), showing a loss of EUR 222,000 (= 7,843,000 − 8,065,000):

Translation loss (P&L)	€ 222,000	
Futures contracts margin (Asset)		€ 222,000

We saw that the FX forward showed a loss of EUR 1,862,000. All this amount was considered effective:

Cash flow hedges (Equity)	€ 1,862,000	
Fx forward (Liability)		€ 1,862,000

3) To record the end of the hedging relationship and the oil purchase on 31 May 20X7:

To keep the case simple, we will summarise all the daily journal entries of the futures contracts since 31 March 20X7 in one. The change in fair value of the futures contracts since 31 March 20X7 was a gain of EUR 7,608,000. All this amount was considered effective and recorded in equity.

Futures contracts margin (Asset)	€ 7,608,000	
Cash flow hedge (Equity)		€ 7,608,000

The initial cash margin of USD 10,000,000 had a previous value of EUR 7,843,000. This is a monetary item and, therefore, had to be revalued at the spot rate on 31 May 20X7 (1.3000). The margin was valued at EUR 7,576,000 (= USD 10 million/1.3200), showing a loss of EUR 267,000 (= 7,576,000 − 7,843,000).

Translation loss (P&L)	€ 267,000	
Futures contracts margin (Asset)		€ 267,000

Let us assume that ABC bought back it futures position, effectively closing its position. The margin account showed a balance of EUR 15,184,000 (= 7,608,000 + 7,576,000) and ABC closed it withdrawing the balance.

Cash (Asset)	€ 15,184,000	
Futures contracts margin (Asset)		€ 15,184,000

The FX forward showed a loss of EUR 1,215,000. All this amount was considered effective.

Cash flow hedges (Equity)	€ 1,215,000	
FX forward (Liability)		€ 1,215,000

The FX forward matured and ABC had to pay EUR 3,077,000 cash settlement:

FX forward (Liability)	€ 3,077,000	
Cash (Asset)		€ 3,077,000

The oil was agreed on 31 May 20X7, so the highly expected purchase became a firm commitment.

4) To record the payment and receipt of the oil on 7 Jun 20X7:

Let us assume that the EUR/USD was 1.3050 on 7 Jun 20X7. The amount in EUR to exchange for USD 118,000,000 was EUR 90,421,000 (= 118 million/1.3050). ABC then paid and received the oil:

Oil Inventory (Asset)	€ 90,421,000	
Cash (Asset)		€ 90,421,000

The amount accumulated in equity (EUR 12,253,000) as a result of the cash flow hedge remained in equity, and was recycled into P&L when the oil was utilised.

9
Hedge Accounting:
A Double Edged Sword

Hedge accounting is optional: it is an elective decision of the management of an entity. Hedge accounting is a special accounting treatment available to ensure that the timing of P&L recognition on the hedging instrument matches that of the hedged item. When hedging, corporations face the choice between entering into hedge accounting compliant hedges and pure economic hedges (see Figure 9.1). At first glance, it seems to be an easy decision as the reduction in P&L volatility stemming from applying hedge accounting provides a powerful argument for adopting hedge accounting compliant hedges. However, in reality the decision whether or not to implement hedge accounting compliant hedges can be a difficult one: hedge accounting requirements are so stringent that they may limit extraordinarily the range of hedging instruments available, to the detriment of optimising cash flows. As a consequence, management is put in a difficult position: shareholders may punish executives for short-term volatility, but will certainly penalise underperforming companies.

The decision to whether or not adopt hedge accounting compliant hedges requires an in-depth analysis at both the entity level and the consolidated level as it may affect earnings, EPS, cash flows, gearing, interest cover, dividend cover, covenants, margins, bonuses and staff payment schemes. This chapter focuses on the main advantages and drawbacks of adopting hedge accounting. In order to highlight some of the hedge accounting weaknesses, we have provided real life examples. Although some of the examples are based on US Gaap reporting companies, the similarities between FAS 133 and IAS 39 make these examples relevant in order to emphasise the issues discussed.

9.1 POSITIVE INFLUENCE ON THE PROFIT AND LOSS STATEMENT

The application, or not, of hedge accounting treatment may have important effects on the income statement (see Figure 9.2), especially when hedging highly expected sales or purchases. Usually these hedges are implemented to mitigate commodity risk or FX risk.

Let us assume that an entity is considering hedging a highly expected foreign currency denominated sale of finished goods with a derivative. The expected sale will not be recorded in P&L until the sale finally takes place. The sale will be recorded in the EBITDA section of the P&L statement.

If the entity applies hedge accounting, the hedge will be treated as a cash flow hedge. The effective part of the change in fair value of the derivative will be recorded in equity. When the hedged item (i.e., the highly expected sale) affects P&L, the accumulated amount in equity will be reclassified from equity to P&L, to the same EBITDA line as the hedged item entry. This is highly relevant as EBITDA is a key indicator for financial analysts and investors. Thus, the application of hedge accounting in this example has two benefits: firstly, it ensures that the

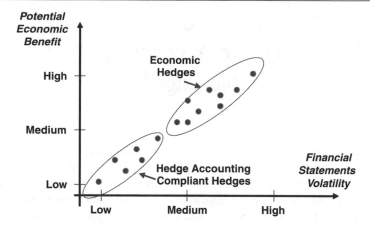

Figure 9.1   Economic Hedges vs Hedge Accounting Compliant Hedges.

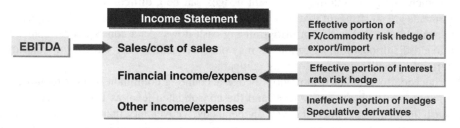

Figure 9.2   Hedges Influence on Income Statement.

P&L recognitions of the hedged item and the hedging instrument take place simultaneously and secondly that the recognitions are made in the same P&L line.

If the entity does not apply hedge accounting, the change in fair value of the derivative for the period will be recognised in the P&L item "other income or expenses" from the derivative's inception. Therefore, there will be a recognition mismatch between the hedged item and the hedging instrument not only in terms of timing but also in terms of P&L line.

Therefore, the use of hedge accounting may not only reduce P&L volatility, but may also reduce EBITDA volatility. For companies for which raw materials price is a very important component of their finished products sale price, the decision to use hedge accounting can be especially relevant.

9.2   SUBSTANTIAL RESOURCES REQUIREMENTS

Implementing hedge accounting is a big challenge as the requirements are far reaching. The administrative load needed to prepare disclosure and presentation requirements, to produce hedge documentation and to test effectiveness can be substantial. A great deal of training is also needed to achieve adequate quality and competence of accounting and treasury personnel. Additionally, strong information systems capabilities are needed in order to process information flows adequately and for reporting. Modelling tools are also frequently needed in order to be able to evaluate financial instruments correctly. Finally, supervision and correct policies and procedures are required in order to determine whether all hedge accounting requirements are met. Lack of appropriate controls can have a real and visible impact on the reported results of an organisation.

> **America West's weak controls**
>
> In 2005, America West Airlines Inc.'s external auditors concluded that America West's fuel hedging transactions did not qualify for hedge accounting under US Gaap principles and that its financial statements for prior periods required restatement to reflect the fair value of fuel hedging contracts in the balance sheets and statements of shareholders' equity of America West. These accounting errors were the result of deficiencies in its internal control over financial reporting arising from the lack of effective reviews of hedge transaction documentation and of quarterly mark-to-market accounting entries on open fuel hedging contracts by personnel at an appropriate level.

9.3   LIMITED ACCESS TO HEDGING ALTERNATIVES

Widespread adoption of hedge accounting compliant hedges may lead entities to undertake hedging instruments that are sub-optimal from an economic perspective. Usually hedging instruments that provide more potential room for economic benefit tend to show lower degree of applicability of hedge accounting.

A good number of hedging strategies are neither fully hedge accounting compliant nor completely non-compliant. As discussed in some of the cases provided in Chapter 3, there are hedging instruments that can be split into a part that meets the requirements of hedge accounting and a part that does not meet these requirements. Figure 9.3 depicts the usual negative relationship between the potential economic value (measured as the participation in potentially favourable market movements) and the degree of hedge accounting compliance in FX hedges of highly expected sales or purchases.

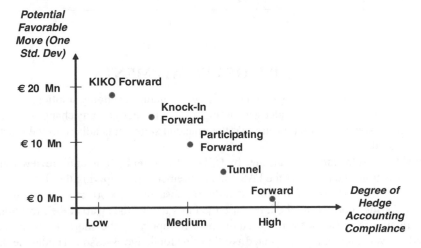

Figure 9.3   Economic Value vs Hedge Accounting Compliance.

9.4   RISK OF REASSESSMENT OF HIGHLY PROBABLE TRANSACTIONS

One potential problem with using hedge accounting occurs when the originally highly probable cash flow being hedged is suddenly no longer expected to take place. In a cash flow hedge of a highly expected cash flow, the change in fair value of the hedging instrument is recorded in equity until the underlying cash flow affects P&L. If the underlying cash flow is no longer expected to take place, the hedging instrument gain or loss deferred in equity has to be transferred to P&L immediately. This transfer can have a devastating effect on P&L if the deferred amount in equity was a very large loss.

EADS and the delivery delay for Airbus 380 superjumbo

In June 2006, EADS – the European manufacturer of the Airbus – reported that it will delay delivery of the A380 superjumbo for the second time. At that time EADS had 159 orders for its A380 planes, which listed for USD 100 million each, for 16 airlines. Some airlines had clauses in their purchase contracts that allowed them to cancel their orders if the aircraft were more than a year late.

Let us assume that EADS hedged one of the USD denominated highly expected sales, and that EADS applied hedge accounting. The changes in fair value of the hedging instrument were then recorded in equity. Assume further that due to the delay, the airline cancelled the plane order. The cancellation may have two different outcomes:

1) If EADS still reasonably expected the sale to take place: the deferred gain or loss that was previously accumulated in equity remained in equity until the sale finally occurred.

2) If EADS no longer expected the sale to take place: the deferred gain or loss that was accumulated in equity was immediately transferred to P&L.

The effects of this second outcome could have a devastating effect on EADS' earnings if the deferred amount in equity was a very large loss.

9.5   RISK OF RESTATEMENTS

For the time being, the accounting treatment of many structured hedging solutions is uncertain. Interpretations of how to apply hedge accounting for specific hedges may change over time and may provoke restatements that ensure that the financial statements adhere to the most recent accounting guidance.

In 2005 GE had to restate its earnings by USD 381 million after an audit review found that certain transactions did not meet the FAS 133 requirements for applying the short-cut method to test hedge effectiveness. GE documented these transactions incorrectly (see Figure 9.4) as qualifying for the short-cut method, because the fair value of the swap at the inception of the hedging relationship was not zero (a requirement for applying the short-cut method). Since these hedges were incorrectly designated as qualifying for hedge assessment under the short-cut method, and GE did not test the hedging relationships periodically for effectiveness, GE was

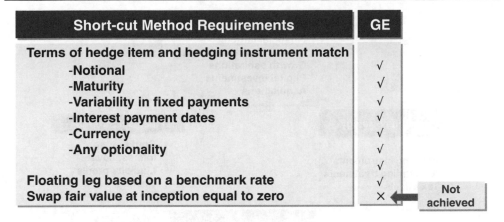

Short-cut Method Requirements	GE
Terms of hedge item and hedging instrument match	
-Notional	√
-Maturity	√
-Variability in fixed payments	√
-Interest payment dates	√
-Currency	√
-Any optionality	√
	√
Floating leg based on a benchmark rate	√
Swap fair value at inception equal to zero	× ← Not achieved

Figure 9.4   General Electric – Wrong Use of Short-cut Method.

required to restate its financial statements as if the hedging instruments were undesignated. The provisions of FAS 133 did not allow GE to apply retroactively the hedge assessments using other methods, although they would have qualified for hedge accounting if other methods to assess effectiveness were used. Although the application of the short-cut method is not possible under IAS 39, restatements may be caused by many other circumstances such as: wrong application of the critical terms method, wrong valuation of derivatives due to faulty models, bad design of prospective tests, etc.

9.6   LOW COMPATIBILITY WITH PORTFOLIO HEDGING

One of the main reasons why entities may choose to ignore using hedge accounting is the current impossibility of applying hedge accounting on a portfolio basis. IAS 39 provided some room for portfolio hedging of interest rates but with a limited applicability.

Most large multinationals centralise their financial risk management in a treasury centre, which is responsible for risk and liquidity management, and funding for the whole group's operations. Frequently, the treasury centre applies a portfolio approach to hedging. This means that it does not consider individual exposures, but combines different exposures, and only enters into hedges with third parties when the residual risk in the portfolio may compromise the delivery of corporate objectives.

The overall risk is usually measured using the value at risk (VaR) and/or earnings at risk (EaR) of the total position. The VaR approach tries to measure the probability that the portfolio does not lose more than a specific amount within a specific time horizon. The hedging strategy then involves limiting the portfolio exposures so the financial and other business targets are not endangered by financial risks. Figure 9.5 depicts the hedging process on a portfolio basis.

To apply hedge accounting to a specific hedging instrument would mean assigning the hedging instrument to an individual transaction between an entity of the group and an outside party, an assignment that may sometimes not be feasible. As a consequence, the entity may end up not applying for hedge accounting for many of the hedging transactions with outside parties.

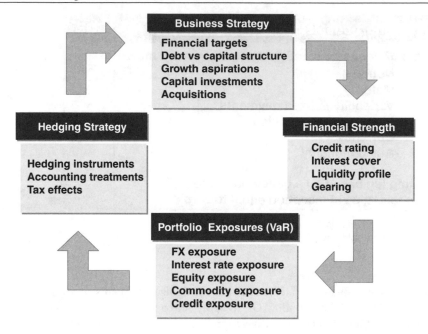

Figure 9.5   Portfolio Hedging – Decision Process.

9.7   LIMITED SOLUTIONS TO BASIS RISK

Sometimes an entity is exposed to a market risk for which hedging is either unavailable or too expensive. The entity may decide to implement a hedge on a different, but notably more liquid, underlying that is highly correlated to the actual risk being hedged.

Although these hedges may work well in the long-term, there may be temporary movements in the underlying of the hedging instrument that are not accompanied by similar movements in the underlying of the hedged item. This risk, called basis risk, may have unexpected effects when a hedge that has been treated under hedge accounting repeatedly fails the retrospective test.

The European airlines dilemma

Most of the time, when hedging their exposure to jet fuel prices, airlines use crude oil derivatives instead of jet fuel derivatives as the former is a much more liquid market. Although jet fuel and crude oil prices are approximately 90 % correlated in the long-term, there have been short-term periods in which they have moved quite independently. Hedging with crude oil price leaves an airline exposed to the price difference between crude oil and jet fuel. Jet fuel price changes are driven mainly by crude oil price changes but are also influenced by other specifics, especially refinery capacities and price switches between diverse oil products.

Using hedge accounting when hedging jet fuel exposure may create great problems for airlines if a hedge relationship is discontinued suddenly because two or more periods the retrospective tests falls outside the 80 %–125 % band.

9.8   FINAL REMARKS

In practice, if a company is contemplating hedge accounting for a specific hedge, careful analysis is required of the costs and benefits of applying it. This can be a complex decision because the main benefit – the added value that comes from reduced earnings volatility – is difficult to measure in practice. Although most companies try to maximise the use of hedge accounting, it is important not to forget that risk management can be a competitive weapon: companies can gain advantage over competitors who suboptimise risk management as a result of excessive emphasis on applying hedge accounting.

The Rolls Royce Decision

When adopting IFRS in 2005, Rolls Royce decided that meeting the strict criteria for hedge accounting was not considered practicable within its FX risk management practices. Rolls Royce believed that its risk management practices were in the best economic interests of shareholders and should not be amended purely to achieve a particular accounting treatment. Accordingly, Rolls Royce decided not to apply hedge accounting to hedges of forecast foreign exchange transactions. Rolls Royce continued to hedge its future forecast US dollar income on a portfolio basis, which it considered was the most efficient economic basis for doing so.

Rolls Royce noted that: "The Group will continue to utilise forward exchange contracts, in the 'portfolio' approach that is well suited to its needs. Contracts may be signed several years in advance of delivery and forecasts of aftermarket sales have to be made. Delivery dates may change and timing of spares sales may vary. It will no longer apply 'hedge' accounting, however, which under IFRS would require the Group to make significant changes to the way in which it operates its hedging policies. Therefore, operating profits will be reported without the benefit of any offset from financial derivatives, as though translated at spot rates only. At the same time, the aggregate value of all the Group's outstanding derivatives will be shown as one asset on the balance sheet, which will be 'marked-to-market' each year, to reflect its fair value. In the profit and loss account, net finance costs will record the net gain or loss on both realised derivative transactions and unrealised, marked-to-market adjustments".

The following table summarises the pros and cons of applying hedge accounting to a specific hedge:

Hedge Accounting Applied	
Strengths	Weaknesses
Reduced volatility in earnings	Limited availability of hedging alternatives.
Reduced volatility of EBITDA	Low compatibility with portfolio hedging techniques.
Improved cash flow forecasting	Systems and human resources to meet hedge documentation, effectiveness testing and disclosure requirements.
Reduced risk of breaching covenants	Potential volatility in reserves (if cash flow or net investment hedge).
Reduced risk of credit rating downgrades	Risk of accounting restatements.

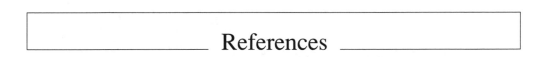

References

Ernst & Young (2005) *Foreign Currency hedges and hedges of net investments in foreign operations.*
Hall, J. C. (2000) *Options, futures, & other derivatives.* Prentice Hall.
PricewaterhouseCoopers (2005) *IAS-39 Achieving hedge accounting in practice.*

Index

Note: Page references in *italics* refer to Figures

Index compiled by Annette Musker